Morality and the Emotions

D0169197

Morality and the Emotions

Justin Oakley

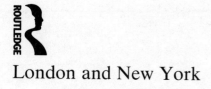

London and New York

First published 1992
by Routledge
11 New Fetter Lane, London EC4P 4EE

Simultaneously published in the USA and Canada
by Routledge
a division of Routledge, Chapman and Hall, Inc.
29 West 35th Street, New York, NY 10001

Typeset in 10/12 Times by Florencetype Ltd, Kewstoke, Avon
Printed and bound in Great Britain by
T J Press (Padstow) Ltd, Padstow, Cornwall

British Library Cataloguing in Publication Data
Oakley, Justin
   Morality and the emotions.
   1. Emotions.
   I. Title
   152.4

Library of Congress Cataloging in Publication Data
Oakley, Justin
   Morality and the emotions / Justin Oakley.
      p.   cm.
   Includes bibliographical references and index.
   1. Emotions—Moral and ethical aspects.   I. Title.
BJ1473.O24   1992
170′.1′9—dc20   91-9497

ISBN 0 415 05661 6

170.19
-011 on 1992

To Laura

Contents

Acknowledgements

I owe debts of gratitude to many people for their help while writing this book. I would like to thank especially John Campbell and Michael Stocker for their willing and insightful guidance throughout the development of the manuscript. They suggested many fruitful avenues to explore, and often helped me find the appropriate 'tone' in which to put my arguments. Their influence on this book will be apparent to anyone familiar with their ideas.

For their extensive comments on the penultimate draft, I am grateful to Genevieve Lloyd, Kim Lycos, Roger Trigg, and an anonymous reader for Routledge, all of whom made suggestions which resulted in many improvements.

I would also like to thank Brian Mooney, and other members of the La Trobe University Ethics Discussion Group, including Dean Cocking, Sue Dodds, Karen Jones, Camille Wood, and Robert Young. Their sustaining discussions during the formative stages of the book brought out many connections and parallels which I would not otherwise have noticed.

I also wish to acknowledge here the Monash University Centre for Human Bioethics, directed by Peter Singer and Helga Kuhse, for providing such a stimulating environment in which to revise the manuscript while I was teaching there during 1990. John A. Burgess, Lynn Gillam, Susan McKay, and Laura Shanner each made valuable suggestions, particularly on virtue theory as an ethical perspective.

Several others are owed thanks for their general support – my parents, Barry and Carmel Oakley, and my brother, Eugene Oakley, for their questions, advice, and encouragement. I would also like to acknowledge my deep gratitude to Robin Pinkney, for initially stimulating my interest in these issues, and for her patience and forbearance.

Finally, I want to express my appreciation to Gai Dunn, Heather Mahamooth, Mary Mulroney, Sue Pollard, and Betty Pritchard, for the administrative expertise they brought to the production of this manuscript. Carmel Oakley also deserves thanks for her work in preparing the index, while Kathryn Bailey kindly helped with the proof reading.

An earlier version of Chapter 3 was read to and benefited from the comments of audiences at La Trobe University, Melbourne, and the 1989 Australasian Association of Philosophy Annual Conference, Australian National University, Canberra. That version appeared as 'A Critique of Kantian Arguments Against Emotions as Moral Motives', in *History of Philosophy Quarterly*, 1990, vol. 7, no. 4, pp. 441–59, and I am grateful to the publishers for permission to incorporate in Chapter 3 some of the material from that paper. Part of Chapter 4 was read at Monash University, Melbourne, and at the 1990 Australasian Association of Philosophy Annual Conference, University of Sydney, and was improved as a result of those audiences' comments. The extract from Schiller in Chapter 3, note 10, is from W. Witte, *Schiller*, Oxford, Basil Blackwell, 1949, and is reprinted by kind permission of the publishers.

Melbourne
December 1990

Introduction

In recent years there has been a welcome reawakening of philosophical interest in the emotions. A significant number of contemporary philosophers have now addressed themselves to questions about the nature of emotions, and about how emotions affect our powers of agency – topics that were dealt with earlier by Plato, Aristotle, Aquinas, Descartes, Hume, and other philosophical luminaries. However, other important issues about emotions, such as the relevance of emotions for morality, which also figured prominently in those historical accounts, have received comparatively little recent philosophical attention.

This general neglect of the moral importance of emotions by contemporary moral philosophy seems largely due to two major (and not unrelated) influences: the predominance of Kantianism, with the devaluation of the emotions which such an approach typically involves; and a preoccupation with moral *action*. Consequently, whenever philosophers discuss moral assessments of people, they usually talk about *agent* evaluations – by which in most cases they mean praise and blame – rather than the broader notion of *character* evaluation, which acknowledges what we *have* and what we *are*, as well as what we *do*.

In this book I hope to make a contribution towards redressing this disorientation. I will argue that our emotions play a fundamental role in our moral lives, and that they are at least as valuable here as the actions we perform. In arguing for this I draw on an understanding of moral value in terms of the Aristotelian notion of living a humanly flourishing life, and I want to show that such a life is importantly an emotional or spirited life. Furthermore, I argue that various kinds of moral assessments, including esteem and disesteem as well as credit and blame, may appropriately be directed at us with regard to our emotions, and these types of assessments may be just as important as evaluations of us as moral *agents*.

My thoughts on these issues were initially inspired by Aristotle's well-known (albeit under-appreciated) claim that moral virtue requires not only acting well, but also having the right emotions in the right way towards the appropriate objects and to the right degree.[1] Now if we were to go by various recent philosophical or psychological theories of the nature of emotions, we should take Aristotle here as exhorting us simply to have the right *beliefs* and/or the right *desires*, or to feel or encourage in ourselves certain *bodily changes*. But this seems mistaken – not only as an interpretation of what Aristotle meant here, but also as an account of the real importance of emotions for morality. These theories of emotion seem to lead to an *under-valuing* of the moral significance of emotions (and the prevalence of these theories of emotion may be another factor which helps explain why the importance of emotions for morality has been so inadequately dealt with recently). For example, could courage still be considered a virtue, if in fact it were just a matter of undergoing a peculiar kind of bodily agitation? Likewise, if compassion is taken as just a feelingless belief that another person is suffering, plus perhaps a desire to help this person, does this really allow us to see the full moral goodness of having this emotion? Indeed, on these descriptions, would we even have courage or compassion here at all? In both cases it seems that the account of the emotion which is being offered leaves us unable to capture its true moral value.

The point here, then, is that in order to gain a proper appreciation of the moral significance of emotions, we first need an adequate account of the nature of emotion. Thus, I begin my argument in Chapter 1 by setting out a theory of emotions as complex phenomena involving dynamically related elements of cognition, desire, and affectivity, and this is the model which I adopt as the basis for discussion throughout this work. As we will see in the following chapters, only a conception of emotion in terms of these three elements can do justice to the central role of emotions in morality. So, in arguing that moral virtue requires having the right emotions, what I believe Aristotle is actually telling us here is that we ought to have the right complexes of cognition, desire, and affectivity.

But while it might be agreed that this conception of emotions is the most instructive in helping us understand their moral significance, to argue for the truth of this theory on such grounds might be construed as question-begging. To avert the possibility of such a charge, I argue for the plausibility of my conception of emotion on independent grounds. That is, in Chapter 1, after presenting my account of emotions as complexes of cognitions, desires, and affects, I then defend this view against rival accounts which reduce emotions to one or two elements of this complex, and the objections which I raise against these accounts are quite independent of my later claims about the moral significance of emotions.

However, establishing a plausible theory of emotion is just a beginning towards a proper understanding of their distinctive moral significance. For even if one accepts that emotions are complexes of cognitions, desires, and affects, one might still undervalue emotions, since one may insist that only one or two of these components of emotions have any *moral* significance. Thus, as we see in Chapter 2, both A.C. Ewing and Jerome Shaffer deny that the affective dimension of an emotion has anything to do with its moral status. According to this view, for instance, compassion is morally good solely because it involves the cognition of another person in distress, and a desire to help her. So, someone who has this cognition and desire in a certain situation is *morally* indistinguishable in this context from a person who actually has compassion here.

In Chapter 2 I argue against these kinds of reductive accounts of the moral significance of emotions, and, taking a broad perspective, I try to show quite generally that all of the three elements which are constitutive of an emotion must be considered in order to determine its moral status. I begin a detailed account of the moral significance of emotions by looking at some characteristics of an emotionally flawed person, and I demonstrate how such a person may thereby have certain *moral* defects. I then show how emotions may be morally good and bad in their important connections with such fundamental and interrelated goods as insight and understanding, strength of will, relationships of love and friendship, and a sense of self-worth. In the remaining sections of Chapter 2, I clarify certain aspects of my account by examining some deficiencies in how utilitarianism and ethical altruism might characterise the moral significance of emotions.

My argument would however be incomplete without a consideration of the Kantian position on the question of morality and the emotions, for Kantianism is well-known for its opposition to allowing emotions a prominent place in our moral lives.[2] So in Chapter 3 I turn to a discussion of whether emotions can be morally good motives to action, and I deal here with some influential Kantian arguments against emotions as moral motives. In this chapter I look at what Kantians themselves think is necessary in order for a motive to have moral worth, and I try to demonstrate that given what Kantians can plausibly require of a morally worthy motive, their favoured candidate of duty has no more claim to be such a motive than do certain emotions, such as sympathy and compassion. I then discuss some recent Kantian views which at least allow some emotions instrumental moral value in so far as they help the motive of duty in leading us to act rightly. However, I criticise these views for their failure to recognise that the moral value of certain emotions may be independent of their motivating right action.

Having shown some important ways in which various emotions can be morally good and bad, in Chapter 4 I consider the practical bearing of my analysis on how we live and how we might improve ourselves morally. That is, I look at the nature and extent of the control which we can have over our emotions, and the implications of this for our responsibility for them. This chapter also provides the background for Chapter 5, where I divide the moral assessments which can be made of us in regard to our emotions according to whether or not we are responsible for having the particular emotion which we are being assessed for.

My general argument in Chapter 4 is that various straightforward ideas about what is involved in being responsible for physical acts also seem to allow that we can often be responsible for our emotions. I reject arguments which deny our responsibility for our emotions on the grounds that we cannot have or stop having them at will, and I then try to show how we can sometimes exercise control over our emotions in a deeper sense, where we attempt to develop our emotional capacities over time, and thereby perhaps shape our character and sensitivity in morally important ways.

In the final chapter I discuss the types of moral assessments which may be directed at us for our emotions. These assessments may be either positive or negative, and, cutting across this distinction, they may be divided into assessments which require our responsibility for the emotion in question, and assessments which do not involve this requirement. Chapter 5 follows naturally from Chapter 4, since I look at crediting and blaming people for their emotions, and these are assessments which do seem to presuppose our responsibility here. I argue that what we understand as credit and blame when applied to us for our actions can also quite properly be directed at us for our emotions, and I demonstrate how a reluctance to accept this because of concerns about meddlesomeness stems from a mistaken account of credit and blame.

To be sure, although I play down the moral importance of many of the differences between emotions and actions, I do not deny that there are some morally relevant differences between them. I just want to see that these differences are correctly located. Thus, while I argue that credit and blame may be directed at us for our emotions as well as our actions, I do acknowledge that the kinds of crediting and blaming *responses* which would be appropriately directed at us in regard to our emotions may differ from those properly directed at us for our actions.

Finally, I turn to the assessments which I call esteem and disesteem, and I argue that we can be the legitimate subjects of these assessments on account of our emotions, even in cases where we are not responsible for having a particular emotion. Further, I argue that contrary to what many philosophers (especially those under the influence of Kantianism) suggest, these assessments can be important *moral* assessments of us, despite the fact that we sometimes lack responsibility for the features with regard to which these assessments are directed at us.

Thus, throughout this book I am concerned to show the falsity of a certain popular view according to which our emotions are merely incidental events in our lives, in that they typically just 'happen to' us, and so cannot reflect well or poorly on us in any important sense. Contrary to this picture, I want to show that our emotions may actually be essential and enduring features of our moral character, and that we therefore have a fundamental reason to seek to develop our emotional capacities in ways which enrich our lives.

1   The nature of emotion

Before discussing the moral significance of our emotions and our
responsibility for them, we need an account of what an emotion *is*. In
this first chapter I shall outline my view of the nature of emotion and
defend it against some important rival conceptions. At the outset I
should say that I am not concerned to discuss epistemological questions about whether and how we can *know* or *recognise* that someone
has an emotion, and if so, what particular emotion it is. Of course,
my conclusions in this chapter will bear upon that issue, but I shall
concentrate here on the conceptual problem of the nature of
emotion.

   In this chapter I argue that an emotion is a complex which
involves dynamically related elements of cognition, desire, and
affectivity. I begin by presenting my account of emotion and
explaining my understanding of the notions of cognition, desire, and
particularly affectivity, which has been neglected by many philosophers. Subsequently, I argue in detail that emotions are in fact
constituted by these three elements, and I do this by showing the
defects of views which analyse emotions in terms of only one or two
of these elements. Of these views, I first discuss that which holds
emotions to be just feelings or affects, and I then examine accounts
of emotions as affective or affectless cognitions. Following this I
deal with the view that emotions are affectless sets of cognitions and
desires, and I then consider briefly analyses of emotions as affective
or affectless desires. We will see that in each case these other
accounts of emotion fail because they are unable to distinguish
consistently between different emotion-types, such as anger and
fear, envy and admiration, and compassion and malice, and also
because they mistakenly conflate emotions and various non-
emotional phenomena.

1. EMOTIONS AS COMPLEXES OF COGNITIONS, DESIRES, AND AFFECTS

I want to argue that emotions are constituted by certain cognitions, desires, and affects, such that these elements are individually necessary and, when dynamically linked, jointly sufficient for emotion. That is, in the absence of any such element in a particular case we cannot, conceptually speaking, have an emotion in that situation. Now this is not really a controversial view of what an emotion is, and indeed, this type of account has been advanced by many philosophers, such as Aristotle, Aquinas, and perhaps also Spinoza, along with various contemporary theorists.[1] However, in setting forth the view that emotions are complexes of cognitions, desires, and affects, it is important to make clear how these elements are to be understood, for those who hold this kind of view may well differ on what they take to be involved in these components of emotion.

Beginning with affectivity, some who advocate this type of account of emotion understand emotional affectivity as purely a matter of *feeling*, where to feel something involves attending to or noticing it.[2] Now it seems that our emotional feelings may be bodily or psychic (or both), depending on whether or not we *take* our feeling to be of certain (not necessarily localisable) bodily happenings. Some typical bodily changes which we may feel when we have an emotion are palpitations, fatigue, epigastric activity, dryness of the throat, shallow breathing, and various other visceral changes. However, it seems that sometimes we do *not* relate our emotional feelings to our bodies.[3] This may be clearest in emotions felt over a period of time. For example, a person who has been feeling hopeful all morning of being offered a promotion by his employer over lunch is unlikely to have been thereby feeling bodily agitation for the duration of the morning. I shall call such non-bodily feelings 'psychic feelings'. Of course, these psychic feelings are not peculiar but are part of our everyday lives. For further examples of these kinds of feelings, consider the joy we feel in reading a good novel, the feelings of excitement at the prospect of seeing an old friend, the ebullience we sometimes feel on certain days when everything seems to go well, or on the other hand, the disappointment we feel when our plans come to nothing, and the feelings of despair and anguish we have when we are struck by a grave personal loss. While such feelings may indeed sometimes be bodily, it seems that the kinds of feelings we have in the above cases need not always be bodily feelings, and in so far as these feelings are non-bodily, then they are psychic feelings.[4]

In allowing for psychic feelings I am not thereby denying that all feelings may have certain (possibly undetectable) neurophysiological correlates, nor am I denying that whenever we are in some conscious state we have at least some kind of minimal awareness of ourselves as embodied beings. Perhaps all feelings require both neurophysiological activity and an awareness on some basic level of having a body; indeed, perhaps certain other kinds of physiological activity, such as visceral changes, are always involved in our feelings also. These issues are too large to be settled here, but we need not decide them in order to understand the difference between bodily and psychic feelings. For as indicated above, what is important in distinguishing between bodily and psychic feelings is whether we *take* a certain feeling we have to be one of bodily activity.

However, while we often do experience bodily and/or psychic feelings when we have an emotion, feelings are *not* essentially involved in the concept of emotion. For as many philosophers have pointed out, it is possible and indeed quite common for us to have emotions without experiencing any *feelings* at all (either of a bodily or a non-bodily variety).[5] For instance, I might be angry with you for arriving late at the cinema since this results in our missing the crucial opening scenes of a Hitchcock thriller, but I might not have any feelings of anger nor indeed any other feelings, because my attention is occupied with trying to pick up the narrative strands of the film. Or, I may be stupefied by fear upon encountering a snake basking in the sun on the track ahead, and only after the snake has slithered away might I become aware of my pounding heart and the weakness in my legs.

We also have emotions over long periods of time without *feeling* them over the whole of that time.[6] Thus, when we are in love with someone for a number of years, we need not, indeed cannot, have feelings of love every moment of that time. And likewise, we may continue to grieve for one whom we have lost without always *feeling* this grief. Indeed, when we have such long-term love or grief, we may on occasions feel an emotion which is, in a sense, contrary to our long-term emotion. Thus, while in love we may feel angry with our beloved for not trusting us, and while grieving we may feel a certain joy in getting the promotion we have always sought. So, since it seems that we can have emotions, both short-term and long-term, without always *feeling* them, feelings cannot be an essential part of the concept of emotion.[7]

Now some philosophers have thought that this point shows that the concept of emotion does not involve an element of affectivity. I believe that such an inference is mistaken. Instead of showing that we can have emotions without affects, the point here suggests rather that emotional affectivity need not be understood solely in terms of *feelings*, as I shall now argue.[8]

It is difficult to give a precise characterisation of the affectivity which seems to be involved in the concept of emotion. Here I shall be concerned just to outline how this notion of affectivity is to be understood, while later in this chapter I shall argue that such affectivity is actually a necessary feature of emotion.

We can begin an account of this affectivity by looking at some of the ways in which we may be affected by an emotion without necessarily feeling it (where to *feel* something, it will be remembered, involves *noticing* it). As many philosophers and psychologists have pointed out, an important way in which our emotions may affect us is in terms of various unusual physiological changes in our bodies. Thus, in the earlier example, when I notice the snake on the path ahead I may undergo certain bodily disturbances which seem intimately connected (in a way to be specified) with my fear. These bodily disturbances will typically include those associated with the activation of the sympathetic nervous system, such as an increase in pulse rate, heartbeat, and respiratory rate, sweating, pupillary dilation, and decreased levels of motility in the gastrointestinal tract. Or, to take a different example, my joy at completing a difficult task might be considered as somehow involving certain bodily changes associated with the activation of the parasympathetic nervous system, such as vasodilation, muscular relaxation, salivation, and an increase in the electrical resistance of the skin.

It is clear that our bodies may sometimes be affected in these kinds of ways when we have such emotions as fear and joy, yet it seems that in having an emotion (especially an emotion like extreme fear), we can undergo these bodily changes without *feeling* them at the time. Our awareness of some of these changes in emotion, such as increased heartbeat, respiratory rate, and salivation, may come and go, depending on what our attention is focused on, yet there are other bodily changes in emotion among those mentioned above, such as pupillary dilation and increased electrical resistance of the skin, of which most of the time we are likely to be unaware. And when we do seem to have an emotion without feeling it, as when we are stupefied by fear upon discovering the snake ahead, our emotion would still have an affective dimension if we were undergoing certain unusual bodily changes which were here associated with our emotion.

Now although the affective element of emotion may consist in unfelt bodily changes of the kind mentioned above, I do not want to argue for the view held by a variety of philosophers and psychologists that emotions necessarily involve such physiological changes.[9] It is beyond my concerns to investigate the truth of this view, but it does seem to me that sometimes when we have emotions, especially emotions we have over long periods, we may not thereby undergo any associated *bodily* changes. Here the affective dimension of emotion may just consist in our undergoing certain *psychic* modifications.

But what is it to undergo these 'psychic modifications'? Earlier in this section I gave some examples of the psychic feelings which we sometimes experience when we have emotions, and I mentioned there certain feelings of joy and despair, among others. To introduce what I shall call 'psychic affects', I want to look more closely at what, if anything, we might be feeling when we have these psychic feelings. In the case of joy, for instance, we may feel a certain 'lightness', 'buoyancy', or energy permeating the mind, and affecting the way we see the world, the thoughts and desires we have, and the manner in which we act. In despair, on the other hand, we may feel 'weighed down' and drained of mental energy or strength, and again this may affect our perceptions, thoughts, desires, and actions. (Of course, feeling buoyant and drained may sometimes or even often be bodily feelings. But I suggested that such feelings need not always and only be bodily, and it is in these kinds of cases that I speak of psychic feelings.) Now the point which I want to stress here is that we can have these emotions without necessarily feeling them, for it seems that we can be affected in the above kinds of ways by emotions such as joy and despair without noticing our being thus affected at the time, and here I want to say that what remains are *psychic affects*. That is, when we are (for example) joyful or despairing without necessarily feeling so, it seems that we may thereby be (*inter alia*) mentally 'buoyed' or 'drained' respectively, and our perceptions, thoughts, desires, and actions may well express these psychic modifications without our realising it.[10]

For more detailed examples of psychic affects, consider being proud of having written a good story, or being envious of our friend's new car. Here again it appears that we can have these emotions but not be feeling them – we may be concentrating on reading the story to an audience, or on driving our friend's car in busy traffic. But we still seem to be affected by our emotions here in certain ways. Thus in being proud of our story we may be elated and in high spirits, and we may see the audience as kindred, read loudly, and sit up straight. In being envious of our friend's new car we might be slightly crestfallen and anxious to reassure ourselves of our own abilities, while also noticing how many passers-by stop to admire the car. And it seems clear that we need not *feel* (i.e. notice) either the elation and high spiritedness which we are affected by when proud here, nor our being crestfallen and anxious when envious here.

A better illustration of what I mean by psychic affects might be provided by emotions had over an extended period of time, such as marital love and profound grief. After all, as the writings of Aristotle, Heidegger, and Sartre remind us, emotions seem to be character-istically enduring rather than episodic phenomena, so it is perhaps to such long-term emotions that we should look in giving an account of emotional affectivity. A man's long-standing love of his wife does not involve continuous feelings of love nor constant bodily agitation. Instead of these feelings and bodily changes, his love would involve being interested in her and warming to her while in her company, seeing her and her projects as important, having 'heartfelt' desires to be with her, and so on. Likewise, a man's grief for his long-lost mother may continue unabated, even though he is not always feeling it nor undergoing any prolonged bodily turmoil. Rather, his grief may continue to affect him psychically such that he is downcast and languid, goes about his life in a subdued and withdrawn manner, sees the world as cold and uncaring, and so on.

As these examples suggest, the psychic dimension of emotional affectivity is the mental 'tone' which affects us when we have an emotion, and which characteristically permeates our perceptions, desires, and actions in ways which we are not always aware of. This emotional tone can affect our lives for extended periods, as in cases of enduring emotions such as the love and grief mentioned above.

Now contrary to what some philosophers may suggest, this endur-ing emotional affectivity is not satisfactorily analysed in terms of *dispositions*.[11] It is one thing to say that a person is *disposed* to have a certain kind of emotional affect over an extended period, and quite another thing to say that they actually *are* emotionally affected in a certain way over that period. For example, it is misleading to describe a person who is still grieving for his long-lost mother as having a 'disposition' to grieve for her which is 'actualised' when he talks about her and recalls his happy memories of her. For his grief is not something which is present only on such occasions: it also infuses and directs much of his thought and action in the first place. The person who has a *disposition* to grieve for his lost mother would tend to think of her and have grief on such occasions, but his grief may not colour his life in general – he may be able to overcome his grief when it occurs and get on with things without being affected by grief. But the life of the person who is still grieving for his mother is *suffused* with grief. That is, grief forms the dominant tone of his life, affecting much of what he thinks about and does, in ways such as those mentioned above.

To clarify what I mean by non-bodily emotional affectivity, let me dwell for a moment on this contrast between being *disposed* to have a certain type of emotional affect over some period, and actually *having* an emotional affect over that period. For it may seem, particularly to those who take seriously Ryle's critique of Cartesianism about mental states,[12] that there is nothing to an enduring emotion apart from a disposition to have certain affects, and that talk of such affects having an enduring 'presence' is just obscurantist metaphysics.

A useful way of bringing out the contrast I want to draw here is through an analogy with the difference between having a thought 'at the back of one's mind', so to speak, on the one hand, and on the other hand, the familiar phenomenon of having a word 'on the tip of one's tongue'. Take the thought that it is time to have morning tea with my colleagues. I can have this thought at the back of my mind while concentrating on the task at hand, but the 'presence' of the thought means that I am disposed to take appropriate action given certain kinds of stimuli: thus, I shall leave my desk immediately a colleague reminds me that it is time for tea. My thought and its link with my behaviour here is a causal mechanism which is triggered or actualised when certain events (such as my colleague's reminder) occur. Compare this with the state one is in when trying to remember a word or name which is on the tip of one's tongue. William James describes this familiar experience well:

> Suppose we try to recall a forgotten name. The state of our consciousness is peculiar. There is a gap therein; but no mere gap. It is a gap that is intensely active. A sort of wraith of the name is in it, beckoning us in a given direction, making us at moments tingle with the sense of our closeness, and then letting us sink back without the longed-for term. If wrong names are proposed to us, this singularly definite gap acts immediately so as to negate them. They do not fit into its mould. And the gap of one word does not feel like the gap of another, all empty of content as both might seem necessarily to be when described as gaps. When I try vainly to recall the name of Spalding, my consciousness is far removed from what it is when I try vainly to recall the name of Bowles; . . . our psychological vocabulary is wholly inadequate to name the

differences that exist, even such strong differences as these. But namelessness is compatible with existence . . . The rhythm of a lost word may be there without a sound to clothe it . . . Everyone must know the tantalizing effect of the blank rhythm of some forgotten verse, restlessly dancing in one's mind, striving to be filled out with words.[13]

The difference between being *disposed* to have a certain kind of emotional affect, and actually *having* that emotional affect, I suggest, corresponds roughly with the above distinction in the cognitive sphere. That is, in the case of grief, for example, a person who has a *disposition* to grieve for his lost mother over an extended period has various causal mechanisms in place which are set off by certain stimuli – a visit from an old friend of hers, a passing car which resembles hers, a familiar-sounding voice, and so on. He is, in other words, 'sensitised' to certain features of some situations, as is someone who has a particular thought at the back of his mind. The person who has enduring grief for his lost mother, on the other hand, is not merely sensitised to particular features of situations which may 'set off' his grief. Rather, his grief *guides* his attention to various motherly scenes and colours his perception of those scenes, in much the same way as James describes how the blank rhythm of a word or a line of poetry which now escapes us beckons our consciousness to run through various possible words to fill the gaps. And, just as we may, without realising, be searching our minds for a certain word which is on the edge of our consciousness, so too our perceptions, desires, and actions may be directed and coloured by a certain emotional tone, sometimes for long periods, without our necessarily being aware of it. This emotional tone is what I am referring to as the psychic dimension of emotional affectivity.

Indeed, recognising the nature of this emotional affectivity is important for another reason: it enables us to make sense of and give a rational explanation for what might otherwise appear to be merely a succession of disparate episodes.[14] Thus, a person who remembers happy occasions spent with his mother, perceives the world as cold and indifferent to him, feels mentally drained, and acts in a subdued and withdrawn manner, may not thereby be undergoing or carrying out four detached episodes. If we allow that emotional affectivity can persist and condition our thoughts, desires, feelings, and actions, then we can give a deeper explanation of the occurrence of these features here as signs of our underlying grief. In fact, as I argue in Chapter 2, it is partly because of this perception-guiding function of emotional affectivity that emotions of various kinds can be seen as morally significant. For emotions such as love, sympathy, and compassion enable us to see certain morally important features of the world as salient features of certain situations.

To sum up my account of emotional affectivity then, an affect is a bodily or psychic condition which we are in, but which we need not feel, in having an emotion, and this condition is linked dynamically with the elements of cognition and desire in that emotion.

Turning to the cognitive element of emotion, it is important that this is not construed too narrowly. Many philosophers explicate this cognitive component of emotion in terms of *beliefs*. However, as some have recently argued, the notion of belief may in some ways be too strong as a general characterisation of the kind of cognitions involved in emotions.[15] When we *believe* some proposition p, we are not merely entertaining the thought of p or imagining that p, but we in some sense are convinced that p or give our 'assent' to p, and we perhaps also hold p true or at least justified by the evidence. But it seems that sometimes we may not assent to the cognitions involved in our emotions, nor need we take these cognitions to be true or evidentially warranted. One example of this may be seen in cases of emotional 'inertia', where our emotion does not correspond to our professed beliefs or judgements: e.g. in certain dog phobias we avowedly believe that the neighbour's dog is harmless yet still seem to fear him when he approaches.[16] Perhaps here our fear of the dog does not involve a *belief* that he constitutes a threat to us, since we are convinced that he is harmless, so the cognition involved in our fear here might rather be said to take the form of a *thought* that the dog will harm us. Other examples where we might have emotions without beliefs may be the emotions which we have towards fictional characters, and the emotions we have in our dreams, daydreams, and fantasies.[17]

In the light of this it might appear better to understand the cognitive component of emotions in terms of say (following some philosophers' suggestions), thoughts, apprehensions, or imaginings, rather than beliefs. However, it would seem that the cognitions involved in emotions cannot be generally characterised in terms of these phenomena either. For thoughts, apprehensions, and imaginings (like feelings) are *conscious* phenomena or ways of being aware of (in the sense of noticing) something, but as I argued above, we can have an emotion without always being aware of having it (such as when we are angry at someone for years, or are obviously jealous on a certain occasion without realising it), and sometimes this is because we are unaware that we have the cognition involved in the emotion. In this respect, 'belief' may be a better description of our cognition here, since we can have beliefs both on particular occasions and over a period of time, without necessarily being aware of them. Perhaps all we can say, then, is that while emotions always have a cognitive component, there is no particular kind of cognition which we always have when having an emotion. Therefore, the cognitive component of emotion should be read as encompassing a variety of ways of apprehending the world, ranging over beliefs, construals, thoughts, and imaginings.

Regarding the element of desire in emotion, this need not of course be expressed in behaviour, nor need it always be a conscious, felt striving.[18] We often have emotional desires without being aware of them, although in many cases we would admit to having such desires if we were asked. I might be angry with you about something and so want to retaliate next time I see you, but at the moment I am preoccupied with something else. But sometimes our emotional desires that we are unaware of are subconscious in a deeper sense. For example, I may strongly deny envying someone their luxurious house, because I claim to have no desire for such things, but to others it may be abundantly clear from my behaviour that I am indeed envious of this person, and thus that I do actually desire the luxurious house. Similarly, although a person may profess to be motivated to stay with their partner out of love, others might find strong indications that they are really acting out of a suppressed desire to shun loneliness, and thus that they are really motivated by fear here.[19]

Let me briefly illustrate the account of emotion which I have outlined above by looking at how it would characterise some particular emotions. On my view, fear would be analysed as a cognition of imminent harm to someone and a desire to avoid this harm, along with certain appropriate affects, such as being alarmed or feeling 'hyped up'. Anger I would take as equivalent to being pained by the cognition that we (or others we care about) have been injured or wronged, and having a desire to retaliate against the offender. Jealousy, on my account, would be characterised as a painful cognition that we have lost or are in danger of losing something we want and care about (such as the attentions of another person).

So far I have been describing emotions as combinations of cognitions, desires, and affects. However, putting the view in this way may give the impression that I am proposing that when all the appropriate elements of a certain emotion-type simply coexist in us, then we actually have that emotion. But this is false. For if we have each of the components of a particular emotion but these components have radically different causes, then we do not in this case have that emotion.[20] For instance, I may notice my friend's being insulted by someone, while at the same time wanting to injure the person responsible, and feeling agitated. However, my state as so far described would not necessarily amount to being angry with the person who insulted my friend, nor even perhaps would I have *anger* at all. For my desire to injure the offensive person and my feelings of agitation might have nothing to do with my cognition of the insult – I may have wanted to injure this person for different reasons (e.g. in order to make them wary of me), and I may be feeling agitated because of a stomach upset.

This shows that in an account which explicates emotions in terms of components, it is important to emphasise that these components must be dynamically linked with each other in order to constitute an emotion. Thus in the above example, my desire to retaliate and my feelings of agitation must be dynamically related to my cognition of my friend's being insulted, in order for my state to count as being angry with the offensive person.

2. AFFECTIVE THEORIES OF EMOTION

Having outlined my own view of the nature of emotion, I now want to defend it by showing how some important rival theories of emotion are inadequate, because they omit one or more of what I hold are the three components of emotion: i.e. cognitions, desires, and affectivity. The first account of emotion I will discuss holds that emotions are bodily and/or psychic *feelings*, or at least bodily and/or psychic *affects*. Some version of this view has been held by various philosophers and psychologists, and it is also a view of emotion immediately suggested by common sense. But as we will see in this section, this view fails because in the absence of any element of cognition, it is unable to distinguish between various emotions. Proponents of this view may allow that particular emotions are *typically* linked with certain cognitions, but we will see that the connection between emotions and cognitions is stronger than this, and is in fact a *conceptual* connection.

An unambiguous affective theory of emotion was put forward by William James, and a similar view was proposed by James's contemporaries Carl Lange and Alexander Sutherland. James believed that an emotion is the feeling of certain bodily changes, mainly of a visceral nature (such as fluttering of the heart, epigastric activity, and

shallow breathing), which are produced immediately by our perception of certain features of the world.[21] He puts the view plainly in his
essay, 'What is an Emotion?' 'My thesis . . . is that the bodily
changes follow directly the PERCEPTION of the exciting fact, and
that our feeling of the same changes as they occur IS the emotion.'[22]

According to this view, different emotion-types involve feelings of
distinctive sets of bodily changes, and thus emotion-types are distinguished from each other by their different bodily feelings.[23] For
example, Lange argues that fear differs from anger in that fear
involves feelings of palpitations (produced by convulsions of the
constrictor muscles), dryness of the mouth, and trembling of the
limbs, whereas anger involves feelings of the swelling of the blood
vessels, an increase in the secretion of certain bodily fluids (such as
saliva), and the onset of irregular breathing.[24]

A somewhat different affective theory of emotion is the view that
emotions are what I have called 'psychic feelings', rather than bodily
feelings, and in the accounts of emotion given by Descartes and
Hume, there is a strong suggestion of the view that emotions are such
non-bodily feelings.[25] Thus in *The Passions of the Soul*, Part I,
articles 24–5, Descartes distinguishes the perceptions which we relate
to our body or to some of its parts – such as hunger and thirst – from
the perceptions which we refer exclusively to the soul – such as joy
and anger – which we feel as though they are in the soul itself. He
then goes on to define emotions or passions in article 27 as: 'the
perceptions, feelings, or emotions of the soul which we relate spe-
cially to it, and which are caused, maintained, and fortified by some
movement of the [animal] spirits'. So according to Descartes, an
emotion is the perception of an event in the soul.[26]

Hume seems to hold a similar view of the nature of emotion, for in
his definition of the passions in *A Treatise of Human Nature*, Book I,
Part i, section 2, and Book II, Part i, section 1, and also in his
discussions of the passions in the *Treatise* generally, Hume speaks of
passions or emotions as simple non-bodily feelings. At the beginning
of the *Treatise* Hume divides all our perceptions into impressions and
ideas, and he includes sensations and emotions in the former category, and thoughts and beliefs in the latter category. Hume then
distinguishes between emotions and bodily sensations, and proceeds
to describe the manner in which emotions are produced in us. That is,
Hume classifies emotions as 'impressions of reflexion' which are
caused by the ideas that we form of our impressions of sensation (e.g.
hunger, thirst, and various kinds of bodily pleasure and pain).[27]

Most of Hume's discussion of the passions is contained in Book II

of the *Treatise*, and here Hume deals mainly with the passions of
pride and humility, and love and hatred. His description of these
emotions illustrates well the view of the nature of emotions found
throughout the *Treatise*:

> The passions of PRIDE and HUMILITY being simple and uni-
> form impressions, 'tis impossible we can ever, by a multitude of
> words, give a just definition of them, or indeed of any of the
> passions. The utmost we can pretend to is a description of them by
> an enumeration of such circumstances, as attend them.[28]

Hume makes a similar statement about love and hatred when he
introduces them at the beginning of Part ii of Book II, describing
them as 'simple impression[s], without any mixture or compo-
sition'.[29] Thus, Hume seems to hold that emotions are simple, unanalysable impressions of a non-bodily variety, or, in other words, a type
of psychic feeling.[30]

However, an affective theory of emotion need not be cast in terms
of feelings.[31] As I argued in Section 1, it seems that we can have
emotions without feeling them, but an unfelt emotion still has an
affective dimension in the bodily and/or psychic modifications we
undergo in having the emotion. In the light of this, it may be argued
that emotions are just these bodily and/or psychic affects (which may
often, but need not, be felt).[32] So for example, this view would hold
that joy is essentially nothing more than perhaps the peculiar mental
'lightness' or 'buoyancy' which we have (and sometimes feel) on
certain occasions, while fear would perhaps be analysed as the complex set of changes our bodies undergo upon activation of the sympathetic nervous system.

Of course, few proponents of affective theories of emotion would
deny the important role of perceptions, thoughts, beliefs, and desires
as causal factors which may produce (and be produced by) emotions.
But what *all* affective theories of emotion have in common is a denial
that these causal antecedents and effects of feelings or affects are an
essential part of the *definition* of emotion. That is, those who hold
affective theories of emotion are all agreed that emotions are in
essence feelings or affects, and that particular emotions are essentially differentiated from each other by their feelings or affects. As
Hume puts it in the *Treatise*, the pleasant sensation of pride and the
painful sensation of humility 'constitute their very being and essence
. . . Of this our very feeling convinces us; and beyond our feeling, 'tis
here in vain to reason or dispute'.[33] Therefore, in their definitions of
particular emotions, proponents of affective theories can recognise

such phenomena as beliefs and desires only as (some of the) causal antecedents and effects which *typically* or *characteristically* produce or result from the affective states in question.

But whatever form of the affective theory of emotion is proposed, there is a fundamental objection which seems to refute any version of this theory. This objection is that emotions cannot be simply various kinds of feelings or affects, because it can be shown that different emotions may have the same feelings or affects. Thus, against the James–Lange theory of emotions as bodily feelings, the experimental evidence from the famous studies by Cannon and by Schachter and Singer indicates that we may undergo the same set of bodily changes in having what are clearly different emotions, and so an emotion *cannot* be identified with our feelings of these bodily changes.[34] For example, Cannon demonstrated that the same bodily changes produced by the activation of the sympathetic nervous system – including acceleration of both heart and respiratory rates, inhibition of gastro-intestinal activity, sweating, and pupillary dilation – occur in such readily distinguishable emotional states as fear and anger. Indeed, Cannon also found that these bodily changes may also be felt in various non-emotional states, such as chilliness, hypoglycaemia, and fever.[35] So contrary to the James–Lange theory, the case of fear and anger shows that emotions cannot be just the feelings of bodily changes.

A parallel objection confronts the view that emotions are psychic feelings, which I attributed to Descartes and Hume, among others. That is, emotions which are obviously different (and which are acknowledged as different by those who have them) may nevertheless have the same psychic feelings.[36] For instance, when jealous we often feel a certain non-bodily distress or anxiety, but these psychic feelings are also typically felt in anger, resentment, indignation, and in some varieties of envy. Likewise, benevolence and gratitude may both involve psychic feelings of affection and warmth. And perhaps there are certain feelings, such as interest and satisfaction, which may be experienced in both the otherwise contrary emotions of love and hatred. But if one emotion can feel like another, different emotion, then the distinctions between emotions cannot always be drawn in terms of feelings, and so the version of the affective theory which attempts to do this is mistaken.

Note that these points are distinct from the observation that the same emotion may have many different feelings. Love, for example, may on various occasions involve feelings of concern, longing, tenderness, concord, exhilaration, and so on. Now those who hold that emotions are feelings might well recognise this diversity of feelings in particular emotions. But they might argue that this is not a problem for their view, since none of the feelings of one emotion-type is ever involved in another emotion-type. That is, their claim would be that the range of feelings in love, say, never overlaps with the range of feelings in hatred. But as I suggested above, this seems false, for whether we are speaking of love and hatred, or jealousy and anger, the feelings of one emotion-type may sometimes be just like those of another emotion-type. So, because the view which holds that emotions are feelings is unable to distinguish between these different emotions in such cases, it is therefore inadequate.

Further, even if the affective theory of emotion is reformulated in terms of the view that emotions are perhaps unfelt psychic and/or bodily affects (in the sense explained above), the same problem would still show it to be mistaken. One form of this view equates emotions with the unusual bodily changes which we are thought to undergo (but do not necessarily *feel*) when we have an emotion. On this view, each emotion-type involves a unique pattern of bodily changes, and so, for example, grief and despair, on the one hand, are distinguished from love, on the other hand, in that the former are held to involve a slowing of respiration, heartbeat, and metabolic functions, while the latter is said to be characterised by a slight increase in respiration and heartbeat, muscular relaxation, pupillary dilation, and so on. However, the experiments of Cannon and Schachter and Singer mentioned above show that the same bodily changes may be involved in different emotions, and so it is *not* the case that distinct emotion-types involve unique patterns of bodily changes.[37] So the view which equates emotions with bodily affects is to be rejected because it fails to distinguish between emotions which are clearly quite different.

The other version of the view that emotions are affects takes affectivity in a psychic sense, but this view also seems to be refuted by the same kind of objection. As explained above, recognising that emotions may affect us psychically instead of (or sometimes as well as) bodily, this view claims that an emotion is nothing more than the characteristic psychic affects which we have (but need not feel) in that particular emotion. For instance, joy would be characterised as a certain lightness or buoyancy of the mind, whereas shame would essentially be a peculiar kind of mental distress or dejection. But while it is important to bring attention to the ways in which emotions can affect us psychically, it seems implausible to hold that we can distinguish between emotions purely in terms of their psychic affects, for it would appear that different emotions may involve similar psychic affects.[38] Thus, it seems that the lightness or buoyancy which might be thought characteristic of joy may also affect us when we are proud, and likewise, both shame and embarrassment may involve a certain possibly unfelt mental distress or dejection. So, when faced with the problem of distinguishing between emotions, none of the affective theories of emotion we have considered seems to have the conceptual resources to draw such distinctions adequately, and these theories must therefore be regarded as mistaken.

What all this suggests is that even when broadly construed as involving feelings and affects, *affectivity* alone is insufficient for emotion. For while we can sometimes explicate distinctions between emotions exclusively in affective terms, it seems that in many cases we need to refer to something apart from affectivity in order to adequately draw conceptual distinctions between different emotions. I shall argue, as do many other philosophers, that this added factor is usually the beliefs or cognitions (and sometimes also the desires) of the person having the emotion. That is, cognition is part of the concept of emotion.

For example, while the bodily feelings of fear and anger may sometimes be indistinguishable, we can capture the distinction between these emotions by adverting to the beliefs or cognitions which are associated with them: fear seems to involve the thought of imminent harm to someone, whereas anger involves the belief that we have (or another person has) been injured or slighted in some way. Likewise, jealousy and envy may involve similar psychic feelings, but we can distinguish between these emotions because jealousy involves thoughts of something desirable which one has or has had (such as the attentions of one's beloved) being threatened or lost, while envy seems to involve the thought of something one desires but has never had. Again, although we can be psychically affected in similar ways by pride and joy, there is a distinction between these emotions in that pride seems to require a belief in something worthwhile which is related to ourselves, whereas joy requires the thought merely of some possible state of affairs which we view favourably (whether or not we regard it as reflecting well on ourselves). Similarly, shame and embarrassment may often be indistinguishable in terms of their affects or feeling-tones, but shame is distinct from embarrassment in that shame requires an awareness of oneself somehow falling below some accepted standard of behaviour, while embarrassment requires the recognition just that one has been or is involved in something unfortunate, quite apart from any reference to such standards.

Now, some of those who hold affective theories of emotion might admit that cognitions are important for distinguishing between particular emotions, at least in so far as there seem to be certain cognitions which are typically associated with particular emotions. That is, proponents of affective theories can accept my analysis of the cognitions associated with various emotions as an account of the *typical* causal antecedents of particular affective states, but (to be consistent) they would still insist that emotions are in essence just feelings or affects. However, although this position shows some appreciation of the importance of cognition for emotion and so is thereby an improvement on those affective theories which do not allow even this much, it is nevertheless inadequate. For such a view still holds that emotions are just affects, and that in fact we sometimes do have the affect which in itself constitutes a particular emotion without also having the cognition with which it is characteristically associated (or indeed, without having *any* cognition linked with that affect at all).[39] So for example, this view would allow that the affectivity involved in the emotion of anger might conceivably be caused in some cases by a cognition quite different from the cognition that someone has been injured or slighted – such as the belief that kangaroos are marsupials – or perhaps by no cognitions at all, and what we are affected by here could still properly be described as 'anger' because of its 'characteristic feel'.

But this is implausible, for the connection between emotion and cognition is stronger than this. That is, unless our state essentially involves (along with certain affects) the cognition that someone has been injured or affronted, then it would not be anger at all. The connection between cognition and emotion is *conceptual*, for without the appropriate cognition, we cannot (logically speaking) have a particular emotion. Indeed, if our affective state was not linked with *any* cognitions at all, then our state here would be better characterised as a bodily sensation or other feeling rather than an emotion, for unlike emotions, sensations and feelings need not involve cognitions.[40]

3. COGNITIVE AND COGNITIVE–AFFECTIVE THEORIES OF EMOTION

Let us now move on to accounts which analyse emotions in terms of cognitions, or complexes of affects and cognitions. I will argue that both of these views are inadequate, mainly because they fail to recognise the importance of *desire* in the concept of emotion, and so they are unable to explicate distinctions between certain emotions, such as fear and interest, and between emotions and non-emotional phenomena.

We may begin by introducing the view which takes emotions to be combinations of affects and cognitions, or perhaps 'affective cognitions'. This seems a natural position to hold, given the inadequacies of purely affective theories of emotion. Indeed several writers, after arguing for the importance of cognitions in distinguishing among emotions, propose this type of account. Thus, according to Lyons's 'causal–evaluative theory' of occurrent emotional states, 'X is deemed to be an emotional state if and only if it is a physiologically abnormal state caused by the subject of that state's evaluation of his or her situation',[41] where an 'evaluation', for Lyons, does not involve desire but is a judgement that something is in some way good or bad. On Lyons's view then, 'Grief . . . might be defined simply as evaluating something as a great loss and that this affects the person physiologically.'[42] Similarly, Schachter and Singer define emotion as 'a joint function of a state of physiological arousal and an appropriate cognition',[43] and Stuart Hampshire speaks of emotions as feelings along with beliefs or imaginations about their causes, suggesting, for example, that 'Regret is a mode of unhappiness, or unpleasure, conjoined with a thought about the past'.[44]

There are also others who hold this kind of view of emotions, but these writers speak not so much of emotional affects being 'accompanied by' or 'conjoined with' certain cognitions, but of emotions as 'affectively charged' cognitions. So C.D. Broad claims that 'Emotions . . . are *cognitions* with a certain kind of psychic quality'.[45] That is,

> To be fearing a snake, e.g. is to be cognizing something – correctly or incorrectly – as a snake, and for that cognition to be toned with fearfulness. In general, to be fearing X is to be cognizing X fearingly; to be admiring X is to be cognizing X admiringly; and so on.[46]

Sartre also seems to characterise certain emotions, such as horror, in terms of affective ways of seeing the world.[47] This version of the cognitive–affective account brings out an important way in which we can be affected in having an emotion, which we discussed earlier in this chapter.

However, some philosophers who see the problems with purely

affective theories of emotion claim that affectivity is actually quite superfluous to the concept of emotion, and they argue that emotions are really just a form of *cognitive* phenomena. An unequivocal statement of this kind of view is provided by Robert Solomon, who holds that 'emotions are judgments – normative and often moral judgments'.[48] Solomon says, for instance, that

> I cannot be angry if I do not believe that someone has wronged or offended me. Accordingly, we might say that anger involves a *moral* judgment . . ., an appeal to moral standards and not merely personal evaluations. My anger *is* that set of judgments. Similarly, my embarrassment *is* my judgment to the effect that I am in an exceedingly awkward situation. My shame *is* my judgment to the effect that I am responsible for an untoward situation or incident. My sadness, my sorrow, and my grief *are* judgments of various severity to the effect that I have suffered a loss. An emotion is an evaluative (or a 'normative') judgment, a judgment about my situation and about myself and/or about all other people.[49]

But 'cognition' need not be taken as involving only the rather formalised notions of belief and judgement, and indeed, some who have given a purely cognitive account of emotions have analysed them in terms of such phenomena as thoughts, construals, and apprehensions, and these accounts might seem more promising than the suggestion that emotions are just a type of judgement. Thus, some philosophers have claimed that at·least some emotions are constituted by certain thoughts or complexes of thoughts, and so an emotion like jealousy, for instance, would be defined just in terms of our having thoughts of (say) our own inadequacies and our rival's strengths and weaknesses.[50]

A somewhat different kind of cognitive account is advanced by Sartre, who argues that when the things which we seek appear unattainable in reality, we attempt to resolve the situation by transforming the real world into an imaginary world, where the obstacles disappear or where what was sought is seen as no longer desirable; and according to Sartre emotions are, in general, the apprehensions which we have of the world in transforming it in these ways.[51] So for example, passive sadness or grief is characterised by Sartre in terms of our seeing the world as uniformly bleak in order to evade the new demands which carrying on our projects would otherwise place on us.[52] Influenced by Sartre, other philosophers have claimed that emotions are interpretive patterns of attention or 'construals' of the world and the people in it.[53]

Of course, those who analyse emotions in terms of cognitions may well recognise that affects and desires are importantly related to emotion. But these theorists can allow that affects and desires have only a *contingent* relation to the cognitions which they take as constitutive of the various emotions. For example, cognitive theorists would regard psychic and/or bodily agitation and the desire to flee as some of the possible causal manifestations of fear, as this emotion would be held to be essentially just a belief or thought of danger to someone, or a construal of something as dangerous.

However, while cognition is indeed essential to emotion and often provides a basis for identifying and differentiating emotions, and while it is important to recognise that emotional cognitions often do involve seeing the world in certain ways, the view that emotions are just cognitions of various kinds faces serious problems. An initial problem for cognitive accounts of emotion is that it does not always seem possible to distinguish between emotions solely on the basis of the cognitions which they involve.[54] For example, the cognition of another person in distress seems to be involved in compassion, but we may well have this cognition and feel *Schadenfreude* or malice instead. Similarly, we may construe a certain situation as dangerous with feelings of either fear or excitement. What seem to distinguish the emotions here are their feelings or affects rather than their cognitions. Thus, compassion involves being pained by another's distress, while in *Schadenfreude* and malice we find this cognition pleasurable. So also excitement, unlike fear, involves taking what we see as dangerous to be a pleasurable thrill.

Cognitive theorists may insist that emotions can always be distinguished in terms of cognitions, given that the appropriate cognitions are specified in sufficient detail.[55] So they might argue that in excitement we see the danger as a challenge, whereas in fear we see it as a threat. But instead of pursuing this rejoinder, I will bring out a fundamental problem which seems to be fatal to any purely cognitive account of emotion.

That is, emotions cannot be just cognitions, for as many philosophers have pointed out, we can and indeed often do have the particular cognition which is taken by cognitive theorists as constitutive of an emotion, yet at the same time not have that emotion.[56] For instance, a person may judge himself responsible for an untoward situation or incident, but contrary to Solomon, he may not have any shame about it because he could be too arrogant to let *this* bother him. And I may well recognise that I have suffered a significant loss without thereby feeling any sorrow or grief, for I may be quite inured to such losses. The same point can be made when cognition is understood in terms of thoughts or construals. Thus, we may be struck by thoughts of our own inadequacies in comparison with our rival, or we may construe the world as bleak and uninviting, but we might not be jealous or grief-stricken, respectively, because we may be preoccupied with other things or too tired to care. In all of these cases we judge or construe the world in some of the ways which cognitive theorists take to be equivalent to emotion, yet we do so quite unemotionally, so it seems that cognition alone is insufficient for emotion.

Perhaps cognitive theorists will deal with this problem by arguing that emotions are actually *sets* of judgements, thoughts, or construals (etc.), and so, given the appropriate set of cognitions, we will indeed have an emotion.[57] So for instance, it might be claimed that love is an emotion consisting in the complex of the following cognitions: the construal of another individual as attractive, the judgement that they are a worthwhile person, that their welfare should be promoted, and that they are stimulating company, are trustworthy, and should be accorded equal rights in a relationship. But this approach will not rescue the cognitivist position, for it is still possible to have the set of these cognitions in an unemotional way. That is, I might make these observations about another person without *loving* that person – e.g. I may be drained of emotional energy after a long and difficult break-up, or I may well be in love with someone else instead. Further, the problem here does not seem to be something which the cognitivist might resolve by adding more cognitions to the set which is thought to constitute a particular emotion, but rather, it seems to indicate a fundamental difficulty with purely cognitive theories of emotion. That is, no matter how much complexity is built into a cognitive set, it would always seem to be possible for those cognitions to be had in affective or affectless ways.[58] For what is always left out in cognitive accounts of emotion is the dimension of affectivity. But affectivity cannot be taken as superfluous to the concept of emotion since, for example, it is only when we are actually *pained* by a loss or an unfortunate incident that we can have grief or shame, respectively, and likewise, we must have *warmth* towards one whom we regard as a suitable companion, in order to have the emotion of love.

Apart from the cognitive account's neglect of the affective dimension of emotion, there is another weakness of this view, which also shows the inadequacy both of accounts which analyse emotions as combinations of cognitions and affects, and, it might also be noted, of affective theories of emotion. That is, all these views fail because they do not recognise the importance of *desire* for the concept of emotion.

The involvement of desire in emotion can be shown in various ways.[59] We can begin by taking some of the analyses of particular emotions given by cognitive and cognitive–affective accounts, and pointing out how they are unsatisfactory in ignoring desire. For instance, take the analysis of anger given by these theorists. Now this emotion cannot be defined simply as a judgement that we or others have been injured or affronted, because we might make such judgements and perhaps be moved to try to help the offender overcome their unfortunate tendencies, but here it would seem incorrect to describe our state as one of *anger*. Much the same could be said if we were pained by the acknowledged injury or affront, but nevertheless wanted only to help the offender. The reason that we do not have anger in these cases, I would argue, is because we lack the appropriate desire. That is, anger seems to involve not just being pained by what we take as an injury or a slight, but also a desire to retaliate at who or what is responsible.

Of course, anger is not the only emotion which seems to require a certain desire. Consider jealousy. As seen, those who give cognitive or cognitive–affective accounts of emotion characterise jealousy in terms of such things as having certain (perhaps affectively charged) thoughts about one's inferiority in relation to some third party and about the possibility of losing the exclusive attentions of one's spouse or companion. But one might indeed picture the loss of one's partner, and one may well find this somewhat distressing, without thereby being *jealous*. For one might recognise that the relationship has deteriorated to such a stage where it is beyond salvaging, and one might actually prefer one's partner to become interested in someone else. The point is then, that neither cognitions nor cognition–affects seem sufficient for jealousy, because jealousy also requires a desire to keep what it is one thinks one is in danger of losing. Consider also love. Would it be accurate to describe someone as *loving* another if he had no desire to be with her, benefit her, or make her happy, even if he at the same time believed that she was attractive, that her welfare was important, and he had feelings of warmth towards her? I would say not: whatever this man does have here, it would not seem to be love, unless he also has some of the appropriate desires. It would seem therefore a conceptual impossibility to have various emotions in the absence of having certain desires.

We can further demonstrate the importance of desire for the concept of emotion by pointing out that different emotions may sometimes be indistinguishable unless we make reference to desires.

For example, take fear, say, of a snake. If this fear is defined as having the cognition of a snake and being in a state of agitation, then it would not be distinguished from being interested in or excited by the sight of the snake – imagine a field naturalist catching their first glimpse of a rare species. In order to draw a distinction between these emotions here, it seems that we must also refer to the desires had by the people involved: the person who is afraid of the snake wants to flee, while the interested naturalist wants to stay and examine the snake.

The involvement of desire in emotion is also shown when emotions are cited as motives for behaviour, for it seems that when we act out of an emotion, we are usually motivated by a certain desire. For instance, compassion is sometimes given as a motive for helping others in distress, but would such action be explained if compassion was analysed just as the cognition of others who are in difficulty, or as being pained by this cognition? I would say not, because one might have this cognition or cognition–affect, and yet have an inclination to turn away (perhaps because one believes people should fend for themselves), and here one would not seem to have compassion. It appears that we need to postulate a desire to help those whom we take to be in distress as part of compassion, in order to account for the place given to this emotion in explanations of helping actions.[60] On cognitive and cognitive–affective accounts of emotion, it may well appear rather mysterious that emotions characteristically motivate us to act in certain ways, since on these views, emotions are presented as more akin to passive affective states rather than the often powerful motives which we typically find in our phenomenological experience.

4. EMOTIONS AS COGNITIONS AND DESIRES

Now, some who argue as I have that cognition must be accompanied by desire in emotion would dispute my claim that emotions require affectivity, for they hold that emotions are actually just affectless combinations of various cognitions and desires. Thus, Marks argues for a theory where 'emotions are *identified* with (certain sets of) beliefs and desires',[61] while affects are relegated to the status of 'manifestations . . . [or] effects of (some set of) the emoter's beliefs and/or desires',[62] as it is belief/desire sets themselves that constitute emotions. For instance, fear of a dog, on this view, is analysed as having not only the belief that the dog is threatening to bite us, but as having both this belief plus a desire to avoid the dog and for it not to bite us. Similarly, anger is characterised as having the cognition of an affront to someone along with the desire to punish the person responsible, whereas love consists in just, say, believing that someone is attractive and that their welfare should be looked after, while wanting to benefit them for their own sake.

The view that emotions are just affectless complexes of cognitions and desires might seem a natural position to take, once it is recognised that we can have emotions without necessarily feeling them. However, acknowledging the possibility of unfelt emotions should not lead one to conclude that emotions are essentially affectless phenomena, for there are other important ways in which we are affected in emotion, apart from having various feelings. That is, sometimes we may undergo abnormal bodily changes or be affected by certain kinds of unfelt psychic 'buoyancy' or 'heaviness' in having emotions (such as joy and grief, respectively). So, in being emotionally affected we may experience certain feelings, but sometimes we may just undergo various psychic and/or bodily modifications.

I will argue here that we cannot, conceptually speaking, have an emotion unless we are thereby actually affected in some such ways. So, in regard to the view which defines emotions as affectless complexes of cognition and desire, while I agree that emotions do involve cognitions and desires, I believe that a general characterisation of emotions exclusively in terms of these phenomena is inadequate, for such an analysis does not recognise that emotions require affectivity.

Thus, I shall suggest that sets of cognitions and desires are insufficient for emotion by attempting to show that we can have the cognitions and desires appropriate to a particular emotion, without yet having that emotion, and much less *feeling* it.[63] Consider an example where we have the cognitions and desires involved in the emotion of grief: that is, we believe that we have lost someone important to us and we wish that the lost one would return, or at least that the loss had never occurred. Now it seems that, for various reasons, we may have this complex of cognition and desire without necessarily having (nor, *a fortiori*, feeling) *grief*, or any other emotion at all. Perhaps we are not concerned or upset about the loss, for we may have been expecting it for a long time, as is often the case when we lose someone who has had an extended and debilitating illness. Or, on the other hand, we may have been grieving about the loss for some years, but now reached a stage where we are unable to grieve any longer. Something has changed in this latter case, but surely it need not be our cognitions and desires about the loss. Rather, I would suggest that what are missing when we lack grief in these cases are the *affects* appropriate to grief, such as being downcast and languid, feeling subdued, seeing the world as cruel, and so on.

Similarly, if a colleague of ours notices that we are grieving and has an inclination to help alleviate our distress, this is not yet to say that they have compassion for us. For they may not be roused by or be upset about our situation, but rather might view our plight in a cold and detached way. Here it would appear that in spite of their having the appropriate cognitions and desires, they do not have compassion because their response to us lacks an affective dimension.

To take another case, there seem to be important differences between a person who has the cognitions and desires involved in love and a person who actually has the emotion of love. Both people see another individual as attractive, both believe that she is a sincere and worthwhile person, and that her welfare should be promoted, and both people want to benefit that other person and share in her company. But the person who *loves* another seems to have more than just a certain set of cognitions and desires, as above. That is, he also cares about another individual, shares her pleasures and pains, has concern for her welfare, is interested in her projects and priorities, enjoys her company, feels warmly disposed towards her, and so on. Further, these affects may well be manifested in his behaviour, especially towards her: he may speak keenly of her, have a cheerful manner, and pursue his activities with 'heartfelt' desire.

The important point for us here is that in the absence of these affects, there is no love. For we often indicate the passing of our love for another with such comments as 'being with you no longer does anything for me', 'I cannot get enthusiastic about what you do and consider important', and 'I do not feel anything inside for you any more'. And surely we can make such claims about another individual while continuing to acknowledge their attractiveness, and to believe that they should be cared for, and while still wanting to see them flourish, and to spend time with them (only now as an associate, rather than a lover). Although we retain these cognitions and desires, we no longer *love* this person, because the affective dimension of our relationship has faded. What these examples of grief, compassion, and love suggest about emotions in general is that cognitions and desires taken together appear to be insufficient for emotion, unless there is also an element of affectivity. So it would seem to be the case that emotions require affectivity.

This conclusion is also suggested by consideration of a further problem which might be noted for the view of emotions as cognitions and desires. That is, those who hold this view sometimes seem unable to distinguish between two emotions which clearly are different, for two emotion-types may involve the same set of cognitions and desires, and be distinguishable only in terms of their affects.[64] For instance, certain kinds of admiration and envy both involve the cognition of another person possessing what one considers to be a fine quality, and both may involve a desire to have that quality oneself. However, when we feel *admiration* for someone on account of something, such as admiring a mountain climber for their courage, we are pleased by their having this quality without necessarily being pained by our lacking it, whereas in *envying* the mountaineer for their courage, it seems that we are actually pained about not having it. Affectivity seems essential to distinguishing between these emotions here, for they seem to share a common set of cognitions and desires. But because the view which analyses emotions as sets of these cognitions and desires does not allow that emotions involve affectivity, this view cannot draw a distinction between the emotions in the above example, and therefore seems inadequate.

What this also brings out is that certain affective states may well be characteristic of particular emotions, and moreover, it seems to be a conceptual requirement of having various emotions that we are affected in certain determinate ways. So for instance, grief and indignation require not just any affects but involve our being *pained* by the thought of our loss or of the other's undeserved good fortune, while pride and joy require our being *pleased* at what we value.[65] But the affectivity appropriate to a particular emotion cannot be specified too narrowly, for we can be pained and pleased by something in different ways, and in fact some emotions, such as love, seem to involve a very broad range of possible affects (e.g. being delighted by the presence of our beloved, worrying at their unexplained absence, and so on).[66]

5. EMOTIONS AS AFFECTIVE OR AFFECTLESS DESIRES

In Section 3 we saw the importance of desire for the concept of emotion, and how a reference to desire is sometimes necessary in order to distinguish certain emotion-types. Recognising this, some theorists may be inclined to dispense with any cognitive element and analyse emotions just in terms of desire and affectivity. That is, cognitions would be considered inessential to the concept of any particular emotion, although perhaps some cognition – such as a belief or thought that the object of our emotion at least exists – might be regarded as *causally* necessary for the production of an emotion.

Thus on this view emotions would be characterised as types of affective desires.

Before examining this view, I want to briefly consider the possibility of a further reduction of emotions to forms of *affectless* desire. The notion of desire would here be understood simply as having an inclination to pursue something, or in other words, as what stimulates goal-directed, intentional action. It is desire uninvested with affective significance, which is to say that it involves neither yearning nor a pleasure of fulfilment (when what is aimed at is attained). Now it is somewhat difficult to find any philosophers who actually propose a general characterisation of emotions in terms of such affectless desires, and this may already give rise to suspicions about its plausibility. However, Hume and Spinoza sometimes appear to suggest this kind of view about certain emotions, such as anger, which they both define as just the desire of misery or punishment to an adversary.[67] But whether or not Hume and Spinoza can therefore be taken as claiming that some emotions are equivalent to affectless desires, we can in any case ask if such a view could be correct as a general account of emotion. To mention some other examples of how this view might analyse particular emotions, love might be defined as just the desire to be with or benefit another, and envy could be defined as the desire to have something possessed by someone else.

While desire is indeed an important element of emotion, a theory of emotion based exclusively on desire seems inadequate, since it fails to recognise that being *affected* seems to be a conceptual requirement of our having an emotion at all. Having merely an inclination or an aim to injure an opponent, benefit some individual, or possess something had by another is not yet to have anger, love, or envy, respectively. These emotions require at least desiring with affect, such that we long to fulfil our desire and are perhaps pained at its frustration, or in any case pleased at attaining the object of our desire.

In the light of this, an analysis of emotions in terms of *affective* desires might appear more promising than the above view, but a consideration of this suggestion reveals further problems for any desire-based account of emotion. The idea now would be that emotions are to be understood as various passionately held, or 'heartfelt', desires, essentially requiring no cognition (although perhaps a minimal belief or thought about the existence of a certain object would be allowed as a contingent causal antecedent of emotion). Thus, desire would here be construed as involving more than just an inclination to seek – it would be inclination which is invested with psychic energy, as in hoping, longing, yearning, coveting, and so on. Further, desire in this sense is characterised by disappointment at dashed hopes, and satisfaction and contentment upon fulfilment.[68] So, for example, fear would on this view be analysed as having a passionate and urgent desire to flee, while courage might be held to be just a vigorous desire to protect oneself and others, come what may. Similarly, grief would be defined as a kind of painful longing, while pride might be equated with a keen desire to parade oneself in front of others.

However, any attempt to define emotions in terms of affective or affectless desires fails, because while emotions do involve affects and desires, emotions also involve cognitions. For instance, having an urgent desire to flee does not constitute fear, since we may well have this desire just because we are bored or disgusted by something, and in neither case would we actually be afraid. Along with the appropriate desire and affects, it seems essential to fear that we have a belief or thought of imminent harm to someone. Likewise, anger cannot be equated with a passionate desire to injure an adversary, since, for example, professional boxers may have such a desire towards their opponents, without being angry with them. Anger seems to require not only this affective desire, but also the belief that whom or what we want to injure has harmed or slighted us in some way. Indeed, it is *because* we have this belief that we want to injure the other person. That is, in anger the belief that we have been harmed or slighted explains our having the desire to injure the person responsible.

Another problem with desire-based accounts of emotion is that these views are sometimes unable to distinguish between various emotions, because different emotions may have the same desires and affects. For example, jealousy, anger, and hatred may all involve a perhaps passionate desire to injure someone, and so might be indistinguishable in such terms, but the cognitions involved in these emotions enable distinctions to be drawn between them. Thus, in jealousy the one whom we want to injure is a person we take to be a rival (say, for our partner), in anger this person is simply one who has harmed or affronted us, while in hatred we want to injure one whom we find repulsive and perhaps worthless, and whose welfare we believe ought not be promoted. So, accounts of emotion based solely on desire or on desire and affectivity seem inadequate, and are therefore to be rejected, because the omission by these views of any cognitive component in emotion leads to serious problems.

6. CONCLUSION

We have seen in this chapter the deficiencies of theories of emotion which omit cognition, desire, or affectivity. The conclusion, then, to be drawn from this is that an adequate account of emotions must explicate emotions as complexes involving these three elements in dynamic relations with each other.

This conclusion is also supported by an explanatory point which shows the weakness of those views which characterise emotions in terms of only some of the various phenomena which I believe constitute emotions. That is, while it may be analytically useful to speak of separate 'elements' or 'components' of emotion, we might well wonder at the extent to which the elements which I have argued are involved in emotion are really separable at all, at least in a mentally and morally healthy individual.[69] For it seems that in explaining the way people are and what they do, we normally attribute to them *complexes* of cognitions, desires, and affects together. Indeed, we usually take these elements as entering into and 'enlivening' each other, rather than as independent mental entities which sometimes happen to coexist. Now the point here is, perhaps individuals and their actions would be largely inexplicable were their emotions taken to involve only certain parts of the complexes which I understand as emotions. That is, accounts which analyse emotion just in terms of say, cognition, or cognition and affectivity (or other parts of what I regard as emotions), may well be deficient in their explanatory power, particularly when applied to our *emotional* behaviour. For instance, is a person's fleeing at the sight of a snake adequately explained by attributing to them a certain state of bodily and/or psychic agitation and the belief that they are in danger? It would seem not, for they could have held this belief while in an agitated state, and yet they might have been moved to drive the snake away instead of fleeing, perhaps because they wanted to make the way safe for others. Thus, along with cognitions and affects, we must also attribute to them an appropriate desire in order to explain what they do here.

While the view of emotions as complexes of cognitions, desires, and affects seems able to deal with the problems confronting the theories of emotion considered above, and thereby seems to be an improvement upon them, it also has much else to recommend it. As I hope the following chapters show, this account has substantial explanatory value in various contexts. For first, emotions are often appealed to as explanations of actions, and because my account portrays emotions as involving desires, it brings out a clear sense in which emotions can be motives to action. Second, since I characterise emotions as having an important affective dimension, this explains why we are often said to be 'touched', 'aroused', 'stirred', or 'fired' by emotions. Third, this view allows for the different ways in which emotions may be subject to assessments of rationality. For instance, fear may be irrational because it involves a mistaken belief (as in persistent fear of a dog which obviously left the neighbourhood long ago), or because the intensity of the affect is ill-proportioned to the object (as, for example, where the dog is still around and I am in a constant state of alarm), or perhaps because the desire involved seems inappropriate (as in, say, continuing to fear the dog when I am already well away from it).

Another advantage of an analysis of emotions as complexes of cognition, desire, and affectivity is that it accounts for the various ways in which different emotions can be related to and contrasted with each other. Thus, emotions may be classified as active or passive according to their desires; and so anger might be regarded as an active emotion because it involves the desire to seek out the offender for retaliation, while grief might be thought a passive emotion because it involves perhaps the desire to be left alone and for the past to be different. Also, we may classify emotions as calm or violent in terms of their affective element. For instance, felt admiration seems to be a calm emotion, involving relatively stable feelings of interest and fascination, whereas fear would seem to be a typically violent emotion, given the state of agitation which characterises it. And further, it is possible to find conceptual similarities among emotions by adverting to their cognitive component. So, certain kinds of envy can be seen as related to indignation, in so far as both emotions involve a cognition of another's undeserved good fortune, and analogously, pride can be contrasted with shame, because in both emotions we have a cognition of a certain quality which we see as associated with us, only that in pride we consider this quality estimable, while in shame we regard it as discreditable.

Now, this analysis of emotions as complexes of cognition, desire, and affectivity helps us gain a deeper understanding both of the moral significance of emotions, as we shall see in the following chapter, and of the possibilities of having control of (and thus being responsible for) our emotions, as we see in Chapter 4. But of course, this is not to argue that my analysis of emotions should be accepted because it enables us to better appreciate their moral importance and how we can be responsible for them. For while my view does seem to have such consequences, I have argued for it in this chapter on quite independent grounds.

I shall conclude this chapter with an important qualification about what might be called the limits of emotion. Throughout this book I talk about a variety of emotions such as care, concern, interest, sympathy, compassion, courage, and so on. Now without questioning my argument in this chapter that complexes of dynamically related cognitions, desires, and affects are emotions, it might be doubted whether some of the phenomena I speak of as 'emotions' are properly located in this category. In particular, it might be thought that, say, care, concern, and interest may be quite unemotional and dispassionate, and should not therefore be grouped with such phenomena as sympathy and compassion.[70]

This is a perfectly legitimate doubt, and I shall make three points in response to it. First, we sometimes use terms such as 'dispassionate' and 'disinterested' to denote an absence of emotional turbulence or agitation, or to denote an impartial attitude towards certain people. Thus, some talk about a scientist's dispassionate commitment to her work or a judge's disinterested attitude towards those brought before him. But both impartiality and an absence of emotional turbulence towards something are compatible with and may indeed be expressive of our having a variety of emotions towards it, and so these would not, in themselves, be sufficient to show an absence of *emotion* here. A scientist's dispassionate lack of emotional turbulence in regard to her work and a judge's disinterested impartiality towards those who stand accused before him may express a passionate commitment to seek truth and justice, respectively. As I pointed out when discussing emotional affectivity (and as Hume recognised), there are 'calm' passions or emotions, which guide and colour our thoughts in more subtle ways than typically violent emotions such as fear and anger. And as Hume also noted, there are emotions, such as benevolence, which are compatible with an impartial view of their objects.[71]

Second, it should of course be acknowledged that there are genuinely *unemotional* forms of care, concern, and interest. For example, we speak of caring or not caring for poetry, and of having 'day-care', or 'nursing care', and of something being 'a concern of mine' or being 'in my interests', which may be 'taken care of', and in all of these cases we need not be speaking in terms of our having any *emotions*. Rather, these notions of care, concern, and interest refer here to various attachments, commitments, and preferences we may have, or activities we may be involved in. To be sure, it may be that, as I argue in the following chapter in relation to self-worth, we cannot give an adequate account of notions such as attachment and commitment without involving emotions. Nevertheless, attachments, commitments, and preferences are not as such necessarily emotions, and in so far as certain of these phenomena are seen as features of a virtuous person, then it would follow that emotions are not the only psychological states or conditions which ought to be cultivated.

Thus, my third and final point here is to acknowledge a qualification in my talk of 'emotions'. That is, where the phenomena I speak of as emotions can be plausibly given a non-emotional interpretation, as is the case with care, concern, and interest, I should unless otherwise indicated be understood throughout as referring only to the *emotional* forms of those phenomena, construed as complexes of dynamically linked elements of cognition, desire, and affectivity.

2 The moral significance of emotions

Emotions occupy a fundamental place in our moral lives. However, especially in recent ethicists' preoccupation with action, this truth has all too often been obscured. Some philosophers have lately been re-emphasising the importance of emotions for morality, providing analyses of the moral significance of particular emotions such as sympathy, compassion, pride, and jealousy. In this chapter I shall take a broader perspective. That is, I aim to show that there are various emotions which are indeed morally significant, and I want to explain how their moral significance is to be properly understood. In undertaking this I want to demonstrate that we can appreciate the full moral significance of emotions only if we accept that, as I argued in Chapter 1, emotions are complex phenomena involving cognitions, desires, and affects; and so accounts which characterise emotions in terms of only one or two of these elements lead to an undervaluing of the place of emotions in our lives. But even if one accepts my account of emotions as complexes of these three elements, one may still not appreciate that each of these elements contributes to the moral significance of emotions, so this chapter also aims to establish this latter point.

I begin by criticising certain forms of the view that the moral significance of emotions derives from only one or two of their component cognitions, desires, and affects. As a point of departure for my discussion of the moral significance of emotions, I consider some features in the life of an unemotional or emotionally deficient person. I then try to bring out the ways in which various emotions may be shown morally good and bad in their connections with such important and interrelated goods as insight and understanding, strength of will, relationships of love and friendship, and having a sense of self-worth, and I argue that certain emotions are essentially involved in our achieving these goods. That is, it may only be through having emotions such as sympathy and compassion that we can make an accurate judgement of another's needs, which is morally good both in itself and in enabling us to act appropriately. Further, our emotions play an integral part in our carrying out our values with psychic harmony, which is the morally best way of enacting our values, and emotions are central to relationships of love and friendship. Also, our deepest attachments, which are crucial to our sense of self-worth, essentially involve emotions. In arguing for such claims, I do not enter into extended discussions of these particular goods, for my aim is to give a general account of some of the important ways in which emotions are involved in our living a flourishing life. And if my arguments are right, they will also show that the lives of unemotional or certain emotionally deficient people will be morally impoverished in various ways.

Towards the end of this chapter, and as a means to clarifying aspects of my account, I consider some deficiencies in how emotions may be seen as significant by certain forms of utilitarianism, and also in an influential recent defence of ethical altruism. This leads to a discussion of the nature of moral value, and I conclude by looking at ways of evaluating particular emotional responses.

Whether and how emotions are thought to be morally significant seems to depend partly on one's account of the nature of emotions, and partly on one's conception of morality. The account of morality according to which I argue that emotions are morally significant is based on an aretaic ethics or ethics of virtue. Such an ethics takes virtue as both self-regarding and other-regarding, although not necessarily in a universalistic sense, and as involving motives, intentions, and character-traits, as well as acts in which these may be manifested.[1] This account is therefore broadly speaking Aristotelian, where the notion of a good life is central, and where morality involves not just doing good acts, but performing such acts both out of good motives and for the sake of good reasons. Indeed, according to the conception of morality drawn on in this book, acting well is only one aspect of living a good life, for living well perhaps more importantly involves the development of a certain good character as an enduring way of being which underlies and informs the actions we perform on particular occasions.[2]

Now it might be thought that to use an Aristotelian conception of ethics to argue for the moral significance of emotions begs the question, since it is already part of this account that emotions play a central role in virtue.[3] But I do not assume from the outset that emotions have moral significance. Rather, my argument for this claim is based on certain observations about how emotions operate in our lives. Further, my argument is also supported by an examination of some deficiencies in the way emotions are characterised as significant by certain other moralities.

In what follows, emotions are understood as complex phenomena involving cognitions, desires, and a dimension of affectivity. This account of the nature of emotions was argued for in Chapter 1, and the points I make in the present chapter might be seen as lending further support to such an understanding. For while some of what I say below may apply equally well on some other models of emotion, I hope to show that the integral part which emotions play in our moral lives can be properly appreciated only if one accepts the account of emotion given in the previous chapter.

1. COMMON MORAL ASSESSMENTS OF EMOTION

A variety of moral assessments linked with emotions are often made in common usage. For instance, love, care, and sympathy are commonly thought good, while hatred, resentment, and malice are thought bad. We are accused of feeling excessive fear, overweening pride, or unjustified anger. We may be admired for our courage, praised for our compassion, or esteemed for our benevolence. This may already suggest that the way such assessments are applied to us and our emotions is highly complex. In this chapter, I shall be concerned largely with moral assessments of emotions themselves, rather than with evaluations of persons on account of their emotions, which I reserve for Chapter 5. But while the moral assessments of emotions found in ordinary language may be suggestive, my arguments for the moral significance of emotions do not rest on linguistic usage. I mention the occurrence of such assessments in this context only to point out that what I am arguing for has, at least in outline, considerable foundation in common sense.

However, our preanalytic evaluations of various emotions are not very illuminating and may in fact be rather misleading. For instance, sympathy and care may not be morally good when felt towards a person known to be thoroughly evil, and likewise, hatred and resentment of such a person may here not be morally bad. Indeed, we might wonder whether there are any particular emotion-types which (to the extent that they are morally significant at all) can be invariably associated with either only goodness or only badness.[4] I shall not discuss this large question directly here, for my more modest aim in this chapter is to indicate some of the ways and circumstances in which a range of particular emotions may be morally good or bad. In doing this I want to develop the idea, which Aristotle was correct to emphasise, that living a good life involves, in an important sense, living an emotional or spirited life.

Before proceeding, it should be acknowledged that some of the assessments which we commonly make of emotions involve standards of rationality rather than morality. For example, when we speak of anger as irrational or unreasonable, we may be referring to the cognitions involved (e.g. that you were being offensive, or that *you* were the one who injured or slighted me) as ill-founded in some way,[5] or to the desires involved (e.g. to retaliate against the table edge) as somehow inappropriate, or perhaps to the feelings as being 'out of proportion' to the situation (e.g. becoming outraged at having been shortchanged a small amount of money),[6] rather than to any moral significance that the anger might have. Other assessments, such as 'justified' and 'unjustified', are perhaps less clear, for they seem able to be used in either a moral or a rational sense.

There are important issues involved here in rational assessments of emotions. We may disagree over how to explicate the notion of feelings being 'in proportion' to a situation, and there may be a problem, parallel to that raised below in regard to moral assessments of emotions, with assessing emotions for rationality in terms of only one or two of their constitutive elements (i.e. cognitions, desires, and affects), rather than all three taken together.[7] There are also interesting and complex issues concerning the relation between rational and moral assessments of emotions since, to mention just one point, it seems that if an emotion (such as resentment of a colleague) is *rationally* justified, this may not in itself be sufficient for it to be *morally* justified, and likewise, to say that some emotion (such as brotherly love) is *rationally* unjustified is not always to say that it is *morally* unjustified. Indeed, as this may suggest, perhaps for at least some emotions, their being rationally justified or unjustified is not even *necessary* for them to be morally justified or unjustified, respectively, so it may be rather difficult to establish general connections between the rationality or irrationality of particular instances of emotion and their moral justifiedness or unjustifiedness.[8] In any case, these issues involving rational assessments of emotions shall largely be left aside in what follows, for to discuss them would lead me too far astray of my concerns in this chapter.[9] Nevertheless, it is important, particularly when referring to assessments of emotions found in common usage, to acknowledge the distinction between rational and moral assessments of emotions.

Quite apart from facts about ordinary language, the claim that emotions are morally significant might be thought uncontroversial for a further reason. For according to a certain traditional view, emotions are disorders of the soul which, if not controlled (by 'reason'), are without exception morally evil.[10] So, Augustine states that the Stoics (such as Epictetus and Marcus Aurelius)

> defend the wise man's intellect and reason against enslavement to the passions . . . [the mind of such a man] permits no perturbations, however they may affect the lower levels of the soul, to prevail in it over reason. No, on the contrary, the mind itself is their master and, when it will not consent but rather stands firm against them, upholds the sovereign rule of virtue.[11]

Thus, in so far as emotions are not under (rational) control they are morally bad, and only to this extent are emotions morally significant.

However, this view seems mistaken for many reasons, of which I will mention only two. First, it understands the relation of emotions to virtue on the model of an ascetic controlling their bodily drives and pleasures and pains, and in doing so, involves an oversimplified and, I argued in Chapter 1, mistaken account of the nature of emotion.[12] Second, while certain emotions may be bad if not controlled in this manner, this is not the case with all emotions, for, as I argue below, there are many important senses in which emotions may be morally *good*, and so are to be valued and cultivated instead of being despised and restrained, as the Stoics would have it. Therefore, emotions may be morally significant on account of their goodness, rather than their badness.

Of course, emotions may be morally bad for many reasons, and in this chapter I will indicate some of the ways in which we can understand their badness. But given the prevalence of the view in traditional moral psychology of emotions as spiritual disorders which are evil if not rationally controlled, I will concentrate on explicating the moral significance of emotions in terms of their goodness, and in doing so, I shall advert to certain corresponding ways in which emotions can be morally bad or wrong.

2. EVALUATIONS OF EMOTIONS IN TERMS OF SOME OF THEIR COMPONENTS

Given my characterisation of emotions in Chapter 1 as complexes of cognitions, desires, and affectivity, perhaps we can begin a philosophical account of the moral significance of emotions by looking for moral significance among their components. Some of those who argue for the moral significance of emotions do so on the grounds of the beliefs, thoughts, or attitudes which they involve. For example, Gabriele Taylor suggests that 'one might plausibly hold that it is always wrong to be jealous at least where the object of jealousy is a person, on the grounds that the emotion involves the belief that another person is a thing to be possessed'.[13] Along similar lines, the goodness of love might be analysed in terms of the belief, which is partially constitutive of love, that the other is a final goal, and, somewhat differently, the moral appropriateness of certain kinds of shame might be seen as deriving from the ashamed person's *admission* of involvement in something immoral. And indeed it does seem that certain cognitions, whether they are involved in emotions or not, can themselves be good or bad. Believing that certain groups of people don't have rights which they do in fact have is regarded as morally reprehensible, while a belief in the value of fidelity between lovers is often thought morally commendable.

Others who argue for the moral significance of emotions focus on the goodness or badness of the desires involved. Thus, according to A.C. Ewing,

> The meaning of 'hatred' commonly includes a desire to destroy or damage its object . . . Now it seems to me that it is always wrong to try to inflict injury on a conscious being as an end in itself, and so the very desire to do so is always open to objection.[14]

Or, for example, sorrow at another's misfortune might be thought good because it involves a desire that the other be happy, and envy thought bad in so far as it involves a desire to deprive others of their achievements. And as such analyses imply, we do regard certain desires, such as the desire to help others, as having moral significance in themselves. Of course, this is not to say that such a desire is *always* good, for, as I discuss later, some desires to help others (such as the desire to help a thief) may be morally bad. Nevertheless, it is clear that in both cases the desires themselves have moral significance.

Another (although less common) approach to understanding the moral significance of emotions may be through a consideration of their affective elements.[15] So, for example, it might be suggested that the goodness of sympathy or compassion as established traits of character derives solely from their exemplifying a capacity for feeling with others (e.g. being upset at their plight), and that this capacity itself is good. Similarly, depression might be thought morally bad on the grounds that it involves feelings or affects which are debilitating to the self. Further, excesses and defects of affectivity in emotion may also have moral significance,[16] and indeed, it might be claimed that certain instances of emotion attain moral significance only because of such affective variations. Thus, a well-proportioned fear of spiders may as such be morally insignificant; however, an irrational fear of spiders, involving severe affective disturbances (such as extreme anxiety, palpitations, nausea, etc., as in arachnophobia) is, at least in so far as rationality is desirable in a good person, clearly a moral defect and therefore to be avoided.

Of course, those who believe that the moral significance of emotions can be shown through their affective elements may also point to the importance here of the link between affects and other components of emotion. Thus it might be suggested that the moral significance of emotions can best be understood in terms of 'affective cognitions'. So for instance, C.D. Broad suggests that the emotion of malice or *Schadenfreude* is morally bad because 'It is [morally] inappropriate to cognize what one takes to be a fellow man *in undeserved pain or distress* with *satisfaction* or with *amusement*'.[17] Likewise, love might be thought good in so far as it is a form of taking pleasure in the good, and envy may be thought bad because it involves being pained at the success of others. Or perhaps the moral significance of emotions might be thought better shown through 'affective desires'. On this kind of analysis, the goodness of courage, for instance, could be explained in terms of its involving a passionate desire to protect oneself and others.

Yet perhaps the most common approach of those who attempt to show the moral significance of emotions is to ignore affectivity and concentrate on the complexes of cognition and desire involved in emotions. That is, rather than looking at only the cognitions or only the desires in emotions, many hold that we can understand the full moral significance of emotions only by considering the way in which such cognitions and desires operate together. According to this view, the moral goodness of, say, compassion is wholly due to its involving the cognition of another person in a state of suffering and the desire for their welfare. A.C. Ewing takes this kind of view when he says, speaking generally of our morally bad emotions, 'in the main we blame a person for his emotions not on account of what he feels but on account of what he sets himself to do, what policy he adopts, [and] what thoughts he voluntarily and habitually dwells on'.[18] Jerome Shaffer makes a similar claim, summarising his account by saying, 'In short, the moral status of the emotion is merely a matter of the moral status of the causative beliefs and desires.'[19]

What the preceding accounts all have in common is the reduction of the moral significance of emotions to the goodness and badness of one or two of their three constituents: that is, the morality of emotions is reduced to the goodness and badness of cognitions or desires or affects, or various pairs of these elements. Now, while such analyses are helpful in pointing us in the right direction and may contribute to our understanding of the moral significance of emotions, nevertheless, as general approaches to demonstrating the true moral significance of emotions these accounts are inadequate, for in order to appreciate this significance properly we must consider emotions in their full complexity. That is, unless the elements of cognition, desire, and affectivity are considered together, we will have only a partial or incomplete account of the moral value of emotions.

If it is only due to certain of their components that emotions are morally significant, then there would be no *moral* difference between having a certain cognition, desire, affect, or some pair of these phenomena, and having the particular emotion which is constituted by the complex of these elements. For example, someone who believes that another person is suffering and/or wants to promote his welfare, but who does not have any accompanying feelings or affects would, on some of the above views, in this regard be no different, *morally speaking*, from someone who has sympathy or compassion for another person. But this seems false, for as I argue in more detail in what follows, a person who is not moved affectively by another's plight, even though he wants to promote the other's welfare, and perhaps believes that he ought to, may nevertheless fail to act on these beliefs and desires when it is morally appropriate to do so. Or, if he does take action to relieve the other's suffering, the nature of his assistance here may itself be inadequate in morally important ways, and, as I shall argue, this is particularly clear when seen in the light of the kind of help which the sympathetic or compassionate person is able to give. But quite apart from their deficiencies as a moral *agent*, the person who, through lacking affectivity, lacks emotions such as sympathy and compassion may thereby have certain moral defects of character, including psychic disharmony, detachment, and insensitivity, for as we shall see, sympathy and compassion, along with other emotions, are morally important in a non-motivational sense.[20]

On another of the preceding views of the moral significance of emotions, a person who is affectively moved by someone's suffering and wants to help them would here be morally indistinguishable from a person who has sympathy or compassion for someone in distress. Now while, as I have suggested, affectivity is indeed a morally important feature of emotion, a recognition of this should not lead us to neglect the moral significance of cognition in emotion. I would say that the person above who has just the affective desire involved in sympathy and compassion is morally inferior to a person who is actually sympathetic and compassionate. For the former person does not have the level of understanding of another person's suffering which I shall argue is so important for showing the moral goodness of sympathy and compassion.

Of course, along with affect and cognition, *desire* is also a morally important component of emotion, and so those who believe that the moral significance of emotions can be properly understood in terms of just affective cognitions are also mistaken. Looking again at sympathy and compassion, the moral goodness of these emotions cannot be adequately shown just in terms of our being pained at the cognition of another in distress (which indeed is consistent with our not having sympathy or compassion at all, but instead wanting to ignore the person in distress): as we shall see, the altruistic desires involved in these emotions are integral to their moral goodness.

Now I do not want to go through each morally significant emotion-type and show how all of its three components contribute to its having this significance. For some further initial evidence in support of this claim, consider briefly the very different emotions of love and malice. In demonstrating the moral importance of love, I shall argue that we must advert to not only the lover's belief that the welfare of the beloved should be promoted and his desire to benefit her for her own sake: we must also emphasise the moral value of the lovers' sharing of each others' pleasures and pains, and the warmth which they have towards each other. And in understanding the moral significance of malice, it is not enough to consider only the malicious person's pleasurable cognition of another in a state of suffering. We must also advert to the malicious person's desire that the sufferer be harmed, in order to properly explicate the moral badness of malice.

As I said above, rather than looking at the whole range of emotion-types in order to support my view that a complex account of the nature of emotion is necessary for understanding their full moral significance, I shall argue for this view by taking some centrally important features of a good life and showing how various emotions, conceived as dynamically related complexes of cognitions, desires, and affects, are integral to our achieving these good features and so to our living a good life. Thus, in demonstrating the place of emotions in a good life, my argument also aims to show that the moral significance of emotions cannot be fully explained by attending to the goodness or badness of only *some* of their components, taken singly or in pairs. For such analyses fail to highlight the distinctive moral significance of *emotions* themselves, concentrating instead on the moral significance of one or two of their components – most commonly, sets of cognitions and desires.

Now, this is not to reject *any* reductive account of the value of emotions, as my account is itself a form of reductionism, given that I analyse the morality of emotions in terms of the goodness and badness of the three elements which I argued in Chapter 1 together constitute emotions. What I do want to reject here are those reductionisms which attempt to understand the moral significance of emotions always in terms of only one or two of their components, even if these views allow that the significance of different emotion-types may not always be due to the same component (e.g. cognition) or pair of components (e.g. cognition and desire) in each case. So I argue that in any case where we aim to achieve a proper understanding of the moral significance of a certain emotion, we must see the goodness or badness of this emotion in its full complexity: that is, we must see the emotion as composed of morally significant cognitions, desires, and affects, taken together.

A point should be clarified before continuing. Some of those who reduce the moral significance of emotions to the goodness or badness of only one or two of the constituents seem to do so because they hold similar reductionist views about the nature of emotion itself. But someone who advocates one of the reductionisms criticised above in regard to the *morality* of emotions need not accept a parallel reductionist *definition* of emotion. So for instance, in arguing that the moral importance of compassion must be explicated in terms of only cognitions and desires, one need not hold that compassion is actually *defined* in terms of just cognitions and desires. Thus, while Ewing and Shaffer (among others) allow no place for affectivity in their accounts of the moral significance of emotions, they nevertheless explicitly acknowledge the presence of an affective element in emotion.[21] I am therefore not concerned in this chapter with issues about the *definition* of emotion, which I have already discussed in Chapter 1.

Of course, the definition of emotion which one accepts will have an

important bearing on one's approach to analysing the moral significance of emotions, and so, looking at some theories which I rejected
in Chapter 1, those views which equate emotions with affects or with
cognitions would (in so far as they considered emotions morally
significant at all) obviously lead to affective- and cognitive-based
accounts, respectively, of the moral significance of emotions.
However, if what I have been suggesting is right, then my argument
will show the inadequacy of the accounts of the moral significance of
emotions which would be yielded by those theories of emotion I
argued against in Chapter 1. Thus, I want to demonstrate that in
order to properly understand the distinctive moral significance of
emotions, we need at least a theory of emotions which defines them
as complexes of cognitions, desires, and affects; but as the views of
Ewing and Shaffer show, establishing this conception of emotion will
not itself ensure a proper approach to understanding the moral
importance of emotions. For we must also see the integral part played
by all of these components in showing the full moral significance of
our emotions.

3. SOME IMPORTANT CHARACTERISTICS OF AN EMOTIONALLY DEFICIENT PERSON

We can begin to appreciate the moral significance of emotions by
noting that the life of an emotionally deficient person may well
thereby be seriously impaired in certain ways. In general terms, such
a person will most likely be characterised by insensitivity, apathy,
listlessness, and detachment, and during their life they would probably be afflicted by feelings of worthlessness, alienation, aimlessness,
and maybe also depersonalisation. Indeed they may be unable to see
any unity and thus perhaps any meaning in their life, and might
therefore have no real sense of their own identity, since our emotions
seem to play an important role in determining what and how much we
are capable of remembering about our lives.[22]

Now, this person's emotional deficiency could be due to their
lacking appropriate cognitions, and so they may have only a superficial understanding of others and of the world in general, and they
might also fail to discern certain important moral features of the
situations they find themselves in. But their emotional deficiency
might also be an indication of a defect of desire, and thus, because
they are unmotivated and lack reasons for action they may, like
Camus's outsider, Meursault, have no real direction or purpose in
their life. Yet even if they do have certain cognitions and desires, so

that, say, they notice injustices suffered by others and want to help them, such a person may fail to respond appropriately here, if they respond at all, since their emotional deficiency might betoken the absence of any meaningful affective dimension to their life. If this were so, then they might likewise observe slights to themselves and perhaps desire to retaliate, but lack the care or interest to do so and, as Aristotle puts it in his description of the 'unirascible' or servile person, would endure these slights or 'put up with' them instead.[23] Thus, an emotionally deficient person may well have no self-respect or respect for others, and such a person may lack integrity and suffer from certain kinds of serious psychic disharmony. If they acted on their cognitions and desires at all, they would perform their activities without 'having their heart in' them – that is, routinely and mechanically – and they would be disengaged from the world around them. Indeed, we might well wonder whether such a person would qualify as a moral agent at all.[24]

It may seem clear enough from the above that the life of an unemotional or emotionally deficient person would, as such, be morally defective, both psychically and in terms of action, and perhaps this is already some indication of the deep moral significance of our emotions.[25] But while this approach is suggestive, it can at best show that emotions are morally important only in so far as they are necessary for us to avoid having certain moral defects. However, the moral significance of emotions can be demonstrated in a more positive way by looking at how they are importantly involved in our achieving certain goods, and those which I will consider in what follows are insight, good judgement, and understanding, strength of will, love and friendship, and a sense of self-worth. This is no mere arbitrary list of goods, for all are central to at least many kinds of good lives, and, as I hope to show, we can discern many important connections between such goods. So, for example, strength of will often requires good judgement, understanding, and a sense of self-worth, as indeed may love and friendship. In attempting to understand such goods and their important connections with emotions and each other, we can gain some idea of what good people may be like.[26]

4. PERCEPTION, INSIGHT, AND UNDERSTANDING

I suggested above that a noteworthy feature of an unemotional or emotionally deficient person might be their suffering from a certain blindness to the way the world is. Both traditional and contemporary moral psychology often portray emotions as typically involving or resulting in some form of impairment of our perceptual and cognitive faculties. We are urged to repudiate or control our emotions as a means to attaining a clear appreciation of reality.[27] Now this depiction of emotions may be true in some cases, and in so far as it is true of a certain emotion of ours, this may constitute grounds for judging our emotion morally bad or wrong in that respect. However, taken as a general account of the way in which emotions operate, this picture seems false. Against this overemphasised account, I want to show that there are important ways in which emotions may actually enlarge and deepen our perception and understanding of the way things are. Concentrating on cases of cognitive distortion in giving a general characterisation of emotions is highly misleading, and presents emotions in an artificially bad light. In what follows I consider only briefly some of the important connections between emotions and insight and understanding, but this should be sufficient both to illustrate how emotions can actually be morally good in this context, and to suggest that the traditional account of these relations is mistaken.

Clear perception and keen judgement are undoubtedly essential to a good person. Insight and understanding have their own value, and further, they are often indispensable to the performance of good actions (as we shall see in more detail in the following chapter). Now to begin with a general point, it is obvious that certain emotions, such as care and interest, will often lead us to a deeper understanding of various features of the world, in the sense that having care and interest in something motivates us to learn about it. This already suggests that the traditional account described in the previous paragraph is wrong, but I want to argue for a stronger claim. That is, I want to show that having certain emotions may sometimes be *necessary* for understanding some features of the world, such that an appreciation of these features would be beyond an unemotional person. This does not appear to be so in the kind of case just mentioned, for it is possible for us (or at least *some* of us) to learn about many things without being motivated by care or interest, or indeed, without being motivated at all.

Nevertheless, it seems that the unemotional person will, as such, have a narrow perception of various features of the world and will lack certain kinds of morally significant knowledge regarding others and the world in general. Several points can be made in support of this claim. First, as Blum and Wallace argue, a sympathetic, compassionate, or kind person is not only apt to perform beneficent acts, but also characteristically perceives more situations as warranting beneficent action when this is in fact the case, than would a person lacking in sympathy, compassion, or kindness.[28] But further, when encountering someone in distress, having such emotions as sympathy and compassion for her often seems necessary in order to understand exactly what her distress involves and what her needs in that situation are.[29] For example, in the absence of sympathy and compassion we might sometimes be unable to imagine or appreciate the suffering of a person who is the victim of racial or sexual discrimination. Similarly, perhaps an unsympathetic or uncompassionate person cannot really understand the despair of someone suffering 'mid-life crisis', whereby the achievement of their youthful goals seems hollow and their current activities seem to lack vitality. Or, consider someone who is mourning the loss of a loved one. It seems unlikely that we can comprehend or even imagine the bereavement and sense of loss experienced by this person unless we have at least some degree of sympathy or compassion for them.

To appreciate the peculiar quality and magnitude of each of these individuals' suffering, it seems that we would need to have a certain *feeling-with* them. But this does not mean simply that we must, in a certain sense, share their pain – we might share their pain for any number of reasons, not all of which would be morally significant or appropriate. It also means that we must believe that they ought to be given support and we must want to help them. Without this complex of cognition, desire, and affectivity we would not have sympathy or compassion for them (but perhaps only distant pity, resignation, or maybe just indifference instead), and without these emotions, it seems doubtful that we could appreciate the nature of their suffering.

To be sure, since one's sympathy or compassion may be weak or ill-informed, I am not saying that having these emotions is always *sufficient* for understanding the plight of the person at whom they are directed. What I am saying is that the unsympathetic or indifferent person (or, as we shall see in the next chapter, the Kantian moral agent acting from duty), to the extent that they perceive the distress of others at all, will often be incapable of understanding the nature of that distress.

Along with such emotions as sympathy and compassion, *love* may also enlarge our perception and understanding of others in a manner that may not be available to an unemotional person.[30] For since loving another involves caring for them for their own sake, in love we contemplate the nature of the other's well-being, and through this contemplation we may reach a deeper understanding of human needs and human nature in general. But further, love may lead us to profound insights about other aspects of the world which would otherwise be unattainable, for love gives us the opportunity to adopt the viewpoint of our beloved – i.e. to, as it were, 'see things through their eyes', and experience with them.

Indeed, this kind of point can be made about many emotions, in the following way. No doubt our understanding of various significant features of the world is importantly developed by our encounters with fictional works (novels, plays, films, etc.), but it is worth noting that a fundamental way in which fiction enlightens us is through our responsiveness to and identification with the plight of various fictional characters in emotions such as sympathy, admiration, pity, and fear which we have in regard to them. Perhaps we would not learn much about the world or the 'human condition' through fictional works if we were not emotionally moved by such works. The novelist and literary critic C.S. Lewis asks, 'What then is the good of . . . occupying our hearts with stories of what never happened and entering vicariously into feelings which we should try to avoid having in our own person?' Lewis's response to his question illustrates my point:

> The nearest I have yet got to an answer is that we seek an enlargement of our being. We want to be more than ourselves. Each of us by nature sees the whole world from one point of view with a perspective and a selectiveness peculiar to himself . . . . But we want to escape the illusions of perspective . . . We want to see with other eyes, to imagine with other imaginations, to feel with other hearts, as well as with our own.[31]

Thus, 'seeing through another's eyes' in love, and the enlargement of understanding we may thereby gain can be thought of as the deepest form of a perfectly general way of reaching insight, as is shown in the enlightenment we may find through our emotional responses to fiction.

Now it might be thought that I have overstated the point here, since some people (such as psychoanalysts and literary critics) can be trained to adopt the viewpoint of other people or fictional characters, without having love or sympathy (or maybe any other emotions) towards them. I would not dispute this, and so I would not argue that love and sympathy are *essential* for the type of enlargement of understanding which I am speaking of. Nevertheless, perhaps we can still say that the kind of depth and breadth of insight which is attainable through *loving* another could not be achieved by a purely intellectual approach. But whether or not this is true, loving another person is still morally important at least in so far as we are thereby given the opportunity to take up a different perspective to our own in a profound way. The traditional account of the bearing of emotions on morality therefore seems misguided in its emphasis on cognitive impairment, for as the above points indicate, emotions may contribute in important ways to our achieving the virtues of clear perception, keen judgement, and depth of understanding, and this shows an important dimension to the moral significance of emotions.

5. STRENGTH OF WILL

As well as lacking insight and understanding, an unemotional or emotionally deficient person may also suffer from a certain kind of weakness of will, for failing to do what one believes good (and indeed, sometimes doing what one believes bad) is a natural consequence of lacking emotions such as care, concern, interest, sympathy, compassion, and courage.[32] This suggests that, as I will argue in this section, having certain emotions is important for doing and being moved to do what one believes good, and not doing or not being moved to do (or being moved not to do) what one believes bad. I want to show here that various emotions may be morally significant in so far as they play an integral part in the transformation of our values into action, or in what we might call our having *strength of will*.

To illustrate the importance of various emotions here, consider the following examples. A student may genuinely believe that keeping up with their work is valuable, and they may perhaps want to do so, but they might well nevertheless fall behind if they lack care and interest in their subject, which they find 'leaves them cold'. Similarly, a person who values helping others in distress and has the desire to do so, but who is emotionally unmoved by the suffering of others, may fail to actually help here because of his 'moral ineptitude'. That is, given the insight into others' needs which we saw in the previous section is attainable through sympathy and compassion, the assistance offered by this person may be inappropriate because he has no *emotional* understanding of the nature of another's distress, nor of what needs to be done in order to help them. Consider also a person who wants to and believes he ought to stand up and defend his humanitarian values against his hostile father. Unless this person has the *courage* of his convictions, he may well fail to successfully defend himself from his father's challenges – perhaps because he would be overcome by fear of his father (or maybe he would be overconfident and so present inadequate arguments).

Now I am not denying that we can, at least on occasions, act on our values in the face of contrary desires and emotions, or without emotions altogether. It is, of course, possible to pursue what one believes good without say, caring for it or having interest in it, and indeed, as we shall see in the following chapter, this may be Kant's view of how the good moral agent will act. So we cannot claim that having certain emotions is *necessary* for strength of will. Nevertheless, we can still argue that emotions such as care, interest, sympathy, and courage play an *important* part in preserving action in accordance with our values, for it is an undeniable psychological fact about us that, without these emotions, our commitments to uphold our values in action may falter. And where what we value is in fact morally good, such emotions might be shown morally right to this extent, whereas if an emotion is integral to our transforming a morally bad value into action, this emotion may be shown morally wrong in this context.

However, I want to argue for a deeper claim. I want to suggest that where what we value accords with what is morally good, we may be *morally better* if in carrying out what we believe good, our emotions harmonise with our values, than if our emotions and values are in disharmony. As Aristotle points out in his contrast between the good person and the merely continent person, while both value and act on what is right, the continent person is morally inferior because he suffers from emotional disquietude in doing so, whereas the good person acts rightly with harmony between his emotions and his values – that is, they 'speak with the same voice'.[33]

Given that we value the right things, there are at least four reasons why we may be morally better if our emotions harmonise with the values we enact, than if they do not. First, in many cases we may be more reliable in successfully carrying out what we value if we care about it. The best examples of this are those discussed earlier, where sympathy and compassion lead us to act appropriately towards those in need, where we might not otherwise have done so.[34]

Second, and perhaps more importantly here, to have our values and our emotions in harmony is to have a certain moral *integrity* or wholeness, which is itself a morally good trait.[35] Consider here a person who values helping others but is emotionally unmoved by their suffering, or perhaps has to struggle against contrary inclinations in order to help them, and does so with regret about the self-regarding pleasures which he has thereby forgone. Although this person may be admirable for his effort and for the assistance he does manage to provide, his lack of emotional support for his values indicates a kind of lack of integrity on his part. For while he does value helping others and he does act on this, he helps only with reluctance, and we might well wonder how seriously he takes the value of helping others. Indeed, this bifurcation between his values and his emotions may be a serious impediment to his flourishing, for if this dislocation persists, it may well lead to his having such psychic disorders as alienation and detachment, especially in situations where he is called upon to help others. For in contrast to the psychic harmony which characterises the better person, the soul of the above person seems, as Aristotle puts it, 'rent by faction'.[36] Martin Benjamin explains well the moral importance of this notion of integrity:

> it [i.e. integrity] provides the structure for a unified, whole, and unalienated life. Those who through good fortune and personal effort are able to lead reasonably integrated lives generally enjoy a strong sense of personal identity. They know who they are and what they stand for; they will experience the satisfaction and self-respect that comes with living in accord with their deepest and most highly cherished values.[37]

This leads me to my third point. That is, a person who values the right things and is emotionally moved to act on them seems morally better than someone who has and acts on these values in the face of conflicting inclinations, because the former person's emotions are an indication that these values are *really his*. Let us look again at two people who both seem to value helping others, but only one does so with 'cooperating' emotions, such as care and compassion, while the other is pained by or regrets his helping others. The split between the latter person's values and his emotions in this context might well be an indication that he does not really value helping others at all – perhaps he is just 'caught up in' the spirit of giving at a concert for charity, or maybe he regards his valuing beneficence as an unfortunate legacy of his Catholic upbringing. But the person who *cares* about helping others and does so without emotional conflict shows that he is acting on 'heartfelt' values – that is, we might say that he *identifies* with them.

Finally, acting on one's values with psychic harmony is morally better than doing so without cooperating emotions because without this harmony we would be unable to achieve many of life's most important goods, such as love and friendship. For example, love involves valuing the beloved for her own sake, and as Stocker argues, acts of love conceptually involve acting both out of love and for the beloved's sake as a final goal. Therefore, in an act of love, one's motives and reasons must, conceptually speaking, be in harmony. For unless our reason for acting in such cases is also our motive for acting, we are not performing an act of *love* – e.g. to the extent that we act for the good of the beloved because it is valuable to maximise pleasure, self-interest, or even perhaps because it is the moral thing to do, we are not yet acting from love.[38]

Thus, where our values accord with what is morally good, the integral part which certain emotions play in our transforming our values into morally good action shows an important way in which these emotions may be morally significant.

It is important to remember, however, that while psychic harmony and strength of will, in enabling us to achieve many great goods, are important for various kinds of good lives, they may also feature in certain bad lives. For what one believes is good may in fact be bad, and so to act on and be emotionally moved to act on such values may also be morally wrong.[39] For example, it seems morally wrong that South African whites exercise political control to maintain black subordination, while believing that they ought to do so, but it seems even worse that they are emotionally moved by paternalistic care and concern to do so. In such cases as these, psychic conflict and weakness of will may be morally preferable to harmony between evaluation, emotion, and action. Thus, to the extent that one (for example) cares and is concerned about doing what is actually bad, care and concern here may themselves be morally wrong emotional responses, and performing a morally bad action out of these emotions might thereby be made worse because of such motivation. However, I am quite prepared to admit this point, since I am arguing that emotions are morally *significant*, not that they are always morally good or right.

Indeed, attending to the notions of psychic harmony and strength of will indicates a further sense in which various emotions might be morally wrong. For just as certain emotions may be integral to our having such harmony and strength, other emotions may sometimes interfere with or prevent our doing or being moved to do what we believe good. Thus, a coward may be prevented by their fear from actually taking or wanting to pursue a dangerous course of action which they nevertheless believe they ought to take.[40] Similarly, a person may be moved by resentment to refrain from helping his more successful colleague, even where he believes that he should help. Again, such cases demonstrate a sense in which some emotional responses may in certain circumstances be morally wrong.

So, our emotions are morally significant because they play an important role in enabling or preventing our acting with psychic harmony in accordance with our values, and this type of strength of will is essential for various good lives, as well as for certain bad lives.

6. LOVE AND FRIENDSHIP

Another important shortcoming in an unemotional or emotionally deficient person would be their failure to achieve such morally significant human relationships as love and friendship. For as I will argue in this section, relationships of love and friendship essentially involve emotions, and these relationships are central to various kinds of good lives.

We might wonder what sort of relationships an unemotional person would be capable of forming and sustaining, for his dealings with others, to the extent that he had any at all, would seem to be somewhat shallow, lifeless, mechanical, and without direction. One point here is that people might be unwilling to form friendships with such a person. It may be common enough for someone to temporarily 'go cold on' his friends. For example, he might not feel like visiting any of them, or he might occasionally be unaffected by some of their trials and tribulations (such as the failure of yet another affair which to him seemed doomed from the beginning). And perhaps it is when our affections towards our friends lapse that duties of friendship may figure appropriately in our motivation.[41] But in any case, it seems unlikely that anyone would want to begin or maintain a friendship with someone who was lacking in emotion as an established feature of his personality.

However, the point here is not only an empirical one concerning people's preferences. It seems that no matter what relationships with others were undertaken by an unemotional person, it would be incorrect to call them friendships. For relationships of love and friendship conceptually require that those involved have a certain understanding of each other, are motivated to promote each other's good, and have certain feelings or affects towards each other. In other words, two people cannot have a relationship of love or friendship with each other, unless they each have certain *emotions* about the other, so a person without emotion could not have such relationships at all.

These claims indicate another important dimension to the moral significance of emotions. That is, emotions are morally significant because they constitute in various ways human relationships of love and friendship, and such relationships are among the most valuable things that we can have. There are several ways in which emotions may be construed as constituting relationships of love and friendship. To begin with, the emotions we both feel towards each other in a sense determine the form our relationship takes. That is, our love or friendship for each other is embodied in our caring about promoting each other's welfare, our feeling sympathetic towards each other in regard to our respective problems, and our feeling angry and indignant at injustices suffered by the other, to name only several. Further, emotions may be thought of as constituting relationships of friendship and love in so far as our mutual affection unifies and bestows a certain significance on our joint activities. We see films and go on walks together out of love and friendship, and many such activities, which might otherwise seem separate and isolated, come to be seen as a complex whole in which our love and friendship are manifested.

In fact, the connection between certain emotions and relationships of love and friendship appears to be conceptual, and the nature of this link can be explicated in the following way. I argued earlier that emotions such as care, concern, interest, and sympathy are important for achieving a certain kind of psychic harmony and, in particular, that such emotions are essential for attaining the psychic harmony which is conceptually required in relationships of love and friendship. Thus, in friendship we must not only value the good of our friend for their own sake, but we must also be affected and motivated by what contributes to or impedes their good, so understood. That is, we must *emotionally* value their good. Without this kind of harmony, one's relationship would not qualify as friendship. For example, two people who perceived and valued what would promote each other's good, and wanted to and indeed perhaps sometimes did promote each other's good, but who typically felt nothing in either the contemplation or execution of such good, would not be correctly characterised as friends. Although we can portray them as in a sense 'taking care of' each other, they lack the *emotional* attachment to each other which seems to be involved in friendship. As Aristotle pointed out, good will, i.e. *eunoia*, is insufficient for friendship because it may lack the affective intensity or warmth necessary for friendship.[42] Instead of friendship the kind of relationship just described would be like that which exists between two associates or allies, or between a guardian and their ward, or a benefactor and their beneficiary.

Of course, if two people simply have certain affectionate feelings for each other, even if they do see each other sometimes, this is also insufficient for love and friendship. For each might regard the other as a pleasant diversion or plaything, and neither might have any desire to benefit the other for his or her own sake, nor might they make any attempts to understand what the other's flourishing would consist in. So too, two people who do understand what would contribute to each other's welfare and who each believe it ought to be promoted would not thereby necessarily have a relationship of love or friendship. For they might not be motivated to benefit or spend time with each other, as is sometimes the case following the dissolution of loving relationships and friendships.

Thus, the mutual care in which love and friendship are embodied involves perceiving and valuing what is conducive to the good of the other, wanting both to promote this good for the sake of the other and to be with the other, and also being affectively moved by what we see conduces to the good of the other. If any or all of these elements are missing, and if this is a typical feature of our relationship, then it would be false to describe our relationship as friendship or as love. So, caring for the friend or beloved for his or her own sake (where this is understood as involving emotion, and not just 'taking care of') can be seen as one of the emotions which is constitutive of friendship and love in that it is an embodiment of these relationships which is necessary in order for them to count as such.

Given that emotions are central to the constitution of relationships of love and friendship, the moral significance of these relationships themselves remains to be seen. That love and friendship are among the greatest and most fundamental human goods is a view which has been held by many philosophers.[43] Indeed, it may even be the case that they provide the touchstone of all other values. As Peter Railton puts it:

> We must recognize that loving relationships, friendships, and group loyalties . . . are among the most important contributors to whatever it is that makes life worthwhile; any moral theory deserving serious consideration must itself give them serious consideration . . . If we were to find that adopting a particular morality led to irreconcilable conflict with central types of human well-being . . ., then this surely would give us good reason to doubt its claims.[44]

We can appreciate some of this value by attempting to imagine what a life without love and friendship would be like. Such a life may well be impaired by certain kinds of alienation, discontinuity, and purposelessness, as well as certain related failures in perception and understanding, for love and friendship are necessary to achieving a certain good kind of continuity, sense of purpose, and knowledge in life. If these claims are correct, love and friendship are among the greatest goods we are capable of achieving, being of value both in themselves, and in terms of their connections with other goods, and emotions are morally significant because they play an important role in the constitution of such fundamentally significant relationships.

However, it might be thought that this is to overemphasise the goodness of love and friendship, for we can imagine lives which are good but which nevertheless lack love and friendship. For example, here we might consider a slightly modified version of the now much discussed case of (a perhaps somewhat fictionalised) Gauguin, who was led by his devotion to his art to abandon his family in Paris in order to live and paint in Tahiti. As the example is described, Gauguin's commitment to his art was inseparable from his deserting his family, such that anyone pursuing Gauguin's artistic goals would necessarily have to do without love and friendship, at least to a large extent.[45] Now instead of focusing as others have on what this example shows about 'moral luck', I want to consider how this case bears on the question of the relation between love and friendship and good lives. For our purposes then, suppose Gauguin's artistic devotion was such that he was unable to form relationships of love and friendship in Tahiti. It might then be suggested that because of his single-minded and guiding commitment to his art and because of the value of what he actually produced, Gauguin had a good life and achieved a good kind of continuity, sense of purpose, and knowledge, but he did so without love and friendship. Thus, the objection to my claims might be that, as the Gauguin example shows, (i) love and friendship are not necessary for a good life and so (ii) the moral significance of emotions cannot be seen in terms of love and friendship. From this it might then be inferred that (iii) emotions therefore have no moral significance.

Such an argument, however, is mistaken on several counts. First, (iii) does not follow from (ii), for as I argue elsewhere in this chapter, the moral significance of emotions can be explicated quite apart from their role in love and friendship. For instance, we can see the moral significance of emotions in terms of psychic harmony and strength of will. Indeed, this may be evident in the Gauguin example itself, for we can understand Gauguin as driven by a passion for his art to do what he believed good (i.e. leave his family to go and paint in the comparative isolation of a tropical island), and so Gauguin's artistic passion may be thought morally significant.

Second, if (i) were true, (ii) would not follow, for something need not be necessary for all forms of good lives before it can have moral significance. Thus, there may be cases of people living good lives, and indeed, the best they are capable of living, but nevertheless being afflicted by serious psychic disharmony, such that the overcoming of that disharmony might not improve and might even substantially diminish the value of their lives. For example, the various kinds of psychic conflicts and torments undergone by Gauguin's contemporaries Van Gogh, Dostoevsky, and Nietzsche might each in its own way be seen as integral to the greatness which these men attained. However, if there are good lives which can be achieved without psychic harmony, this does not entail that psychic harmony lacks moral significance. For we have already seen that psychic harmony has considerable moral significance. Similar remarks, I want to claim, can be made about love and friendship. Thus, in arguing for the moral significance of love and friendship (and so of the emotions in which they are embodied), I am not arguing that love and friendship are necessary for all forms of good lives, for, as Gauguin-type examples show, such a claim would be mistaken. Rather, I want to argue that love and friendship are necessary for certain kinds of good lives.

Finally, regarding (i), admittedly it seems true that some people may be able to live good lives in the absence of love or friendship.[46] Thus, we may take it that Gauguin's life was good, and further, perhaps the best he was capable of living, even though he decided that at a certain stage of his life he would do without love and friendship.[47] However, be this as it may, his life may still be thought of as morally lacking in so far as he did not have love and friendship, for such relationships constitute great human goods in themselves, and they are central to our achieving certain other goods. It should be noted here that to think of Gauguin's life as morally lacking in so far as it was without love and friendship is not to be taken as implying that his life would have been better had he had love and friendship (i.e. stayed with his family in Paris), for *ex hypothesi*, an artistic life in Tahiti without love and friendship was the best life possible for him. That Gauguin's life may be thought morally lacking means that it was a life from which certain fundamental goods (love and friendship) were missing. That is, while there are various kinds of good lives with many different good features (including being passionately committed to an important project, as Gauguin was), love and friendship occupy an especially significant place in the range of these goods, for unlike many other good features of lives, the absence of love and friendship in any life would be a grave loss.

Further, no doubt the sense of purpose, continuity, and the knowledge which Gauguin's artistic passion bestowed on his life were good, but this does not impugn my claims about the necessity of love and friendship for achieving certain other goods, and about the consequent centrality of love and friendship among the range of good features of lives. For I did not claim that love and friendship are necessary for achieving *any good* sense of purpose, continuity, and knowledge. Indeed, quite apart from what is shown by the Gauguin example, perhaps a strong, independent, career-oriented person who avoids love and friendship can achieve a good sense of purpose and continuity in life. Much less did I (or would I) claim that love and friendship are necessary for achieving *any* sense of purpose, continuity, and knowledge, for clearly, certain kinds of continuity, purpose, and knowledge may be morally indifferent (e.g. those involved in making the quest for the perfect meal one's project in life) or morally bad (e.g. those given in planning to assassinate a benevolent head of state), and love and friendship may not be necessary to achieving these. My claim, rather, is that, as seen below, love and friendship are necessary for achieving a *certain good* sense of purpose, continuity, and knowledge in life, so that a life devoid of love and friendship, such as Gauguin's, will fail to have *these*, and so may be morally lacking in these respects, as well as with regard to the value of love and friendship in themselves.

That relationships of love and friendship are necessary for achieving a certain good sense of purpose, continuity, and knowledge in one's life can be seen in the following way. As Aristotle argues, because love and friendship involve an appreciation of the other for their own sake, we reflect on what the well-being of the other consists in, and consequently become aware of their life as a complex and unified whole. Further, in relationships of friendship and mutual love the other can function as a mirror towards our self, reflecting qualities of the self that are otherwise inaccessible. So, through seeing the life of the other as forming a complex unity, we may achieve an awareness of our own life as itself unified and continuous, in a manner that is unavailable to a person whose life lacks love and friendship.[48] Also, the close association with another person in love and friendship can produce an increased knowledge of human needs and desires in general, in terms of which one may see one's own requirements and aspirations. If these arguments are right, love and friendship are of substantial value not only in themselves, but also because of their important connections with other goods, and they are essential to various kinds of good lives, but perhaps not all good lives. Nevertheless to the extent that any life is devoid of love or friendship, it is morally lacking in that respect. Thus, the moral significance of emotions can be seen in terms of their roles in love and friendship. To be sure, not all emotions help constitute relationships of love and friendship. Indeed, for various reasons, certain emotions seem typically rather seriously detrimental to such relationships.[49] For instance, envy is a competitive emotion focusing on others' gains and involving a negative assessment of oneself compared with them, a dissatisfaction with one's 'lot'. Malicious envy would seem particularly destructive here, since it involves a desire not to benefit the other but to deprive them of their valued quality or qualities. Another emotion which might be mentioned here is resentment, which involves having a certain bitterness towards others and a desire to annihilate, shunning intimacy in favour of defensiveness. Of course, I do not deny that sometimes it is better for the friendship or from some other point of view if we resent our friend, e.g. for their bad qualities and actions. Thus, resenting our friends may sometimes be morally justified. But in other cases where we resent a friend, including some cases where this is justified only in a rational sense, this resentment seems clearly detrimental to our friendship (and perhaps also undesirable from some broader perspective). Other examples of emotions which typically inhibit or preclude relationships of love and friendship might be guilt, contempt, fear (e.g. of intimacy), and self-pity.[50]

However, the acknowledgement of the deleterious effects of these emotions on love and friendship does not tell against my general contention. For I have argued that emotions are morally significant, and that one aspect of this significance can be seen in terms of their roles in love and friendship, which seem essential to various kinds of good lives. To the extent that certain emotions are typically destructive of such relationships, they might in those circumstances be regarded as morally bad or wrong (although much more would need to be taken into account to make any general claim about the moral badness of these emotions here). Thus, acknowledging these emotions gives us some idea both of the range of emotions which are morally significant, and of the ways in which they may have such significance.

7. SELF-WORTH

Another distinguishing feature, related to the points in the foregoing discussion, of an unemotional or emotionally deficient person might be their lacking any sense of self-worth. For emotions are importantly connected with our own and others' sense of self-worth. In this section I will show this by arguing that our attachments to our projects and to others are central to our sense of self-worth, and that our emotions are essentially involved in the deepest types of attachment.

To introduce these connections in a general way it might be said that, as Solomon emphasises (following Sartre, who in turn was here influenced by Heidegger), it is through our emotions that we constitute ourselves – i.e. through our emotions we bestow meaning to the circumstances of our lives and invest ourselves in the world, providing opportunities for fulfilment and frustration, and it is in such constitution and involvement that an appreciation of our self-worth can be reached.[51] That is, since (as we saw in Chapter 1) emotions can be thought of as involving a certain manner of apprehending or viewing the world, our emotions create interests and purposes for us in the world, and our interests and purposes are clearly important for determining who we are and how we see ourselves. For example, a sympathetic or compassionate person views the suffering of others with distress and is guided by a concern to help others, and his sense of self-worth may be grounded partly in what he sees as his capacity and ability to help others. So our emotions may be integral to our self-concept, and indeed, they may provide an important key to our identity, for many of our characterisations of particular people are often put in emotional terms.[52]

We can introduce the significance of our emotions in connection with our sense of self-worth through seeing the role of psychic harmony and strength of will in preserving a sense of our own worth. For as David Sachs points out, effectiveness in pursuing one's wishes is central to the notions of self-respect and self-worth,[53] and we have already seen that emotions such as care, interest, sympathy, and courage play an important role in our doing and being moved to do what we believe good. Whether our sense of self-worth depends on our succeeding in our desire to provide for our family, improve our education, write good novels, or simply to be able to effectively defend what we believe in when challenged, it seems that being moved by such emotions as care, interest, sympathy, and courage is crucial to our achieving what we aim at and value here, and thus to our achieving a sense of self-worth in this way. It is an all too familiar experience where the failure of these kinds of endeavours, due to our lacking appropriate emotional attachments to them, results in our having doubts about our self-worth.

Now, given that both our being involved in and carrying out what we consider important and also our being engaged with the world are central to our achieving a sense of self-worth, we can argue that having certain emotions is essential to our reaching an appreciation of our own worth. For we cannot give a rich and deep account of *attachment* without involving emotions.

In support of this claim, consider initially people's attachments to certain impersonally conceived projects or objects. For example, could a person really be regarded as *committed* to fighting for multilateral nuclear disarmament unless they were taken up by care, concern, and interest for that cause, such that they respond with disappointment to breakdowns in arms talks between the major powers, and with hope and encouragement to the groundswell of support for what they believe in? Or, could we adequately describe Gauguin as single-mindedly *devoted* to his art unless we saw this in terms of a passionate attachment?

Of course, we might be able to give some account of these attachments in non-emotional terms. So, we could say that the person seeking nuclear disarmament shows their commitment by attending meetings and rallies for the cause, and perhaps by discussing disarmament with their friends. Likewise, we could say that Gauguin displayed his devotion to his art in the fact that he spent many hours of each day painting. But these accounts would be inadequate, for the actions described in these examples may not show an *attachment* to the projects in question at all. A person may attend rallies and discuss nuclear disarmament with their friends not because of any underlying commitment, but because they want to oblige their friends or win their favour. And the Gauguin portrayed in this example might have spent his days painting not because of any devotion to art, but simply because he found it relaxing or therapeutic.

I am not denying that we can have unemotional or 'cool' attachments to various things, but this is usually an indication that we regard such attachments as insignificant. For describing an attachment in emotional terms is the way we normally mark its importance to us. Thus, consider here our interpersonal attachments. We usually indicate the importance to us of the people we know or are acquainted with in terms of ever-expanding concentric circles of diminishing emotional concern and intimacy. So, our close friends occupy a circle near the centre, and our close attachment to them is shown by our delighting in their company, worrying about them and missing them when they are abroad for long periods, and responding with sympathy and grief when misfortune befalls them.

It might be objected that many scientists, for instance, regard their commitment to seek truths about nature as of fundamental importance in their lives, even though this commitment may, or it might be said, must, be unemotional. But to take this as an objection to my claim would be to misunderstand the way in which our attachments are importantly emotional. In claiming this, I do not mean simply that to be attached to X is thereby to be disposed to have various emotional 'episodes' with regard to X. This may sometimes be the case, but the emotionality of attachment which I am trying to bring out is more importantly an enduring phenomenon. That is, our having care about and interest in what we are attached to underlies and explains our being drawn to it on particular occasions, and also what we do and may feel on those occasions. Thus, as I pointed out at the end of Chapter 1, the 'detachment' which a scientist may aim for in carrying out their investigations and experiments may well express an underlying *passionate* commitment to seek the truth.[54]

Another problem for any attempt to give a non-emotional account of attachment is that it would not seem able to adequately capture the sense of loss we have when an attachment is severed.[55] For example, our friendships are for many of us among our most important attachments, and so when the bond between us is broken by prolonged absence, betrayal, or the death of the friend, we naturally have a deep sense of loss. Now surely this sense of loss consists in more than just *noting* that we have suffered a loss. Or perhaps what I should say is that if this is all that our sense of loss involves, this would suggest that our attachment was not very important to us or was in some way deficient, and so maybe not correctly described as 'friendship'. Rather, the sense of loss which naturally follows the breaking of an important attachment is an *emotional* one – that is, we *feel* the loss, and we typically experience a range of associated emotions, including grief, wistfulness, and perhaps even anger. Indeed, sometimes the emotions we feel about our less significant losses indicate that our attachments here were importantly emotional. Thus, when we say after moving house that we were 'really attached' to our old house, we are not merely *noting* the loss; we are feeling a kind of sorrow which suggests that we were affectionately disposed towards our old house.

If these arguments are right, then our emotions are essentially involved in our important attachments to our projects and to other people. Indeed, even our attachment to ourselves, if I may put it so, seems importantly emotional, for many of the ways in which we see ourselves cannot be adequately explicated in other than emotional terms. Thus, as Stocker argues, notions such as 'taking things personally' need to be understood at least partly in terms of various forms of self-care and self-concern.[56] Therefore, without certain emotions it seems that we would be detached and dissociated in various ways from ourselves, from others, and from the world around us, and our sense of self-worth may well suffer as a result.

Of course, to say that an unemotional person will be detached from the world in various ways is not to say that an emotional person will necessarily be attached to worldly concerns.[57] Whether or not this is the case will depend on the emotion and its object. However, it is to say that in order to adequately express a person's attachment to something we need to refer to, among other things, their emotions. And, given the importance of our involvements and attachments for our achieving a sense of self-worth, we can thereby gain some idea of the role emotions play in our attaining this sense.

We can discern a further connection between emotions and self-worth by looking at the emotions that others have towards us. In this regard, James Wallace argues that kindness and compassion from others tend to foster and support our self-esteem and sense of worth, because the benevolent concern for the other which is involved in such emotions is an affirmation that we matter.[58] If people lacked such altruistic emotions towards each other, our sense of self-worth might be seriously threatened, for as Wallace says, 'the feeling that everyone around one is indifferent toward one is truly demoralizing'.[59] Indeed, it might be through an awareness of the benevolent concern that others have for us that we sometimes feel prompted to care about and take interest in our own activities. In summary then, it seems that caring for and taking an interest in ourselves and our welfare, as well as having altruistic emotions towards others, are (normally) fundamental to developing and maintaining a sense of our own and others' unique importance and worth.

These claims are relevant for showing the moral significance of emotions because the notion of individuals as valuable is central to morality. Indeed, such a notion is taken by certain moralities such as Kantianism as the hallmark of moral value, from which all other values proceed.[60] I do not wish to speculate on this issue here. For in any case, whatever its place in relation to other values, the concept of personal worth is indisputably an important moral concept, and an appreciation of this worth is of unquestionable moral significance. I have been arguing that our emotions are central (at least for most of us) to our achieving such an appreciation.

But given the importance of the notion of individual value for morality, we might now look to what may obscure a recognition of this value in order to explicate a certain kind of moral badness. In this regard, certain emotions sometimes seem detrimental to one's sense of self-worth, and to this extent may (*ceteris paribus*) be morally bad. For example, that form of resentment which is founded on a sense of one's ineluctable inferiority to others and a desire to reduce others to one's own miserable level involves a kind of devaluation of the self. Resentment also severs one's relations with others, preferring to view them from a distance, and so precludes the affirmation of one's self-worth that may come from others. Of course, it should be acknowledged that resentment need not *always* undermine our sense of self-worth, for keeping others at a distance in resenting them may sometimes be morally right, especially in the case of evil people, and our sense of self-worth may here in fact be maintained by resentment. Irrational feelings of guilt, especially when strong, also threaten to undermine our sense of self-worth, particularly in so far as such guilt involves self-condemnation, initially in the light of a specific act but ultimately embracing the whole of one's being.[61] To be sure, focusing on the function of a certain kind of guilt in relation to self-worth is to look at only one aspect of the moral significance of that emotion. It is not to make a blanket denunciation of guilt, for there are of course some things about which (if we do or have them) we ought to feel guilty, and indeed, as Williams (among others) points out, guilt can have a creative or reparative function in leading a person to seek rectification of their transgressions.[62]

However, emotions may be detrimental to our sense of self-worth in yet other ways. For given the importance of our involvements and attachments in developing and maintaining our self-worth, we might consider here how certain emotions work in various ways against such involvements and attachments. Thus, in depression and despair we tend to withdraw ourselves from the world, lacking the energy to pursue what we may consider worthwhile, or, at a more advanced stage, regarding such activities as 'not worth it'. We relinquish our engagement in the world and our effectiveness in pursuing our wishes, and so lose an important means of affirming our self-worth.[63] In so far as these and other emotions involve or lead to the destruction of our sense of self-worth then, they may be morally bad, and this is a further illustration of the variety of ways in which emotions may have moral significance.

It should also be acknowledged that there is of course another way in which some emotions may be shown to be morally bad in their connections with our sense of self-worth. That is, there are certain emotions we may have regarding ourselves, such as overweening pride or inordinate self-concern, which give us an *excessive* sense of our own worth, and further, various emotions which others may have towards us, including envy and adulation, may also lead us to have such an inflated conception of ourselves. Now here it seems clear that to the extent that they lead to such conceit, these emotions would indeed be morally bad, but nevertheless we can still claim that other forms of, say, pride and self-concern may be shown to be good if and in so far as they contribute to our achieving a *proper* sense of our own worth. For as Aristotle saw, there is a morally legitimate form of self-concern which lies between the morally defective extremes of having too much or too little sense of our own worth.[64]

Let me clarify a point before continuing. That is, in arguing for the moral importance of emotions in our lives, I do *not* (as I hope is clear) thereby mean to endorse any form of sentimentality or emotional self-indulgence as moral ideals. Some (such as Kant and the Stoics) who see little or no place for emotions in the moral life seem to argue for their view here by pointing to the moral defectiveness of a sentimental or 'showy' person. But while I agree that a moral person should avoid sentimentality, I think that, far from showing the unimportance of emotions for morality, this rather indicates the moral importance of having appropriate emotions to a proper degree in the right situations. Yet in any case, it is highly misleading to use a flawed emotional person as a foil for demonstrating the (alleged) moral superiority of a dispassionate life,[65] for as I have attempted to show, the life of an emotional or spirited person need not and typically will not thereby be like that of the flawed emotional person depicted in such arguments. Thus, the conception of an emotional or spirited person which is elaborated in this chapter is that of someone who has insight and understanding, psychic harmony and strength of will, cares for their friends, and has a sense of their own worth, and this person seems unlikely to be a sentimental or emotionally self-indulgent person.

Rather than examine other features in the life of a person incapable of emotion, I will develop my account of the moral significance of emotions further by looking at how emotions might be characterised as morally significant (or insignificant) by certain other moralities. For the view that emotions are morally significant might as such be thought uncontroversial, since indeed, there may be other moralities, such as utilitarianism, which are compatible with this view. Thus, in order to explicate further my understanding of the moral significance of emotions and to contrast it with other accounts, I will discuss the manner in which emotions may be given moral significance by several prominent moralities. I devote my attention initially to certain views on the morality of emotions which might be taken by utilitarianism (following an important recent defence of that theory in the context of moral psychology), after which I consider the place of emotions in the ethical altruism of Lawrence Blum, particularly as found in his book, *Friendship, Altruism and Morality*. I shall also discuss Kant's views on the moral insignificance of emotions, along with some attempts by Kantians to accommodate emotions in morality; but given the complexity of those views, and because Kantianism looms as a major opponent to my account of the moral significance of emotions, my discussion of Kantianism will (apart from some brief references shortly) occupy a chapter in itself, which follows after the present chapter.

8. UTILITARIAN ACCOUNTS OF THE MORAL SIGNIFICANCE OF EMOTIONS

It is often claimed that utilitarianism is concerned exclusively with the morality of actions, thereby neglecting motives. Indeed, this overconcentration on action has commonly been regarded a serious fault in utilitarianism as an ethical theory. However, in an important paper, Robert Merrihew Adams argues that this need not be the case, by defending a form of utilitarianism which allows for moral assessments of motives. According to Adams's theory, one motive is morally better than another to the extent that the former has more utility than the latter, where 'utility' is understood in terms of happiness or satisfaction.[66] So for example, seeing an exhibition of Impressionist paintings out of an interest in art for its own sake may, on balance, lead to more enjoyment than seeing it out of a concern to please one's wife or to maximise utility, so the former pattern of motivation is better here, by 'motive-utilitarian' standards, than the others.[67]

Given this account, it might be thought that utilitarianism can allow for the moral significance of emotions. That is, the goodness and badness of emotions would be determined by whether they conduce to or detract from utility, respectively. And in making such assessments of utility, we would need to include some estimation of the effect of a particular emotion on others, as well as considering how it affects ourselves.[68] According to motive-utilitarianism then, we might say that, for instance, compassion towards another is morally good when, taking into account the happiness of both ourselves and the person to whom the compassion is directed, it leads to more happiness than misery. Motivation by emotion may also be compared with other patterns of motivation using motive-utilitarianism. So, visiting a sick friend out of sympathy might be morally better than doing so purely out of duty, for motivation by sympathy here might lead to more happiness, all things considered, than motivation by duty.

However, the moral significance of emotions cannot adequately be captured by motive-utilitarianism, understood in the above sense, for the goodness or badness of an emotion is not determined by the amount of utility it results in.[69] For example, consider cases where we have sympathy or compassion for another whom we cannot help or console, because they are isolated from us and we cannot communicate with them. Here our sympathy and compassion may have little or no utility for us or for the person in distress, yet this would hardly seem to diminish or undermine their moral goodness. Conversely, imagine a person who feels malicious joy upon contemplation of the undeserved sufferings of some of the religious martyrs of the past. While this person's joy here would have considerable utility for them, it is obvious that it would not thereby be morally good here – rather, it would be profoundly evil.

Nevertheless, motive-utilitarians may insist that their theory can give an adequate account of the moral significance of emotions, for they may propose a modification to their view which would allow it to accommodate the above counterexamples. That is, they might argue that in assessing the goodness or badness of a certain emotion, we are not (or at least not primarily) concerned with the utility which it *actually* leads to. Rather, what is important here is whether the emotion is *directed at* consequences which do or do not have utility (quite apart from the utility or disutility of the particular consequences, if any, which the emotion actually results in). Thus, on this version of motive-utilitarianism, love and compassion would be morally good even where they cannot be expressed in action, because these emotions involve intentions to perform acts of great utility, even though these intentions might not always be acted on.

Now, this form of motive-utilitarianism would indeed be an improvement on the earlier version of that view, as it now recognises the moral importance of what we might call the 'content' of a motive, as distinct from looking only at its outcome. Yet even this utilitarian account fails to give a satisfactory analysis of the moral significance of emotions, since there seem to be some emotions which may be morally good or appropriate, even though they are neither directed at nor productive of consequences which have any utility. Thus, consider the emotion of grief. It seems part of living a moral life that we grieve at the passing of those close to us, such that a failure to experience this kind of grief in these circumstances would indicate a serious moral deficiency. However, in grieving we typically do not thereby have any intentions directed at producing consequences which have any utility. Sometimes our grief might have a certain utility in that we may want to show others that they are not alone in their loss, but where this is not the case, such as when *we* were closest to the lost one, or when there is nobody with whom we can share our grief, surely our grief does not then become morally insignificant. Also, grief may assist us in coming to terms with bereavement, and therefore have some utility in this sense, but its moral significance seems not to consist in this fact. For even where our grief is of no help to us in coping with our loss, nor of any help to others in coming to terms with theirs, it may still be morally appropriate, for lacking such grief can be a significant moral defect.

Maybe there are other forms of utilitarianism which might yield a more adequate account of the moral significance of emotions. So, as a beginning towards such a view, it might be suggested that the utility and disutility of consequences be understood as referring to something broader than pleasure and pain, happiness and unhappiness, or satisfaction and dissatisfaction (as we shall see shortly in my discussion of Blum's view). Of course, to move in this direction may lead to an abandonment of what would be a recognisable version of utilitarianism, perhaps in favour of some other form of consequentialism. But it is utilitarianism, not consequentialism as such, which I am concerned to reject here with regard to the issue of the moral significance of emotions. And I think I have given reason to believe that, in so far as utilitarianism considers motives morally important at all, on certain common and straightforward conceptions of 'utility', the moral significance of emotions cannot properly be demonstrated and understood in terms of utility.

9. ETHICAL ALTRUISM, EMOTIONS, AND THE NATURE OF MORAL VALUE

In *Friendship, Altruism and Morality*,[70] Lawrence Blum provides a well-argued and thorough critique of Kantian views of emotions as morally insignificant, and of the related idea, prominent in recent forms of Kantianism, that our psychological states are morally valuable only considered as motives which lead us to perform right acts. Against these Kantian views (which I discuss in detail in the following chapter), Blum offers us an explication of the moral significance of emotions in terms of ethical altruism, and an examination of his account is instructive for attaining a proper understanding of how emotions are morally significant. According to Blum, an emotion is morally important if it is directed at or grounded in the weal and woe of another (pp. 9–15, 163–4), and so, for example, sympathy, compassion, and concern are morally valuable because they are other-directed in this way. Further, Blum argues that such altruistic emotions are 'intrinsically valuable', in the sense that they are morally good apart from whether they actually issue in beneficent action.

Now, Blum's account is important in drawing attention to the moral value of altruistic emotions, and also in showing how emotions may be good even when they are not expressed in action. In emphasising this latter point, Blum's view is an advance over the first form of motive-utilitarianism considered above, which held that motives are morally good only where they *actually* lead to consequences of optimal utility. Indeed, as I argue in Chapter 3, this exclusively action-oriented approach to understanding the moral significance of psychological states is misguided, for moral goodness and badness sometimes derive from psychological states themselves, and this can importantly affect the moral status of the acts to which they lead (although as we shall see, to argue for the non-motivational value of various emotions is not thereby to argue that they have value in *all* situations). Blum's account is also an improvement on the second version of motive-utilitarianism discussed above, according to which motives that did not actually result in consequences of optimal utility could be morally good if they were directed at producing such consequences. For Blum's notion of being grounded in a person's *weal and woe* as what determines the moral goodness of a particular psychological state is a broader concept which accords better with what we believe is morally valuable than does the utilitarian notion of being directed at what produces happiness and satisfaction.

However, despite these strengths, Blum's account is open to three objections which are of importance for our purposes.

First, Blum's analysis is at best only an incomplete or partial account of the moral significance of emotions in general, for it overlooks the moral value of self-regarding emotions. That is, I would argue that emotions which take one's self as their object may have a certain moral significance. Living well, understood in one way, involves more than caring about the welfare of others, for, as we saw earlier, caring about and taking an interest in oneself and what one values are essential to at least many good lives. And, as Aristotle pointed out, this legitimate sense of self-regard, *philautia*, is importantly distinct from the excessive self-love or selfishness found in certain people, for it is only the former that is normally essential for human flourishing.[71] Further, the moral significance of such emotions as pride and shame, among others, can be seen in the light of this care and interest. That is, taking pride in oneself and one's achievements involves a certain self-directed care and concern,[72] and shame involves a similar self-care and self-concern, a sense of some feature or action reflecting badly on oneself, and a desire to atone for it. Of course, self-regarding emotions do not exhaust the sphere of what is of self-regarding moral significance – they are but one, albeit important, part of this sphere, which includes various self-regarding actions, character-traits, motives, and other psychological states.[73] Yet in failing to recognise the importance of this realm for morality, Blum's account of the moral significance of emotions is seriously incomplete.

The second problem with Blum's analysis which I want to mention can be brought out in the following way. Underlying Blum's account of the moral significance of emotions is his claim that an emotion is morally valuable if it is directed at or grounded in the weal and woe of another. This claim, we might note, could also be held by a motive-utilitarian who understands 'utility' in terms of welfare or well-being (instead of the usually more narrowly construed notions of satisfaction or happiness). However, quite apart from its neglect of the self-regarding, it seems that this account fails to capture the moral importance of some emotions which need not be directed at or grounded in a person's *weal and woe*. For instance, here we might again consider my earlier example of grief. It seems morally appropriate that we grieve at the passing of a loved one, for indeed to lack this grief would be to have an important moral defect. Yet, especially when *we* were emotionally closest to the deceased, our grief is not directed at or grounded in anyone's weal and woe. Grief is not an *altruistic* emotion, but then it does not seem to be an egoistic emotion like say, self-pity, either: rather, these categories do not seem applicable to grief at all. Similarly, we normally regard it as morally appropriate for people to feel some degree of *guilt* about their transgressions. But guilt need not be directed at or grounded in some person's weal and woe – e.g. I may feel guilty about spying on you without thereby believing that I have caused you any distress.

Perhaps Blum and those motive-utilitarians who construe 'utility' in terms of welfare could find ways of dealing with such cases, but their handling of them might well involve some rather strange interpretations of what it is for a psychological state to be directed at a person's weal and woe. So the problem here for Blum is that while this notion is an improvement on some utilitarian accounts, it still seems too narrow to capture the various ways in which emotions can be morally significant. In order to achieve a proper understanding of the moral significance of emotions in their full complexity, we need to invoke the notion of living a good life, detailing the virtues that this involves and showing how emotions are related to them, and in this chapter I have attempted to make a beginning towards such a project.

The final and for our purposes perhaps the most important point which I want to make against Blum's account concerns the connection between emotions and moral goodness and badness. As I noted earlier, Blum argues that altruistic emotions such as sympathy and compassion have a certain intrinsic value – that is, they are good whether or not they actually lead to beneficent action, for it is conceptually true of such emotions that they are grounded in the weal and woe of others. Aside from its failure to show the moral importance of self-regarding emotions, we might wonder whether this is a sufficient explanation of the moral goodness of altruistic emotions, for we can ask what it is about a regard for the weal and woe of others that makes such a regard morally good.

It is not clear what Blum's answer to this question would (or could) be. In some places (e.g. pp. 5–6, 85, 163–4), he seems to suggest that the goodness of an altruistic regard has sufficient intuitive appeal to support his claim. Yet in other places, he argues that the concern for others involved in altruistic emotions is morally good because it conveys a good to the recipient – that is, the person at whom the emotion is directed values (or would value) being regarded altruistically by others. For example, Blum argues that supporting striking farmworkers out of sympathy for them and their cause is morally good because they appreciate the concrete assistance and value the sympathy which it expresses (pp. 144–5). Or, it is morally better that we visit a sick friend out of sympathy or compassion than out of a sense of obligation, because our friend would prefer to be visited out of the former motives (pp. 37–8, 142–3, 159).

Now clearly, how we prefer to be thought of and treated by others is an important sign of what may be morally valuable. But to base morality merely on personal preference is to invoke a form of preference-utilitarianism, and to leave oneself open to the many problems which confront that view. As Kantians, among others, are apt to point out, one cannot always move from the fact that we find attractive being thought of and treated by others in certain ways to the claim that being regarded in such ways is as such *morally* valuable.[74] For what a person finds attractive might itself be bad. Thus, a successful screen actress may take great delight in the all-consuming envy felt towards her by her less successful associates, yet even if her delight in such envy, on balance, has optimal utility here, the envy is not thereby reduced in badness, much less made morally good.

But more importantly, a similar point can be made about the regard for the weal and woe of others which is involved in altruistic emotions. I agree with Blum that it is often morally good to be concerned for others' weal and woe. However, it nevertheless seems that having such a regard might in certain situations be morally bad or wrong. For example, feeling sympathy towards one who we acknowledge to be a notorious thief, because of the difficulties they experience in carrying out their illicit activities, may itself be bad or wrong. Therefore, the moral goodness of altruistic emotions is not adequately explained in terms of their satisfying the preferences of those at whom they are directed, nor in terms of the regard for others' weal and woe which they involve.

However, nowhere in his account of the moral significance of altruistic emotions are the above kinds of examples discussed by Blum. Perhaps this omission results from a failure to notice an important ambiguity in the term 'intrinsically good'. As Blum uses the term, an emotion is intrinsically good if it has value quite apart from whether it actually leads to beneficent action. But there seems to be another application of this term, which is to things (e.g. psychological states) that have value in all situations, and this is quite a different notion. Blum may think that the former entails the latter; but if anything, the reverse is the case, as I argue below. In order to distinguish them, I will refer to the former, non-motivational sense of the term as 'intrinsic goodness', and call the latter, universal sense, 'unconditional goodness'.[75]

An emotion may have value independently of its motivating morally good action, that is, it may be intrinsically good, without its necessarily having such value in all situations, and so it may not be unconditionally good. For instance, as we have seen in this chapter, the intrinsic goodness of care may be explicated in terms of its involvement in our having psychic harmony and a sense of self-worth, yet this does not imply that its goodness holds across all possible situations, for care may be morally bad or wrong when it takes evil as its object (such as a person's caring about their racist principles and policies being upheld). Indeed, perhaps there are no emotions which are morally good in all situations – in any case, I shall remain agnostic about this. However, if some psychological state was held to be unconditionally good, then it seems to follow that it would also be intrinsically good. Thus, Kant thought that the motive of duty had unconditional worth as a motive to action, and so when the duty motive was ineffectual or (we might allow) when it led to bad action, the duty motive itself remained morally valuable, as we shall see in the following chapter. Indeed, considered in this manner, it may be difficult to conceive of a motive that is unconditionally good without its being intrinsically good; but clearly, that a motive is good in the latter sense does not entail that it is good in the former.

It might be wondered how an emotion can be intrinsically good and yet not be unconditionally good. But whether this question is found puzzling may depend on how the moral goodness of emotions is explicated in the first place. On Blum's account, this goodness is seen in terms of a conceptual feature of altruistic emotions – that is, in terms of their being grounded in the weal and woe of others. Thus, in order for an emotion to qualify as altruistic at all, it must have such an orientation, which, according to Blum, is good in itself. On this account then, any altruistic emotion must necessarily be morally good. However, as we have seen, a regard for the weal and woe of others, considered as such, may not always be morally good, so an explanation of the goodness of altruistic emotions just in terms of such a regard is inadequate. We need a deeper explanation of how emotions are connected with moral goodness (and badness), which goes beyond their formal characteristics and allows consideration of their *substantive* objects. Given such an explanation, we may begin to see how emotions can be morally good beyond their being motives to action, without its necessarily being implied that they are good in all situations (which I do not want to claim is true of any particular emotion).

The account of the moral significance of emotions given in this chapter may be seen as one step towards such an explanation. For on this account, the moral goodness and badness of emotions and the character-traits which they express is not settled by attending to personal preferences, nor by an exclusive consideration of whether the emotions involve certain formal characteristics, such as a regard for the weal and woe of others. It is not so much because emotions may be agreeable to those at whom they are directed that they can be morally good, but because, as I have tried to show throughout this chapter, they are importantly connected with such great goods as psychic harmony, strength of will, love and friendship, a sense of self-worth, and knowledge and understanding. Indeed, as I hope has become clear, these goods are themselves importantly interrelated, and they make key contributions to the goodness of many good lives. According to James Wallace, 'In order for a trait to be a virtue, it must tend to foster good human life in extensive and fundamental ways. It must be the perfection of a tendency or capacity that connects and interlocks with a variety of human goods in such a way that its removal would endanger the whole structure'.[76] The above-mentioned goods may be considered as virtues in this sense, and what I have been arguing in this chapter is that a person whose life was altogether lacking in emotions would be seriously defective, as they would thereby be denied the opportunity to achieve these and perhaps other goods. Thus, it is in the light of their connections with these goods that we may determine the various situations in which emotions may be morally good or bad. And this perspective is more illuminating and, I believe, brings us closer to the truth than any such pre-analytic claim, which is often heard, to the effect that love as such is morally good, while hatred as such is morally bad.

10. MORAL DIFFERENTIATION BETWEEN PARTICULAR EMOTIONS

In this chapter I have explicated the moral significance of a variety of emotions by demonstrating how they help constitute or undermine such central human goods as understanding, strength of will, psychic harmony, love and friendship, and a sense of self-worth. My approach has been to show how certain emotion-types, such as sympathy, compassion, care, concern, and courage, are essentially involved in the achievement of such goods, while other emotion-types, such as fear, resentment, envy, and self-pity are inimical to our attaining these goods in our lives. Now, while this helps sketch an overall picture of the place of emotions in morality, some details about moral differentiation between particular emotions need to be filled in, as a basis for what I shall say in the following chapters about the relations between emotions, actions, responsibility, and evaluations of persons as emotional subjects. Specifically, are *all* emotion-types morally significant, or is it only those mentioned above? And, since we have seen that even those emotion-types which are essential to the virtues mentioned above can go wrong, how can we differentiate between particular manifestations of these emotion-types as right or wrong?[77]

Let us begin with the first question. If care, concern, sympathy, compassion, and courage, on the one hand, and fear, resentment, envy, self-pity, on the other hand, are all morally significant emotion-types, do my arguments about the moral significance of emotions apply to *all* emotions? Is there anything distinctive about these types of emotions, compared to emotions generally? Are emotions which I have not mentioned, such as embarrassment, awe, nostalgia, and intrigue, morally significant? If not, why not?

In fact, the answers to these questions have already been suggested by my arguments in this chapter. That is, from a moral point of view, there is an important difference between, say, compassion and resentment, on the one hand, and embarrassment on the other hand. Compassion enlarges our understanding of the world and plays an important role in love and friendship; resentment undermines interpersonal relationships and one's sense of self-worth. But embarrassment has no such relation to human goods. A capacity for embarrassment (which should not be confused with a sense of humility) seems neither essentially involved in, nor a serious threat to, our achieving any of the above-mentioned goods. And so too, I would argue, for emotions such as awe, nostalgia, and intrigue. To the extent that these latter emotions do not figure importantly in relation to human virtues and vices, they are not morally significant. So, the first step to establishing the moral significance of particular manifestations or occurrences of emotions is to determine whether this emotion is an instance of an emotion-type which helps constitute or undermine one of the goods which are central to human flourishing. Let us call this 'first-level moral significance'. If my arguments in this chapter are right, then care, compassion, resentment, and envy count as morally significant at this level, whereas embarrassment and intrigue have no such moral significance.

But if we are to go beyond this level of moral significance, and say more about when and how particular manifestations of emotion-types may be morally significant, we need to look more closely here. For there may be no emotion-types which are invariably right or invariably wrong in all their manifestations. Even those emotion-types

which are characteristically good at the first level of moral significance, such as sympathy, care, and love, may nevertheless be morally
bad or wrong in some contexts. For example, I claimed that sympathy
for a thief in their difficulty in carrying out their illicit activities is
morally wrong, as is the paternalistic care which South African whites
have towards their black compatriots, and (as discussed later in this
chapter) the possessive love which a mother may have for her adult
daughter. So what criteria should we use for evaluating the rightness
or wrongness of particular manifestations of emotions? Let us call
this rightness and wrongness 'second-level moral significance'.

Two points must be borne in mind in regard to these second-level
evaluations of emotions. First, we are still dealing here with evaluations of *emotions* themselves, and not with evaluations of *persons* on
account of their emotions, which I discuss in Chapter 5. So, I will not
examine here the connection between our having good or right
emotions, and the character-evaluations which might be made of us
in that respect. Second, the move from first- to second-level moral
significance of emotions is not a move to talking about occurrent
emotions instead of enduring or 'dispositional' emotions. I have been
concentrating in this chapter on showing how certain emotion-types,
impersonally conceived, are essentially involved in certain virtues,
just as one might discuss the general question of how a trait such as
honesty might be a virtue. But in moving to the second level of
emotional moral significance, I now want to discuss how particular
enduring or occurrent emotions, as examples of these emotion-types,
might be right or wrong, given what they are specifically directed at.
Given that care, for instance, helps constitute virtues such as strength
of will and friendship, how can we evaluate care, say, which is
directed at a thief, either as an enduring emotion (i.e. having a
disposition to care for a particular thief) or an occurrent emotion (i.e.
caring for a particular thief on a certain occasion)? The analogy with
evaluating honesty would thus be that if one had shown that honesty,
impersonally considered, is essentially involved in certain virtues,
one might then go on to examine how to evaluate honesty which is
directed towards particular objects, as a disposition (as in 'I am
always honest with my father'), or as an occurrence (as in 'I must be
honest in acting as executor of my father's will and estate').

Now, at this second level of moral significance, my claim is that a
particular emotional response of ours is *right* if what we take it to be
directed at is *in fact* morally *good*, whereas an emotional response of
ours is *wrong* if what we take it to be directed at is *in fact* morally *bad*,
where 'goodness' and 'badness' are understood here according to

virtue ethics: i.e. in terms of what contributes to or detracts from a flourishing life. So at this level, the rightness or wrongness of the particular emotional responses we have is determined by comparing how the person who experiences the emotion views the particular or (in Aristotle's terms) 'material' object of his or her emotion, with what the right or wrong material object of this emotional response would be here.[78] But how can we tell what the right or wrong material object of an emotion would be in any particular case? This is determined, I suggest, by reference to the Aristotelian notion of *phronesis*, or 'practical wisdom'. Following Aristotle, *phronesis* is a kind of deliberative capacity which helps guide our emotional responses towards the right particular or material objects in particular situations. My claim about the rightness and wrongness of our emotional responses can therefore be put as follows: an emotional response is right if we take it to be directed at the particular object which *phronesis* would direct it towards here, while an emotional response is wrong if we take it to be directed at a particular object which *phronesis* would direct it away from in this context. So, the *rightness* or *wrongness* of a particular emotional response is dependent on whether it is *in fact* aligned with an appropriate object, in the manner of a practically wise person.[79]

Let me clarify the criterion of emotional rightness and wrongness which I am suggesting here, by explaining the nature and guiding role of *phronesis* as an indicator of rightness and wrongness from the perspective of an ethics of virtue. As Aristotle makes clear in Book VI of the *Nicomachean Ethics* (*NE*), *phronesis* is neither scientific knowledge of demonstrable empirical facts, nor is it theoretical knowledge of first principles and necessary truths, nor is it the technical knowledge of a craft; rather, *phronesis* is the capacity to see what in general is good for man, and to see what this entails one ought to feel and do in the variety of situations one finds oneself in.[80] In other words, it is a capacity to deliberate well such that one realises virtuous ends in one's responses to particular situations. It may be possible to see in some purely intellectual sense what is virtuous without understanding the implications of this for what one ought to feel and do in particular situations (see *NE*, VII, 3, 1146b30–1147a24), and it may also be possible to feel and act rightly 'by accident', that is, without having deliberated properly (see *NE*, VI, 9, 1142b23–6, VI, 12, 1144a18, VI, 13, 1144b26); but *phronesis* is a capacity which integrates these perceptual, deliberative, affective, and practical faculties so that they operate well together. So, through *phronesis* we can understand the features and activities which are characteristic of human flourishing, such as psychic harmony, strength of will, love and friendship, and a sense of self-worth; and we can also understand how these virtues (and their corresponding vices) bear on what we ought to feel and do in a certain situation. In other words, with regard to our emotions, *phronesis* guides our particular emotional responses towards morally good objects (and away from morally bad objects).

But *phronesis* is not simply a disposition to act and feel in certain ways, which is activated when the appropriate situations arise. For as Nancy Sherman points out, *phronesis* also actively directs our perception to certain ethically salient particulars of situations. Through *phronesis* we become sensitive to when characteristic human goods are 'at stake' in various situations, and certain emotions play an indispensable role in helping *phronesis* discern the ethically salient features of situations.[81] Thus, in Section 4 of this chapter I argued that emotions such as love and sympathy may lead us to a deeper understanding of certain human needs, and may alert us to when those needs are at stake in a particular situation in the first place, so that we can respond more appropriately. So too, as Sherman argues,

> a sense of indignation makes us sensitive to those who suffer unwarranted insult or injury, just as a sense of pity and compassion opens our eyes to the pains of sudden and cruel misfortune . . . We notice through feeling what might otherwise go unheeded by a cool and detached intellect. To see dispassionately without engaging the emotions is often to be at peril of missing what is relevant.[82]

But love, sympathy, and compassion can also be misdirected to morally bad objects, unless they are guided by *phronesis*, so in good character, *phronesis* works hand in hand with certain emotions to highlight when the virtues and vices are at stake.[83] In summary then, *phronesis* coordinates our perception of and response to a certain situation with what we ought to feel and do in that situation, in the light of the virtues and vices which are relevant there.[84]

So, how does this help provide a criterion of emotional rightness and wrongness, at the second level of moral significance? What we must do, in assessing a particular manifestation of an emotion-type as right or wrong, is determine what emotional response a *phronimos*, or practically wise person, would have in this situation. More specifically, we must determine whether the object of our emotion here is an object which the *phronimos* would have this emotional response towards in this situation. If our particular emotional response and its object are consistent with those of a *phronimos* here, then our emotional response is *right* in this situation; whereas if our emotion and its object are those which the *kakos* or *akolastos*, or person afflicted by some vice (such as profligacy, weakness of will, apathy, or an excessive sense of self-worth), would have in this context, then our emotional response here is *wrong*.

In explaining this claim, it will be helpful to consider some examples of particular emotions evaluated in these ways. In earlier sections I argued that *care*, as an emotion-type, is essentially involved in achieving such important human goods as strength of will, love and friendship, and a sense of self-worth, and therefore care has significant first-level moral goodness. But I also allowed that care may be morally wrong when it takes evil as its object. For example, if I care about the welfare of one who I acknowledge to be a murderous dictator, and I care about him considered as an evil murderous dictator, then my care here is *wrong*, because this emotional response is consistent with one which a vicious person would have here: murder is an act which is inimical to the attainment of most of the central human goods dealt with in this chapter, and to regard as valuable the welfare of a person who has committed such an act would itself be vicious.[85]

Or consider love, which I also argued has significant first-level moral goodness. Now a mother's love for her daughter, whose interests the mother takes to be morally good, is itself thereby morally good, and in so far as what the mother takes to be the daughter's interests are in fact morally good, or at least not evil, her mother's love here is also right. However, where this motherly love fails to develop along with the daughter into a mature form of love but instead becomes possessive, and based on an inadequate conception of just what is in the daughter's interests, then the love itself would be wrong, since it is contrary to what a *phronimos* would feel here. That is, the mother loves her daughter *qua* dependent, but a *phronimos* would see that the daughter's ability to carry out her values and hence retain her sense of self-worth would be seriously threatened by this possessive form of love, which is directed at a narrow conception of the daughter's interests, and so would recognise the moral wrongness of this emotional response here.

Consider also sympathy, which at the first or general level of moral significance is essentially involved in such goods as friendship, understanding, and certain forms of strength of will. Now, despite the importance of the emotion of sympathy in virtue, we may sometimes have sympathy for those who we take to be or in fact are morally bad, and so at the second level of moral significance, our sympathy for a particular person may itself be morally wrong. Suppose we have sympathy for a former company director convicted of fraud, as he tries to shield his face from the cameras gathered outside the court-room. If, on account of his humiliation, we sympathise with him here, considered as a thief, then our sympathy here is itself morally wrong, for a *phronimos* would recognise that this sympathy was directed at a profligate person who had acted unjustly, and so would not take such a person as the object of his sympathy. Finally, consider grief felt towards the loss of one's beloved. The *phronimos* would recognise the grief as an appropriate indication of the depth of one's love and attachment to one's beloved, which are themselves important human goods, and so this grief would be the right emotional response here.

Notice that I have not said that in order for one's particular emotional responses to be right or wrong, one must actually *be* a *phronimos*, or a vicious person, respectively. To be sure, the pres-ence of *phronesis* as a motive regulating our emotions may indeed be necessary for having a creditworthy or estimable *character*, as I suggest in Chapter 5. As Aristotle puts it, 'in order to be good one must be in a certain state when one does the several [virtuous] acts' (*NE*, VI, 12, 1144a18). 'For it is not merely the state in accordance with the right rule, but the state that implies the *presence* of the right rule, that is virtue; and practical wisdom is a right rule about such matters' (*NE*, VI, 13, 1144b26–8). However, since in this chapter we have been concentrating on evaluations of emotions *as such*, rather than evaluations of persons on account of their emotions, it is suf-ficient for emotional rightness (or wrongness) that our emotional response to a particular situation is directed at an object *in accord-ance with* (or contrary to) that which *phronesis* would direct it at, even if our response does not 'imply the presence' of *phronesis* here.[86]

Before concluding, it should also be noted that a particular emotional response which is directed at an appropriate object may nevertheless be wrong because its *intensity* is inappropriate to the situation. For example, as Aristotle says (*NE*, IV, 5, 1125b32–3), there are indeed things, such as a friend's insults, at which we ought to be angry, but if our anger here is of an intensity that is dispro-portionate to the gravity of the insult, then our emotional response here is wrong. It is in *this* context that Aristotle's somewhat contro-versial 'Doctrine of the Mean' should be understood. In Book II, Chapter 6, of the *Nicomachean Ethics*, Aristotle claims that virtuous emotions lie in a 'mean' between the opposite vices of excess and defect; but this should not be misunderstood as a general endorsement of emotional moderation. Rather, Aristotle is claiming that our emotional responses can be too strong or too weak, relative to the particular situation, and so it may be right to have intense anger towards a friend for a significant betrayal of trust, but wrong to respond with such anger to a minor slight. Thus, the rightness or wrongness of particular emotional responses is also partly a function of their *intensity*, which must be adjusted to the situation, and here again *phronesis* plays a crucial role in helping a person of good character discern the ethically salient particulars of a situation, so that he can respond with the right emotional intensity here.

Now, I do not claim that the procedure I have suggested for evaluating emotional responses will be easily and straightforwardly applied in particular cases. It may be difficult to determine just what human goods are at stake in a certain situation, and even if this is established, it may also be unclear what particular emotional response would have been in accordance with *phronesis* here. But I submit that such a procedure is no more difficult in application than the general approach to evaluation taken by its two main rivals, Utilitarianism and Kantianism. For it may be equally difficult to determine just what among the alternatives in a particular situation would result in consequences of maximal utility, and there may be similar problems in determining whether what one proposes is permissible according to the universalisability procedure of the Kantian categorical imperative, as we shall see in the next chapter.

Of course, an ethics of virtue may face certain irresolvable conflicts among values, so I do not want to be taken as in any way claiming to have shown that such an ethics offers a coherent picture of the broad and complex spectrum of what has moral significance in our lives. Nevertheless, I hope that the foregoing account has not only demonstrated that our emotions are morally significant, but also that it has given some idea of the variety of important ways in which emotions may have such significance, and of how this significance is to be properly understood.

3 Kantian arguments against emotions as moral motives

In the previous chapter I attempted to bring out the moral significance of our emotions by examining their connections with various
important features of good lives. Because I wanted to highlight the
distinctive moral importance of *emotions*, which, especially given the
action-oriented approach of much recent ethics, is often overlooked,
I concentrated mainly on the morality of emotions themselves, rather
than on the morality of action motivated by emotion. But since our
emotions can be morally significant in their own right, it would seem
that action motivated by our emotions may thereby be morally good
or bad, at least to some extent, and may thus reflect well or poorly on
us. In other words, it follows as a natural consequence of my account
of the moral significance of emotions in Chapter 2 that emotions can
be moral motives.

However, in arguing that our emotions and the acts they motivate
can as such be morally good and can reflect well on us, I encounter
an important Kantian objection which needs to be examined. That
is, a central claim of Kant's ethics is that only acts which are done
from duty have moral worth, and in the course of arguing for this
claim Kant explicitly asserts that, apart from one important exception, motivation by emotion cannot be morally good.[1] The emotion
which Kant excludes in making this assertion is respect (*Achtung*)
for the moral law, since in his view this is the only emotion which
involves a recognition of the determination of the will by the moral
law.[2]

Quite apart from what Kant himself said, it might be thought that
the claim that only acts which are done from duty are morally good is
compatible with allowing that emotions *other than* respect for the
moral law can be morally good, since it is possible, for instance, that
one could be motivated to act from *love* of doing one's duty.[3] If the

possibility of such cases is admitted, the view might then be that only motivation by duty, or by emotions which somehow involve an attachment to duty, is morally good. Indeed, as we shall see, this kind of view has recently been defended by several writers in giving Kantian or quasi-Kantian accounts of moral agency. Such a view may include Kant's, since respect can be one of the emotions which is held to involve an attachment to duty, and therefore to be morally good. But the view here seems to go beyond Kant's, in so far as it allows that emotions other than respect can involve attachment to duty in a manner that is morally good.[4]

This chapter is therefore directed at those who claim that only motivation by duty, or by emotions which involve attachment to duty, rather than motivation by emotions which do not involve attachment to duty, is morally good. Since the arguments which follow apply equally to both types of Kantian view above, I shall henceforth ignore the difference between them, and speak only of motivation by *duty* (which may be taken as either that alone, or as including motivation by *emotions* which involve attachment to duty), on the one hand, and motivation by *emotion*, which on the other hand refers to emotions that do not involve attachment to duty.

I am not concerned to discuss whether acting from duty can be morally good. Rather, my aim in this chapter is to show the falsity of the arguments advanced by Kant (particularly in the *Foundations*) and by some recent Kantians *against* emotions as moral motives, in their attempts to establish duty as *the* moral motive. I argue that there is at least as much reason to believe that emotions can be morally good motives as there is to hold this of duty, and further, that the moral importance of emotions goes beyond their value as motives in any case. Thus, I want to demonstrate that the claims made by Kant and his followers about moral motivation do not refute my arguments in Chapter 2 that emotions can be morally good in various ways, and in examining these Kantian views here, I hope also to illuminate the ways in which emotions can motivate morally good actions.

Before going any further, let me add a clarificatory note about my understanding of the term 'moral'. In the previous chapter I argued that we can see the moral significance of emotions by looking at their important connections with certain features of a flourishing life. Now it might be said that Kant's notion of the 'moral' is somewhat more circumscribed than this, and so one cannot use my arguments in Chapter 2 to show that Kant should have thought emotions morally significant, on *his* understanding of 'moral'. But let me say that while I do take the previous chapter as indicating how our emotions can be morally significant in an important and widely used sense of 'moral', I concede that nevertheless some moralists, particularly Kantians, may resist characterising this significance in *moral* terms (although as we see later in this chapter, some Kantians may still attempt to capture the moral significance of emotions in certain ways). It is beyond the scope of this book to embark on a general discussion of the relative merits of aretaic and Kantian approaches to morality (if indeed we ultimately even need to decide between them); in any case, I do not argue here that Kant should have regarded emotions as morally significant in *his* sense of 'moral'.

My aims in this chapter are more modest. I will argue for the negative thesis that Kantian arguments against emotions as moral motives are unsuccessful, and I also suggest that Kant's requirements for moral motives may be too strong, such that even the duty motive itself may perhaps be ruled out by those conditions. Indeed, I want to show that given what Kant and Kantians can *plausibly* require of a moral motive, duty has no more claim to be such a motive than do certain emotions. It is characteristic of Kantians to take *reliability* as a necessary condition of a moral motive, and then argue that since only duty can meet this requirement whereas emotions cannot, duty is therefore the only moral motive. Against this, I argue that in the various ways in which this condition may be understood, it does not favour duty over emotion. I also show that Kantians beg the question against their opponents in arguing that duty is the only moral motive on the grounds that duty, unlike other motives, is in a certain sense 'internally connected' with right action. If we were to decide between duty and emotion as moral motivation, what we would need is some kind of *independent* comparison between them. Now, in arguing for these claims I do not presuppose the substantive account of the moral significance of emotions given in Chapter 2, but of course, once we see the failure of these Kantian arguments, then the way is left open to consider in detail how emotions might be morally significant motives. And it is as a beginning towards demonstrating this significance that the previous chapter is intended.

It is not my purpose here to become involved in exegetical disputes concerning the nature of Kant's views on moral motivation. I want to show that no matter which of the several prominent interpretations of Kant's remarks (especially in the *Foundations*) on duty, emotion, and moral worth is accepted, his position on motivation by emotion involves serious errors, and is therefore to be rejected. I begin with a brief point about the kind of value embodied in the Kantian notion of moral worth, after which I look at four different accounts of how

Kant's view that duty is the only moral motive bears on motivation by emotion. I then examine some of the principal arguments given by Kant and his supporters against emotions as moral motives, and in my criticisms of these arguments I challenge the alleged superiority of duty over emotion in this respect. Following this I consider a possible way in which a Kantian who is perhaps persuaded by some of my arguments might characterise certain emotions as morally significant. In the penultimate section I discuss an important Kantian argument against emotions as moral motives which appeals to a connection between morality and freedom in order to show that duty is the only moral motive. Finally, I examine an interpretation of the notion of moral worth which attempts to defuse the issue between Kant and his critics.

1. KANT'S ACCOUNT OF MORAL WORTH, ACTING FROM DUTY, AND THE PLACE OF EMOTIONS IN MORAL MOTIVATION

In order to understand the nature of the value which Kant attributes to acting from duty and denies to acting from emotion, we need to look at just what Kant has in mind by the notion of moral worth. It has been taken as uncontroversial by many that the possession of moral worth, for Kant, is a supererogatory good: that is, it is better to have moral worth than not to have it, but lacking moral worth is itself no moral defect.[5] However, some recent commentators have understood Kant as holding not only that it is better to have moral worth than to lack it, but also that lacking moral worth may for various reasons be morally defective.[6]

Yet there is a third position on Kantian moral worth which has also been defended recently. Richard Henson suggests that Kant's notion of moral worth in the *Foundations* is analogous to a citation for gallantry in winning a hard battle. That is, although we praise such feats, we do not thereby

> mean to encourage people to search out or create situations in which this sort of praise is warranted. On the present interpretation of moral worth, it would in a way be better if a person's acts never had it, because it would be better not to be in the sort of situation in which it is possible.[7]

As Henson understands Kant then, lacking moral worth is no moral defect, for while it may be better once in situations of battle or struggle to perform acts that have moral worth,[8] nevertheless, since it is desirable that such situations are avoided, it is better, all things considered, not to have moral worth in the first place.

I shall not decide between these competing interpretations of Kantian moral worth here.[9] For I want to show that on any of the above accounts, Kant's views on morality and the emotions are faulty. In much of what follows, I will assume that it is on the whole better to have moral worth than to lack it, but whether or not lacking moral worth can be morally defective is an issue which I need not settle in order to make my point (although I do think that Kant actually held that lacking moral worth can at least sometimes be morally defective; but I shall not try to show this). At the end of this chapter I will discuss Kant's views with Henson's 'battle-citation' model of moral worth in mind.

So far as I can see, there are at least *four* possible interpretations of how Kant's claim that only acts which are done from duty have moral worth bears on the role, if any, that inclinations (emotions) are permitted to play in motivating such acts. To begin with, there is the interpretation offered by Schiller, in his notorious mockery of Kant, where an act has moral worth only if it is done from duty in the face of *contrary* inclinations. Thus, Schiller takes Kant as claiming that, for example, it is only when I act out of duty towards my friend while also despising him that my act has moral worth.[10]

Second, there is the view Henson attributes to the Kant of the *Foundations* (in conjunction with the battle-citation model of moral worth): an act has moral worth only if it is done from duty, but only when one acts without any cooperating inclinations present is one acting from duty at all, since it is only then that one may be properly said to have won the battle to act in spite of one's inclinations.[11] (The notion of 'cooperating inclinations' involved here refers to any inclinations which would lead one, in the absence of the duty motive, to perform the act in question.)[12] Thus, on Henson's interpretation, for an act to be done from duty (and therefore have moral worth) it is not sufficient that our motivation in performing the act seemed to us to be a sense of duty – irrespective of what other potential motives were present. According to Henson, Kant held that in order to act from duty at all (and thereby gain moral worth), no cooperating inclinations may even be *present* in the agent at the time of acting.[13]

Notice that this is not necessarily to require the total absence of inclinations in acting from duty, for on this interpretation, acts may be done from duty (and so have moral worth) with inclinations present that are contrary to or irrelevant to the act in question.[14] Thus, Henson's Kant is in this sense less extreme than Schiller's, for the latter requires the presence of contrary inclinations in action that is morally worthy, whereas the former requires only the absence of cooperating inclinations. As mentioned earlier, Henson makes his interpretation of Kant here palatable by attributing to him a battle-citation model of moral worth, according to which there is nothing morally wrong with failing to perform acts that have moral worth. So, if we perform a dutiful act from inclination, or with cooperating inclinations present, instead of from duty, this is not morally defective, it is just that such an act has no moral worth.[15]

However, in a reply to Henson, Barbara Herman advances a third interpretation of Kant's remarks on duty, inclination, and moral worth. According to Herman, if we look at Kant's arguments for the moral worth of the duty motive, he does *not* claim that acting from duty involves the absence of cooperating inclinations (understanding the notion of 'cooperating inclinations' as defined earlier). As long as it is duty that *actually moves one to act*, the act has moral worth, regardless of whether cooperating inclinations are present.[16] As Herman puts it, Kant holds that an act has moral worth if and only if duty is its primary motive. Further, Herman argues that since Kant claims that only morally required acts can be performed from duty as a primary motive,[17] then it is only such (dutiful) acts that can have moral worth. Thus, only dutiful acts that are done from duty as a primary motive have moral worth.

Herman also rejects Henson's claim that according to Kant, it is better, all things considered, that one's acts lack moral worth. For, against Henson, Herman claims that Kant does not hold that it is better that we avoid situations where morally worthy action is possible. But this does not mean that Kant urges us to constantly seek out opportunities to perform morally worthy acts. According to Herman, Kant believes that situations where we are called upon to act dutifully arise as part of normal everyday life, and instead of trying to somehow engineer things so that we would rarely be confronted with such situations, it is morally better that we face these situations, that we carry out our duty, and moreover, that we do so from a sense of duty rather than from inclination, for it is only duty which, unlike inclination, is reliable in moving us to do the right thing. Indeed, because inclinations are unreliable in this sense, acting from them instead of from duty may even be morally defective.[18] I will discuss this part of Herman's position shortly. Here it is sufficient to point out that Herman takes Kant as holding that it is on the whole better if one's acts have moral worth, and further, that lacking moral worth through acting from inclination may itself be morally defective.

Yet while this is the interpretation offered by Herman regarding moral motivation of *dutiful* acts, she proposes a different account of Kant's views concerning morally *permissible* acts, which suggests the possibility of a fourth position on what Kant saw as the proper relationship between moral value and motivation by duty and inclination. Now, although only dutiful acts could, for Kant, be *morally worthy*, morally permissible acts could, depending on their motives, indicate an 'attitude of virtue' in the agents who perform them.[19] Morally permissible acts are those such that neither their performance nor their omission violates the universalisation test of the categorical imperative when proposed as maxims. Dutiful acts, of course, are those which pass the test but whose omission would fail it. As Herman explicates Kant, a morally permissible act can indicate this attitude of virtue in the agent if and only if duty is one of the conditions with regard to which the agent acts. That is, morally permissible acts which reflect well on the agents who perform them are those which are in a sense motivated by duty in conjunction with other motives. For in the good Kantian agent, duty plays the role of (what Herman calls) a 'limiting condition' in the motivation of such acts, whereby it regulates their acting on some other motive, such that they do not contravene the universalisation test of the categorical imperative.[20] Thus on this account, where helping another is in fact permissible (but not actually morally required), there is nothing wrong, and indeed, much that is admirable and praiseworthy (although not yet *morally* worthy), in acting out of compassion regulated by a sense of duty. But if we performed such an act out of inclination, such as compassion, without regard for its permissibility, then our action here would fail to attract this kind of Kantian praise (and it may even be considered morally deficient).

Now, it is not my purpose here to decide among the foregoing interpretations. Rather, I want to point out that whichever interpretation of Kant's remarks on duty, motivation, and moral worth we take, his position accords no value to either act or agent for an act that is performed out of emotion where the duty motive is absent. That is, on each of these interpretations of the implications for the emotions of Kant's claim that only acts done from duty have moral worth, it is clear that he saw acting with regard to duty as a precondition for value in his assessment of motives for actions. And if, as we assumed at the beginning of this discussion, we take a person's possessing this value (in the form of moral worth or an attitude of virtue) as a mark of their goodness, and on the whole better to have than to lack, then, quite apart from the further issue of whether failing to possess such value can be morally defective, Kant's view clearly devalues acting out of emotion, at least considered as such.

To be sure, it should be acknowledged that there are passages in the *Foundations* where Kant seems to allow that certain emotions may have some kind of value. For example, along with such qualities as intelligence, resoluteness, and perseverance, courage and other emotions may be valuable in the sense and to the extent that they make life easier and happier, and also in that we tend to appreciate and admire such features in others. But Kant argues that without a *good will*, these qualities and emotions may well become harmful and contemptible, and he claims that therefore they may be *morally* admirable and desirable only in so far as they are influenced by the presence of a good will.[21] So the point remains that Kant denied moral value to acting from emotion in the absence of the duty motive. For Kant held that something cannot have moral value to any degree unless it is combined with good willing (i.e. being moved by the idea of duty), and so, whatever value Kant accorded to acting from emotion in the absence of duty, it seems that he did not regard this as *moral* value.[22]

2. THE ALLEGED SOVEREIGNTY OF THE DUTY MOTIVE – KANTIAN ARGUMENTS AGAINST EMOTIONS AS MORAL MOTIVATION

My strategy will be to examine some of the main arguments which Kant and his followers use to deny that emotions can be moral motives, in order to uncover some of the criteria which *they* consider important for moral motives to satisfy. I then compare motivation by duty and by emotion with regard to those criteria, and I will argue that, in so far as those requirements themselves are plausible, duty has no more claim to be considered a moral motive than do various emotions.

If we look at certain passages in the *Foundations*, Kant appears to be arguing that emotions cannot be moral motives because they are unreliable and capricious, whereas duty is dependable and stable, and is always available to us as a motive to action.[23] That is, a moral motive must be something which we are all capable of having, and it must reliably lead us to act in a manner that is consistent and steady, but emotions are transitory and impulsive, and therefore cannot meet this requirement.[24] Thus, *reliability* is considered by Kant to be an important criterion of an acceptable moral motive. I want to show that, in the various ways we might take Kant here, his claims are mistaken.

We can begin by distinguishing between two elements of reliability according to which motivation by duty is alleged to be superior to motivation by emotion: they are summonability and efficaciousness.[25] The reliability of a motive is, in part, a function of its summonability – that is, the extent to which we are capable of bringing it before our mind. Kant and his followers claim that the sense of duty, since it proceeds from the faculty of reason, is always available to us to be called upon as a motive to action, whereas emotions, being part of our lower, sensual self and therefore transitory and capricious, are not, and so cannot be moral motives.

Before examining the plausibility of this claim, we might cast doubt on its implicit assumption that universal accessibility is a necessary condition of a moral motive,[26] for perhaps there is no such thing as a motive which we are all capable of having. In any case, there seem to be some motives which are thought paradigmatically morally good, such as being motivated by great courage and bravery in an act of heroism, but which few of us seem capable of having.

But, granting universal accessibility as a necessary condition of moral motives, the Kantian claim that the duty motive is always available, while emotions are capricious, seems to be false, for several reasons. First, beginning with the latter half of this claim, the Kantian criticism of emotions as impulsive and capricious is an unjustified generalisation.[27] It is not surprising that Kant made such claims, since his view seems to be based on a simple sensation model of emotions as non-cognitive phenomena over which we have little if any control. Kant regarded emotions (other than respect for the moral law) as belonging to the causally determined empirical world of sense, and as such, amenable to natural scientific description and explanation. Thus, Kant held that the study of the nature of emotions 'belong[s] to an empirical psychology, which would be the second part of physics if we consider it philosophy of nature'.[28] Kant usually refers to emotions as simple feelings, by which he seems to mean bodily sensations, and he often speaks of emotions in terms of bodily illnesses.[29] For example, in *The Doctrine of Virtue*, Kant says that 'Sympathetic joy and sorrow are really sensuous feelings of a pleasure or pain at another's state of happiness or sadness (shared feeling, feeling participated in)', and he likens the generation of such sympathy to 'the communication of warmth or contagious diseases . . ., since it spreads by natural means among men living near one another'.[30] To be sure, Kant's last major work, *Anthropology from a*

Pragmatic Point of View, did attempt to formulate (among other things) a rudimentary schema of types of emotions according to their duration and intensity.[31] Yet even here it was in terms of their opposition to reason that Kant *defined* these types of emotion: 'to be subject to both affects and passions is probably always an illness of the mind because both affect and passion exclude the sovereignty of reason'.[32] However, as I argued in Chapter 1, this view of emotions as mere affects is an oversimplified picture of the nature of emotions, for emotions are complex phenomena involving cognitions and desires as well as a dimension of affectivity. Perhaps if Kant had had a more adequate account of the nature of emotions, he would not have regarded them as so lacking in moral value.

But in any case, there are many emotions which, because of their susceptibility to development and training, fail to fit Kant's model of emotions as 'pathological' phenomena which are largely beyond our control. For example, as I argue in the following chapter, there is often much that we can do to cultivate a sympathetic and compassionate responsiveness to the plight of others, whereby we can adjust our responses according to their distress. Indeed, I suggest in Chapters 4 and 5 that a failure to develop such capacities can sometimes in itself be blameworthy. Emotional capriciousness may not be a sign of the inadequacy of emotions themselves as moral motives, so much as an indication of a kind of moral failing in the particular person whose emotions are typically capricious.

Yet aside from the merits or otherwise of these arguments, there is a second reply which can be made to the Kantian claim that the duty motive is superior to emotion in terms of summonability. That is, we can ask whether the motive of duty itself is in fact always available in the manner which Kantians claim. Notwithstanding some of the rather dogmatic assertions of Kant and his supporters in this regard, it does not seem too difficult to imagine cases where even the most well-trained Kantian agent (let alone those of us who are not well-trained Kantians) is unable to summon a sense of duty as a motive for action that is in fact required by universal law.[33] Indeed, such a failure may be the direct result of strong emotional motives which tend in the same direction as or away from the act in question. Or perhaps the agent just suffers from a lack of care or energy in this particular case.

It might be replied here that, rather than showing any fault in the summonability of the duty motive, this merely indicates that the agent in question is not rational. So, the Kantian claim would now be that the duty motive is always summonable by all *rational* beings. But this modified claim is open to two further objections. First, it seems possible that even a rational person may sometimes be unable to summon the motive of duty. Second, if the Kantian will not admit the possibility of such cases, it seems that whether or not an agent is able to summon the duty motive is being used as a criterion for his rationality, which is a move that is not obviously justified.[34] So it begins to appear doubtful whether duty is at all superior to emotion with regard to their summonability as motives.

Yet even if we grant the Kantian claim that duty, unlike emotion, *is* always available as a motive to action, it remains to be seen whether duty is more reliable than emotion in terms of *efficaciousness*. For another aspect of the alleged reliability of the duty motive is that, once summoned, it can be depended on to be effective in action. That is, the presence of the sense of duty is, according to this view, always sufficient to outweigh the influence of inclinations away from the dutiful act. But again, it does not seem too difficult to imagine cases where contrary desires are strong enough to prevent the motive of duty issuing in action. For example, many a professor would have given way to their desire to dine out with friends instead of marking their students' assignments, despite their sense that duty bids them to do the latter. Indeed, even apart from such familiar cases of weakness of will, it seems that we can simply choose to ignore or act against what we know to be our duty.[35] The view which holds that it is logically impossible for an agent to recognise that he has an obligation to do something without thereby being motivated to do it (which is often called 'internalism') seems to me to be mistaken.[36] Moreover, many emotions, including some of which I argued in Chapter 2 are morally significant, may themselves be strong enough to defeat quite powerful contrary inclinations, and succeed in motivating the acts at which they aim.[37] For example, acting out of compassion or love towards another may be done in the face of quite stubborn self-regarding inclinations and desires. Therefore, it is questionable to say the least that duty is superior to emotion as an effective motive to action.

However, rather than dispute the preceding arguments, Kantians might claim that there is a deeper sense of reliability which tells in favour of duty, rather than emotion, as the proper moral motive. Thus, Barbara Herman argues that it was not in terms of summonability or efficaciousness in action *as such* that Kant considered the duty motive as substantially more reliable than emotion, but it was in terms of efficaciousness in leading to *right* action. She maintains that Kant argued that emotions could not be moral motives because they lead to right action only through a fortuitous alignment of motives and circumstances, which could have been otherwise. However, in acting from the motive of duty, one has an *interest* in the moral *rightness* of one's action, which therefore makes the rightness of the action that is performed a 'nonaccidental effect' of one's concern.[38] Thus, Herman's argument on Kant's behalf here is that emotions cannot be moral motives because, unlike duty, they do not provide the agent with an interest in the moral rightness of his actions; an interest, that is, which will 'guarantee that the right action will be done'.[39]

Before responding to this argument, it will be instructive to clarify just what Kant might have had in mind by the idea that in acting from duty one is acting with an interest in the moral rightness of one's actions. Several critics have understood this to imply that the good Kantian agent acts out of duty *for the sake of* a moral principle. The criticism which is then made of such an account is that the agent seems concerned about the wrong thing. That is, in a situation where a person recognises that he could easily give urgently needed help to another, the Kantian would appear to give help for the sake of fulfilling his duty, which is seen as defective. For the *object* of such an act should be to help this person, rather than to fulfil a moral requirement.[40]

Herman herself has recently responded to this criticism, and her reply elucidates the idea that the motive of duty involves a moral interest in the rightness of actions. She maintains that it is a mistake to think of the good Kantian agent on the model of a 'rule-fetishist'. For if the *motive* of an action is properly distinguished from its *object*, then it is clear that in acting from duty, the object of one's action need not be to do what moral principle requires. In being motivated to help another by duty, one can be directly concerned with the welfare of that person as the *object* of one's act. Indeed, this can be regarded as the typical picture of the good Kantian agent.[41]

The distinction between motives and objects of actions which is invoked here is quite commonplace. For example, consider a person who has resolved to put aside $100 each week for a holiday abroad. When payday comes around, they are motivated by their resolution to deposit a further $100 in their holiday account; but clearly, *keeping their resolution* is not the aim or object of their action here (i.e. they save the money not for the sake of keeping their resolution) – rather the object is to have enough money for their holiday, or, simply, to have a holiday. (Of course, they are also motivated by their desire for a holiday abroad, so the object of an action can serve as a motive; but the important point here is that an action may have motives which are not also among its objects.) So, acting from the motive of duty guarantees right action because it involves a moral interest in the rightness of one's actions as part of the *motive*. It is part of being *moved* to act from duty that one acknowledges the constraints of universalisability. Thus, on Herman's interpretation, Kant did not deprive acting from emotion of moral worth because such acts lacked a moral interest as part of their *objects*, but because acting from emotion involves no moral interest as part of the *motive*. It is in this sense that Herman takes Kant as claiming that motivation by emotion is merely fortunate to 'hit upon' right action.

There are complex issues underlying Herman's argument, and these can best be brought out, I suggest, through a closer examination of the charge, mentioned earlier, that the nature of the help provided for others by the Kantian agent is somehow morally defective. Rather than accusing the Kantian agent of rule-fetishism, perhaps what these critics find morally objectionable in Herman's picture of the good Kantian agent is that such an agent seems unable to care for and offer help to others in a manner which is steady, strong, and dependable, because of the way in which his attachment to others is conditional: that is, in ceasing to help the other simply because (from a Kantian point of view) it is wrong to help her, he abandons the other too easily.[42] The issue would then be about the *conditionality* of the helping motive, and not about its *object*. For while it might be agreed that a Kantian agent can take another person's welfare as the object of his helping motive, the conditionality of the Kantian agent's attachment to those he benefits (i.e. its dependence upon permissibility, by Kantian standards) would be thought to make the Kantian an unreliable benefactor.

It might be replied that there is a sense in which acting from emotion is also conditional, in so far as my helping you depends on the absence of more pressing constraints on me (such as my brother being in danger of his life, or my house being on fire). Nevertheless, it might be allowed that helping another out of emotion involves more of an unconditional attachment to that person than does helping another out of duty. Indeed, it might be said that this is exactly the point. If we look at Herman's arguments, we find that she has a serious objection to help given out of altruistic emotions involving comparatively non-contingent attachments to another. That is, acting out of emotion lacks moral value *precisely* because of the relative unconditionality (compared with acting from duty) of the motive which may thereby be involved. Since the agent who acts out of, say, sympathy or compassion towards another is not concerned with whether his action is morally correct or required, he may be acting immorally in helping the other.[43] For example, he may be helping an escaped prisoner to elude the authorities, or a thief with his load of stolen goods. According to Herman, only the duty motive is reliable in leading to right action, because in acting from duty, we acknowledge the constraints of morality. Thus, Kant rejects emotions as moral motives on the grounds that (especially because of the nature of the attachments which they may involve), they can lead us to perform immoral actions.

Now I shall not dispute the claim that, in acting from emotion, we may sometimes be acting immorally. Rather, I shall challenge the assumption that a motive cannot be morally good if it *may* lead us to perform immoral actions. To begin with we might note that throughout the *Foundations*, Kant emphasised the moral assessment of motives *apart from* the actions in which they may be involved, and indeed, he argued that the motive of duty has unconditional worth, even though he allowed that we may act from duty and yet fail to act rightly:

> The good will is not good because of what it effects or accomplishes or because of its adequacy to achieve some proposed end; it is good only because of its willing, i.e. it is good of itself . . . Usefulness or fruitlessness can neither diminish nor augment this worth.[44]

So Kant himself does not seem to require a moral motive to be infallible, and so he seems to reject the very view which Herman is attributing to him. Perhaps then, in comparing motivation by duty and motivation by emotion, we should in both cases examine the moral worth of the motive as such, instead of looking at their efficaciousness in leading to a certain kind of action. However, even if Herman appears to be arguing for the moral superiority of the duty motive from rather un-Kantian premises, we should still consider whether these premises are correct.

Turning to this question then, I would argue that just because a motive *can* lead us to perform immoral actions does not entail that this motive cannot be morally good. There are two points here. First, when we act from a motive which, on some substantive account of morality (such as that given in the previous chapter), seems morally valuable, why should the mere *possibility* of this motive's being involved in immoral action rule out its moral value in cases where the

100 Morality and the Emotions

actions it leads us to perform are *not* immoral? Second, is such a motive no longer morally good when it *is* actually involved in immoral action? I shall concentrate mainly on the first question, for there are complex and difficult issues arising out of the second, which we need not settle in order to reject Herman's argument for duty instead of emotion as moral motivation. Nevertheless, I shall make some brief comments shortly in regard to the second question.

Consider a person who, out of compassion, helps another whom he sees is genuinely in need, and imagine further that he acts with the depth of appreciation of the other's needs which, as I explained in Chapter 2, is characteristic of a compassionate person. Herman would claim that this person's helping the other from such a motive cannot be morally good because he might have been led by this motive to act immorally. Now, given that this person is not acting immorally in acting out of compassion here, I venture that many of us would regard the fact that compassion *can* motivate immoral action as irrelevant to the evaluation of his motive here. But let us focus on the general view underlying Herman's claim – that is, the view that a motive cannot be morally good if it *may* lead us to perform immoral actions. This requirement seems too strong, for if this were a condition of moral motives then it is likely that there would be *no* moral motives whatsoever, for there seems to be no motive which is such that it can *never* be involved in immoral action. Certainly, the emotional motives which I argued in Chapter 2 are morally good may nevertheless motivate immoral action in some cases. And indeed, as Kant himself recognised, even the duty motive is not infallible in this sense, for it is also possible to act wrongly from duty (although in Kant's view, this did not diminish the value of the duty motive, for Kant believed that motivation by duty is always morally good, even where we thereby act wrongly).

Thus I believe it can be shown that Herman's claim about the sufficiency of the duty motive for right action is in fact mistaken. For a person who acts on the motive of duty and thereby (we may suppose) has an interest in the moral rightness of his action may nevertheless be acting on *false beliefs*, and therefore be acting wrongly, even if his duty motive is both summonable and efficacious. False beliefs can enter into and affect (what would otherwise be) dutiful action in various ways. An agent may make errors in the calculations which are involved in the universalisation test of the categorical imperative, or in his application of it to the situation at hand. Thus, in acting from a duty of beneficence, the Kantian agent may have false beliefs about what the recipient needs. He may therefore fail to carry out his duty here, and so he may act wrongly. Indeed, in Herman's own example, which she uses to argue that sympathy cannot be a morally good motive, where we are motivated by sympathy to help a person whom we do not realise is a thief with his heavy load, it is equally possible that someone may help this person out of a duty of beneficence, and so regard himself as acting rightly, even though he is actually acting immorally. To act out of duty may well be to have a moral interest in the rightness of the action performed, but having such an interest does not ensure that it will be infallible in executing its aim.[45] Therefore, contrary to Herman, motivation by duty does not seem in itself sufficient to guarantee the rightness of the actions which are thereby performed. So, while motivation by emotion may sometimes suffer from vicissitudes in terms of reliability, this had better not preclude emotions from being moral motives, since motivation by duty may itself be plagued by similar difficulties. It seems then that infallibility cannot be required of moral motives, for to retain this condition would seem to undermine Herman's own argument for duty as the moral motive. And without this condition, Herman's examples of the involvement of various emotions in immoral action fail to show that emotions cannot be moral motives.

Now, Herman would most likely respond to this by insisting that since motivation by duty involves a moral interest in acting rightly, the duty motive is 'internally' or conceptually connected with right action, and so duty therefore qualifies as a moral motive; whereas motivation by emotion cannot be morally good because it involves no such moral interest or conceptual connection and so leads us to act rightly only as a matter of luck.[46] However, this response is unconvincing, for in what sense is the duty motive conceptually connected with our acting rightly, when, as we have seen, we may act on this motive and yet fail to act rightly? Since motivation by duty and motivation by emotion both seem to be fallible in this regard, in both cases there would seem to be an element of luck involved in whether the motive in question succeeds in leading us to act rightly.

However, perhaps what is meant by saying that the duty motive is 'internally connected' with acting rightly is that this motive *aims at* right action (even though motivation by duty may not always lead us to act rightly). But to rely on this as an argument for the moral goodness of the duty motive instead of other motives would be to beg the question against those who hold that motives other than duty can be morally good. For one could with as much justification reply that motivation by certain emotions is morally good because they are in this sense internally connected with morally good action (given some other substantive account of moral goodness, such as the aretaic conception of morality elaborated in Chapter 2). Thus for example, one could argue that motivation by compassion is morally good because it *aims at* action which would relieve the suffering of others, and this action is morally good (even though, like duty, acting out of compassion may not *always* lead us to act rightly). Now the issue here is not whether this would be a plausible argument for compassion as a moral motive. The point is, it would be question-begging to assume without further argument that any motive which does not aim at the type of action which compassion aims at cannot be a moral motive. What is needed is some kind of *independent* comparison between motivation by duty and motivation by emotion. But in the absence of this, the arguments we have been considering for duty instead of emotion as moral motivation seem unconvincing.

Indeed, the inadequacy of Herman's argument against emotions as moral motives can be demonstrated further by noting that the moral goodness of a certain motive may not be annulled when it is actually involved in immoral action. This is the second point I adverted to earlier, but because it raises complexities which are beyond the scope of this chapter, I shall discuss this second point only briefly here. Consider again the example where, out of sympathy, we help a person who is struggling with a heavy load which unknown to us contains stolen property. According to Herman, acting out of sympathy here cannot be morally good because we are performing an immoral act – i.e. we are helping a thief. However, it is far from clear that our acting immorally here shows that our motive of sympathy here cannot be morally good. Consider a parallel case: I notice that you are struggling with your maths homework and, since I have an aptitude for maths, I offer to help you; but in helping you with your homework here, I am actually unwittingly helping you to cheat in the exam tomorrow. Now surely this latter fact does not prevent my intention to help you with your homework being morally good. And if my intention here can be morally good, could not the same be said of motivation by sympathy in Herman's example?

To be sure, I am not claiming that the moral goodness and badness of motives is always unrelated to the moral significance of the acts in which they are involved, and indeed, in the previous chapter I allowed that emotions which might otherwise be morally good may actually be morally bad or wrong when they motivate actions which aim at evil ends. For instance, to have and act out of care may be morally bad or wrong when it takes evil as its object. But there are many different views about the bearing of acting immorally on the goodness or badness of one's motive in so acting. One view which would be taken by some in regard to the example of helping a thief out of sympathy is that this proves nothing about the failure of sympathy as a morally good motive, since the act may still be good *qua* act-of-sympathy.[47] Another view here, which relies on some notion of the unity of the virtues, is that sympathy which motivates immoral action is not really true sympathy at all, as our idea of what such emotions are is based on some conception of what the good person, who displays virtues such as justice and good judgment, does and feels.[48] Now, I do not want to argue for these views, as in any case they introduce complexities which cannot be examined in this chapter. But I mention them here in order to show that Herman's argument from the involvement of a motive in immoral action to the claim that such a motive cannot be morally good is highly controversial, and would be rejected by many (including Kant himself, as we have seen). That Herman's argument (at least in the context of motivation by duty and by emotion) *should* in fact be rejected is what I have been urging in the preceding paragraphs.

In the foregoing I have been responding to certain Kantian arguments for duty instead of emotions as moral motivation which attempt to establish this claim by appealing to some notion of *reliability*, and thus far my response to these arguments has been that, even if we allow reliability as a condition of moral motives, it does not seem to favour duty over various emotions, for duty has not been shown more reliable than various emotions with regard to motivating us to perform right acts. Both duty and emotion are fallible here. Yet while emotions may sometimes lead us to act immorally, nevertheless, as we have seen in this and the previous chapter, certain emotions, such as care, sympathy, and compassion, may reliably lead us to perform morally good actions.

Indeed it might even be suggested, as a further reply to the above Kantian arguments, that motivation by emotion may actually be *more* reliable than motivation by duty in leading us to perform what *Kantians* themselves regard as right acts. For the person motivated by certain emotions may sometimes be more likely to have true beliefs about the situation in which he acts than the person motivated by duty, and so the former may thereby have a better idea of when he is called upon to act dutifully and of what such action involves. For example, compare someone who helps another out of sympathy with someone who helps her out of a duty of beneficence. Thus, consider a Kantian agent on the one hand, and a sympathetic person on the other, who encounter a colleague who is grieving over the loss of a loved one. Now, given that both the Kantian agent and the sympathetic person could do something to help relieve the suffering of their colleague, they would both have a duty of beneficence towards her. Let us assume that the Kantian agent is able to summon and act on his sense of duty here. Now despite this, the Kantian agent's attempts to alleviate his colleague's grief seem likely to be far less successful than those of the sympathetic person in this situation, at least in so far as the Kantian agent's capacity for sympathy is undeveloped. For in the absence of such sympathy, the Kantian agent's attempts to relieve the suffering of his colleague may well be inappropriate. For example, he may suggest that she takes a holiday in order to divert her mind from the tragedy. However, a sympathetic person would probably see that this would be unlikely to alleviate her grief, and might perhaps offer to relieve her of the painful task of informing friends and other associates of the tragedy. Therefore, in this case, as in many others, the sympathetic person seems able to perform an act that is more beneficial and appropriate to the recipient, and so is more likely to fulfil his duty of beneficence, than is the act that is performed by the person motivated by duty.

However, Kantians may respond to such examples with a different line of argument. Kantians may concede that acting from the motive of duty cannot in itself guarantee that the action thus performed will not be wrong, and thus they may abandon their insistence on infallibility as a requirement of moral motives, as a means of distinguishing between duty and emotion. Instead, the argument might be that when we act from duty but nevertheless act wrongly, our failure here is due entirely to the intervention of *external* factors, rather than because of any *inherent* problem with the duty motive; whereas in contrast, it is characteristic of warm-hearted motives that, when unmediated by duty, they lead us to overlook conflicting moral considerations. For example, it might be argued that in acting out of love for a particular person, without regard for duty, one is thereby inclined to neglect considerations of fairness which come appropriately into play in the context of various institutional roles, such as those of doctor, teacher, and magistrate. Yet when motivation by duty is led astray by such factors as false beliefs, this is simply an indication of our necessarily imperfect rationality as moral agents, and is not an indictment of the duty motive itself.

Nevertheless, this defence fails to safeguard the Kantian position on motivation by duty compared with emotion. Let us agree with the claim that it is a characteristic feature of motivation by emotion

unregulated by duty that one is thereby led to overlook considerations of rightness (even if this does seem to be overstating things, in
the case of emotions such as sympathy and compassion). What can be
shown, I think, is that where acting from duty involves acting
wrongly, this failure is not always due to external factors but can
sometimes be traced to features internal to the duty motive itself.
When the criticism of duty is put in terms of 'false beliefs', this to
some extent obscures the real problem with duty compared to emotion, which becomes particularly apparent in duties of beneficence.
For even duties of promise-keeping and truthfulness can fail to be
fulfilled, despite our scrupulous efforts to keep our duty motive free
from immoral influences, simply because, for example, we may incul-
pably have false beliefs about the particular person to whom we are
here duty bound. But the failure of the duty motive in certain duties
of beneficence cannot be accounted for simply in terms of the intervention of these external factors. For in cases where one is called
upon to fulfil a duty of beneficence, there is a certain kind of 'moral
ineptitude' which is characteristic of motivation by duty uninformed
by sympathy or compassion.

Consider again the case of those who attempt to help a colleague
who is grieving over the loss of someone dear to her. I argued that,
without sympathy, the Kantian agent's attempts to help his colleague
out of duty here may well fail, whereas a sympathetic person would
be likely to make more appropriate efforts to relieve his colleague's
distress. Now, an important reason why a sympathetic or compassionate person may be better able to carry out a duty of beneficence is
that, as I argued in Chapter 2, having sympathy or compassion for
another is often necessary to gaining a proper understanding of what
actually needs to be done in order to help them. But even apart from
the superior insight into the situation which the sympathetic person
seems likely to have, the help they provide to the recipient may be
more appropriate than that given by someone motivated by duty,
because what the person in distress may need is *action-from-
sympathy*, that is, action which is motivated by a *feeling-with* the
other, rather than action done out of duty.[49] Without such emotional
motivation, one may fail to provide what the person in distress needs
to alleviate their suffering, and so one may fail to carry out one's duty
here. Thus, there seems to be an inherent problem with motivation
by duty which is unaccompanied by sympathy and compassion, in the
case of certain duties of beneficence; for, paradoxically, it is *the very
fact* that one acts from duty uninformed by sympathy or compassion
which entails that one fails to fulfil one's duty here.

Indeed, the degree of confidence in the duty motive shown in the Kantian argument here suggests a further internal difficulty with duty. For the Kantian view here is that it is only the undue influence of external factors which prevents the duty motive from issuing in right action, and the implication of this view is that in seeking to improve ourselves morally, we should concentrate on keeping our motive of duty pure by suppressing motives which may lead us astray. In fact, if we accept Kant's view of emotions such as sympathy and compassion as unruly forces which can spread uncontrollably like an illness, then perhaps we should attempt to eradicate our propensities for these emotions, lest they interfere with the reliable operation of duty. As Kant himself put it in the *Foundations*, 'The inclinations themselves . . . are so lacking in absolute worth that the universal wish of every rational being must be indeed to free himself completely from them'.[50]

However, it is this very imperialism of the duty motive which may well undermine the efficacy of duty itself. For, if my arguments about the importance of sympathy and compassion in fulfilling our duties of beneficence are correct, then in curbing or eliminating our capacities for these emotions, we would thereby deprive ourselves of the ability to effectively carry out many of our duties of beneficence. Thus, we might recognise that we have such a duty towards a relative, a friend, or a colleague in emotional distress in a certain situation, but we would have so disabled ourselves that we would be capable of providing little real assistance here. Indeed, it is questionable whether, having cultivated our sense of duty at the expense of our emotional capacities, we would even be able to *recognise* our duties of beneficence in many of these types of cases. For the proper cultivation of a certain type of motivation itself involves developing an awareness of aspects of situations where acting from such a motive would be appropriate,[51] and a natural consequence of neglecting one's capacities for sympathy and compassion is a form of perceptual 'blindness' to certain kinds of human suffering. Instead of being encouraged by duty to suppress our capacities for sympathy and compassion, we should in our quest for moral improvement make attempts to cultivate these emotional motives, since our beneficent action would thereby be more appropriate, and we would be likely to have a more developed awareness of the situations where we are called upon to act beneficently. For it is characteristic of the sympathetic or compassionate person not just to perform beneficent acts, but also to perceive more situations which warrant beneficent action in the first place, compared with a person who acts purely from duty.[52]

Now, Kantians will probably reply that the greater awareness of the sympathetic person here means that, generally speaking, there is a greater likelihood of their acting immorally than the person who acts from duty. But this need not be true. For first, as we saw earlier, a person acting from duty may none the less be acting wrongly. Thus in the above case, one may act from a duty of beneficence, but without sympathy one may have an inadequate understanding of the other's plight and so provide little real assistance for them, and therefore fail to carry out one's duty here. And second, given that the sympathetic person characteristically has a more highly developed awareness of when beneficent action is called for, and since when they see they can help they are more likely to perform actions which really count as *helping* the other (due to their deeper understanding of and empathy with the other's plight), they may more reliably and more thoroughly do what the duty of beneficence requires of them than a person who acts from duty. Indeed, it could be argued that in so far as the sympathetic person is more likely to fulfil their duty of beneficence than is the person motivated by duty, this may outweigh the sympathetic person's possible failures to act dutifully in *other* areas where the person motivated by duty may be relied upon to carry out their duty, so that motivation by sympathy may perhaps be on the whole more reliable in leading a person to act rightly than motivation by duty. But in any case, apart from the merits of such an argument, it seems that if reliability in motivating right action is taken as a criterion of what motives can be morally good, a Kantian might at least sometimes do better to act not from duty but from emotion instead, since the latter might be more reliable than the former in this respect.

It is worth noting in passing the implications of my argument for the various so-called 'caring professions', such as nursing and social work. In these areas, emotions have been traditionally contrasted not so much with reason but with some notion of 'professionalism', where maintaining a sense of 'professional detachment' demands that one avoid becoming 'emotionally involved' with one's patients or clients, and that one instead is motivated to act by one's special duties of beneficence here. But in many ways this is a false and somewhat superficial contrast, which can seriously mislead those working in such areas about what is appropriate in these contexts. Part of what seems to underlie this contrast is a quasi-Kantian conception of emotions as typically partial, unreliable, and difficult to control. It is one of my major concerns in this and the next chapter to show that such a characterisation of emotions is false. So far I have argued that

108 Morality and the Emotions

emotions such as sympathy and compassion may be at least as reliable as duty; and, as Lawrence Blum has persuasively argued, these emotions need not compromise our impartiality in situations where such an attitude is appropriate.[53] Indeed, my argument in this and the previous chapter suggests that sympathy and compassion may be *indispensable* to the proper fulfilment of certain duties of beneficence. A nurse or a social worker, for example, may have to act from sympathy or compassion in order to adequately understand their patient's or client's needs, and so provide the care which is appropriate for them. So, far from it being the case that professionalism in the caring professions requires an *unemotional* attitude to one's patients or clients, it would seem that those employed in these areas may sometimes actually be neglecting their professional responsibilities to the extent that they do not act from emotions such as sympathy and compassion.[54] And, as I go on to argue in Chapter 4, there are various ways in which one can attempt to cultivate and develop one's capacities for sympathy and compassion, such that one is *empowered* rather than 'overcome' by these emotions.

Of course, being motivated by sympathy or compassion does not in itself guarantee that one will act with sufficient depth of understanding to adequately fulfil one's duties of beneficence, for it is possible for a person acting out of sympathy or compassion to misconstrue just what the recipient's good consists in. This would be true, for example, of a person who had inadequately inculcated these emotional capacities. Thus, while acting from sympathy or compassion is often *necessary* for fulfilling our duties of beneficence, it may not be *sufficient* for this. But this does not mean that it is a sense of *duty* (and the universalisability principle thereby involved) which must constrain or regulate our sympathy or compassion in order to lead us to act rightly. Rather, as I suggested in the previous chapter, sympathy and compassion, like all morally significant emotions, need to be guided by practical wisdom or *phronesis* to be reliably directed to the right objects, and so to reliably lead to right action.[55] Like duty, motivation exclusively by emotion is also fallible.

To conclude this section then, we can say that in so far as duty is argued to be a superior motive to emotion on the grounds of *reliability*, such arguments are to be rejected, for motivation by emotion can be at least as reliable as, if not more reliable than, motivation by duty, according to each of the various senses of reliability which Kant and his followers offer. So motivation by duty seems to have no more claim (and may indeed have less claim) to be regarded as moral motivation than does motivation by various emotions.

3. KANTIANISM AND THE NON-MOTIVATIONAL VALUE OF EMOTIONS

In the previous section I argued that in cultivating a reliable disposition to perform right acts, a Kantian may be well advised to develop their capacity for having and acting out of emotions such as sympathy and compassion, instead of concentrating exclusively on developing their sense of duty and their ability to act out of duty. Now, this suggests a possible way in which Kantians might allow that certain emotions may be morally significant and may be considered as morally worthy motives. That is, a Kantian may regard certain emotions as morally good in an *instrumental* sense: i.e. in so far as they can assist the motive of duty in leading us to act rightly. Indeed, some Kantian theorists, perhaps from an awareness of the kind of points I have raised, have recently begun to recognise the moral importance of emotions such as sympathy and compassion, and some have actually allowed that these emotions may sometimes qualify as moral motives (given that the person who acts from them has an underlying commitment to acting in accordance with duty). Thus, in a recent article Herman herself admits that there might be a 'Kantian argument for the development of the affective capacities and Kantian grounds for valuing them. Not, of course, valuing them for themselves, but as morally necessary means [to] . . . the realization of moral intention in [right] action'.[56] And as she and these other Kantian theorists point out, there is textual evidence in Kant's *later* writings to suggest that even Kant may have allowed that certain emotions may be morally valuable in this instrumental sense.[57]

These modifications to the Kantian position on emotions are certainly an improvement on the views considered above, which accord emotions no moral value whatsoever. Yet despite this, Kantianism is fundamentally incapable of appreciating the full moral significance of emotions, for this significance goes deeper than the efficacy of emotions as motives to right (or wrong) action. That is, emotions may still be morally good and bad when they do not motivate us to perform morally significant actions, and indeed, when they are not expressed in action at all. In other words, emotions can be morally significant in a *non-motivational* sense.[58]

In order to see this, let us consider a person, physically isolated from others, who feels compassion for a terminally ill relative in the throes of death who has lost all touch with others. Now, although the former's compassion cannot be expressed in beneficent action towards their ill relative nor, let us assume, towards concerned others, surely it may still be morally good. For the compassionate person *values* their ill relative, and, as I argued in the previous chapter, to be affectively moved by what and whom one values is integral to the goodness of a good life. Further, their compassion is an important indication of their sense of *connectedness* with others, which, while it may be under increasing threat from the kind of individualism prevalent in many contemporary Western societies, is nevertheless itself morally desirable.[59]

To bring out the moral significance of this compassion in another way, let us look at how it might be regarded by Kantians. Since, as I have described the situation, there is no possibility that this compassion can be expressed in beneficent action, it seems that even a Kantian who allows emotions instrumental moral value (i.e. in so far as they help us carry out our duties) would regard such compassion as morally insignificant. Indeed, remarking on the kind of situation I have described, Kant himself advises: 'If . . . there is no way in which I can be of help to the sufferer and I can do nothing to alter his situation, I might as well turn coldly away and say with the Stoics: "It is no concern of mine".'[60] However, Kant here seems to countenance a kind of emotional indifference and detachment which many of us, I suggest, would rightly find morally defective, particularly in cases such as that outlined above, where the suffering person is someone dear to us.

Of course, this is not to say that failure to feel compassion in any case where we realise we cannot help a person we notice is in distress indicates a moral defect on our part. Rather, what is at issue is the kind of *character* endorsed by Kantians here. That is, there seems to be something morally defective about a person who turns away without emotion whenever they see they are unable to help another in distress, and the deficiency of such a reaction is especially apparent where the person in distress is one whom we cherish. If this claim is correct, then this is further evidence that having compassion towards those we see suffering, even where we cannot help them (when perhaps regret is also appropriate), is a morally desirable feature of character. And as I argued above, whether or not it can be acted on, this compassion importantly embodies our association and kinship with other people. But the view that emotions may be morally significant only in an instrumental sense as motives to action seems unable to capture the moral goodness of our having this kind of emotional character, and so even if Kantianism allows for the *instrumental* value of certain emotions, its account of the moral significance of emotions nevertheless seems to be inadequate.

However, Kantians might use the notion of character which I have invoked here to reply that an instrumental account of the moral significance of emotions can accommodate the foregoing type of example in an indirect sense. That is, Kantians might argue that compassion which cannot be expressed in beneficent action may be morally good because it is the sign of a character trait which *generally* issues in beneficent action, even though it does not do so always.[61] We could attempt to resist this account by arguing that even if the compassionate person in the above example could *never* express his compassion in beneficent action (e.g. because of prolonged physical isolation, such as imprisonment), we would still regard his compassion as morally good, such that, moreover, its absence may constitute a moral defect. But the reply might now be that even here, where a certain person's compassion is *never* expressed in beneficent action, the moral goodness of that compassion is still parasitic on its generally leading to beneficent action, even if it never does so in *this* person.

Nevertheless, there are several reasons for rejecting a purely *instrumental* account of the moral significance of emotions. Before setting out these reasons, however, we might note that the reply suggested above on behalf of the instrumental account, where a character trait of a certain person which never leads him to perform beneficent action can nevertheless be morally good because it generally leads to such action, seems to have come a long way from Kantianism, and we might wonder whether Kantians (in so far as they allow emotions instrumental value at all) could consistently hold such a view. For here efficaciousness in leading to right action would as such no longer be regarded a necessary condition of the moral goodness of motives, since on the above view, a compassion which never leads to right action may still be morally good. Yet as we saw in Section 2, efficaciousness in leading to right action is often considered by Kantians (although perhaps not by Kant himself, at least in the *Foundations*) to be a necessary condition of the goodness of motives, in their arguments for the moral goodness of the duty motive.

But whether or not it can be seen as a consistent form of Kantianism, the truth of the instrumental view itself remains in doubt. For it assumes that moral goodness is applied primarily to action and only derivatively to motives, and that the moral goodness of actions is always determined independently of motives (otherwise it would have to admit that psychological states may themselves have a certain non-instrumental value). But moral goodness does not derive solely from good action, for sometimes moral goodness (and badness) derives from psychological states themselves, and this can affect the moral status of the acts in which these states are expressed.[62]

Now there is indeed some truth in the instrumentalist view that the moral significance of psychological states can be seen in terms of the actions which they typically motivate; and thus, part of the moral goodness of sympathy is undoubtedly due to the acts of helping which it characteristically initiates. However, we ought to avoid taking this truth as a reason for holding that emotions are morally significant *only* in terms of the actions to which they lead, for often the reverse is the case. That is, many actions only *become* morally significant because they are performed out of morally significant emotions, and so it cannot be the case that action is the sole source of moral significance. For example, there might be nothing morally significant about our pursuing many activities together, considered as such, but if we pursue such activities out of love for each other, then they may well become a morally significant feature of our lives. A similar point may be made about various omissions prompted by emotions. For instance, my deliberately failing to send you a Christmas card may be morally insignificant, although if my omission here is motivated by malice, it would seem to have some moral significance. As Green argues, 'Love and hatred are ethically important because they issue in acts of helping and hurting, but these are acts which are ethically important also because they are acts of love and hatred, even apart from any benefit or harm done.'[63] If this is right, then the instrumental view that emotions are morally significant only in their connections with independently characterised good action must be false. For as Kosman, explicating Aristotle, puts it, 'it is with respect to how one feels and not simply how one acts in the light of one's feelings that one is said to be virtuous'.[64]

The second reason for rejecting an instrumental account of the moral significance of emotions is related to the above point about this account's exclusive focus on *action* as the source of moral value. That is, the instrumental account, particularly in the form proposed recently by Kantians, deprives us of an important distinction between two kinds of moral assessments which we make of motives. As Robert Adams points out in regard to desires, we normally distinguish between desires which are only 'accidentally' good or bad (i.e. good or bad only if acted upon), and desires which are 'intrinsically' good or bad (i.e. desires which are good or bad whether or not they are acted upon). For example, there is nothing bad in waking up with the desire to go surfing instead of going to work, at the same time judging that the latter is one's duty; although presumably *acting* on such a desire would be bad, and could thereby render such a desire bad in this case. In contrast, there seems in general something bad about desiring for its own sake the suffering of another person, whether or not one acts on such a desire.[65] However one regards the moral status of a desire such as that in the latter case, and whatever terms one uses to describe it and a desire like that in the former example, there does seem to be a morally important distinction here between two kinds of desires.

Moreover, a parallel distinction seems applicable to emotions: that is, using Adams's terminology, certain emotions may be only accidentally good or bad, while others seem intrinsically good or bad. For instance, there may be nothing morally significant about my having a little affection for you, although presumably many acts done out of that affection would be morally good, and could reflect this goodness on the affection itself in such cases. But on the other hand it seems that altruistic emotions such as sympathy and compassion can be morally good quite apart from whether they are manifested in altruistic action, as I argued earlier. As with desires, there appears to be a distinction between the way in which the emotions in these two cases are valuable, but it is a distinction which an instrumental account of the moral significance of emotions seems unable to draw. For the instrumental view assimilates all cases of morally significant emotions to the category of emotions which have only 'accidental' moral significance, and this gives a distorted picture of the variety of ways in which emotions may be morally good and bad.

To be sure, in arguing that certain emotions may be intrinsically or non-motivationally good and bad (i.e. good or bad even if they are not expressed in action), I am not thereby arguing that such emotions are thus *unconditionally* good and bad (i.e. good or bad in all situations), since as I pointed out in Section 9 of the previous chapter, the former type of goodness or badness does not entail the latter. For example, while care for another may often be morally good even when it cannot be acted on, none the less if our care here is directed towards someone whom we know to be thoroughly evil, then it would be morally bad or wrong here. But in any case, the important point for us is that the instrumental account of the moral significance of emotions, which some Kantians want to allow for, seems to be inadequate, for it incorrectly locates the source of moral value exclusively in action, and in doing so it overlooks the non-motivational moral value of certain emotions, and conflates two importantly different types of moral assessments of our psychological states.

4. OBLIGATIONS CONCERNING EMOTIONS?

I noted above that Kant in his later writings suggests that certain emotions may be morally valuable in so far as they can assist us in acting in accordance with duty. In fact, Kant holds not only this, but in these later works he even claims (rather surprisingly, given his denial in the *Foundations* of the moral importance of emotions) that we have a *duty* or *obligation* to cultivate emotions such as love, sympathy, and concern, since these emotions may help us carry out our duties towards others.[66] In this section I will make some brief comments on the question of whether there are duties or obligations regarding emotions themselves.

While Kant's recognition here of the moral significance of certain emotions is an important correction to his earlier views, perhaps Kant has overstated the point in claiming that we therefore have a *duty* or *obligation* to cultivate such emotions. For we can allow for the moral significance of emotions, even in Kant's sense as aids to acting dutifully, without committing ourselves to holding that there are obligations concerning emotions themselves. Thus, in Chapter 2 I explicated the moral significance of emotions in terms of an aretaic ethics or ethics of virtue, and nowhere did I argue that we are ever morally *required* to have certain emotions. Maybe this is sometimes the case, for example, with love in marriage,[67] but I want to leave this issue open. For in any case an ethics of virtue still allows one to claim, as does Aristotle, that (for instance) there are things at which we ought to be angry,[68] where this 'ought' counsels us about how to act and feel if we want to live a good life and avoid various bad lives.[69]

However, it might be thought that in claiming, as I have in several places, that lacking emotions can be morally defective, I have introduced some notion of obligation concerning emotions. Let me make clear that failing to have a certain morally good emotion, where this goodness is explicated aretaically, may indeed be a moral defect, but this does not entail that we have obligations concerning our emotions. To see this, consider a case involving virtuous action, such as action characteristic of generosity. In performing such action, the agent shows his concern for the good of the recipient in his intention to benefit her. Further, the agent gives up something of value to himself, and gives more than is generally expected in such circumstances. Now it is clear, especially from this last feature, that refraining from a particular act of generosity is unlikely to be a moral failing or to violate any obligation; moreover, a person who never acts generously may violate no moral obligation. However, it seems to me that, as Wallace argues, *never* acting generously is none the less symptomatic of a certain moral failing.[70] Similar considerations apply, I suggest, to lacking emotions which are important to various good lives. Thus, while a person who lacked emotions such as love and care in a certain situation may simply fail to be good in this respect, a person whose life was consistently devoid of this good through the absence of such emotions would be seriously morally defective. And this seems different from claiming that there are obligations concerning emotions.

Yet it might be suggested from the above that there is still some notion of obligation regarding emotions which is implicit in my claims. One might agree that we cannot have obligations to have certain emotions in particular situations, but one might think, as Kant held in his later writings, that we have obligations to have certain emotional *dispositions*, and this is why, as I have said, never having certain emotions can be morally defective.[71] However, I am not arguing that there are obligations concerning emotional dispositions. Perhaps there are some such obligations, but again, I shall leave this issue open. For even if we do not have obligations regarding emotional dispositions, a person who never had emotions such as love and care because he lacked such dispositions may nevertheless for that reason be considered morally defective, as these emotions both constitute and contribute to great human goods.

In explicating the moral significance of emotions in terms of an ethics of virtue, I do not mean to deny that an ethics of obligation may be appropriate in other contexts. For example, in legal and institutional contexts it may be perfectly acceptable to speak of certain kinds of action, such as murder and nepotism, as absolutely prohibited and liable to some form of legal and/or moral sanction. Of course, the domain of virtues and vices and that of obligation and prohibition are importantly related, as Alasdair MacIntyre has succinctly pointed out:

> An offence against the laws destroys those relationships which make common pursuit of the good possible; defective character, while it may also render someone more liable to commit offences, makes one unable to contribute to the achievement of that good without which the community's common life has no point.[72]

An ethics of obligation may also have a certain role in personal relations. So for instance, as I noted in Chapter 2, relationships of love and friendship may involve certain duties towards each other which come appropriately into play when our affections for each other lapse. Undoubtedly, such relations between virtue and obligation are complex and difficult to make out, and I do not wish to speculate on them further here. For as I hope to have shown in this and the previous chapter, the moral significance of emotions can be adequately captured only by an ethics of virtue.

5. THE ARGUMENT FROM THE CONNECTION BETWEEN MORALITY AND FREEDOM

But quite apart from anything I have argued so far, some Kantians may appeal to a different kind of argument in their attempts to establish duty instead of emotion as moral motivation. It is a central claim of Kant's ethics that when we are acting from duty or reason we are acting freely, whereas in acting from our emotions or inclinations our conduct is thereby unfree and beyond our control.[73] This claim has its roots deep in Kant's metaphysics. That is, according to Kant, we gain our autonomy as self-legislating beings, for it is only *qua* such beings that we liberate ourselves from the contingencies of the deterministic world and become free and rational agents subject to the moral law in the intelligible or *noumenal* world. Our emotions, on the other hand (with the exception of respect for the moral law), fall completely within the sensible or *phenomenal* realm, among the causally determined forces that uncontrollably buffet us, and, to the extent that we suffer from them, deprive us of our freedom. Thus, according to this argument, to be a moral being is a mark of our freedom, so emotions cannot be moral motives because they are beyond our control: in acting from them we are acting unfreely. However, since in acting from duty we are acting freely and independently, only duty, and not emotion, can be an acceptable moral motive.[74]

This argument involves profound issues about the metaphysics of freedom which I do not intend to explore here. For there are several replies which can be made to this Kantian argument without broaching such large issues. To begin with, it should be made clear that the argument can be interpreted in two different ways, depending on what view is attributed to Kant concerning the relationship between free will, reason, and emotion. According to one prominent interpretation, Kant held that acting freely and acting from reason are one and the same thing: that is, acting from reason is both necessary and sufficient for acting freely.[75] Now many recent accounts of what motivation by reason is understand it as being motivated to act by one's beliefs or judgements, as opposed to being moved by one's desires or inclinations. But Kant's account of motivation by reason seems somewhat narrower than this, since Kant understands such motivation as being moved to act by a universal principle which we have ourselves willed as law. Further, the concept of duty has its source in the practical faculty of reason. Therefore, since motivation by duty arises from the faculty of reason, which alone is the basis of our freedom, in acting from duty, we are acting freely. Thus, in so far as a requirement for an acceptable moral motive is that it motivates free action, duty automatically becomes the preferred motive on this view.

However, this version of the argument, as it stands, involves some rather implausible consequences. For if, as this view holds, morality is concerned only with free action, and we are acting freely only when we are acting from duty, which alone is good, then this seems to make both free *immoral* action and free *morally neutral* action impossible. On this view we are always acting either freely and morally, or unfreely, but never immorally or morally neutrally and freely; but to rule out these last two possibilities seems implausible.[76] For surely a thief may be acting freely in taking what belongs to someone else, just as we may be acting freely in flipping a light switch or closing a door. One response which a Kantian could offer here is to admit that reason can be mistaken, such that to act from duty is not yet to act morally, which is a possibility I argued for earlier in this chapter. But this response would seem to undermine the alleged superiority of motivation by duty to motivation by emotion which this very argument attempts to establish. So the consequences of this version of the argument then are either that free immoral action and free morally neutral action are impossible, or that motivation by duty, considered in itself, is not yet morally good. Neither consequence can be comforting for the Kantian view.

Perhaps a Kantian can respond to the foregoing problems by offering a different interpretation of the argument under consideration. The claim might now be that free will is not to be *identified with* reason or duty but rather in a sense *stands outside* both duty, on the one hand, and inclination, on the other, such that we can choose whether to be moved by duty or enslaved by inclination.[77] Further, the argument might continue, while acting from duty is then not *necessary* for acting freely, nevertheless in being moved by duty we preserve our freedom, and so acting from duty is *sufficient* for free action; whereas in contrast, acting from emotion or inclination always deprives us of our freedom and so is sufficient for acting *unfreely*.[78] It would then be concluded that since acting from a moral motive requires acting freely, acting from duty qualifies as moral motivation, while acting from emotion or inclination cannot be acting morally. On this version of the argument then, unlike the previous interpretation, we are free to act immorally since (for example) we can choose to submit or 'give in' to our emotions, which are seen as without exception bad.[79]

In reply to both versions of the above Kantian argument, I shall not here dispute their claim that a requirement of an acceptable moral motive is that it leads to free action. (I argue against moral motivation having such a requirement in Chapter 5.) For the validity of this criterion may be granted, while rejecting the claims, made by both arguments, that in acting from duty we are acting freely, and that in acting from emotion we are acting unfreely. On the first point, it seems that we sometimes find what we believe to be our duty constraining and restrictive of our freedom.[80] For example, we might well acknowledge that we have a duty to visit our elderly parents tonight, even though we might much rather stay at home and read some philosophy instead. Where we nevertheless carry out our duty here, it does seem that we may be acting unfreely at least in some important sense of that notion. But in any case, whatever we make of such apparent counterexamples to the Kantian thesis that acting from duty is sufficient for acting freely, the second of the above Kantian claims – i.e. the claim that acting from emotion is sufficient for acting unfreely – seems to be false. That is, as I argue in detail in the next chapter, the picture embodied in the Kantian view of emotions as tempests which we suffer and which therefore deprive us of our freedom and responsibility is seriously mistaken, for we can be and often are at least as responsible for our emotions as we are normally held to be with regard to many of our actions. And it follows from this that we can be responsible for actions motivated by our emotions.

The Kantian argument under consideration here involves a certain distortion of the issues anyway. For contrary to the claims of Kant and many of his followers, the traditional distinction between reason and emotion and the idea of these 'faculties' as opposing forces is in various ways false and misleading. For one thing, emotions involve cognitions, as well as desires and a dimension of affectivity, but cognitions are usually thought of as an integral part of the faculty of reason. Indeed, as I argued in Chapter 2, emotions are open to assessments of rationality, such that it may sometimes be rational for us to have a particular emotion in a certain situation. Further, many emotions can involve intellectual problems and projects as part of their objects, and may be essential to good intellectual activity, such as scientific activity, which is often held up as the paradigm of rationality.[81] Also, I argued in the previous chapter that emotions can sometimes reveal to us important truths about others and the world which might well be inaccessible to a 'purely rational person' (at least in so far as they are unemotional). Against the Kantian tradition which holds the rational and passional aspects of our nature in opposition and regards morality as a function solely of our reason, I believe that, as Aristotle realised, our emotions themselves can express our moral or evaluative outlook.

To conclude this section then, it seems that neither version of the Kantian argument from the connection between morality and freedom succeeds in showing that moral motivation must be motivation by duty instead of emotion. Thus, again we see that, as I have argued generally in this chapter, the criteria which Kantians consider must be satisfied by an acceptable moral motive fail to establish duty as superior to emotion in this regard. It seems that motivation by emotion can do at least as well, if not sometimes better, by those requirements as motivation by duty. Therefore we can say that, in so far as moral worth is understood as the hallmark of Kantian value and is thus on the whole desirable, Kant and his followers not only devalue the emotions and acting from emotion but they do so without good reason.

6. MOTIVATION BY EMOTION AND HENSON'S INTERPRETATION OF KANTIAN MORAL WORTH

Before concluding this chapter, let us briefly consider Henson's attempt to soften Kant's view that only acts done from duty have moral worth by attributing to him a 'battle-citation' model of moral worth, where, as we saw in Section 1, moral worth is awarded for valour, but lacking such worth is no moral defect, and we do not encourage people to seek moral worth as on the whole it is better not to have it. For with this model in mind, one might reply to my arguments by claiming that Kant does not *devalue* actions performed out of emotion in denying them moral worth. But aside from the question of its merits as an interpretation of Kant, it can be shown that this model involves a mistaken view of the relation of emotions to morality and has unacceptable implications in any case, and should therefore be rejected.

Initially, we might wonder whether the battle-citation model of moral worth defuses the issue between Kant and those who, like myself, want to defend the value of motivation by emotion, to the extent that it is no longer an issue. For if acting from emotion is not necessarily morally defective and may indeed on the whole be better than having to act from duty, what could be objectionable about Henson's account?

But there are several reasons why Henson's battle-citation model ought to be rejected. We should remember what this model involves: moral worth is pictured as a reward for winning the battle to act from duty alone, in the face of either contrary inclinations or a complete lack of inclinations directed towards that act. So although we may not be censured in losing such a battle and acting from our inclinations, to win the battle is certainly to merit an important form of praise. But if my arguments in Chapter 2 are right, not only is having and being motivated by certain emotions *not* morally defective, it may actually be morally *good*, and so my first criticism of the battle-citation model is that it fails to acknowledge the moral value of emotions.

But second, winning the struggle against recalcitrant inclination seems to be no special mark of moral virtue anyway.[82] Even if Henson is correct in taking Kant to hold the contrary, no reasons are given, by either Kant or Henson, to support the view that we should earn moral praise for defeating our emotions in acting from duty. Indeed, as I argued in the previous chapter, a person who has to act against their emotions in carrying out their values may thereby actually have a certain moral defect. At least, such a person seems morally inferior in this regard to one whose emotions harmonise with their values in acting on what they believe is right. But the problem with Henson's account of Kantian moral worth here is that it does not allow us to say this, for it denies the moral goodness of a person who does not need to struggle to act rightly, and in this it deprives us of what seems to be an important moral exemplar.

It might also be useful to consider some of the implications of the battle-citation model of moral worth here. Now although Henson's Kant sees nothing morally defective in acting from at least certain emotions, nevertheless agents would presumably be at fault for failing to perform dutiful acts – i.e. acts that are right in accordance with the categorical imperative – when required to do so (otherwise Kant's ethics would lose its imperative character altogether). So on this view, rather than strive to perform morally worthy acts, when we are called upon to act dutifully we should try to do so, without having to act from the morally worthy motive of duty.[83] Thus in so far as we should, morally speaking, attend to our motives at all, we should concentrate mainly on eliminating our morally bad motives, although we perhaps should make at least some attempt to cultivate the duty motive (which on this account is the only morally worthy motive), since we may sometimes need it to help us in the struggle against our inclinations.

But while I believe Henson is correct in restricting the proper role of the duty motive to cases where we must act rightly even though we lack the inclination to do so, Henson's battle-citation model of moral worth seems to carry with it the undesirable implication that in seeking to be moral, we should not in normal circumstances attempt to act from or cultivate morally worthy motives. Indeed, according to Henson, we should try to avoid getting into situations where it is possible to act from morally worthy motives,[84] and, rather paradoxically, on Henson's view there would be something wrong with a person who (in normal circumstances) strives to perform morally worthy acts. However, all this seems to do violence to our notion of moral worth, for surely there are normally many motives which, morally speaking, we ought to attempt to cultivate and act on, and which others should be encouraged to cultivate and act on; yet Henson's battle-citation model leaves us with no way to capture the moral importance of such endeavours, and should therefore, I believe, be rejected.

I cannot pursue these issues further here. Nevertheless, what I hope to have shown in this chapter is that no matter which of the prominent interpretations of Kant's remarks on moral worth and motivation by duty and emotion is adopted, his arguments and those of his followers considered here against emotions as moral motives are mistaken. There is at least as much, if not more, reason to hold that emotions can be morally worthy motives as there is to believe this of duty.

4 Responsibility for emotions

Now that we have seen some important ways in which various emotions can be morally good and bad, it is natural to turn to the questions of whether and how we can be responsible for our emotions. For if my account of the moral importance of emotions is to have any significant bearing on how we live our lives and on the attempts we can make to improve ourselves morally, then we need to investigate both whether and how we can cultivate emotions which I argued could in certain circumstances be morally good or right, and also the question of whether and how we can exercise some control over emotions which I portrayed as morally bad or wrong in certain contexts (given that cultivation and control of something are two ways of being responsible for it, at least in the sense of 'responsibility' which I will be dealing with in this chapter). Indeed, those who take the still rather widely held view of emotions as characteristically states which we suffer and which we therefore cannot be responsible for – a view taken by many Kantians in their rejection of emotions as moral motives – may question the practical value of my earlier analysis of the moral significance of emotions. In the present chapter, I want to provide answers to these questions by showing that such a picture of emotions is seriously mistaken.

In seeking a proper understanding of the role played by emotions in our moral lives, then, it is crucial that an examination of the question of our responsibility for our emotions is undertaken. A discussion of this issue is also important for understanding the various ways in which our emotions may reflect on us morally, for as we shall see in Chapter 5, whether we are responsible for a certain emotion of ours helps determine the *kind* of moral assessment that is properly made of us on account of it.

In this chapter, then, I examine our responsibility with regard to our emotions by looking at the nature and extent of the control which we can have over them, and the implications of this for our responsibility for our emotions. I will argue that there are various important kinds of control which we can have over our emotions which amount to our being responsible for them. In arguing for this, I do not propose a fully articulated account of responsibility, nor will I address those who are sceptical about the metaphysical foundations of responsibility. To attempt such tasks would be beyond the scope of this book. Rather, my argument proceeds by demonstrating that certain widely accepted and straightforward ideas about responsibility for physical acts also show that we can be responsible for our emotions, so that if we allow responsibility for many common physical acts, we must also often allow responsibility for emotions.

I begin by examining some common arguments which are used to show that we cannot be responsible for our emotions, and I reject these arguments on the grounds that they presuppose implausibly strong conditions of responsibility. These conditions would rule out our responsibility for most *actions* which we are usually thought responsible for. Here my aim is the negative one of showing that these arguments do not *preclude* our responsibility for our emotions. Having established this, I then turn to the more important task of arguing for the positive claim that we can in certain circumstances be responsible for various emotions which we have. I argue for this by looking at certain conditions which many take to be sufficient for responsibility for *actions*, and I show that these conditions may also be met in many cases by our emotions.

In order to avoid arguing at cross purposes, it is important to briefly outline the notion of 'responsibility' with which I am concerned. Note that I am not here offering a *definition* of responsibility, but merely indicating the place in our discourse occupied by the sense of 'responsibility' involved in my discussion. Here I want simply to make clear the significance of what would be achieved if one were to provide a plausible account of 'responsibility', in the way the term is used in this book.

We can distinguish between three important ways in which the significance of the expression 'A is responsible for X' can be understood. First, to say that A is or was responsible for something sometimes indicates no more than that A *caused* it. As Hart points out, this sense of 'responsibility' need not carry any implication of credit or blame, is typically (but not always) used in the past tense, and is often associated with actions and events, rather than agents, as causes.[1] Thus, 'the drought was responsible for the failure of the wheat crop' means no more than that the drought *caused* the crop's failure.

The second sense of 'responsibility' goes well beyond mere causality. In this second sense, to say that someone is responsible for something amounts to saying that they are *blameworthy* for it. This sense of responsibility can be further subdivided into two categories, depending on whether it is *legal* or *moral* responsibility that is in question. In the former case, to say that someone is legally responsible for some action is to say that according to the law they are liable to be penalised or punished for it as the law deems appropriate, whereas in the latter case, moral responsibility equals moral blameworthiness.[2] The sense of 'responsibility' involved here seems more commonly used in contexts of legal responsibility.

The third way of understanding the significance of the expression 'A is responsible for X', and the sense which I use throughout this book, also denotes more than merely 'A caused X', but is not equivalent to 'A is blameworthy on account of X'. In this third sense, which is quite commonplace, to be responsible for something is to be *open to* creditworthiness or blameworthiness for it, but whether one is actually creditworthy or blameworthy for it depends also on its goodness or badness (or rightness or wrongness).[3] Understood in this way, being responsible for something is, in itself, a necessary but not sufficient condition of being creditworthy or blameworthy in regard to it. To illustrate the distinction between the second and third senses of 'responsibility', suppose I give you a gift which you find offensive. We could establish that I was responsible for giving you the gift, in the sense that I am *open to* creditworthiness or blameworthiness for this, without going into the rightness or wrongness of my action. But if I gave you the gift because I knew it would offend you and I wanted to offend you, then I would be responsible for giving you the gift, in the sense that I would be *blameworthy* for this. These three senses of 'responsibility' are sometimes conflated, but it is important to recognise that they are distinct.[4] It is views about what is required by this *third* sense of responsibility which I want to examine here.

1. RESPONSIBILITY AND DOING OR HAVING AT WILL

It is sometimes held that being able to do or have something at will is a necessary condition of responsibility for it. So, for example, in part because I can sit, stand, or hold my breath at will, I can be responsible for these acts, whereas since I cannot sneeze at will, I cannot be responsible when I do so. On this view, I can do or have something at will if all that is required for it to be the case is that I will it. To be sure, this notion of 'at will' is not very well defined. For instance, it is controversial whether, if I can do X at will, and, unknown to me, X extensionally involves Y, I can thus do Y at will. Maybe this just points to a general indeterminacy with the notion of ability. But in any case, it is taken for granted by many that we cannot have emotions simply at will in the way we can perform many physical acts simply at will. Indeed, many who believe we can perform various physical acts at will hold that it is in principle impossible to have emotions simply at will.[5] While this last claim may be too strong, rather than dispute it here, let us examine the implications of such views for the issue of responsibility for emotions.

That we cannot have emotions simply at will is sometimes taken as sufficient to show that we cannot be responsible for them.[6] However, such a move is far from justified. For even if it were generally true that we could not have emotions simply at will, the ability to do or have something at will is *not* a necessary condition of responsibility for it. As Michael Stocker and others have argued, many acts, such as driving a car or winning a game, are of a kind that cannot be done simply at will, since they rely importantly on external factors in order to succeed, yet we can still be responsible for them.[7] Indeed, it might be wondered whether 'simply willing' is sufficient for the success of *any* acts, even those as basic as raising one's arm or holding one's breath. If doing or having at will were a necessary condition of responsibility, we would be denied responsibility for much in our lives that we are normally thought responsible for, and in fact there would remain little – or little of any significance – that we would be responsible for.

But perhaps a modified version of the claim might be thought more promising. That is, it might be held that I can be responsible for something only if I can do or have it successfully at will *given a suitable background*.[8] For example, I can be responsible for driving a car if, given that I know how to drive a car, I am not incapacitated, and I have a fully operational car at my disposal, I can perform the act of driving a car at will. The argument would then be that we cannot have emotions at will in this sense, and therefore we cannot be responsible for them. In response to these claims, we should ask two questions. First, are we unable to have emotions at will given a suitable background of, say, appropriate thoughts and dispositions? Second, is *this* notion of doing or having at will itself a necessary condition of responsibility?

Clearly, this modified notion of doing or having at will makes it more difficult to exclude emotions from the realm of what we can do or have at will. Indeed, it may seem that we can sometimes have emotions 'at will' in this sense. For example, given the following background: I believe that, compared with my brothers and sisters, I was treated unjustly as a child by my parents, and I know from past experience that I become angry and resentful towards my parents when dwelling upon such thoughts, perhaps I can in fact be angry and resentful 'at will' just by deciding to think about those childhood injustices. However, those who deny that emotions can be had at will, even in the modified sense of that notion, might counter that despite the above background obtaining, thinking about such childhood maltreatment might not make me angry and resentful. I may be unable to rid myself of distracting thoughts, for example, or I may be too tired to concentrate on such unfortunate features of my upbringing.

Maybe this objection could be accommodated by providing a more detailed description of the background (including, for example, that I will not be plagued by distracting thoughts, and I am not too tired to concentrate), such that, given this, I can work up anger and resentment just by deciding to think of my childhood ills. In a sense though, this misses the point of the objection. For the claim is that in the case of physical acts such as driving a car, the 'suitable background' can always be described in such a way that my willing to do the act is sufficient for its success, whereas no matter how the background for having an emotion is specified (without getting to the point where our having the emotion is completely determined, i.e. nothing to do with our willing or not willing it), it still remains possible in those circumstances that we may will the emotion and yet it does not come about.[9] So, even if I believe that I was treated unjustly as a child, and I know that thinking about this makes me angry and resentful, and my concentration is unaffected by tiredness or distracting thoughts, I may decide to think about my childhood maltreatment and yet fail to become angry or resentful. As may happen with all emotions, the anger and resentment just may not 'cooperate'. We must wait for emotions to 'act on us', for to have an emotion is essentially to be in a state of *passivity* – that is, to be acted on, rather than to be active. But we need not pursue this particular objection any further. For even if this objection is sound (which it may not be), it will be beside the point if the modified notion of doing or having at will is not a necessary condition of responsibility. So let us now consider this issue.

Stocker argues that responsibility does not require being able to do or have successfully at will, even if we assume a suitable background, for there seem to be many acts, such as flying a kite or finding a cure for cancer, that we can properly be held responsible for, but which are not guaranteed of success, even given a suitable background.[10] In fact, as we shall see shortly, there are other acts which we are responsible for that rely on *luck* for their success. It would seem then that neither doing or having simply at will, nor doing or having at will given a suitable background, is necessary for responsibility. Therefore, to demonstrate that we cannot have emotions at will in either of these senses is not to show that we cannot be responsible for them. For as Stocker puts it, 'activity and responsibility are compatible with an important amount of passivity, of not being in total control, of waiting for and depending on the uncertain hand of outside elements to which we must defer and with which we must cooperate'.[11]

2. RESPONSIBILITY AND AVOIDABILITY

Instead of arguing that we cannot be responsible for our emotions because we lack control of them in the sense that we are unable to have them at will (in either of the above-mentioned ways), it might be argued that there is a passivity of a different kind which is incompatible with responsibility, and that it is because we lack control of our emotions in *this* way that we cannot be responsible for them. That is, the ability to *stop* or *not to do or have* something is often thought to be a necessary condition of responsibility for it. The view here is that if we cannot stop something that we do or have, or give it up just by deciding to give it up, then we are not responsible for it. Regarding the emotions, it is sometimes claimed that we are unable to stop ourselves having them at the time we have them, and that therefore we are not responsible for them.[12]

A proviso needs to be added to this view. It is true that, in a sense, we can almost always avoid doing or having something in so far as, for example, we can knock ourselves unconscious or commit suicide instead. But the sense of 'avoidability' which is involved in the above view cannot of course normally be taken to include what can only be avoided by such extreme means.[13] Otherwise the point of the avoidability condition would be lost, since it would rule out little, if any, of our lives from the realm of responsibility. So the view here is that we are responsible for doing or having something only in so far as we could have then and there taken *reasonable* means to stop ourselves doing or having it at that time. Now, what means are considered reasonable ways of avoiding something, and what means are considered extreme, will often depend upon the person and the circumstances they are in. That is, as I discuss in Section 8, in deciding whether the kind of avoidability is relevant to determining responsibility, we need to look at both what may be expected of this particular individual and what may be expected of a sound moral agent in this situation. But in any case, the ability to control and be responsible for something which is supposed to be attained in part by being able to avoid it is not normally attained simply by having the ability to extinguish all behaviour.

Now as we are no doubt at times painfully aware, it is often the case that we cannot stop ourselves having an emotion just by deciding to give it up. Rarely is our emotional life subject to this kind of immediate control by the will. However, contrary to the above view, it does not follow from this that we cannot be responsible for our emotions, since, as we can see in many cases of physical acts, the ability to stop something we do or have just by deciding to give it up is *not* a necessary condition of responsibility for it. For example, I cannot stop myself from driving off a cliff due to the failure of my car's brakes, but I can still of course be responsible for driving off a cliff if I have never had my car's brakes checked. And in any case, this requirement of immediate avoidability would pare back our responsibility for most of the consequences of our actions, for, once we have acted, it is rarely possible for us to prevent various foreseeable consequences of our action from ensuing (wherever we decide to draw the line between action and consequences), *simply* by deciding to prevent them. And yet surely it is reasonable to hold that we can be responsible for some consequences of our actions which we cannot immediately prevent. So, since the ability to stop something at the time of doing or having it does not seem to be a necessary condition of responsibility for physical acts, showing that we lack such an ability in regard to our emotions is insufficient for denying that we can be responsible for them.

In any case, why should we be particularly interested in what we can have or prevent ourselves having *at will*? Little of what we do or have is amenable to such direct control, and moreover, the acts and conditions over which we might have this control, such as raising our arm or holding our breath, are of little significance in our lives. We would expect any worthwhile theory of agency and responsibility (especially *moral* agency and responsibility) to single out more than just these kinds of things. To focus only on what we can have or prevent at will is to look at life in terms of a succession of episodes, whereas it would seem more accurate and profitable to consider our lives and much of what we thereby do and have as continuous and enduring.[14]

So, let us consider avoidability as a necessary condition of responsibility from this perspective. In determining whether a person is responsible for something which they cannot simply at will prevent themselves from doing or having, what we should consider is how they came to be in a position where their doing or having it is now unavoidable. Being unable to avoid doing or having something can have various causes.[15] The view would now be that if we could not have avoided having our present inability to avoid doing or having something, then we are not responsible for it. Put another way, the view is that we are responsible for something only if we could have at some time avoided doing or having it. This view commands wide philosophical support,[16] and indeed, may well be true – if so, it would certainly allow some important distinctions to be made. In Section 7 I discuss the adequacy of this notion of avoidability as a condition of responsibility. The important point for our present purposes is not to argue for or against the truth of avoidability as a condition of responsibility, but, given its widespread acceptance as a condition of responsibility in cases of physical acts, to see how the emotions would fare with regard to such a condition.

If responsibility for something requires that we were at some time able to avoid our now having it, it becomes difficult in many cases to see how people could plausibly be *denied* responsibility for their emotions, at least on those grounds. For even if it is true that we cannot repudiate our emotions at will once we have them or arrest their hold on us as and when they arise, and so are in these ways passive with regard to our emotions, it seems hard to deny that there is often much we could reasonably have done to affect, control, and even avoid altogether our now having certain emotions. For example, a parent who knows he becomes uncontrollably angry with his daughter when (as usually happens) she defeats him at chess is not thereby relieved of responsibility for becoming angry here, for perhaps he could have avoided his anger by deciding not to play chess with his daughter. Similarly, I may not now be able to avoid having care and concern for my friend, but I may still be responsible for having these emotions in so far as they are manifestations of an emotional attachment which I could earlier have quite easily prevented from developing. So, if the present notion of avoidability is held to be the most plausible *necessary* condition of responsibility, there would be strong doubt about any claim that, according to this condition, we cannot be responsible for our emotions.

3. WHY DO WE LACK DIRECT CONTROL OVER OUR EMOTIONS?

So far I have argued that although we may be passive with regard to our emotions in so far as we cannot have them or stop ourselves having them at will, this passivity does not preclude our being responsible for our emotions, since neither the ability to have at will nor the ability to stop at will is necessary for responsibility. But let us pause to consider briefly some of the reasons why we lack this kind of direct control over our emotions.

We can gain some idea of why emotions cannot typically be directly controlled by the will through a consideration of their constitutive components: that is, cognitions, desires, and a dimension of affectivity. It seems possible to trace the kind of passivity which distinguishes emotions from, for example, physical acts to the *affective* element involved in the former. Various writers disagree over the extent to which affectivity is subject to control by the will.[17] Nevertheless, there is broad agreement that, as Kenny holds, (quite apart from whether we can control the *behavioural* expression of an emotion at will) it seems that the affective elements of emotions, 'though sometimes checkable at will, are not normally producible at will'.[18] Even Sartre and Solomon, whose accounts of emotion emphasise activity, seem to allow for the passivity of affectivity.[19] Indeed, while it may perhaps be possible to arouse 'pangs' of jealousy in ourselves, or to 'work ourselves up' into feelings of rage, it seems that we cannot be as confident about the success of such attempts as we can be about the success of many (simple) physical acts, such as raising our arm. Even if a suitable background for the emotion is provided, its affective element may not arise. And further, it seems unlikely that we can rid ourselves of, for example, the fearful palpitations which we experience at the approaching confrontation with a foe, or the sense of listlessness and dullness at being depressed about our future prospects, just by deciding to give up these feelings.

To be sure, even though we do not seem to have the sort of control over affectivity that can be had over certain physical acts, it is highly misleading to represent affectivity (as some have done) as an 'accidental concomitant' of emotion, or to claim (as many also have) that it renders emotions by nature capricious and unpredictable, for as I argue later in discussing foresight, there is much we can do to regulate and control our emotions and their constituent feelings. Nevertheless, if there is an element of emotion that is least susceptible to manipulation and control by the will, it would appear to be affectivity.

But it may also be because of features which emotions have in common with other phenomena, including physical acts, that we normally lack the kind of direct control over our emotions which is characterised by being able to have or stop something at will. Emotions involve a cognitive element, which is often some form of belief about the world, and adverting to this can give us another reason why emotions cannot normally be controlled at will. For while we can have a great deal of control over our beliefs, they do not normally seem to be (and indeed should not be) the sort of things which can be had or given up simply at will, because they normally require the world to be a certain way.[20] For example, it is usually not easy to believe at will that danger is imminent, or to stop believing at will that one is disliked by one's colleagues.[21]

Now perhaps certain beliefs which are involved in emotions *can* be had or given up simply at will, but it is still a further question whether the emotions involving those beliefs can be had or given up simply at will, for, as we saw in Chapter 1, emotions involve more than beliefs or cognitions, and our inability to directly control our emotions may sometimes be due to those other features. So, even if I can have a belief involved in an emotion simply at will, I may not be able to have that emotion at will. And, as is all too familiar, we may decide to give up the belief which is part of an emotion, but find, much to our dismay, that the emotion or feeling nevertheless persists.[22]

Along with beliefs and an element of affectivity, emotions also involve desires. Perhaps there are some desires, such as wanting to have our neck massaged, which we can have at will, and some, such as wanting an extra chocolate, which we can give up at will. But in the case of many or even most desires, we do not have such direct control.[23] The kind of direct control which we lack with regard to desire may depend partly on the individual, and partly on the nature of the desire itself. Thus, some may be unable to give up their deep-seated desire for understanding, while others need to work at developing such an inclination, and addicts cannot give up their craving for heroin just by deciding to, while most of us would find it difficult to have such a craving just by an act of will. Looking at some typical desires which partly constitute particular emotions, we often seem unable to have or stop ourselves having, say, the desire to strike back at someone that is involved in anger, or the desire to flee that is involved in fear, simply at will, and at least to this extent we would be unable to have or stop ourselves having those emotions at will.

It is worth noting here that it is often a good thing that we cannot (or cannot usually anyway) have or stop ourselves having emotions at will, for this reminds us of the importance of the authenticity and responsiveness of our emotions in relation to the world around us.[24] Indeed, the acknowledgement of this lack of cooperation between emotions and the will is also significant for other reasons. Perhaps it is true that, for instance, we are unable to love another person, care about what we value, or rid ourselves of irrational fears just by an act of will. If so, then adverting to these facts brings our attention to the possibility of such moral and psychic disorders as self-deception, weakness of will, and neurosis, and hence to the difficulties in achieving a good life.

Of course, there are immensely complex issues here concerning the relations between belief, desire, affectivity, and the will. For example, perhaps there can be a link between certain beliefs and desires such that being able to have one (e.g. the belief that danger to oneself is imminent) at will is sufficient for being able to have the other (e.g. the desire to flee) at will. Or, working up certain affective states (e.g. having fearful palpitations, sweating palms) may sometimes be sufficient for having certain beliefs (e.g. about the approaching danger) and desires (e.g. to flee). This is because, as I explained in Chapter 1, the elements of emotion stand in 'dynamic' relations to each other. But I cannot speculate further on these issues here. What I have been suggesting is that our inability to have or give up our emotions at will may often be due to our lacking such direct control over any or all of the cognitive, desiderative, and affective elements which together constitute our emotions. Nevertheless, if my arguments in the two preceding sections are correct, lacking this direct control of our emotions for such reasons does not in itself preclude our being responsible for them.

4. WHEN IS LACKING CONTROL COMPATIBLE WITH RESPONSIBILITY?

We have seen above the implausibility of arguments which deny our responsibility for our emotions on the grounds that we lack immediate control over them. But I have not yet said enough to show that we *can* be responsible for something in spite of lacking this kind of control over it. In this section I suggest that the absence of direct control can be compatible with responsibility, and I will do so by briefly considering two types of cases where lacking direct control over our *actions* is compatible with our being responsible for them. This introduces my positive argument in the following section that, despite the absence of direct control, there are certain other kinds of control – which we can have with regard to our *emotions* – which are sufficient for responsibility.

Thomas Nagel has pointed out that there are many physical acts which we are responsible for, despite their very occurrence, or the nature of their occurrence, being due partly to luck.[25] This point is particularly clear in cases of *legal* responsibility. So, for example, if two people take the risk of driving home while intoxicated, and one swerves onto the footpath in a usually quiet street and knocks over a pedestrian, while the other swerves onto the footpath and affects no one, the first driver's responsibility or culpability is much greater than that of the second. Yet each driver, we may take it, had the same degree of control over their vehicle as did the other. The first driver is responsible for knocking over the pedestrian, even though the latter's presence was out of the driver's control and, we might say, to this extent a matter of bad luck. Indeed, when we reflect that the law is strongly influenced by ulterior practical purposes and contains an irreducible margin of vagueness and arbitrariness, it might be expected that factors beyond our control can significantly affect what we are legally responsible for. A good example of this arbitrariness which may allow luck to enter into determining what we are legally responsible for is the so-called 'year and a day rule', noted by Joel Feinberg:

> If the victim of an assault dies within a 'year and a day', his assailant can be charged with homicide; if the victim lingers on for more than a year and a day, then responsibility for his subsequent death must officially be located elsewhere.[26]

However, luck can also play an important role in *moral* responsibility. For example, if I take it upon myself to invest the family savings in gold shares, but there is an unaccountable collapse in the value of gold the next day, I can legitimately be held responsible for the hardships and deprivations that we now have to endure, even though the loss of my investment was due partly to bad luck.

Moreover, luck can often be seen as influencing the success or failure of our endeavours in general (i.e. quite apart from whether they involve situations of moral or legal significance), without thereby precluding our responsibility for such endeavours. Thus, the wildlife photographer is responsible for his photograph of a rare bird in flight, and a footballer for kicking a difficult goal, as a chef can be responsible for the failure of his dish, and I for my humorous anecdote failing to make an impression on my audience. None of this is to say that we remain responsible no matter how luck is involved in what we do. Nevertheless, it seems that at least in these types of cases, what we are responsible for can be importantly affected by luck.

A second kind of case where we can be responsible for something despite our lack of direct control over it is found in many cases of compulsion, since, as Robert Audi points out, responsibility need not presuppose complete lack of compulsion. Audi gives the example of a missile guard of high endurance and keen respect for duty, who, in a moment of physical and moral weakness (which he fails to muster the courage available to him to resist), reveals the combination of the launching mechanism to his enemies while under strong but not irresistible duress. It seems that the guard may be responsible for revealing the combination, even though it was given only under a considerable degree of compulsion, and to that extent unfreely.[27] There may indeed be other kinds of compulsion which are compatible with responsibility. But we need not discuss such issues here. For the point being made in the above examples is that there appear to be many kinds of physical acts which an agent can be responsible for, despite their importantly lacking direct control over them.

But while it might be agreed that these examples show that we can be responsible for *actions* which we cannot directly control, it could be argued that this will not help my argument that we can be responsible for our *emotions*, for our emotions are beyond our control in a deeper sense than are our actions here. That is, it might be allowed that in the examples given, the person in question is responsible for what they cannot now directly control because they are responsible for some prior activity which is connected with their present action. For example, the wildlife photographer is responsible for his lucky photograph because it is in part a result of earlier training which he undertook. But, the argument would run, we cannot gain control over our emotions even through prior activity, and therefore we cannot be responsible for them. In the next section I will argue for the contrary view, and I will introduce the argument via the notion of foresight.

5. RESPONSIBILITY, FORESIGHT, AND THE CULTIVATION AND CONTROL OF OUR EMOTIONS

Having (or culpably lacking) foresight of something is often thought to be a necessary condition of responsibility for it. That is, unless we foresee (or should foresee) what we are about to do or have, we are not responsible for doing or having it. For example, a person who fires a gun in a crowded area is responsible for wounding or maiming others partly because he would have (or should have) foreseen what he has done here. However, it is often thought that we do not, indeed cannot, have such foresight of our emotions, because it is thought that they are capricious and unpredictable, and this has been taken by many as sufficient evidence that we cannot be responsible for our emotions. Further, because it is held that we cannot have such foresight of our emotions, it would be claimed that there can be no such thing as a culpable lack of foresight in regard to our emotions, for no emotions are such that we can be expected to have foreseen our having them.

Earlier I said that it was worth remembering that emotions cannot usually be had or given up at will, for this brings attention to the importance of the receptivity, sensitivity, and responsiveness to the world which may be involved in emotions. Similarly here, it is a good thing that we are unlikely to have such complete foresight of our emotions as we can have of many (simple) physical acts such as raising our arm and holding our breath, for otherwise emotions could lose their spontaneity and authenticity. But need we have the kind of complete foresight which precedes many simple physical acts (such as those above) in order to be responsible for something?

In answering this question, I want to make use of an important distinction developed by Michael Stocker between what he calls *act foresight*, which is the kind of foresight we have only when what we do or have, or are about to do or have, is present and clear to the mind in or before doing or having it, and 'character foresight' (or what I will henceforth call *schematic foresight*), where we have and can use some skill in doing or having something, without necessarily having the complete foresight involved in act foresight. Schematic foresight involves knowing how and what to do to try and bring something about, and an ability to bring it about and recognise it when it comes about, even though we may not know in advance exactly *when* it will happen, or exactly *what* form it will take if it does occur, or even *if* it will occur at all (since, among other things, there may be an element of luck affecting the outcome).[28]

Now, returning to the question, it seems that we need not have the kind of complete foresight of something which is involved in act foresight in order to be responsible for it. It is often sufficient, for us to be responsible for something, that we have schematic foresight in regard to it. For consider physical acts such as exploring and creating, and endeavours such as conducting an inquiry and trying to find a cure for cancer. The fact that I am uncertain about the outcome of such ventures is quite compatible with my being responsible for what turns out, given that I am using my skills in performing such activities.[29] Therefore, in showing that we cannot have *act* foresight with regard to our emotions, it is not established that we cannot be responsible for them. In order to provide support for such a conclusion, it would also have to be shown that we cannot have *schematic* foresight of our emotions. In what follows I will argue that any such claim would be mistaken.

As argued above, the kind of foresight which is sufficient for our being responsible for many physical acts involves having some skill in doing and producing something, without necessarily knowing in advance exactly when it will be done, or exactly what form it will take when it is done, or even whether it will be produced at all. We can often have such foresight with regard to our emotions, for there is often much we can deliberately do to cultivate, affect, and control them.[30] The first step which we can take towards cultivation and control of our emotions is to attend to and reflect on the nature of their occurrence. For example, we can look at the situations in which they are experienced: I might feel joy in helping others, jealousy at seeing you engaged in animated conversation with someone else, and anger at having been defeated by you in a game. Thus, we can identify the types of situations where a particular emotion of ours characteristically arises, and then endeavour to put or avoid putting ourselves in such situations.

But this is of course just a beginning. We can attempt to see what elements of a situation are more strongly linked with the emotion than others, and try to cultivate or eliminate those elements. We can make attempts to understand why we feel one way about something rather than another, and in doing so, perhaps learn something about what it is in ourselves that contributes to our feeling that way, thus attempting to modify our emotions by changing ourselves. For example, Iris Murdoch describes a mother-in-law (M), who, despite behaving impeccably towards her daughter-in-law (D), feels hostility and resentment towards D because she (M) feels that her son has married someone unworthy of him. But M decides to look at herself and attends carefully to her values and prejudices, and realises that she has projected various unfavourable qualities onto D because she (M) jealously guards her close relationship with her son, and she fears D as a possible threat to this. So M tries to look at D from a new perspective – that is, without prejudice, and M begins to regard D as 'not vulgar but refreshingly simple, not undignified but spontaneous, not noisy but gay, not tiresomely juvenile but delightfully youthful', and through this reorientation M develops a love for D which is appropriate to their relationship.[31]

But while we might in the foregoing ways attempt to modify the emotions which we have towards certain people and in particular situations, we can also take steps to cultivate and inhibit our emotions in a deeper sense, which is more difficult to achieve: that is, we can endeavour to develop or avoid developing certain emotional *capacities*. There are various ways in which we might attempt this. We could begin to develop our emotional capacities through reading the works of writers such as Dostoevsky and James, and seeing the films of directors such as Bergman, in order to enlarge our perspective on life.[32] But as Aristotle suggests, we might be able to develop our emotional capacities in a more deliberate way. Following Kosman's interpretation of Aristotle, we cannot inculcate emotional capacities directly, in the manner in which we can acquire the virtues which are states (*hexeis*) concerning action (*praxis*) by habituation. Nevertheless, Aristotle suggests, it is possible to develop various emotional capacities by engaging in actions which are characteristically associated with particular emotions, and by doing so in such a way that is deliberately aimed at the inculcation of the capacities for having those particular emotions, and, after some time and effort, the emotions themselves may come more naturally.[33] One might usefully compare this with the way in which a 'method' actor of the Stanislavsky-Strasberg school may attempt to develop the emotional aspect of a character by immersing themselves in the type of situations and lifestyle of such a person, in order to feel and act more naturally from the emotions which are appropriate to that character.[34] Also, cultivating capacities for certain emotions, such as sympathy and interpersonal love, might involve resisting temptations to settle for perhaps easier alternatives, such as becoming more self-interested or being content with a rather superficial kind of relationship,[35] and so a refusal to accept such alternatives can be a move towards the inculcation of those emotional capacities.

Further, we can order our emotions in relation to each other, and decide that some are those of which we approve or reflect us as we are or want to be, and commit ourselves to encouraging these, while other emotions are those of which we disapprove or do not reflect us as we are or want to be. Or we can come to see that some of our emotions are compatible with our own nature or human nature in general, while others are not so compatible, and attempt to modify them accordingly.[36] As Lawrence Blum points out, the cultivation or extirpation of deep-rooted emotional capacities may well require critical examination of our fundamental values and attitudes – i.e. our 'moral character' – since our emotional capacities typically reflect and embody our basic values. Without such self-reflection, the attempts to cultivate or prevent various emotional capacities through action may fail.[37] Thus, a person who is trying to overcome his excessive capacity for anger must look at *why* he is so easily slighted. Does he take himself to have certain rights over others which he does not in fact have? Does he think that the world 'owes him something'? Of course, even if he takes appropriate action in the light of his answers to such questions, he still might not succeed in repudiating his excessive anger; but a reorientation of our values is the most important step we can take towards developing and repudiating various emotional capacities.

Nancy Sherman's discussion of the way in which children, as part of their moral education, may be taught to feel appropriately is instructive here. Elaborating on Aristotle's remarks about habituation and moral education, Sherman explains that in teaching a child to have appropriate emotions,

> part of what the parent tries to do is to bring the child to see the particular circumstances that here and now make certain emotions appropriate. The parent helps the child compose the scene in the right way. This will involve persuading the child that the situation at hand is to be construed in this way rather than that, that what the child took to be a deliberate assault and cause for anger was really only an accident, that the laughter and smiles which annoy were intended as signs of delight rather than of teasing, that a particular distribution, though painful to endure, is in fact fair – that if one looked at the situation from the point of view of the others involved, one would come to that conclusion.[38]

Thus, an important part of cultivating our emotional capacities so that we feel the right emotions on the right occasions is learning to compose and discriminate various aspects of what we perceive so that we are led to respond in appropriate ways.[39]

However, as Sherman also points out, it is important to understand that in teaching a child how to feel, one is not thereby engaging in *manipulation* of their cognitions and emotions, for otherwise a child would find it difficult to react appropriately to new situations, since they would have no *independent* understanding of what it is that makes a particular emotional response fitting here.[40] An analogy with learning a foreign language may be illuminating in this context. A good language teacher will not simply use *repetition* to inculcate a capacity in their students to speak a new language, but will use a combination of careful prompting and skilful questioning to eventually elicit responses from students which suggest a grasp of some of the underlying grammatical principles of the language. Without this grasp, one would be unable to extrapolate reliably from one's knowledge of these principles to deal with novel situations outside the pedagogical context.

Of course, in arguing that we can and ought to acquire and develop various emotional capacities, I am not claiming that we ought to consciously monitor our emotional states and the situations we find ourselves in so that we might 'switch on' and 'switch off' various emotional responses as circumstances require. There is something about such a person which many of us, I think, would rightly find rather precious. Rather, I am suggesting that we can and ought to develop our emotional capacities so that we respond naturally and spontaneously with emotions which are appropriate to various situations. Now this notion of 'learned spontaneity' might be regarded as somewhat self-contradictory. But the appearance of contradiction can be dispelled by considering an analogy with how one learns to play a musical instrument. Suppose a person is taking lessons in how to play jazz saxophone. She spends many hours quite deliberately practising various scales, phrases, and progressions. But her deliberate efforts here are undertaken with the aim of eventually being able to improvise spontaneously around what she has learnt, *without* having to deliberate. Indeed, to have to stop and consider each phrase in a saxophone solo before playing it would be counterproductive, and would show that she had not yet properly acquired the relevant capacity. So too, I want to say, with emotional cultivation. That is, my suggestion that we can and ought to make certain deliberate efforts to develop our emotional capacities should not be viewed as an endorsement of a precious or self-conscious kind of character as a moral ideal. Rather, as with learning a foreign language or a musical instrument, if one needed to constantly monitor and adjust one's emotional responses to various situations, this would indicate that one had not yet properly inculcated the relevant emotional capacities.

Now none of this should be taken as suggesting that the cultivation and control of our emotions is a particularly simple and easy task. On the contrary, the regulation of our emotions is highly complex and can be difficult to achieve, given their potential for lack of cooperation with the will. Indeed, the cultivation of various *abilities*, such as learning to speak a foreign language or to drive a car, seems at least as complex and as difficult to carry out as the cultivation of our emotions, but we can nevertheless be responsible for developing these abilities. So, in the absence of good reasons to the contrary, it seems reasonable to argue that we can also be responsible for the results of our attempts to develop and regulate our emotions.

It is important to emphasise the efforts and attempts that we can make to cultivate and control our emotions, because the possibility of such endeavours tells against the view that we are always passive with regard to our emotions; that emotions are akin to mere accidents, things like tempests that we suffer or that come over us, and that therefore repudiate our responsibility. As the foregoing cases show, while we perhaps cannot directly control our emotions, we can often gain control over them through prior activity. In Section 8 I discuss in more detail the kinds of prior activity which allow for present responsibility. The important point here is that all of the above is some indication that we can achieve *schematic foresight* with regard to our emotions, and since such foresight seems sufficient for responsibility, at least in so far as we can have such foresight of our emotions, it seems that we can be responsible for them.

But this is only a partial outline of the scope of our responsibility for emotions, for culpably failing to have or exercise schematic foresight with regard to our emotions is also sufficient for being responsible for them. That is, given the possibility of our acquiring skills in dealing with our emotions, we may be held responsible for not acquiring or not exercising such skills in cases where we ought to have and could have. Much of the point of Aristotelian moral psychology, for example, seems to be that we should learn how to become properly skilled with our emotions, and we shall then be praised where it is appropriate; whereas if we fail to develop such skills where we could have and ought to have, we shall in some cases fail to be praised, and in others we shall be blamed. As Irwin puts Aristotle's view:

we ought to have certain kinds of emotional and appetitive desires: someone can reasonably advise us to acquire them, and we can be praised or blamed for having or lacking them. These are the sorts of things we can affect by our deliberation, and to that extent we are responsible for them.[41]

To be sure, some emotional capacities of ours may resist any efforts we might make to repudiate them, for it must be admitted that our emotions are *sometimes* capricious and unpredictable. But we might still be able to develop certain skills in dealing with these emotions, and in some cases we may be culpable for failing to have or to exercise such skills. For example, if we occasionally suffer from unpredictable bouts of deep depression we may resolve to use various strategies for dealing with our depression when we feel it overtaking us. Thus, we might resolve to try turning to our favourite novel, putting on a record we usually enjoy, going out to a movie, or visiting close friends, and where these actions are successful in relieving our depression, we can be responsible for this. Conversely, where we could have and should have used such strategies to deal with our unpredictable depression but simply did not bother to do so, we might thereby be responsible for being overcome by depression here.

I have been arguing that we are responsible for a present emotional state of ours if we could at some prior time *reasonably* have avoided getting into it. But what exactly would the upshot of this claim be in practice? Does this mean, for example, that a woman suffering from depression induced by pre-menstrual tension, which she can avoid only through taking a drug, is responsible for her depression if she chooses not to take the drug? And am I responsible for my post-separation depression because I could have avoided getting involved in the relationship in the first place?

In practice, our responsibility for particular manifestations of emotions will depend to a large degree on how we explicate the notion of what we could *reasonably* have done or avoided. This notion of 'reasonableness' enters into determining responsibility for emotions at two levels. At the first level, we need to ask whether there was some prior action which we could *reasonably* have been expected to perform or avoid performing, which would have averted (or did actually result in) our present emotional state. Of course, there will very often be many things we could have done in the past which would have prevented our now having certain emotions. But the question is, could we *reasonably* have been expected to act or avoid acting in this way? Where we have failed to do only what it was *unreasonable* to expect of us in the situation, there is no omission here at all on which responsibility might be predicated.[42] At the second level of analysis, we need to ask whether, given that we are responsible for some prior action or omission, we could reasonably have foreseen the emotional consequences of this action or omission. For where it is unreasonable to expect us to have foreseen the emotional consequences of our prior action or omission, then there are no grounds for extending responsibility from that prior action or omission to our present emotional state.

Let us apply this brief analysis to the two examples mentioned above. Suppose in the the first example that it is reasonable to expect a woman who regularly suffers from PMT-induced depression to foresee that, prior to her next cycle, she will again suffer from this depression unless she takes a certain drug. None the less, if she fails to take the drug this does not yet establish that she would be responsible for her depression. For we need to answer the first-level question of whether she could reasonably have been expected to have taken the drug in the first place: that is, the question of whether there is an omission of hers here at all. And the answer to this question will be highly context-dependent. It seems that we would not normally expect a woman who suffers from mild PMT-induced depression, which she is quite prepared to 'put up with', to control this through drugs; and so if she did not take such a drug she would not be responsible for her depression, as there is no omission here upon which her responsibility could be predicated. However, suppose she suffers from severe depression as a result of PMT, and she normally controls this through drugs, as she prefers. Then in a situation where she simply cannot be bothered to obtain the necessary drugs, there might be an omission which she could be held responsible for here, and she might be responsible for her depression which thereby ensues. This would be akin to a case of negligence, where we are responsible for those consequences of an omission which we should have prevented from occurring.

In the second example, where I could have avoided my post-separation depression by not becoming involved in the now-ended relationship in the first place, we can answer the question of whether I am responsible for my depression by appealing to the same types of considerations. Here, however, it is not a question of whether my emotional state resulted from some past *omission*, since we are assuming that my depression is a consequence of my becoming involved in the relationship in the first place, which is an *action*, let us assume, that I could reasonably have avoided. So, at the first level of analysis, there does seem to be an antecedent action here which I am responsible for. But can my responsibility for this action be extended to my consequent post-separation depression? This will depend on our answer to the second-level question of whether I could reasonably have foreseen these emotional consequences of my action. If I justifiably believed that the relationship would be very precarious, and that there would be a good chance that getting involved would eventually result in my becoming depressed at our separating, but I decided to go ahead with it anyway, then I would seem to have some share of responsibility (along with you, perhaps) for my post-separation depression. Where one version of the first case can be viewed as akin to negligence, since there was a culpable omission on the part of the woman suffering from PMT-induced depression, the present case involves a form of recklessness, since I am acting here in spite of the reasonably foreseeable bad consequences. Of course, where the relationship is more promising, and there seems less chance that becoming involved will lead to such post-separation depression, then those emotional consequences would not be reasonably foreseeable, and so I would not be responsible for them if, against the odds, they do eventuate. Thus, which consequences it is reasonable to expect us to foresee at the time of our prior actions or omissions depends partly on the likelihood of those consequences ensuing, given our action or omission.

Now this notion of what is 'reasonably expected' of us needs further analysis, and it may be that the more we acquire knowledge of and skills in dealing with our emotional patterns, the higher our reasonable expectations move with regard to our emotions. In Section 8 I shall discuss the notion of what it is reasonable to foresee, as a condition of extending responsibility to the emotional consequences of our actions and omissions.

To speak, as I have, in terms of emotional 'skills', may give the impression that we can and ought to know how to bring about certain emotions on the appropriate occasions. But the point I have been making in the present section goes further than this. That is, I have been suggesting that we can and ought to cultivate our emotional capacities as traits of character, which involves not just knowing how to produce certain emotions, but involves the development of a whole emotional outlook, an appreciation of situations in terms of one's own and others' emotions, and a capacity to respond naturally with and act out of emotion. In other words, I am suggesting that we can and ought to become emotionally sensitive people. I discussed in Chapter 2 some important reasons why we should cultivate our emotional capacities in these ways. Here I have been suggesting that we can make such efforts at emotional cultivation, and that where we do actually make such attempts or we fail to try when we ought to have and could have, this is sufficient for our being responsible for the emotions we now have as a result.

6. RESPONSIBILITY FOR ACTIONS BUT NOT EMOTIONS

However, there is an important objection to my argument so far which has not yet been addressed. It may be granted that we can make the foregoing efforts to cultivate or inhibit our emotions, and it may even perhaps be granted that such efforts can succeed, yet it might be claimed that this shows nothing in support of the view that we can be responsible for our emotions. All that we are responsible for in such cases, so the objection goes, are the *actions* by which we attempt to modify our emotions. We still lack responsibility for the emotions themselves.

One might begin a reply to this objection by wondering about the plausibility of its motivation. For in so far as it is based on the view that responsibility requires direct control, it might seem that we could not be responsible even for the actions by which we attempt to modify our emotions, as I argued earlier. But this objection can be attacked more directly. I want to give several reasons why such a view seems mistaken.

First, we are often responsible for the consequences of our actions, whether those consequences are conditions, states, beliefs (etc.), or other actions of ours, and further, they do not have to be consequences which are under our control at the time they occur.[43] In order to be responsible for the consequences of what we do, it seems sufficient that in acting, we had foresight,[44] or could reasonably have been expected to have had foresight, of the consequences of our action. Perhaps the most obvious cases of such responsibility are recklessness and negligence, where we act in spite of the consequences which we foresaw or should have foreseen. We can also be responsible for the consequences of things other than our acts and omissions, such as our beliefs. Therefore, since the objection considers cases where emotions are among the consequences of our actions, and further, those actions may involve not just mere *foresight* of their emotional consequences, but may in fact *be deliberately aimed* at cultivating or preventing those consequences, it is highly implausible to restrict responsibility to the initial actions themselves in such cases, rather than extend it to the emotions which are their intended consequences.

Indeed, we can be responsible not only for the consequences of our physical acts, but also for the consequences of our beliefs, decisions, and values, and we can attempt to cultivate and prevent our emotions through these as well. As Sankowski puts it: 'Much more than a person's overt behaviour goes to modify and determine his emotions. His evaluations and beliefs generally, his habits of thought, many of his choices and decisions – all these, and more, affect his capacities and tendencies in emotion.'[45] To Sankowski's list we might also add that emotions can be importantly modified and determined by other emotions. For example, as Hume recognised, our love for another can make it 'easier' to feel sympathy towards them, and more difficult to dislike them.[46] However, the point here does not depend on presupposing responsibility for our emotions. That would be an unacceptable reply to the objection under consideration. Rather my point is that, given that we can make efforts to cultivate and inhibit our emotions through our beliefs, decisions, and values, as well as through our physical acts, and given that we can be responsible for these cognitive and evaluative states, we can be responsible for their consequences, including emotional consequences.

Second, it is worth remembering the potentially uncooperative nature of our emotions in our attempts to cultivate and modify them. But the objection, in so far as it is based on this, is ill-founded, for this ignores or underrates the skills and control, and the capacities and dispositions, which we can have with respect to our emotions. The objection would have more force if the connections between the actions and their emotional consequences were merely accidental or coincidental. For if this were the case we could hardly foresee, much less intend, or be expected to foresee, such consequences of our actions. So a link between acts and their consequences which is important for responsibility with regard to the latter would be missing.

However, as I have already urged at some length, this is often not the case. The connection between acts and the emotions which are their consequences in our attempts at cultivation and inhibition is hardly accidental or coincidental. Given the knowledge that we can acquire of our emotional patterns, this is rather far from the truth. As I have said, cultivation and inhibition of our emotions can be much more than just acting with foresight of the possible consequences – it can be acting in certain ways which are deliberately intended to have a certain emotional effect. As Kosman puts Aristotle's account of how we can acquire virtuous dispositions for feelings, 'it is . . . possible to engage in a certain range of conduct deliberately designed to make one the kind of person who will characteristically feel in appropriate ways, at appropriate times, and so on'.[47] Therefore, given the strength of the link which is possible between the actions by which we can modify the emotions, and the emotions themselves, it seems rather strange to insist that our responsibility is limited only to those actions. In fact, such an insistence cuts us off from an important part of our lives. As Sankowski says, 'declining to apply the notion of responsibility for their emotions to persons out of misguided humanitarianism could actually be harmful. It obscures the extent to which persons create their own emotional lives'.[48]

This second point is worth pursuing further. Certain emotions can often become so natural for us that we tend to forget our responsibility for them. However, in so far as our having certain emotional habits is due to our active efforts to acquire such habits or dispositions, our responsibility for them cannot be forgotten, and indeed, must be emphasised. Aristotle had a point in linking what is voluntary with what is natural for us to do or have.[49] We should not lose sight of the fact that we often create necessities for ourselves. In his discussion of care, Harry Frankfurt develops the notion of 'volitional necessity', which is the kind of necessity we are subject to when we have the actual capacity to forbear from a certain course of action, but we prevent ourselves from mustering the will to forbear from that action.[50] In such a case we may be responsible for that action. (This might be contrasted with the kind of necessity or compulsion we feel in performing a certain action where we lack not only the will but also the capacity to forbear from that action, in which case we would not normally be responsible.) As Annette Baier in her comments on Frankfurt says, 'we display our wills more in what we cannot but do and feel than in what we can directly control, or do "at will" '.[51] Thus, an anti-nuclear activist who feels he cannot prevent himself from rallying in support of his cause is not, in virtue of the necessity he feels, thereby relieved of responsibility for his action. For it may be a necessity he has created for himself because of his concern for the issue. And his concern itself may be something which he has cultivated – he might have resisted strong temptations to devote his energies to lesser, more achievable, projects.

So, the fact that we may feel compelled to experience certain emotions does not necessarily rule out the possibility of our learning to cultivate or inhibit our emotions, and therefore of our being responsible for them. For the necessity we may feel to have certain emotions and not to have others may itself be something that we have created through our prior efforts at cultivation and inhibition. For example, a sympathetic person who feels that he cannot but have sympathy for the plight of those in distress does not thereby lack responsibility for his sympathy. If he has worked at developing his capacity for sympathy, perhaps in some of the ways suggested earlier, then the compulsion for sympathy which he now feels, far from precluding his responsibility, is a sign of the success of his earlier efforts.

One final comment in relation to the objection that urges a restriction of responsibility attributions to actions (by which we attempt to modify our emotions) themselves, is that such a restriction seems rather ironic. One of the implications of the objection seems to be that, in so far as we are concerned about what we can be credited and blamed for, we should attend to our actions, rather than our emotions. However, our emotional capacities can importantly affect our ability to act.[52] For example, as I argued in Chapters 2 and 3, a sympathetic person may well be able to perform more acts of beneficence than one who is unsympathetic. Therefore, if one is concerned with acting creditworthily and not blameworthily, it seems that one should also concern oneself with learning how to cultivate and inhibit one's emotions and emotional capacities, making such deliberate attempts which I have suggested betoken responsibility.

Indeed, not only do emotions affect our *ability* to act, but, as I will argue in the following chapter, when embodied in motives, they can also affect our creditworthiness and blameworthiness in the light of the act.[53] And if it is agreed that our emotions can in this way influence the morality of our actions, then given the objection's concern with our being credited and blamed in the light of our actions, those who make the objection should also want to allow that we can modify our emotions in ways I have suggested amount to responsibility. Of course, neither this point nor that of the foregoing paragraph are intended as telling replies to the objection at hand. Rather, I mention them only to point out some curious consequences of holding the view that, in our attempts at coming to grips with our emotions, it is only the actions involved in those attempts for which we can be responsible, and not the emotions which may be their intended consequences.

7. TWO ACCOUNTS OF RESPONSIBILITY

So far my strategy in this chapter has involved taking certain common
ideas about responsibility for physical acts and showing that these do
not preclude, and in fact often support, our responsibility in many
cases for our emotions. Therefore, in arguing that we can be responsible for our emotions, it has not been necessary to offer a fully
articulated account of the notion of responsibility (which would in
any case be beyond the scope of this book). Indeed, were I to argue
from such an account, my conclusions might be disputed on the
grounds of the explication of responsibility upon which the argument
would be based. But my argument is not open to such an objection,
for, as may already be clear from my discussion of some common
ideas about responsibility for physical acts, my claim that we can be
responsible for our emotions does not rest on presupposing a certain
special account of responsibility. Indeed, my claim is quite compatible with rival accounts of the notion of responsibility. I want to show
this by looking briefly at two prominent but competing attempts to
provide a fully articulated account of responsibility, and demonstrating that the most plausible version of each allows that we can be
responsible for our emotions. Following this I consider how prior
activity can affect our responsibility for what is presently not under
our control.

According to many philosophers, I am responsible for Z if and only
if my beliefs and desires, as reasons, *cause* my doing or having Z.[54]
Thus, if I scream out because I believe that by doing so I will attract
your attention, and I want to attract your attention, I am responsible
for screaming, whereas if I scream because I am pricked by a needle,
I am not responsible for screaming, because my beliefs and desires
played no causal role in my screaming. I will call this the 'causal'
account of responsibility.

But while this account may seem to reflect our intuitive ideas about
responsibility, it is not without its problems. First, how can such an
account allow that we are responsible for certain omissions? For
example, if it simply slips the railway signalman's mind to change the
signal and his omission results in a fatal accident, it seems that he
should not be exonerated from responsibility (and blame) just because his omission was not caused by any of his beliefs and desires.
Second, the beliefs and desires which caused Z may themselves be
beliefs and desires which we are not responsible for having, as in the
case of a person who becomes addicted to heroin because others are
secretly adding the drug to his food. Third, this account faces the

notorious problem of deviant causal chains. That is, my beliefs and desires may cause Z, but I may not be responsible for Z because my beliefs and desires did not cause Z in the 'right way'. For example, I may go to a party in order to verbally insult the host, whom I dislike, yet before I have the opportunity to speak to him, I discover that he is already insulted by my dressing too casually, for (unknown to me) the party was intended as a formal affair. Thus, the causal account of responsibility, as it stands, seems to imply both that we are responsible for too little (as the first problem shows) and that we are responsible for too much (as shown by the second and third problems).

In the light of such problems, the causal account might be made more plausible by adverting to prior beliefs and desires. So, the unwitting heroin addict may not be responsible for his present addiction, as his present desire for heroin and belief that a certain course of action will (temporarily) appease that desire which cause his taking heroin were not caused by prior beliefs and desires of his, but by others adulterating his food. Perhaps such moves can help save the causal account of responsibility, although the issue of deviant causal chains remains a problem. (But given its notoriety for causal accounts in general, maybe it is unfair to single out the causal account of responsibility for criticism on the grounds of this last problem.) In any case, since I am not primarily interested in finding an adequate explication of the notion of responsibility, I will leave it open whether modifications along such lines are successful defences for the causal account.

A common response to the difficulties of the above account is to offer what I will call a 'counterfactual' account of responsibility. On this account, I am responsible for something if and only if I could have done otherwise (or, could have avoided doing it), where 'I could have done otherwise' is understood in terms of 'I would have done otherwise if I had chosen'.[55] Thus I am responsible for getting wet in a shower of rain if I could have taken shelter and stayed dry. This account has the advantage that it eliminates the troublesome reference (in the causal account) to the causal role of beliefs and desires. Yet the counterfactual account of responsibility also has its problems. For as we saw earlier in my discussion of avoidability, there are many things that we are now unable to avoid doing, but which we nevertheless seem responsible for, if our present inability to avoid something was created by past activity. Cases of negligence and recklessness provide the most obvious examples here. However, as we also saw earlier, the counterfactual account can accommodate this problem by modifying the notion of avoidability to include both past and present avoidability. So, the view would now be that I am responsible for something if and only if I could at some time reasonably have avoided doing it (i.e. I would have done otherwise if I, at some time, had chosen).

At first sight, this view might seem quite plausible, for it seems to account for our responsibility in cases of negligence (such as the railway signalman) and recklessness; however, this modified version of the counterfactual account has problems of a different sort. First, it is now notorious that the parenthetical counterfactual statement in the above view may be true, even though I could not have done otherwise and am not responsible.[56] That is, it may be true that I would have done otherwise if I had chosen, but also be true that I could not have chosen (and hence, could not have done otherwise). Thus, the counterfactual account, at least in so far as it explicates avoidability in the above manner, is not a *sufficient* condition of responsibility.

But second, and here more importantly, the counterfactual account is not a *necessary* condition of responsibility, either. That is, in order to be responsible for something, it is not necessary that I could have (at some time) done otherwise, for there are cases where I am responsible for an act of mine that is causally *overdetermined*. For example, if I decide to stay in a room, and the only door to this room is locked after I go in (but this latter fact does not figure in my decision to stay in the room, either because it is unknown to me, or because, although I am aware of it, I have other reasons for staying), I can be responsible for staying there, even though I cannot do (and we may take it, could not have brought it about that I could do) otherwise.[57]

This seems to lead us back to the explication of responsibility in terms of beliefs and desires as causes of action – i.e. the causal account – but as we saw, this account has problems of its own. I shall not attempt to resolve this dilemma, as this would lead me far astray of my concerns in this book. So I again leave it open whether the counterfactual account of responsibility can be suitably modified to deal with these problems. It remains to be seen, however, whether either account allows that we can be responsible for our emotions. So let us consider this question.

On the initial understanding of the *causal* account of responsibility, it may be difficult to see how we can be responsible for our emotions, for some have thought that the causes of our emotions have nothing to do with our beliefs and desires – we 'just feel' a certain way. While

I disagree most strongly with this view, it is not necessary to argue for its falsity here, for I need only point out, as I did earlier, that many omissions (among other things) which we do seem responsible for may appear to be similarly uncaused by our beliefs and desires. If, however, in response to this, the modified causal account (where prior beliefs and desires are allowed as causes of what we presently do or have) is invoked, then it becomes difficult to see how we can be *denied* responsibility for our emotions. For as I have already indicated while discussing foresight, prior beliefs and desires (and actions) often play an important causal role in what we may presently seem to 'just feel'. For instance, my present depression may seem simply to 'overcome me', and I may attempt to explain it by attributing it to, say, a lithium deficiency. However, if I look closely I may discover that my depression is perhaps due to my underlying belief that I have achieved little by comparison with my friends. Therefore, on the most plausible understanding of the *causal* account of responsibility, it seems that we can be responsible for our emotions.

Given the original formulation of the *counterfactual* account of responsibility – that is, as a claim about present avoidability – it may again be difficult to see how we can be responsible for our emotions, for, as we saw in my earlier discussion of avoidability, we often seem to lack this present avoidability with regard to our emotions. However, as we also saw in that discussion, we seem to lack present avoidability with regard to many acts and omissions which we nevertheless seem responsible for (especially in cases of negligence). If the counterfactual account is modified to allow for past and present avoidability, then, in accommodating the acts and omissions which were previously left out, it now appears difficult to exclude responsibility for emotions; since, as I have shown in some detail (in discussing avoidability and foresight), it is often the case that there is something in the past which we could reasonably have done to avoid our now having a certain emotion. Therefore, it seems that whichever of these prominent accounts of responsibility is preferred, the most plausible form of each allows that we can be responsible for our emotions. Thus, unless otherwise indicated, no particular explication of the notion of responsibility is presupposed in what follows.

8. RESPONSIBILITY FOR EMOTIONS AS CONSEQUENCES OF OUR ACTIONS

In the preceding discussions of avoidability and foresight, I have claimed that even if what one presently has or does is not then and there under one's control, one may still be responsible for it because of prior acts or omissions that were under one's control, and are 'relevantly linked' to what one is presently having or doing. Paradigmatic cases of such extended responsibility are recklessness and negligence. Yet there are other kinds of cases, perhaps more apt for my purposes. For instance, Aristotle speaks of people whose character and what arises from it are now fixed and not under their immediate control, but because of prior voluntary acts which led to their having such a character, they may be responsible for what they cannot now help being and doing.[58]

However, the nature of the link between what was previously under our control (Y) and what is now out of our control (Z), which allows responsibility to be extended to the latter, needs to be examined more closely. It seems clear that the first condition for such a link is that Z must in some sense be a consequence of Y. But maybe we can specify more precisely what is *necessary* for extending responsibility from Y to Z. And since agents are not held responsible for *all* of the consequences of their actions, no matter how distantly related, there is also a question about what kind of consequence is *sufficient* for such extended responsibility. (I shall not go into issues here about what it means to say that 'Z is a consequence of Y' – i.e. issues of causality, and so on. I take it for granted that the notion of a 'consequence' has a certain common use in the realm of action, and assume that it is suitably transferable in speaking of emotions. I look briefly at some problems of causal selection at the conclusion of this chapter.)

In my discussion of foresight, I did not attempt to argue that we need to have a certain kind of foresight in order to be responsible for something in the first place, although I did argue that having various sorts of (what might be called) foresight were *sufficient* for this initial responsibility. However, when we are considering extending responsibility to the consequences of something which it has already been established that we are responsible for, then having (or culpably lacking) some form of foresight of those consequences may perhaps be required. Thus, we might say that in order to be responsible for Z, where Z is a consequence of Y (and we are responsible for Y), then in doing Y, we must foresee (or culpably fail to foresee) that Z (or Z-like consequences) might follow. As Eric D'Arcy, in discussing creditworthy acts and consequences, puts it, 'It is not necessary that the agent foresee in detail the precise consequences that emerge, but simply that he had some idea that a certain kind of good result might be anticipated.'[59]

This condition must be weak enough to allow our responsibility to extend to Z for the variety of beliefs and attitudes we may have towards Z in performing Y, where we do seem responsible for Z. For example, it would appear that we can be responsible for Z not only where, in doing Y, we believe that Z is *likely* to follow, but also in cases where we believe that Z is *unlikely* to follow, but we do Y in the *hope* that Z will follow. Indeed, we may be responsible for Z even in cases where although we believe that Z is unlikely to follow and hope that Z will not follow, we nevertheless believe that Z *might* follow, and that Z is of sufficient importance that we do Y in order to be prepared for it (as, for example, in learning an emergency driving technique). However, the condition I have suggested is in most cases too weak to be alone *sufficient* for extending responsibility to Z, as we may foresee that our performing a certain action *might* have all sorts of consequences, yet we do not (normally) in virtue of this seem to be responsible for them. Thus, I might realise that every time I step outside there is a slight chance of my catching a cold, but if my doing so does actually lead to such a consequence on a certain occasion, I do not because of my 'foresight' seem responsible for catching a cold.

In terms of the earlier distinction between act and schematic foresight, the condition I have suggested is weaker than either of these, since it requires neither a clear preview of, nor skills and capacities with respect to, the consequences of one's actions. But I do not want to continue debating the adequacy of the condition which I think may be *necessary* for extending responsibility from prior activity to what is presently not under our control. For it is enough for our purposes to show that certain ways of regarding the consequences of our actions are *sufficient* for such extended responsibility.

As I have already indicated, there are various attitudes and beliefs which we can have towards the consequences of an action, where we are responsible for that action, which are sufficient for extending our responsibility to those consequences. Certainly, having schematic foresight of the consequences of what we do would seem sufficient for our responsibility here, as would, at least in many cases, having act foresight of those consequences, believing those consequences are likely to occur, hoping that they will occur, or even being prepared for consequences which one believes unlikely and hopes will not occur. And of course, culpably lacking such foresight, beliefs, and attitudes with regard to the consequences of our actions is often sufficient for our being responsible for those consequences. Henceforth, unless otherwise indicated, for reasons of clarity I shall speak of the various ways in which we may stand in relation to the consequences of our actions, which allow responsibility to be extended to those consequences, simply in terms of 'foresight' (though it is to be acknowledged here that the use of such a term may be misleading in some cases).

It seems clear, then, that we can be responsible for the consequences of our actions when, in acting, we either had foresight or culpably lacked foresight of those consequences. However, before looking at this in the context of emotions, it should be pointed out that there are serious problems with analysing the notion of culpably lacking foresight as a ground for extended responsibility. According to D'Arcy, responsibility for Y can be legitimately extended to responsibility for Z where, in doing Y, Z is actually anticipated by the agent as a consequence of Y, or could have been anticipated by an 'informed observer' as a consequence of Y.[60] Audi takes a different approach: if we are to be responsible for Z, where Z is a consequence of Y, then in doing Y, it must be the case both that the agent could 'reasonably be expected to believe' that he would or might do Z, and that there were some other action(s) which the agent had the ability and opportunity to perform, and 'could reasonably be expected to see' would or might have prevented Z (where what the agent could reasonably be expected to see and believe is determined partly by reference to what a sound moral agent would have seen and believed in the circumstances).[61] Others speak in terms of exercising a 'reasonable degree of prudence',[62] 'the point of view of the standard man',[63] 'what is foreseeable with ordinary care',[64] or what is 'expectable human behaviour'.[65]

However, on D'Arcy's analysis, where we are responsible for the consequences of our actions which could have been anticipated by an informed observer, it will turn out that we are responsible for far too much, since, *ex hypothesi*, an informed observer would presumably be able to foresee most if not all of the consequences of our actions. Indeed, despite the hopes of Kantians here, it may be, through no fault of our own, that we are unable to take up the perspective of an informed observer in assessing the consequences of our actions. The analysis provided by Audi, where what is reasonably expected of us is explicated partly in terms of the notion of a sound moral agent, although an improvement on D'Arcy's account, is also unsatisfactory. For again, through no fault of our own, we may be incapable of sound moral agency; but in such a case we may, according to Audi, nevertheless be held culpably ignorant of the consequences of our actions. Clearly, it seems implausible to determine our responsibility for the consequences of what we do solely by reference to such 'objective' standards.

Perhaps our responsibility here can more plausibly be measured against a more 'subjective' or individualised account of the consequences it is possible to foresee. The suggestion here might be that my responsibility for Y can be extended to responsibility for Z if, in doing Y, I could have foreseen that Z would (or might) follow. That is, whether or not my failure to foresee the consequences of my action is culpable would be determined by whether or not I have the skills or capacities for such foresight which I failed to exercise in this case. However, while in deciding responsibility we must make allowances for what an individual is capable of foreseeing, an exclusive reliance on such an account will entail that we are responsible for too little. For sometimes a person's inabilities regarding foresight are themselves culpable.[66] So, for example, a self-styled builder who constructs houses which they fail to foresee will not withstand a moderate gale may be unable, given the level of their training, to foresee such unfortunate consequences of their work. Yet they would nevertheless be responsible for the collapse of their houses during the first storm which hits the area, since builders are expected to have enough skill to construct houses that will withstand expected storms. Taking a more general example, a tactless person who is incapable of realising (at least without the help of others) the hurtfulness of their comments to others may be responsible for such consequences, since we expect most people to develop at least a modicum of 'common decency'.

Further, accepting a purely individualised account of culpability with regard to the consequences of our actions, where we are held culpable only for consequences that *we* are able to foresee, would obscure the important point that an individual's ability to foresee the consequences of their actions can be seriously underdeveloped, and therefore needs encouragement to become more like that of a morally sensitive person.[67] For in both institutional situations and in everyday life, we are often expected to have a certain ability to foresee the consequences of our actions.

So it seems that in deciding when we are responsible for consequences of our actions which we failed to foresee, a suitable balance between the perspective of the actual agent themselves (taking into account their particular skills, capacities, background, etc.) and the perspective of what the moral agent would see and do in that situation needs to be found. Neither perspective alone appears to be sufficient.[68]

I do not know how to resolve this problem satisfactorily. Perhaps it does not admit of a clear resolution. Indeed, this problem of balancing the individual's viewpoint and that of a moral person also occurs in trying to find an adequate analysis of the notion of avoidability, as we saw earlier. Nevertheless, there are two points of relevance here for our concerns.

First, in so far as our responsibility in cases of culpable ignorance of the consequences of what we do or have is dependent on the perspective of the moral person, this problem may to some extent be illuminated by what I have said in Chapter 2 about the aretaic conception of morality from which this book draws. That is, a morally sound person would be one who has good judgement and understanding, cares about their friends, and has a proper sense of self-worth, among other qualities. And a *phronimos*, or practically wise person, would see when and how these abstract goods are at stake in particular situations, and would foresee various emotional consequences of their actions. For the purposes of determining when ignorance of the emotional consequences of our actions is culpable, there is some similarity between the standard of the Aristotelian *phronimos*, and that of John Rawls's 'competent moral judge'. For the latter has a normal degree of intelligence, foresees those consequences of their actions which it is reasonable to expect of a person of normal intelligence, and has sympathetic knowledge of various fundamental human interests.[69] And so one might determine what emotional consequences of our actions we culpably failed to foresee partly by reference to what a *phronimos* or a competent moral judge would have foreseen here.

Second, the problem of balancing subjective and objective viewpoints is not limited to cases where we are considering the *emotional* consequences of an action; it is a difficulty which also occurs when we consider other kinds of consequences of our actions, such as the harms which are caused in many cases of negligence.[70] There are no *special* difficulties inherent in saying of someone that they culpably failed to foresee certain emotional consequences of their action, and those problems which do arise in using such a notion where the emotions are concerned might be answered by looking at its use in parallel cases which do not involve emotions.

We have seen, then, that the link between what was under our control and what is now out of our control which is sufficient for responsibility to extend from the former to the latter, is that we foresee, in one of the various senses of 'foresight', or culpably fail to foresee, that the latter would be a consequence of the former. Thus, it is worth repeating here that in order to be responsible for our emotions, it is not necessary that they be under our control at the time we have them. If we had (or culpably lacked) one of these kinds of foresight of certain emotions as consequences of something prior that was under our control, then we can be responsible for those emotions when they occur. And as I have already argued at some length, we can often have such foresight of the emotional consequences of our actions.

Further, since we can often foresee the emotional consequences of our actions, we can often reasonably be expected to have foreseen those consequences at the time of acting. As Sankowski and Adams, among others, have pointed out, ignorance of our emotional patterns can itself be culpable, if it is ignorance that we could reasonably have done something about.[71] Indeed, being responsible for our emotions often can and should involve more than mere foresight of the emotional consequences of our actions. For, as I have said, we can (and sometimes should) make deliberate attempts, through our actions, beliefs, and evaluations to cultivate, control, and prevent our emotions, and we can do so in ways that amount to our being responsible for the latter.

Apart from the difficulties already mentioned, looking for prior voluntariness to account for present responsibility also involves problems of causal selection. That is, in speaking of our responsibility for the consequences of something prior that was in our control, we are citing the latter as an important causal factor in the production of those consequences, but what to select here as a significant cause of those consequences (and hence, how we assign responsibility) is not always clear. Obviously, this question cannot be settled simply by reference to actions of which, if we had not performed them, certain consequences would not have occurred (which we might call the 'terminating conditions' of those consequences), as there are many such actions, the consequences of which we are not responsible for merely on those grounds. Thus, if I had not decided to take you on a skiing holiday you might not have broken your leg, but I am not in virtue of this decision responsible for your accident.

In making causal citations, we may be tempted to look for the newly intervening force in a course of events. However, as Feinberg points out, this is sometimes misleading, as the newly intervening force may just trigger, precipitate, or ignite some elaborate process which has already been set up.[72] Thus, another's trivial act may set off a latent emotional capacity of ours, but, although we commonly believe otherwise of ourselves in such situations, it is to our own emotional capacity which we should turn in looking for the significant cause which is relevant to deciding responsibility here. And it is when our attention is properly directed in this way that we are apt to make such familiar admissions as: 'It's not your fault I'm so angry, it's mine, for I shouldn't get so angry over such little things.' In these kinds of cases, rather than focus on the immediate voluntary act which triggered the reaction, we should look at the creation of the capacity or mechanism which was there to be triggered, in order to settle the question of responsibility.

On the other hand, however, there are cases of trivial acts setting off an emotional reaction where it is proper to concentrate on the former as the important causal factor, and hence as the locus of responsibility. The most familiar example of these kinds of cases is provocation, where a series of what (considered in themselves) can seem like trivial acts, extended over a period of time, set off an angry reaction in another person. The preceding kinds of cases show that, in assigning responsibility for emotions that are not presently under our control on the grounds that they are the consequences of prior voluntariness, there can be several causal candidates between which it may be difficult to decide, and the task of attributing responsibility may thereby be complex and problematic.

Now, none of what I have said is intended to deny the fact that our emotions are subject to the larger causal influences of biological, social, cultural, and other factors. While this is not the place to begin a discussion of such important topics, the following at least can be said. In many cases, as with actions, holding people responsible for their emotions seems quite compatible with there being these larger explanations of their having certain emotions (and may indeed presuppose such larger explanations).[73] But, one might ask, if all our emotions were caused, say, by biological factors, how could this leave room for our being responsible for our emotions? On this question I should say that I am a compatibilist. That is, I believe that if all our emotions were biologically caused, this is compatible with our having responsibility for those emotions we could reasonably foresee as consequences of actions we could reasonably have avoided, assuming that (notwithstanding the difficulties noted in Section 7 of this chapter) a plausible compatibilist explication of 'avoidability' can be given, as I believe it can.[74]

To be sure, there will be cases where emotions of ours are determined by these deeper biological, social, and cultural influences in such a way that precludes our responsibility for those emotions. To take one brief example, given the current worldwide level of unemployment, it may be improper to lay responsibility for the profound depression which is characteristically experienced by those long out of work at the door of the individual. However, the question of whether or not we could be responsible for our emotions if they were *always* completely determined by such external influences is something that cannot, and indeed need not, be answered in a work of this nature. For what I have been arguing is that an examination of many common ideas about responsibility for actions shows that we can also be responsible for our emotions, and just as none of those ideas denies that our actions are subject to such larger causal influences, so too, it may be said, with regard to our emotions.

In the last part of this chapter I have tried to elucidate the idea that our responsibility for prior acts (etc.) can be extended to the consequences of those acts (etc.) that are not under our immediate control, and it seems that, in so far as such extended responsibility is justified where acts issue in consequences which do not involve emotions, it is also justified where the consequences of those acts are emotions. To conclude this chapter then, it seems that none of the conditions which seem properly involved in establishing responsibility for physical acts precludes our being responsible for our emotions, and further, such conditions often actually suggest various ways in which we might indeed be responsible for our emotions. This strengthens my argument in Chapter 2 that our emotions have an important place in our moral lives, and in the next chapter I shall examine the implications of my conclusion here for the kinds of moral assessments which are justifiably made of us on account of our emotions.

5 Moral assessments of persons for their emotions

It is a commonplace that moral assessments may justifiably be made of agents on account of their actions. However, few contemporary philosophers have taken up Aristotle's suggestion that moral assessments may properly be applied to persons in respect of their *emotions*. I argued in Chapter 2 that there is a variety of important ways in which emotions have moral significance in our lives. In this chapter I shall discuss what assessments can appropriately be made of persons with regard to their morally significant emotions, and what the conditions are which affect the nature and legitimacy of those assessments.

These assessments may be divided into four categories: that is, vertically, into those directed at us for our morally *right* emotional responses, and those which focus on our morally *wrong* emotional responses; and horizontally, into assessments which require that we are responsible for the emotion in question, which I take to be true of credit and blame, and assessments that do not require our responsibility, which I discuss as forms of esteem and disesteem. These terms and the notion of moral assessment employed here will be defined properly as we proceed.

Now, some resist the idea of our being morally assessed for the emotions we have because, as seen in Chapters 2 and 3, they deny the moral significance of our emotions. Others oppose at least our being *blamed* and *credited* for our emotions because, as we saw in Chapters 3 and 4, they hold that we cannot be responsible for our emotions. Both of the views on which this opposition is based were rejected in the foregoing chapters. Yet some seem to resist the idea of our being morally assessed for the emotions we have because of their views about the nature of moral assessments, such as credit and blame, esteem and disesteem. In this chapter I want to show the falsity of those views.

Thus, my aim in this chapter is to demonstrate that it is indeed appropriate to blame, credit, esteem, and disesteem people for their emotions, and further, to show that no *special* account of these assessments is needed in order to establish this.[1] In other words, what we understand as blame, credit, esteem, and disesteem when directed at people for their actions may also be justifiably applied to people on account of their emotions. Now, the main worry of those who hold that we can legitimately be blamed, credited, esteemed, and disesteemed for our *actions* but not for our *emotions* seems to be that to apply these moral assessments to people for their emotions is to have a righteous and meddlesome over-concern with what is none of our business. I will demonstrate that this kind of worry is unfounded, and I shall do so by showing that it arises from the erroneous conflation of an important distinction between the justification of blameworthiness and creditworthiness, on the one hand, and the justification of what I call 'blaming and crediting responses', on the other hand. I then apply a parallel distinction to esteeming and disesteeming persons for their emotions, which are assessments that do *not* require a person to be responsible for the emotions in question. A commonly held view in regard to moral evaluations of persons is that *moral* evaluations can be properly directed at us only on account of what we are responsible for. I shall argue that esteem and disesteem show this to be false, since these are moral evaluations which can be legitimately applied to us even for those emotions of ours which we are not responsible for having.

To be sure, in arguing that we may be morally assessed for our emotions as we are for our actions, I am not arguing that there are *no* relevant differences between emotions and actions which we should be responsive to in blaming, crediting, esteeming, and disesteeming people. Rather, I just want to see that any such differences are properly located here. That is, I want to show that for the purposes of moral assessment, the differences between emotions and actions are relevant not to whether a person is in fact blameworthy, creditworthy, estimable, or disestimable in a particular situation, but only to determining the types of blaming and crediting responses, or esteeming and disesteeming responses, which would be appropriately directed at them in that situation.

1. THE NATURE OF BLAMEWORTHINESS AND CREDITWORTHINESS

A standard account of an important category of negative and positive agent evaluations which we may call blameworthiness and creditworthiness runs as follows: X is morally blameworthy or creditworthy[2] on account of some action Z if and only if (i) Z is morally wrong or right; and (ii) X is responsible for Z.[3] In this first section, let me briefly explain the plausibility of (i) and (ii) as conditions of blameworthiness and creditworthiness in the realm of *action*, and I want to look at whether there is anything in this account which precludes our being blameworthy and creditworthy for our *emotions*.

The blaming responses which I shall argue that blameworthiness makes us liable to may consist in acts such as reproaching or censuring, or just in certain attitudes and emotions such as disapproval and indignation. Likewise, the crediting responses which creditworthiness entitles us to may be acts such as commending or rewarding, or various attitudes and emotions such as approval and gratitude.[4]

It should be emphasised at the outset that in this chapter I am concerned with crediting and blaming responses directed at *persons* on account of what they do or have. These responses embody a judgement that a particular action or feature of a person reflects well or poorly upon them, and so the crediting and blaming responses which we have towards a person can be an important indication of what we take their moral worth to be. These responses may express a judgement that the person at whom they are directed shows themselves good or bad in so far as they have some feature or perform some action – although in crediting or blaming a person for something we need not, of course, be making any *overall* judgement of their moral worth.[5] In order to be creditworthy or estimable for one's *character*, I would argue that one would need to have inculcated a form of practical wisdom, or *phronesis*, as a kind of guiding condition or regulatory motive guiding one's emotions towards the right objects, in the manner I explained in Section 10 of Chapter 2.[6] But contrary to Hume and others,[7] it is not only for our character-traits and dispositional features that we may be properly credited and blamed. I believe that we may also be justifiably credited and blamed for actions and emotions which are *uncharacteristic* of us, given that the conditions for creditworthiness and blameworthiness obtain here, and there are no reasons (of the kind discussed in the following section) against the appropriateness of our being the subject of crediting or blaming responses in this situation.

Now, to begin with, the first condition in the standard account of blameworthiness and creditworthiness, that we can be blameworthy and creditworthy only for what is wrong or right, respectively, seems uncontroversial. For whatever else these notions require, it seems that they clearly involve an evaluation of some action or personal feature as wrong or right. This is central to their character as *assessments*, rather than just value-neutral descriptions or observations. The point here is a conceptual one: that is, to hold that we could be blameworthy or creditworthy for what is in no way wrong or right would seem to be a misuse of the concepts of blameworthiness and creditworthiness.

Of course, there may be disputes about the nature of this rightness and wrongness, and I would here defend an aretaic conception of these notions, as explicated in Chapter 2, where rightness and wrongness are understood in terms of what makes for a good or a bad life. So for example, doing a favour for a friend out of friendship is morally right because it is an expression of a character-trait which is central to human flourishing. And conversely, a self-pitying withdrawal from the world such that one feels no longer able to pursue what one values may well be morally wrong, since the erosion of a sense of self-worth which is likely to result is a serious impediment to human flourishing. However, any disputes which may arise about this conception of morality are not important here, for they concern substantive issues, whereas the moral significance condition of blameworthiness and creditworthiness is a *formal* condition, which is neutral among various normative accounts of morality.[8]

Turning to the second condition of the standard account of blameworthiness and creditworthiness, most writers who discuss these notions accept that responsibility is a necessary condition of blameworthiness and creditworthiness. The notion of 'responsibility' referred to here is that dealt with in Chapter 4 – that is, *moral* responsibility rather than merely *causal* responsibility. And again, there might well be disagreements about just what is involved in being morally responsible for something. Thus, as we saw in Chapter 4, many hold that moral responsibility requires avoidability, while some claim that contrary to this, moral responsibility requires that our beliefs and desires play a causal role in bringing about what we are responsible for. I did not attempt to resolve this issue, since both views seemed to allow that we can be responsible for our emotions. Nor shall I attempt to settle this dispute here, for advocates of these divergent views seem to agree that responsibility is a necessary condition of blameworthiness and creditworthiness, and indeed, many of them explicitly acknowledge this connection in stating what they take to be the significance of their analyses of responsibility.

Let me briefly give some motivating reasons for accepting condition (ii) in the standard account of blameworthiness and creditworthiness. Responsibility seems closely linked with these assessments, since in many contexts, both moral and non-moral, it is clear that in allocating blame or credit for something, we are assigning responsibility for it. Thus, in deciding whether to give credit to a prime minister and his government for recent economic recovery, we are deciding whether it is his government's policies or global market forces that are responsible for the recovery. Similarly, in deciding who gets the blame for allowing the opposing team to overwhelm us in the last quarter of a football match, we are trying to determine which players were responsible for letting their opponents wrest the initiative from them. Indeed, as we saw in the previous chapter, there is even a sense in which 'morally responsible' is used as meaning 'morally blameworthy'. Another point which suggests that blameworthiness and creditworthiness require responsibility is that if in performing a faulty or meritorious act it can be shown that we were coerced or in some other way forced to perform such an act, we would thereby be excused from blameworthiness and creditworthiness, and this seems to be because in being *forced* to act faultily or meritoriously, we would not be *responsible* for acting in this way.[9]

Some might object to the claim that *creditworthiness* requires responsibility, since it may be argued that we can credit people for qualities such as beauty, intelligence, and sensitivity, even when it is clear that they are not responsible for having these qualities.[10] But to use the notions of credit and creditworthiness in this way is to confuse them with praise and praiseworthiness. Certainly, we may legitimately praise people for their beauty and intelligence, or for their kindness and courageousness, without thereby implying that they are responsible for having such qualities, as praise and praiseworthiness do not require responsibility. Indeed, as Brandt puts it, 'In many contexts "praiseworthy" is indistinguishable in meaning from "excellent" or "fine".'[11] Yet in contrast to praise, to the extent that we credit people for their beauty, intelligence, kindness, or courageousness, it seems that we do so only in so far as they are responsible for having such qualities. Therefore, credit seems to be closer to the opposite of blame than is praise, because credit and creditworthiness, like blame and blameworthiness, seem to require responsibility, while praise and praiseworthiness do not, and this is why I discuss blame together with credit, rather than with praise.[12]

So the standard account of blameworthiness and creditworthiness in terms of being responsible for a wrong or right action appears to be quite a plausible account of these assessments. But does this account allow that we can also be blameworthy and creditworthy for our *emotions*?

Let us begin with the moral significance condition for blameworthiness and creditworthiness. Emotions can meet this requirement no less than our actions, since, as I argued in Chapter 2, there are many ways in which emotions may have moral significance in our lives. For some brief examples, sympathy and compassion are morally valuable because they often play such a crucial role in our understanding of and responding appropriately to the sufferings of others. Shame is another morally important emotion, in so far as it involves an appropriate form of self-concern and a desire to atone for some defective action or personal feature. On the other hand, resentment towards others seems morally bad or wrong where it is founded on a sense of inferiority and involves a distancing of oneself from others. Likewise, excessive anger at a minor injury seems a moral fault because it evidences a distorted sense of justice.

The second requirement of the standard account of blameworthiness and creditworthiness, the condition of responsibility, can also be satisfied by our emotions. For I argued in the previous chapter that we often do have control of our emotions in one of the various senses which amount to our being responsible for them. So for instance, if we fail to avoid certain situations where we know we are likely to become excessively angry, and we could reasonably be expected to avoid such situations, then it seems that we would be responsible and, indeed, blameworthy if we became angry in such a situation. So too, many of us can take steps to cultivate our capacity to respond appropriately to others with sympathy and compassion, and where we succeed in this, we would be responsible and also creditworthy for having these emotions. Thus, if one accepts the burden of my arguments in the foregoing three chapters, and if one also accepts the standard account of blameworthiness and creditworthiness, one must, it would seem, allow that we can be blameworthy and creditworthy for our emotions.

2. BLAMEWORTHINESS AND CREDITWORTHINESS FOR EMOTIONS, AND THE JUSTIFICATION OF BLAMING AND CREDITING RESPONSES

But some writers would argue, against this conclusion, that while we can indeed be blameworthy and creditworthy for our *actions*, we cannot be blameworthy and creditworthy for our *emotions*, or at least, not when an emotion of ours is not expressed in blameworthy or creditworthy action. Those who hold this view may well allow that our emotions can be morally significant, even perhaps in a 'non-motivational' sense (i.e. independently of being expressed in action), and that we can also be responsible for them, but they object to our being blameworthy and creditworthy for unexpressed emotions because of what they take to be involved in the notions of blame-worthiness and creditworthiness. These writers accept that being responsible for something wrong or right is necessary for blame-worthiness and creditworthiness, but they argue that we cannot be blameworthy and creditworthy for our emotions, because they be-lieve that to allow this would be to condone meddlesomeness. That is, they argue that blameworthiness and creditworthiness involve a *further* condition which in effect excludes the application of these assessments to us for our emotions. The type of restriction which these theorists have in mind would seem to be that blameworthiness and creditworthiness cannot be applied to us on account of what are (in a certain sense) merely 'internal' phenomena, or perhaps, not on account of what is only *self*-regarding. And thus, the argument goes, because such a requirement rules out emotions, we cannot be blame-worthy or creditworthy on account of them. In this section I want to show why such a view ought to be rejected.

There are two versions of this view. One version holds that we can *never* be blameworthy or creditworthy for phenomena such as emo-tions.[13] The other version holds that we *can* be blameworthy or creditworthy for an emotion, but only when it is expressed in blame-worthy or creditworthy *action*.[14] Regarding the latter view, I rejected this 'instrumental' approach as an account of the moral significance of emotions in Chapter 3, where I argued that emotions can be morally significant quite apart from their motivating morally significant action. However, some might agree that emotions can be non-motivationally morally significant, but in regard to morally assessing people for their emotions, they may nevertheless insist on giving an instrumental account of *blameworthiness* and *creditworthiness*.

So let us examine the plausibility of these views about blame-worthiness and creditworthiness.

In arguing against those who hold that we cannot be blameworthy or creditworthy for *having* an emotion which is not expressed in blameworthy or creditworthy action, we can deal with the two versions of this view together. Instead of disputing the premise that emotions are self-regarding or internal phenomena, I want to show that this view of blameworthiness and creditworthiness (in whichever version it is put forward) is mistaken, because it erroneously takes what may sometimes be a factor in the justification of particular blaming and crediting responses to be a condition of blameworthiness and creditworthiness themselves.

My argument in this section runs as follows. I begin by acknowledging that the need to avoid meddlesomeness is an important constraint on the blaming and crediting responses we are justified in having towards people for their emotions. I then argue that where our having blaming or crediting responses towards someone would be meddlesome, this does not affect whether they are in fact blameworthy or creditworthy in that situation. Indeed, when we look at blaming and crediting people for their *actions*, there seems to be a perfectly general distinction between the truth of a person's blameworthiness or creditworthiness, and the justifiedness or otherwise of having blaming or crediting responses towards them. That is, contrary to the suggestion that allowing blameworthiness and creditworthiness for emotions is to legitimise meddlesomeness, it seems that being blameworthy or creditworthy is *not* sufficient for being the justified subject of blaming or crediting responses. Rather, the significance of being blameworthy or creditworthy is that one is thereby *liable* or *entitled* to be the subject of blaming or crediting responses, respectively (where this liability or entitlement is understood in terms of a necessary but not sufficient condition for blaming or crediting responses actually being justified here). Whether one would *then* be the justified subject of blaming or crediting responses, given one's blameworthiness or creditworthiness, is determined partly by reference to other considerations (apart from one's deservedness of blame or credit), such as privacy, charity, and utility. But such considerations do not bear on the *truth* of a person's blameworthiness or creditworthiness for something, and so an appeal to these kinds of considerations is no objection to our being blameworthy and creditworthy for our emotions. Indeed, as we will see, these factors do seem to allow that certain people may sometimes be justified in having various blaming and crediting responses towards us for our emotions.

As noted above, those who believe that blameworthiness and creditworthiness involve a condition which excludes their application to us for phenomena such as emotions (or at least, emotions which are not expressed in blameworthy or creditworthy behaviour) argue for this view because they have a general kind of worry about the claims I make in this chapter. Their worry here is that to allow people to be blameworthy and creditworthy (other than in an instrumental sense) for their emotions is to encourage a righteous and meddlesome over-concern with the affairs of others, which will, as Price puts it, result in 'a perfect orgy of moral indignation and condemnation',[15] and may lead to a quasi-Orwellian scenario of punishing people for the way they feel.

Now, what exactly is the relevance of this worry about meddlesomeness for the claims about emotions which I am making in this chapter? Certainly, it would *often* be improper for us to have blaming and crediting responses towards other people for their emotions – particularly where these blaming and crediting responses consist in acts, such as punishing and reproaching or rewarding and praising, and especially where there is no special relation between us and those people. To punish or reproach people for having morally wrong emotions would seem in many cases to be an unjustifiable interference with their affairs since, as Mill pointed out, it seems wrong to do people harm for things they do or have which do not significantly affect others.[16] So too, while rewarding and praising others for their morally right emotions seems somewhat less objectionable, it may still sometimes be a meddlesome intrusion into what is none of our business.

Indeed, even in situations where reproaching another person for their morally wrong emotional response would not be an intrusive interference, it may still be improper for other reasons. Thus, although it may not be meddlesome for a woman to reproach her husband for his excessive anger at losing a game of chess to his son, nevertheless, her reproach may be unjustified here if her husband is immediately repentant about his anger and is struggling to overcome it.

Now, *if* blaming and crediting are always conceived of as *actions* that we perform, such as punishing and rewarding, there might be good reason to be concerned that allowing blame and credit for emotions may result in objectionable and intrusive practices. But as many philosophers have pointed out, blaming and crediting need not be actions but may sometimes involve just having certain attitudes and/or emotions, such as disapproval and indignation or approval and admiration, about the person we are blaming or crediting.[17]

Nevertheless, even having crediting and blaming *attitudes* and *emotions* towards others for their right and wrong emotions may be objectionable, in so far as it shows an improper over-concern with others' lives. For example, it may be highly inappropriate for me to feel outraged with my boss for his apparent deep-seated resentment towards his wife which he has culpably failed to overcome. Indeed, it may be no business of mine even to *inquire* about or concern myself with his blameworthiness here (and it may equally be none of my business to inquire or be concerned with whether he has any *creditworthy* emotions towards his wife).

We can see from this, then, that in having appropriate blaming and crediting responses, we must acknowledge considerations of privacy, charity, and utility.[18] But, importantly for my argument, where such considerations dictate that having blaming or crediting responses towards a certain person would be improper, this does not, I think, show that this person is not *blameworthy* or *creditworthy* here. For given a person's blameworthiness or creditworthiness, it is in my view always a *further* question whether blaming or crediting responses towards them would be justified or unjustified.

Now, those who dispute this claim hold that being blameworthy or creditworthy is *sufficient* for being the justified subject of blaming or crediting responses,[19] and it is this view which seems to underlie the objection that it is improper for people to be blameworthy and creditworthy for their emotions. On this view, in cases where blaming or crediting responses towards a certain person are unjustified for some reason (such as when having such responses would contravene the constraints of privacy, charity, and/or utility, as most would agree may often be the case where our emotions are concerned), it would follow that this person could not be blameworthy or creditworthy here. But this view is false. It can be shown that blameworthiness and creditworthiness (while indeed necessary) are *not* sufficient for justified blaming and crediting responses, and so where blaming or crediting responses towards someone are unjustified (at least on grounds of privacy, charity, and/or utility), this does not automatically rule out their blameworthiness or creditworthiness here.

Since the claim that allowing blameworthiness and creditworthiness for emotions will lead to meddlesomeness and oppressive practices seems to have more force in the context of blameworthiness than of creditworthiness, in what follows my argument is cast largely in terms of blameworthiness and blaming responses.[20] But a parallel argument can be made in regard to creditworthiness and crediting responses, and I shall indicate this where appropriate.

Let us begin by noting a point made by Mill. As mentioned earlier, some who object to our being blameworthy for our emotions may do so because they agree with Mill that we must not be punished for our self-regarding faults, and, they argue, our morally wrong emotions are examples of self-regarding faults. However, while Mill certainly held that self-regarding faults are not *punishable*, he did seem to allow that we can still be *blameworthy* for faulty emotional dispositions. Mill believed that because they may lead us to improperly harm others, 'malice . . ., envy . . ., irascibility on insufficient cause, and resentment disproportioned to the provocation . . . are moral vices', and may themselves be 'fit subjects of disapprobation which may rise to abhorrence'.[21] But Mill also thought that even those faulty emotional dispositions which he considered were unlikely to lead us to unduly harm others, such as overweening pride and excessive fear, may make us 'properly a subject of distaste, or, in extreme cases, even of contempt'.[22] To be sure, Mill did not regard these latter faults as *morally* blameworthy, but the important point for us is not Mill's substantive account of morality, but rather his recognition of the distinction between the truth of a person's blameworthiness, and the justifiedness or otherwise of punitive responses towards them. As Mill saw, the non-punishability of a person's fault does not entail that they cannot be blameworthy for it, and so while it may well be improper to *punish* people for their faulty emotions, this does not show that they cannot be *blameworthy* for these emotions.

Now, when we turn to our blameworthiness for our *actions*, it seems to be a perfectly general point that the truth of our blameworthiness for some action, while necessary, is *not* sufficient for our being the justified subject of blaming responses on account of it. In other words, given that we are blameworthy for a certain action, whether we would then be the justified subject of blaming responses in regard to it is always a further question. This can be seen most clearly in cases of blaming responses which themselves are overt acts directed at the blameworthy person. For example, if a person who is blameworthy for some action is already contrite and self-punitive in regard to it, others may not be justified in reproaching or otherwise punishing them for their transgression.[23]

There are various reasons why blaming acts towards a blameworthy person may be unjustified in these kinds of situations. One of the important aims of many blaming responses seems to be that of leading the wrongdoer to repent and mend their ways, and this might not be furthered by reproaching a person who is already contrite about their transgression. Indeed, such action may be counterproductive with regard to this aim. But considerations of utility are not the only factors to be taken into account in determining whether blaming responses towards a blameworthy person are justified. For another important aim to be acknowledged in the justification of blaming responses is that of retribution – that is, seeing that the offender gets their due. Thus in some cases where a person is blameworthy, especially if their offence is serious, the fact that they admit they acted wrongly and already show signs of contrition and self-reproach may well not render unjustified certain blaming acts, such as reproach, which others may direct at them (particularly if these others are somehow involved in the situation).[24] (Considerations of utility also play a role in determining the appropriateness of crediting acts towards creditworthy persons. Thus, a creditworthy person who already has a highly self-congratulatory attitude may not need to be encouraged by praise from others to continue to do the kind of thing which they are creditworthy for, but if their good action is very worthy, it may still be appropriate to give them the praise they deserve.)

Other considerations which need to be taken into account in justifications of blaming and crediting responses are charity and privacy. Sometimes when the offence which a person is blameworthy for is relatively minor, it would be uncharitable to reproach them for it and they ought perhaps to be forgiven instead, even if considerations of utility and desert both indicate otherwise. This seems particularly true where the offended party is, say, a friend or spouse. There seem in any case to be special permissions regarding blaming and crediting responses for such persons as spouses, parents, close friends, those who may have a stake in the matter, and of course, the blameworthy or creditworthy individual themselves.[25] Outside one of these relations, it may be none of our business to reproach or praise a person for their blameworthy or creditworthy action, respectively, even if they deserve to be reproached or praised, and even if such action on our part would have a high degree of utility with regard to their future behaviour. For example, if I deliberately insult you, I may perhaps be justifiably reproached only by you and your close friends. Reproach from any others here would indeed seem to be a meddlesome and intrusive interference with our affairs.

Now I cannot undertake a comprehensive discussion of the considerations relevant to determining whether and what kinds of blaming and crediting responses are justifiably directed at a blame-worthy or creditworthy person in any given case. What is important for us is that once a person's blameworthiness or creditworthiness for something has been established, they are not necessarily thereby the justified subject of blaming or crediting responses. For considerations of utility, charity, and privacy may show that blaming or crediting responses would be unjustified, although importantly, where such responses are unjustified *for these reasons*, this does not seem to affect whether the person concerned is blameworthy or creditworthy for what they have done. For instance, if a friend of mine makes a tactless remark, which it is then obvious to me that he regrets (even though he perhaps does not actually apologise), he might not be justifiably subjected to blaming acts from me or anyone else here, but he would nevertheless still seem to be *blameworthy* for his tactless comment.

However, while it might be agreed that blameworthiness and creditworthiness may not be sufficient for justified blaming or credit-ing *acts* of any kind, such as reproach or praise, it might be argued that blameworthiness and creditworthiness are always sufficient for at least some kinds of *private* blaming and crediting responses to be justified. That is, being blameworthy or creditworthy might be thought always sufficient for the justifiedness of being the subject of some kinds of blaming or crediting attitudes and emotions, such as disapproval and indignation, or approval and admiration.[26]

But there seem to be certain cases where a person is blameworthy, and yet *no* blaming responses towards them would be justified.[27] That is, sometimes neither blaming acts nor blaming attitudes or emotions would be justifiably directed at a person who is blameworthy. For instance, if a person of whom people rightly have a high opinion commits a minor offence, they would seem to be blameworthy for this, but in view of their deserved standing in the community and the triviality of their offence, blaming attitudes or emotions (such as disapproval and indignation) towards *them* on account of what they did might not be justified from anyone (although of course, we may still disapprove of their offence itself). An even better case might be one where one's spouse is blameworthy for a slight offence. While one might think poorly of what they did here, one might not be justified in having any blaming attitudes or emotions about *them* on account of their misdeed. Generally speaking, in these and other such cases it may be appropriate to pardon or forgive the blameworthy person for their action, instead of, say, disapproving of or having indignation towards this person because of what they did (although of course, we might still disapprove of their *action*). And in forgiveness here, it seems clear that the person's action would still be regarded as wrong and they would still be *blameworthy* for it, but blaming acts, attitudes, and emotions towards them on account of their action would be unjustified.[28] (Indeed, in cases where it is appropriate to forgive a blameworthy person, we may not be justified in *dwelling* on their offence at all, but we perhaps should instead try to forget about it.)

Thus, it appears that one can be blameworthy for something where no blaming responses towards one would be justified. A parallel point about creditworthiness can be made with a similar example. Imagine people intent on destroying a good habit they have cultivated, who relax their destructive efforts on a certain occasion, and their good habit reasserts itself temporarily, although they are quick to renew their evil project. These people may indeed be creditworthy on that occasion, but they might not be the justified subject of *any* crediting responses, including admiration and self-approval, given their destructive efforts. So I conclude that neither blameworthiness nor creditworthiness alone is sufficient to justify blaming or crediting responses of any kind.

It appears, then, that the relationship between blameworthiness and creditworthiness, on the one hand, and being the justified subject of blaming or crediting responses, on the other, is that being blameworthy or creditworthy makes one only *liable* or *entitled* to be the justified subject of blaming or crediting responses, respectively. For factors such as privacy, charity, and utility may render blaming and crediting responses unjustified without thereby affecting one's blameworthiness or creditworthiness. Given this, the worry that allowing people to be blameworthy and creditworthy for their emotions will lead to oppressive practices and a meddlesome over-concern with others' affairs seems unfounded. For to say that someone is blameworthy or creditworthy for their emotion is to say only that it is a morally wrong or right emotional response which they are responsible for, and that because of this they are thereby liable or entitled to be the subject of blaming or crediting responses from someone on account of their emotion. It is *not* to say, in the case of blameworthiness, that they would be justifiably punished, reproached, nor even privately condemned for their emotion. Likewise, being creditworthy for an emotion is *not* thereby to be the justified subject of rewards, praise, or unexpressed approval on account of it. Indeed, to say that a person is blameworthy or creditworthy for their emotion is not even to say that others have any business to *inquire* about this fact. Just as in cases of action, whether a person who is blameworthy or credit-worthy for an emotion would be the justified subject of any blaming or crediting responses is determined by reference to considerations of privacy, charity, and utility.

Now, as I noted earlier, in many cases it would be improper for us to have blaming and crediting responses towards others for their emotions, particularly in the absence of some special relation between us and them. For in general, the emotional lives of others are simply none of our business. But as we can now see from our study of the role of these kinds of restrictions in the context of action, this point does not bear on the *truth* of our blameworthiness and credit-worthiness for our emotions. Speaking of reproach as a blaming response, Robert Merrihew Adams makes a similar point:

> The rights of privacy and community are such that in general it is likelier to be our business to reproach someone for an action or inaction than for a bad state of mind. But it would be a mistake to infer that the former must be more blameworthy than the latter.[29]

Nevertheless, considerations of privacy, charity, and utility do seem to allow that certain blaming and crediting responses *can* sometimes be appropriately directed at people who are blameworthy or creditworthy for an emotion. For example, a loyal wife may be justified in feeling indignant and disapproving of her husband because of the unreasonable jealousy he has towards her, since she may feel that it indicates an ill-founded lack of trust in her, which he could easily overcome. Indeed, if her husband feels increasingly jealous and simply averts his eyes from the fact of her loyalty, she may be justified in reproaching him for his jealousy. A parallel example involving crediting responses and creditworthiness might be one where a friend who has developed his capacity for altruistic emotions feels deep sympathy and compassion towards a stranger in obvious distress. In this case it might not be inappropriate for me to express to him my approval and commendation of him for his emotional response.

I conclude, then, that since the objection to our being blameworthy and creditworthy for our emotions appeals to considerations which are relevant to the justification of particular blaming and crediting responses, but are *not* relevant to our blameworthiness and credit-worthiness, it therefore provides no grounds for adding a condition of blameworthiness and creditworthiness which excludes their application to us for our emotions. The view which allows that we can be blameworthy and creditworthy for our emotions in an instrumental sense (i.e. when our emotions are expressed in blameworthy or creditworthy action) is, to be sure, an improvement on the view which regards our emotions as wholly outside the domain of blameworthiness and creditworthiness. However, in claiming that being blameworthy and creditworthy for unexpressed emotions is improper, both views are misled by a confusion between the justification of blaming and crediting responses, and the justification of blameworthiness and creditworthiness. It would often be improper for those who have no special relation or involvement with us or the situation at hand to have blaming and crediting responses to us for our emotions, but this is not relevant to whether or not we can in fact be blameworthy and creditworthy for our emotions.

Since no emotion-excluding condition should be added to the standard account of blameworthiness and creditworthiness, and given that this account seems independently plausible, I take it that our ordinary notions of blameworthiness and creditworthiness do actually allow that these assessments can be applied to us in regard to our emotions. So, if we are responsible for having a morally right or wrong emotional response, then it seems that we are in fact creditworthy or blameworthy for it, respectively.

Let us turn our attention now to esteem and disesteem, which are moral assessments that do not require our responsibility for what they are directed at. In this context there is a distinction in justification parallel to that which I have argued for in the case of creditworthiness and blameworthiness. That is, we should distinguish between the justification of estimability and disestimability, on the one hand, and the further question of when and what kinds of 'esteeming and disesteeming responses' are justifiably directed at us.

I shall say more about the conditions involved in being estimable and disestimable in the following section. Here the point is that, as with creditworthiness and blameworthiness, the significance of being estimable or disestimable for something is that one is thereby *entitled* or *liable* to be the subject of esteeming or disesteeming responses on account of it, where this entitlement or liability is understood in terms of being a necessary but not sufficient condition for being the justified subject of esteeming or disesteeming responses. Whether these responses would then actually be justified in any given case is determined by reference to considerations such as privacy, the estimable or disestimable person's attitude to their feature in question, and perhaps their character in general. Thus, in arguing that we may be estimable and disestimable for emotions which we are not responsible for having, I will not thereby be arguing that others would then automatically be justified in having esteeming and disesteeming responses towards us for these emotions. As with any good or bad feature of ours, the justifiedness of others having these responses towards us for our emotions cannot be determined without reference to the above considerations; and in many cases where we are estimable or disestimable for having a particular emotion, considerations of privacy will preclude all but those closely associated with us from having any justified esteeming or disesteeming responses towards us here.

There is a large variety of esteeming and disesteeming responses which people may be entitled or liable to in virtue of being estimable or disestimable. Since esteem and disesteem do not presuppose responsibility, the range of esteeming and disesteeming responses which we can justifiably have towards an estimable or disestimable person will differ from the range of crediting and blaming responses discussed earlier. Thus, thinking well of, approval, admiration, praise, and commendation are esteeming responses which we might legitimately have towards people on account of their good qualities which they are not responsible for having, whereas it may be inappropriate (at least in some cases) to reward or (perhaps) have gratitude towards people simply for their having such qualities. Among the disesteeming responses which we might justifiably have towards people on account of their shortcomings which they are not responsible for having are: thinking poorly of, disapproval, disdain, contempt, lamentation, regret, remorse, shame, and embarrassment; however, it would be inappropriate to punish, censure, or (perhaps) have indignation towards people for their having such shortcomings.[30]

3. THE NATURE OF ESTIMABILITY AND DISESTIMABILITY, AND THEIR APPLICATION TO US FOR OUR EMOTIONS

Given that the significance of being estimable or disestimable on account of something is that one is thereby entitled or liable to be the subject of esteeming or disesteeming responses, respectively, in regard to it, I now want to examine the conditions under which we are estimable or disestimable on account of something, and whether we can be estimable or disestimable for our emotions which we are not responsible for having. I will argue that in order to be estimable or disestimable for something, it must be related to us in the same way that is required for having pride and shame in regard to something, and that this relation allows that we can be estimable and disestimable for those emotions of ours which we are not responsible for having.

Clearly, the first condition which is necessary for a person (X) to be estimable or disestimable for something (Z) is that Z must somehow be right or good, or wrong or bad, respectively. As with creditworthiness and blameworthiness, this is a conceptual point, for this is what determines their character as *assessments*, rather than value-neutral descriptions. Further, since I am concerned mainly with estimability and disestimability as *moral* assessments, the rightness and goodness, and badness and wrongness which I shall be concentrating on here is *moral* rightness, goodness, badness, and wrongness, where again these notions are understood aretaically, in terms of what makes for a good or a bad life, as elaborated in Chapter 2.

But is this all that is required? It seems also that Z must be 'associated with' X in some way, and that the manner in which Z is associated with X needs to be specified, in order for X to be estimable or disestimable on account of Z. For a person would not be estimable merely on account of, say, certain kinds of good fortune befalling them, such as winning a lottery in which a friend has secretly bought them a ticket, and likewise, someone would not be disestimable just because, say, through no fault of their own, they lack opportunities.[31] (Since we are dealing specifically with those good and bad things associated with a person which they are *not* responsible for, it is important to notice this absence of responsibility in these examples. It is in regard to their *winning the lottery* that the former person would not be estimable, and it is with regard to their *lacking opportunities* that the latter person would not be disestimable. But, of course, this is not to deny that each person might be responsible for what they do in response to what has happened to them here.)

With the moral assessments discussed in the previous sections of this chapter, the requisite relation between us and what we could be assessed for was given by the notion of responsibility. So, for example, a person would be *blameworthy* both for their shortcomings and their limited opportunities, if they were responsible for these. However, since we are looking now at how a person (X) can be morally assessed with regard to what they are *not* responsible for having (Z), we here need some account of the kinds of relations between X and Z which would allow such assessments to be made of X.[32] Indeed, this is particularly important in discussing whether these assessments can be applied to us for those *emotions* of ours which we are not responsible for having. For it might well be argued that these emotions just 'come over' or 'happen to' us, and that therefore we cannot be estimable or disestimable on account of them, as this would be like being estimable for winning a lottery in which a friend has secretly entered us, or being disestimable for the limited opportunities that befall us, which as I noted above would be illegitimate.

I want to argue that the manner in which something must be associated with a person before they can be estimable or disestimable on account of it is that it must be a *feature of the person*, rather than a *feature of the situation*. This is a somewhat difficult distinction to explicate, but I suggest that our understanding of it here may be aided by looking at a conceptual requirement involved in the emotions of pride and shame.[33]

As Hume and others point out, pride and shame are directed at something which is viewed by the subject as good or right, or bad or wrong, respectively, and both emotions require that the objects at which they are directed are 'related to the self' in some way.[34] Apart from the question of how the goodness or badness of what we are proud or ashamed of is properly determined, the important point for us is that the relation between a person (X) and something (Z) which is required in order for them to have pride or shame in regard to it seems to be of a similar nature to the relation between X and Z which is necessary for X to be estimable or disestimable on account of Z. Therefore, we can gain some idea of the relation between X and Z which is required for estimability and disestimability by looking at the corresponding relation which is involved in pride and shame.

But what is the nature of this relation between X and Z which is required in order for X to feel pride or shame about Z? Clearly, the relation involved here is *not* that X must be responsible for Z, since, although we are often proud or ashamed of what we are responsible for, we can also quite legitimately be proud and ashamed of certain things which we may not at all be responsible for, such as the fine bone structure of our face, or our clumsiness.

The precise nature of the relation between X and Z which is required for X's being proud or ashamed of Z is difficult to specify. It is at least clear that we may legitimately have pride or shame in regard to our personal qualities, or in regard to various possessions which we may have or lack. For example, a person can take pride in their beauty, strength, intelligence, and wit, as well as in their house, garden, and clothes, and someone may be ashamed of their ugliness, weakness, obtuseness, and dullness, as well as, say, their poverty. It also seems that a person can be proud/ashamed of such things as their fidelity/disloyalty, fame/obscurity, good/bad heritage, and their nationality. But contrary to what Hume seems to think,[35] of course none of this is to suggest that we can be appropriately proud and ashamed only of our *enduring* features, since, for example, a person who is suddenly blessed with great courage and strength in an emergency may well take pride in this, and a priest who occasionally finds himself assailed by adulterous impulses may well be ashamed of his having them.

Yet while the class of things that we can legitimately have pride or shame in regard to seems multifarious, the sense in which something must be 'related to us' before we can feel pride or shame about it is by no means trivial, for there are many things which may be associated with us, but not yet in the manner required for pride and shame. Thus, as Hume points out, simply *being present at* a sumptuous feast may indeed be an occasion for joy, but the relation between us and this event is not yet close enough for pride, unless we tell some story about how we have contributed to the success of the feast, or about it being an honour for us to be invited (e.g. because the host is an important figure).[36] Likewise, we may regret or lament having parked our car in the spot where it was later crashed into by someone else, but we could not properly be ashamed of this unless it somehow showed a defect on our part (such as that we had left the car parked dangerously or illegally). And pride and shame would be similarly inappropriate for such things as winning a lottery in which a friend has secretly bought one a ticket, or lacking opportunities through no fault of one's own, respectively, for like being present at a feast or having one's car crashed into, these are not features of the person but rather are only features of their situation.

The point which I am making, then, is that in order to determine whether the relation between a person and something is close enough for them to be estimable or disestimable in regard to it (given that it is also good, right, bad, or wrong), we can look at whether the relation is of the kind required for their being proud or ashamed of it. If there is this relation between the person and the object, then we may call it a 'feature of the person'; otherwise it will be a 'feature of the situation'. Thus, we may be estimable for our beauty, intelligence, wit, and for our sudden courage and strength in an emergency, as well as for such things as our house and other possessions, while we may be disestimable for our ugliness, obtuseness, dullness, and for the immoral impulses which may on occasion beset us, as well as perhaps sometimes for our poverty. (Of course, being estimable or disestimable for some of these things would not be *moral* estimability or disestimability, given their lack of moral significance.) But we may not be estimable or disestimable for such things as winning a lottery which we have been unknowingly entered in, or non-culpably lacking opportunities, for these are related to us only as features of our situation, and cannot be features of *us*.

To be sure, this is not necessarily to say that whatever we can be proud or ashamed of we can also be estimable or disestimable for, since we may feel pride and shame about things which *we* regard as good or bad, but which are not *in fact* good or bad. Perhaps at most it can be said that, speaking of pride and shame which is directed at what is indeed *morally* good, right, bad, or wrong, whatever we are or would be justified in having such pride or shame about, we can also be (morally) estimable or disestimable in regard to. But I do not want to be taken as suggesting that the reverse is the case – i.e. that whatever we may be estimable or disestimable for, we could be proud or ashamed of. For while there may often be this kind of overlap, there might be various reasons why we in some cases could not have pride or shame about what we are estimable or disestimable for. Perhaps we can no longer see a certain asset or defect of ours as particularly good or bad, right or wrong; or maybe we do see this, but without being pleased or pained by it; or perhaps we view our asset or defect with pleasure or pain, but for various reasons we do not or cannot think well or poorly of *ourselves* on account of it.[37] But such issues need not concern us here. For all I have been suggesting is that pride and shame on the one hand, and estimability and disestimability on the other, are similar in the *relation* which they require between the subject of the emotion or assessment, and the object upon which they are predicated, and that therefore the nature of this link which is necessary for estimability and disestimability can be illuminated by looking at the corresponding link which is necessary in the case of pride and shame.

Regarding those emotions of ours which we are not responsible for having, perhaps enough has been said to show that they are related to us in the sense of being features of *us* rather than features of our situation. And moreover, the constituent cognitions, desires, and affects involved in emotions seem to be features of us in the requisite sense. For unlike such things as winning a lottery in which a friend has secretly entered us or non-culpably lacking opportunities, we can be proud or ashamed of our emotions and their constitutive elements, despite our sometimes lacking responsibility for them, and quite apart from whether a particular emotion which we have is 'in character' for us. For example, having a natural capacity for sympathy would seem to be related to us in such a way that we could be proud of this; and being unexpectedly overcome by strong malicious feelings on a certain occasion may well be grounds for shame. It therefore seems that we can be *estimable* on account of our good or right emotional responses, and *disestimable* in regard to our bad or wrong emotional responses, even where we are not responsible for having them, since our emotions do seem to be features of us in the sense explained. As Robert Merrihew Adams puts it,

> Our desires and emotions . . . are responses of ours, and affect the moral significance of our lives, not only by influencing our voluntary actions, but also just by being what they are, and by manifesting themselves involuntarily. Who we are morally depends on a complex and incompletely integrated fabric that includes desires and feelings as well as deliberations and choices.[38]

Indeed, of the things which may be associated with us that we are not responsible for, our *emotions* (and their constitutive elements) seem to be features of us in a deeper sense than many other things in this class, including our *actions* that we are not responsible for. It is much more difficult to sincerely 'disown' an emotion, having shown that we are not responsible for having it, than it is to repudiate an action which we are excused from responsibility for performing. For as I argued in Chapter 2, our conceptions of ourselves are importantly defined by the emotions and emotional capacities which we have – our emotions express our commitments, or, as we might say, our 'evaluative outlook'. Thus, we are often unsatisfied with a description of another's character which makes no reference to their emotions, for a person's emotional capacities are a significant indication of their nature.

In contrast to this, the actions we perform which we are not responsible for seem to be features of us only in a *derivative* sense, since in order for such an action to be a feature of us (and one might even say, in order for it to qualify as an 'action' – rather than a mere movement – of ours at all), it must in some way proceed from what *are* clearly features of us, such as our beliefs, desires, intentions, or emotions. For example, if a person was (non-culpably) unable to prevent themselves running away from something out of a fear which was itself uncontrollable, their fleeing here may well be a feature of them. But if they could not help running away because they were (non-culpably) unable to prevent themselves being propelled by someone else, perhaps their running away here would not be correctly characterised as a feature of *them* (nor, indeed, would it be correctly construed as an 'action' of theirs at all). *A fortiori*, we may well be *estimable* or *disestimable* for many of the actions we perform which we are not responsible for, but it seems that this would only be in virtue of the connections they might have with such features as our beliefs, desires, intentions, and emotions.[39]

In summary then, a person is estimable or disestimable for something if and only if it is good or right, or bad or wrong, respectively, and it is a feature of them. And the significance of being estimable or disestimable for something is that one is thereby entitled or liable to esteeming or disesteeming responses, respectively, on account of it. In the case of emotions which we are not responsible for having, in so far as they are good, right, bad, or wrong, we may indeed be estimable or disestimable on account of them. But this does not mean we would also be estimable or disestimable for such things as winning a lottery which we have secretly been entered in, or non-culpably lacking opportunities, for unlike these kinds of things, our emotions, even when we are not responsible for having them, are still features of *us*.

4. ESTIMABILITY, DISESTIMABILITY, AND THE NOTION OF MORAL ASSESSMENT

At this stage in our discussion of assessments of persons on account of what they are not responsible for having, there is an important objection which must be faced. That is, while it may be agreed that we can be estimable and disestimable for our emotions which we are not responsible for having, some would argue that these assessments are not *moral* assessments, and thus are not relevant to an estimation of a person on account of their morally significant features (or what we might call their 'moral character'). For it may be argued, following Aquinas, that only what is subject to the will can be of moral significance, and so we can be subject to *moral* assessments only on account of what we are responsible for.[40] Thus, given that I am discussing assessments which are applied to us on account of what we are not responsible for having, these assessments (in so far as they focus on what we are not responsible for) cannot be moral assessments.

Indeed, the Thomistic view that morality presupposes responsibility might be used as a major premise in an argument which concludes that emotions themselves have no moral significance, if the claim that we are not responsible for our emotions is taken as a minor premise. As we saw in Chapter 3, this is an argument which is often used by Kantians. However, this argument fails, for we saw in

Chapter 4 that there are various ways in which we can be responsible for our emotions, and so the minor premise in the above argument is false. Aquinas would also reject this argument because of the falsity of its minor premise, since he holds that emotions can be brought under rational control, and so are to this extent morally significant.[41] But the moral significance of our emotions does not depend on establishing that we can be responsible for them in any case, for the view that morality presupposes responsibility, which forms the major premise in the above argument, is also false.

Against Aquinas, I want to argue that what we are not responsible for having can be of moral significance, and so the assessments which are appropriately made of people on account of what they are not responsible for having can be *moral* assessments, and may therefore be relevant to an estimation of a person's moral character. This will show that the moral significance of our emotions is not contingent on our being responsible for them (although, to be sure, whether or not we are responsible for having a particular emotion may affect the *type* of moral assessment which is properly made of us on account of it, as we have already seen in this chapter).

It is worth noting in passing that, in response to the view which allows estimability and disestimability to be applied to people on account of what they are not responsible for but denies that they are *moral* assessments, one argument which might be deployed here takes issue with this view directly. That is, it could reasonably be argued that to regard a certain assessment as 'moral' is to imply that it has a distinctive kind of importance, such that, when applied to a person (X) in respect of a particular feature of them (Z), this assessment cannot be overridden by *non-moral* assessments of X for Z, but only by other *moral* assessments of X for Z. Then one could attempt to show that estimability and disestimability actually function like moral rather than non-moral assessments in this regard, entering into important and complex relationships with (other) moral assessments in a manner that would be almost impossible to discern were estimability and disestimability only non-moral assessments.[42] Now there are extremely complicated and difficult issues concerning the notion of overridingness, and the focusing of such assessments, which would need to be gone into here.[43] But my case against the view that estimability and disestimability for our features which we are not responsible for are not moral assessments does not rest on this kind of argument.

Let me try a different line of argument. Since the claim that estimability and disestimability, when applied to persons on account of what they are not responsible for having, are not moral assessments is supported by the view that morality presupposes responsibility, what I want to do now is argue against the latter view, thereby undermining the basis of the former claim. Quite apart from the substantive conception of morality which one holds, it seems counterintuitive to argue, as Aquinas does, that a necessary condition of the moral significance of something we have is that we are responsible for having it. We saw earlier that it is characteristic of Kantians to argue for this practical view of morality. Suppose that the Kantian idea of duty as the prime moral motive were correct. Now, if a person were pathologically incapable of acting from a certain duty, such as the duty to be truthful,[44] surely this would be a morally significant feature of their character, independently of whether or not they are responsible for having this inability.[45]

What I am suggesting here is that whether or not the assessments which are made of a person on account of their features are regarded as *moral* assessments, and so become relevant to an estimation of their moral character, surely depends not so much (if at all) on the *kinds* of assessments themselves, but on whether what they are being assessed for (e.g. an emotion, action, or character-trait) is morally significant.[46] Even those who conceive of morality purely in terms of the practical, must concede that whether or not an assessment is regarded as moral is at least partly determined by the significance of what the assessment is directed at. For just as creditworthiness and blameworthiness (which are taken by those who view morality as wholly practical to be paradigmatic of moral assessments) may be directed at a person for their non-moral features (such as their athletic ability), so too estimability and disestimability may be directed at them for their moral features or their non-moral features, as we have seen. And in deciding whether these assessments are moral or non-moral, in each of the above cases we must take into account whether or not they are directed at the person in regard to their moral features. Indeed, given that we can be *responsible* for having various *non-moral* features (such as athletic ability) as well as for our moral features, one must in any case have some way of distinguishing between moral and non-moral assessments of people which is independent of the question of their responsibility for the feature which they are being assessed for. And on the view which I am putting forward, it is the moral significance or otherwise of the person's feature itself which is central here.

Against those who hold that morality presupposes responsibility and who therefore deny that estimability and disestimability for our features which we are not responsible for having can be moral assessments, I want to show that we need not establish that a person is responsible for something they have before we can properly say that it is morally significant. Thus, for example, as Lawrence Blum argues, it may be no fault of his own that a man sincerely holds racist values, yet surely his holding such values is no less relevant to an estimate of his moral character, for they are founded in an entire way of looking at persons of a certain type, and are connected with other important ways in which he regards himself and the world.[47] Robert Merrihew Adams puts it well: 'It matters morally what we are for and what we are against, even if we do not have the power to do much for it or against it, and even if it was not by trying that we came to be for it or against it.'[48]

Now one might agree that estimability and disestimability are *moral* assessments, but object that these are merely *impersonal* moral assessments of what has value and disvalue in the world, so that in disesteeming a racist person, we are just saying that this person's racism is a morally bad thing for the world. However, I am not saying simply that it is a 'bad thing for the world' that this racist person exists or at least that he holds such values, in the sense that the occurrence of floods and earthquakes are bad features of the world. While this person's racism is indeed a bad thing for the world, what I am saying is that this person's racist values reflect badly on *him*, such that they make him, to this extent, a morally bad person.[49] They are integral to what he is and they are related to him in such a way that he could (indeed should) be ashamed of his having them. The point which I want to emphasise here then is that it seems counterintuitive to say that, on discovering that a person is not responsible for his holding racist values, they are no longer morally significant, and so no longer relevant to an estimate of his moral character, and that therefore the assessments which may be directed towards him on account of his racist values are not moral assessments. This discovery would alter only the *kind* of moral assessments which would be properly made of him on account of his racist values – that is, instead of being blame-worthy, he would now be disestimable here.

It cannot be objected that the above claims presuppose a certain substantive conception of morality, which might well not be accepted. For in arguing that the range of what may be morally significant includes what we are not responsible for having, I am not here arguing for a particular account of what it is for something to have moral significance. Rather, I am making the formal point that, in determining which of a person's features (whether we are speaking of racist values, altruistic emotions, or an inability to act from a certain duty) are morally significant, and so whether the assessments which are made of them on account of those features are *moral* assessments, it is counterintuitive to hold that we first need to establish that they are responsible for having them. In order to decide this question of moral significance, a condition other than responsibility is needed: that is, we need refer only to our substantive account of morality. So, in urging those who make the objection which we have been discussing in the foregoing paragraphs to accept that estimability and disestimability can be moral assessments, I am not here asking them to reject their substantive conception of morality.

However, given that moral significance is not determined by responsibility, and that when assessments such as estimability and disestimability are regarded as moral assessments is decided according to the substantive account one gives of the moral significance of what these assessments are directed at us for, we might now look to how this moral significance is to be determined. Concerning this point, in Chapter 2 I defended an account of morality based on the notion of a good life, understood in aretaic terms, and I argued there that since emotions are importantly connected with many great goods, such as relationships of love and friendship, a sense of self-worth, and insight and understanding, emotions are among the things which contribute to a good life, and therefore have deep moral significance. Indeed, I argued that the moral significance of emotions can be adequately captured only in terms of this aretaic conception of morality. Thus, given that our emotions may be morally significant, it seems that when we are estimable or disestimable on account of emotions we may have which we are not responsible for having, these assessments may be regarded as moral assessments, despite our lacking responsibility here. Our emotions are an integral part of our moral character, and so evaluations of persons in the light of their emotions are among the most fundamental moral evaluations of people that can be made.[50] In fact, any overall moral assessment of a person which failed to consider that person's emotional life is likely to be seriously inadequate and potentially misleading.

Indeed, emotions seem to be a subclass of the great variety of personal features for which we may lack responsibility, but which are nevertheless of moral significance, and so may be the appropriate focus of moral assessments. Hume pointed out that

> many of those qualities, which all moralists, especially the
> ancients, comprehend under the title of moral virtues, are equally

involuntary and necessary, with the qualities of the judgement and imagination. Of this nature are constancy, fortitude, magnanimity; and, in short, all the qualities which form the *great* man.[51]

Robert C. Roberts also makes this point:

foresight and psychological insight are characteristics of an ideally moral person, yet it seems wrong to call them determinations of the will. And gentleness, politeness, and friendliness, in some people at least, are unwilled and nonwilling styles of behavioral demeanor. So probably not all morally relevant traits are matters of the will.[52]

Thus, since people do have morally significant features which they are not responsible for having, morality does not presuppose responsibility. And so, given the moral importance of such features, it seems that we may be estimable and disestimable on account of them when they are outside the limits of our responsibility, and these assessments may be regarded as moral assessments. For when we esteem or disesteem a person for their morally good or bad features, we are saying such things as that they are, to this extent, living a good or a bad life, or that they are good or bad company, or that they are worthy of emulation or contempt, respectively. And it seems clear that we can say such things of a person on account of their having a certain morally good or bad feature, without presupposing that they are responsible for having it. Thus, since morality does not require responsibility, the moral significance of our emotions does not depend on establishing our responsibility for them, and so our emotions can be morally significant beyond the extent to which we may be responsible for having them.

Lawrence Blum, who endorses the foregoing kind of argument, takes this as implying that, from the point of view of demonstrating both the moral significance of our emotions and the types of assessments which are justifiably made of us on account of our emotions, it is unnecessary to show that we can be responsible for our emotions.[53] But the fact that morality does not presuppose responsibility should not be taken as implying that it is unnecessary or unimportant to provide an account of how we can be responsible for our emotions. For, as I have suggested in this chapter, whether or not a person is responsible for their manifestation of emotion is important for determining the *kind* of assessment that is appropriately made of them on account of their emotion here. Thus, in the absence of an account of our responsibility for our emotions, it might seem that estimability and disestimability are the only moral assessments it is proper to make of persons in regard to their emotions. But such an impression would be mistaken, for I argued in Chapter 4 that there are various ways in which we can be responsible for our emotions, and so there are other kinds of moral assessments, such as blameworthiness and creditworthiness, which are also appropriately made of persons on account of their emotions, as we have seen in this chapter. In any case, since the view that morality does not require responsibility might still be rejected, and because I believe that we can in fact be responsible for our emotions, contrary to Blum, I think it is important that an account of our responsibility for our emotions is given in a detailed discussion of morality and the emotions.

Conclusion

In this book we have seen that morality is concerned not only with our actions, but in many important ways with our *emotions*. In arguing for this I have thereby attempted to substantiate Aristotle's view that human flourishing requires having appropriate emotions as well as performing good actions, and I have demonstrated how the emotions we have may reflect on us morally.

Contrary to the general denigration and neglect of emotions by Kant and various contemporary ethicists, we have seen that emotions are integral to our achieving such fundamental goods as insight and understanding, strength of will, relationships of love and friendship, and a sense of self-worth. Indeed, I argued that the life of a person who fails to attain these goods through lacking appropriate emotions may well be morally deficient.

Those who accord little moral significance to emotions have often based their views on inadequate accounts of the nature of emotion. A plausible theory of what emotions are therefore seems to be an important prerequisite to reaching a proper understanding of the moral significance of emotions. So, I began by arguing on independent grounds that emotions are complexes of cognition, desire, and affectivity, and I subsequently tried to show how this account enables us to better appreciate the fundamental role of emotions in our moral lives.

Now, in arguing for these views, I have not thereby been endorsing a form of sentimentality or emotional self-indulgence as moral ideals. Indeed, I have acknowledged that various emotions may in certain circumstances be morally bad or wrong, and may reflect badly on us. Generally I have been advocating that we ought to, as Aristotle said, have the right emotions towards the proper objects and to an appropriate degree. Thus, emotional excesses may be morally bad, both in themselves and in the actions which they lead us to perform, just as may emotional deficiencies.

Further, I have tried to show how various emotions, such as sympathy and compassion, may be morally good motives to action, and in arguing for this, I dealt directly with some influential Kantian arguments for duty and against emotion as moral motivation. Using the criteria which Kantians themselves insist must be satisfied by morally worthy motives, we saw that emotions such as sympathy and compassion have as much claim to be moral motives as does duty.

We also considered the practical bearing of my analysis of the moral significance of emotions, by looking at the types of control which we can gain over our emotions, in comparison with the control which we can have over our everyday actions. Here we saw that some important conditions for responsibility in the case of action, such as avoidability and foresight, also allow that we can often be responsible for our emotions. Moreover, I argued that we can be responsible for our emotions not only by gaining various kinds of control over our emotional *episodes*, but also in the deeper sense that we can develop our emotional capacities in ways which lead to our having an enduring and appropriate type of sensitivity as a feature of character.

Turning to how our emotions reflect on us morally, I divided moral assessments of us in regard to our emotions into creditworthiness and blameworthiness, which require that we are responsible for the particular emotion we are being assessed for; and esteem and disesteem, which do not require our responsibility here. I argued that if we distinguish between being *worthy of* these assessments, and being the justified subject of various *responses* which embody these assessments, then it is not meddlesome to allow these assessments to be directed at people for the emotions which they have.

In an important sense, then, our emotions seem to be related to us in a similar manner as are our children – we can sometimes exercise control over them, and they may reflect both credit and blame on us. But at other times they seem to have an uncontrollable life of their own. Nevertheless, we must not abrogate our underlying responsibility for them, because they are both so important in our lives, and in both cases they need to be trained and educated in order to flourish and reach maturity.

Notes

INTRODUCTION

1 See Aristotle, *Nicomachean Ethics*, Book II, Chapter 6, 1106b15–29.

2 Indeed, the prevalence of Kantian ethics might be seen as contributing to ethicists' neglect of the emotions, because of the inherent antagonism in Kantianism towards emotions, and also for a less direct reason. That is, it may be that, as Lawrence Blum has argued, Kant viewed emotions as morally unimportant because he assumed (along with Hegel) that the emotional life is characteristically the life of women, while the rational, dutiful life is properly that of men, and in advocating the subordination of emotions to reason, Kant was expressing (as was Hegel) the superiority of a patriarchal organisation of society. (See L.A. Blum, 'Kant's and Hegel's Moral Rationalism: A Feminist Perspective', *Canadian Journal of Philosophy*, 1982, vol. 12, no. 2.) Thus, it may be no accident that the recent resurgence of interest among moral philosophers in the emotions has occurred at a time when traditional male/female oppositions are being rejected. On the connection between moral rationalism and masculinity, see G. Lloyd, *The 'Man' of Reason: Male and Female in Western Philosophy*, London, Methuen, 1984.

1 THE NATURE OF EMOTION

1 See Aristotle, *De Anima*, 403a2–b4; *Rhetoric*, 1378a20–1388b30 (on Aristotle's account of the nature of emotion, see M.F. Burnyeat, 'Aristotle on Learning to be Good', in A.O. Rorty (ed.), *Essays on Aristotle's Ethics*, Berkeley, University of California Press, 1980, e.g. pp. 70–1, 80; W.W. Fortenbaugh, 'Aristotle: Emotion and Moral Virtue', *Arethusa*, 1969, vol. 2, no. 2; W.W. Fortenbaugh, 'Aristotle's Rhetoric on Emotions', *Archiv fur Geschichte der Philosophie*, 1970, band 52, heft 1; W.W. Fortenbaugh, *Aristotle on Emotion*, London, Duckworth, 1975; and L.A. Kosman, 'Being Properly Affected: Virtues and Feelings in Aristotle's Ethics', in Rorty (ed.), *Essays on Aristotle's Ethics*); Aquinas, *Summa Theologiae*, 1a2ae, Q. 22, art. 1–3, 1a2ae, Q. 23, art. 1–4; Spinoza, *Ethics*, Part III, esp. prop. 1vi, and 'General Definition of the Emotions', Part IV, prop. xxxiii. (On Spinoza's account of emotion, see J. Bennett, *A Study of Spinoza's Ethics*, Indianapolis, Hackett Publishing Co., 1984, Chapter 11, 'Affects'.) Contemporary representatives of this view include W.P. Alston, 'Emotion and Feeling', in P. Edwards (ed.), *The Encyclopedia of Philosophy* (Vol. 2), New York, Collier Macmillan, 1967; W.P. Alston, 'Feelings', *Philosophical Review*, 1969, vol. 78, no. 1, esp. pp. 21–2; M.B. Arnold, 'Human Emotion and Action', in T. Mischel (ed.), *Human Action:*

Conceptual and Empirical Issues, New York, Academic Press, 1969; A. Ben-Zeev, 'The Nature of Emotions', *Philosophical Studies*, 1987, vol. 52, no. 3; L.A. Blum, 'Compassion', in A.O. Rorty (ed.), *Explaining Emotions*, Berkeley, University of California Press, 1980; L.A. Blum, *Friendship, Altruism and Morality*, London, Routledge & Kegan Paul, 1980, e.g. pp. 12–15; D.M. Farrell, 'Jealousy', *Philosophical Review*, 1980, vol. 89, no. 4; O.H. Green, 'Emotions and Belief', in *American Philosophical Quarterly, Monograph No. 6: Studies in the Philosophy of Mind*, Oxford, Blackwell, 1972; O.H. Green, 'Wittgenstein and the Possibility of a Philosophical Theory of Emotion', *Metaphilosophy*, 1979, vol. 10, nos 3 and 4; W. Lyons, 'Physiological Changes and the Emotions', *Canadian Journal of Philosophy*, 1974, vol. 3, no. 4; W. Lyons, *Emotion*, Cambridge, Cambridge University Press, 1980, esp. pp. 53–98 (here Lyons argues that the complex of cognition, desire, and affectivity is necessary only for *some* emotions, such as love and fear); J.A. Shaffer, 'An Assessment of Emotion', *American Philosophical Quarterly*, 1983, vol. 20, no. 2; M. Stocker, 'Psychic Feelings: Their Importance and Irreducibility', *Australasian Journal of Philosophy*, 1983, vol. 61, no. 1; and M. Stocker, 'Affectivity and Self-concern: The Assumed Psychology in Aristotle's Ethics', *Pacific Philosophical Quarterly*, 1983, vol. 64, no. 3.

2 Thus, feeling in this sense is to some extent disanalogous to perceiving, for it seems that we can be *perceiving* a certain object, such as the farmhouse on the hill ahead, in the sense that it registers in our 'perceptual field', without necessarily attending to or *noticing* our perception of it – we may notice just what a beautiful landscape it is.

3 See Alston, 'Feelings', p. 9; B. Aune, 'Feelings, Moods, and Introspection', *Mind*, 1963, vol. 72, no. 286, p. 200; K. Duncker, 'On Pleasure, Emotion, and Striving', *Philosophy and Phenomenological Research*, 1940, vol. 1, no. 4, pp. 403–4; A. Kenny, *Action, Emotion and Will*, London, Routledge & Kegan Paul, 1963, pp. 34–5, 56, 67–8; M. Perkins, 'Emotion and Feeling', *Philosophical Review*, 1966, vol. 75, no. 2, pp. 151, 154; and A.O. Rorty, 'Explaining Emotions', in Rorty (ed.), *Explaining Emotions*, p. 118.

4 These psychic feelings and their importance for emotions have been recognised since the ancient Greeks. For example, both Plato and Aristotle discussed notions of 'mental' pleasure and pain. See Plato, *Philebus*, 47e1–48a9; *Republic*, 439e1–441b1; Aristotle, *Nicomachean Ethics*, Book III, Chapter 10, 1117b28–36. Descartes and Hume also distinguished between bodily sensations and non-bodily emotional feelings. See Descartes, *The Passions of the Soul*, Part I, articles 22, 24–30; David Hume, *A Treatise of Human Nature* (ed. L.A. Selby-Bigge), Book I, Part iv, sec. 2 (pp. 195–6), Book II, Part i, sec. 1 (pp. 275–7). For contemporary accounts, see John Dewey, 'The Theory of Emotion', in C. Calhoun and R.C. Solomon (eds), *What is an Emotion?* New York, Oxford University Press, 1984, e.g. p. 170; Duncker, op. cit., esp. pp. 401–8, 425–6; R. Lawrie, 'Passion', *Philosophy and Phenomenological Research*, 1980, vol. 41, no. 1; G.D. Marshall, 'On Being Affected', *Mind*, 1968, vol. 77, no. 306; Max Scheler, *Formalism in Ethics and Non-Formal Ethics of Values* (trans. M.S. Frings and R.L. Funk), Evanston, Northwestern University Press, 1973, pp. 335–49; Stocker, 'Psychic Feelings', and Stocker, 'Affectivity and Self-Concern'. Psychic feelings are also acknowledged by E.L. Beardsley, 'Moral Disapproval and Moral Indignation', *Philosophy and Phenomenological Research*, 1970, vol. 31, no. 2, pp. 167–8; A.C. Ewing, 'The Justification of Emotions', *Proceedings of the Aristotelian Society*, 1957, suppl. vol. 31, p. 70; and Farrell, op. cit., pp. 538–43.

5 See Alston, 'Emotion and Feeling', pp. 482–3; Alston, 'Feelings', pp. 6n7, 12–18; P.S. Ardal, *Passion and Value in Hume's Treatise*, Edinburgh, Edinburgh University Press, 1966, pp. 22–4; Aune, op. cit., pp. 197–9; E. Bedford, 'Emotions', in V.C. Chappell (ed.), *The Philosophy of Mind*, Englewood Cliffs, Prentice-Hall, 1962, pp. 112–14; Calhoun and Solomon (eds), *What is an Emotion?* pp. 10, 14–15; Lawrie, op. cit., esp. p. 113; Lyons, *Emotion*, pp. 6, 128; Lyons,

'Physiological Changes and the Emotions', p. 616; J. Marks, 'A Theory of Emotion', *Philosophical Studies*, 1982, vol. 42, no. 2, p. 228; A.I. Melden, 'The Conceptual Dimension of Emotions', in Mischel (ed.), *Human Action: Conceptual and Empirical Issues*, p. 219; J. Neu, *Emotion, Thought and Therapy*, London, Routledge & Kegan Paul, 1977, pp. 49, 57–9, 99–100; G. Rey, 'Functionalism and the Emotions', in Rorty (ed.), *Explaining Emotions*, pp. 178, 187; J. Robinson, 'Emotion, Judgment, and Desire', *Journal of Philosophy*, 1983, vol. 80, no. 11, p. 740; Scheler, op. cit., p. 257n; R.C. Solomon, *The Passions*, Garden City, Doubleday Anchor, 1976, pp. 161–3, 179; Solomon, 'Emotions and Choice', in Rorty (ed.), *Explaining Emotions*, p. 254; J. Tietz, 'Emotional Objects and Criteria', *Canadian Journal of Philosophy*, 1973, vol. 3, no. 2, pp. 215–16.

6 Some philosophers call such long-term emotions 'dispositional' emotions, but I find this term misleading here, and so will avoid using it. This term implies that when we speak of a person having an emotion over a period of time, what we really mean is that this person is disposed to have this particular emotion on certain occasions. But for reasons given shortly, I believe this latter notion is quite different from what is meant by our having an emotion for a certain period of our lives.

7 Another, although perhaps more controversial, way of arguing for this point is by adverting to the possibility of our having *unconscious* emotions. That is, as psychoanalysis has shown, it seems that we may sometimes be angry with our superiors, jealous of our fathers, and anxious because of some forthcoming event which sets off an associative chain linking up with an earlier threatening situation, but yet not *feel* angry, jealous, or anxious at that time, because the emotion is suppressed from consciousness. I would not deny that emotions and affects can be unconscious, but I shall not pursue this here. On unconscious emotions and affects, see Calhoun and Solomon (eds), *What is an Emotion?* pp. 38, 184; S. Freud, 'The Unconscious', in Calhoun and Solomon (eds), *What is an Emotion?* Lyons, *Emotion*, pp. 29–30, 168; Neu, op. cit., p. 141; Solomon, *The Passions*, pp. 163–4; and L. Tov-Ruach, 'Jealousy, Attention, and Loss', in Rorty (ed.), *Explaining Emotions*, esp. pp. 469–70.

8 There are several philosophers who, having recognised that the above kinds of examples show we can have emotions without feeling (in the sense of *noticing*) them, want to retain an affective dimension in emotion by speaking of 'unfelt feelings'. See, for example, S.R. Leighton, 'Unfelt Feelings in Pain and Emotion', *Southern Journal of Philosophy*, 1986, vol. 24, no. 1; and D. Palmer, 'Unfelt Pains', *American Philosophical Quarterly*, 1975, vol. 12, no. 4. However, because I want to reserve the term 'feeling' for cases of *noticing*, and I would rather not use any seemingly contradictory locution as 'unfelt feelings', I speak instead in terms of emotional 'affects' (which I take to be much the same as what is meant by those who talk of 'unfelt feelings').

9 For example, Aristotle, *De Anima* (trans. J.A. Smith), 403a2–b4, 403b17–19 (e.g. 403a16–18: 'all the affections of soul involve a body – passion, gentleness, fear, pity, courage, joy, loving, and hating; in all these there is a concurrent affection of the body'); Alston, 'Emotion and Feeling', pp. 482, 486; Aquinas, *Summa Theologiae, Vol. 19, The Emotions* (trans. E. D'Arcy), 1a2ae, Q. 22, arts 2 and 3 (e.g. 1a2ae, Q. 22, art. 3: 'Emotion always involves some physiological modification'); Arnold, op. cit., pp. 172, 184–5; P.J. Koch, 'Bodily Feelings in Emotion', *Dialogue*, 1987, vol. 26, no. 1; Lyons, 'Physiological Changes and the Emotions', pp. 604, 607–9, 612–17; Lyons, *Emotion*, pp. 52–62, 81, 115–19, 123–9 (Lyons holds that unusual bodily changes are required only for what he describes as cases of 'occurrent emotion': i.e. being in the grip of an actual emotional state on a particular occasion); Perkins, op. cit., p. 147; Rey, op. cit., pp. 179–80, 187–9; S. Schachter and J.E. Singer, 'Cognitive, Social, and Physiological Determinants of Emotional State', in Calhoun and Solomon (eds), *What is an Emotion?* pp. 177, 182–3; Spinoza, *Ethics* (trans. R.H.M. Elwes), Parts III and IV (e.g. Part III, Def.

iii: 'By *emotion* I mean the modifications of the body, whereby the active power of the said body is increased or diminished, aided or constrained, and also the ideas of such modifications').

10 Cf. Aune, op. cit., pp. 197–8; Dewey, op. cit.; P.S. Greenspan, *Emotions and Reasons*, New York, Routledge, 1988, pp. 3–36; Lawrie, op. cit.; Leighton, op. cit., esp. p. 74; Marshall, op. cit.; Palmer, op. cit.; R.C. Roberts, 'What an Emotion is: A Sketch', *Philosophical Review*, 1988, vol. 97, no. 2; Scheler, op. cit., p. 257n.

11 For example, J.R.S. Wilson (*Emotion and Object*, Cambridge, Cambridge University Press, 1972, p. 76) suggests that such enduring emotions are dispositions, just as beliefs are dispositions. On this notion of 'disposition', see A. Kenny, *The Metaphysics of Mind*, Oxford, Clarendon Press, 1989, pp. 83–5.

12 See Gilbert Ryle, *The Concept of Mind*, Harmondsworth, Penguin, 1963. For a recent defence of Ryle's critique of Cartesianism, see Kenny, *The Metaphysics of Mind*.

13 William James, *The Principles of Psychology*, (Vol. 1), Cambridge, Mass., Harvard University Press, 1981, pp. 243–4.

14 Cf. Greenspan, op. cit., pp. 28–36; C. Behan McCullagh, 'The Rationality of Emotions and of Emotional Behaviour', *Australasian Journal of Philosophy*, 1990, vol. 68, no. 1, pp. 57–8; and H.F. Nissenbaum, *Emotion and Focus*, Stanford, Center for the Study of Language and Information, 1985, pp. 104–19.

15 See Alston, 'Emotion and Feeling', p. 481; C. Calhoun, 'Cognitive Emotions?' in Calhoun and Solomon (eds), *What is an Emotion?*; Green, 'Emotions and Belief', p. 28; P.S. Greenspan, 'Emotions, Reasons, and "Self-involvement" ', *Philosophical Studies*, 1980, vol. 38, no. 2; P.S. Greenspan, 'Emotions as Evaluations', *Pacific Philosophical Quarterly*, 1981, vol. 62, no. 2; P.S. Greenspan, 'A Case of Mixed Feelings: Ambivalence and the Logic of Emotion', in Rorty (ed.), *Explaining Emotions*, esp. pp. 224, 234–9; Greenspan, *Emotions and Reasons*, pp. 3–9, 16–22, 33, 41–62, 79–107, 148–51; S. Hampshire, 'Sincerity and Single-Mindedness', in *Freedom of the Mind and Other Essays*, Princeton, Princeton University Press, 1971, pp. 239–40; J.M.E. Moravcsik, 'Understanding and the Emotions', *Dialectica*, 1982, vol. 36, nos 2–3, pp. 213–15; Neu, op. cit., p. 36; G. Pitcher, 'Emotion', *Mind*, 1965, vol. 74, no. 295, pp. 332, 336; R.C. Roberts, 'Solomon on the Control of Emotions', *Philosophy and Phenomenological Research*, 1984, vol. 44, no. 3; Rorty, 'Explaining Emotions', p. 115; R. Scruton, 'Emotion, Practical Knowledge and Common Culture', in Rorty (ed.), *Explaining Emotions*, p. 534n11; M. Stocker, 'Emotional Thoughts', *American Philosophical Quarterly*, 1987, vol. 24, no. 1; Stocker, 'Psychic Feelings', p. 8n9. Also, Aristotle seems to hold that emotion requires *thought*, which he distinguishes from imagining, on the one hand, and judgement, on the other.

16 See Greenspan, 'Emotions, Reasons, and "Self-Involvement" '; Greenspan, 'Emotions as Evaluations'; Greenspan, *Emotions and Reasons*, pp. 16–20. For similar examples, see Calhoun, op. cit.; O. Hanfling, *The Grammar of Feelings*, Milton Keynes, Open University Press, 1976, pp. 41–2; P.J. Koch, 'Emotional Ambivalence', *Philosophy and Phenomenological Research*, 1987, vol. 48, no. 2; Roberts, 'Solomon on the Control of Emotions'; Rorty, 'Explaining Emotions'; and Stocker, 'Emotional Thoughts'.

17 Of course, it might be replied here, following Kendall Walton ('Fearing Fictions', *Journal of Philosophy*, 1978, vol. 75, no. 1), that at least in cases of emotions had towards fictional characters we do not 'really' have emotions here at all (but as Walton puts it, we only 'make-believedly' have them), since emotion *does* involve belief, which is lacking here. Indeed, it has been argued by Robert Gordon, in a series of papers ('Emotions and Knowledge', *Journal of Philosophy*, 1969, vol. 66, no. 13; 'Judgmental Emotions', *Analysis*, 1973, vol. 34, no. 2; 'The Aboutness of Emotions', *American Philosophical Quarterly*, 1974, vol. 11, no. 1; and 'Fear', *Philosophical Review*, 1980, vol. 89, no. 4), culminating in his book, *The Structure*

of Emotions (New York, Cambridge University Press, 1987), that the cognitive component of certain emotions, such as anger, must be understood in terms of *knowledge*, rather than mere thoughts or beliefs. (On this kind of view, see C. Provis, 'Reason and Emotion', *Canadian Journal of Philosophy*, 1981, vol. 11, no. 3; and J. Tietz, 'Knowledge Requiring Emotions', *Southwestern Journal of Philosophy*, 1975, vol. 6, no. 3.) But this latter claim seems too strong, as for one thing, it would exclude the possibility of our ever having *unfounded* anger (i.e. anger which involves a false belief), which seems counterintuitive. With regard to the former claim, it seems at least as plausible to hold that we can have *real* emotions about fictional characters and thus allow that emotions may involve cognitions only in the sense of thoughts, as it would be to endorse Walton's view that emotions about fiction are only make-believe on the grounds that real emotions involve beliefs. In any case, I shall not pursue this issue, for the example of emotional inertia already suggests that we can have emotions without beliefs.

18 Cf. Ardal, op. cit., pp. 126–8; Lyons, *Emotion*, pp. 25–32, 167–9; Neu, op. cit., pp. 73–5, 99–100; and M. Vadas, 'Affective and Non-affective Desire', *Philosophy and Phenomenological Research*, 1984, vol. 45, no. 2, esp. pp. 275–6.

19 Since we may not always be aware of the constituent affects, cognitions, and desires in having an emotion, it is a consequence of my view that we can have unconscious emotions, and be mistaken about what we take an emotion of ours to be directed at. On these issues, see R. de Sousa, 'Self-deceptive Emotions', in Rorty (ed.), *Explaining Emotions*; Hampshire, op. cit., pp. 239–40, 251–6; and Provis, op. cit., pp. 446–7.

20 Cf. Gordon, 'The Aboutness of Emotions', esp. p. 29; Hanfling, op. cit., p. 44; and Lyons, *Emotion*, pp. 48–9.

21 See William James, 'What is an Emotion?' esp. pp. 11–13, 15–21, 23, 25–6; William James, 'The Emotions', esp. pp. 100–5, 118–21; and C.G. Lange, 'The Emotions: A Psychophysiological Study', esp. pp. 37, 60–6, 72–3, 79–83; all in K. Dunlap (ed.), *The Emotions*, New York, Hafner, 1967. A recent attempt to defend this kind of view, using a functionalist analysis of feelings, may be found in R. Kraut, 'Feelings in Context', *Journal of Philosophy*, 1986, vol. 83, no. 11. See also R. Kraut, 'Love De Re', in P.A. French, T.E. Uehling, and H.K. Wettstein (eds), *Midwest Studies in Philosophy*, 1986, vol. 10; and S.G. Clarke, 'Emotions: Rationality Without Cognitivism', *Dialogue*, 1986, vol. 25, no. 4. Some of the psychologists who have held this view are mentioned by Kenny, *Action, Emotion and Will*, Chapter 2; and Lyons, *Emotion*, pp. 15–16.

22 James, 'What is an Emotion?' p. 13. See also James, 'The Emotions', p. 100.

23 See James, 'What is an Emotion?' pp. 15–17; James, 'The Emotions', pp. 95, 101–3; and Lange, op. cit., pp. 40–60. For example, on p. 15 of 'What is an Emotion?' James says: 'no shade of emotion, however slight, should be without a bodily reverberation as unique, when taken in its totality, as is the mental mood itself'.

24 Lange, op. cit., pp. 46–54.

25 This view also had its adherents among psychologists, such as Wundt and Titchener. (See Alston, 'Emotion and Feeling', pp. 480, 483; Alston, 'Feelings', pp. 7–12; Green, 'Wittgenstein and the Possibility of a Philosophical Theory of Emotion', p. 257; Kenny, *Action, Emotion and Will*, p. 29; Solomon, *The Passions*, pp. 135–7.)

26 Descartes, *The Passions of the Soul* (trans. E.S. Haldane and G.R.T. Ross), Part I, arts 28–39, 45–7, 50; Part II, arts 51, 70–3, 79, 86, 91–137; Part III, arts 160, 199–202, 211–12. This interpretation of Descartes's view of emotion is also taken by Alston, 'Emotion and Feeling', p. 480; Calhoun and Solomon (eds), *What is an Emotion?*, pp. 11, 54–5; Kenny, *Action, Emotion and Will*, pp. 2–13; Lyons, *Emotion*, pp. 2–8; Neu, op. cit., p. 79; A.O. Rorty, 'From Passions to Emotions and Sentiments', *Philosophy*, 1982, vol. 57, no. 220, pp. 161–6, 171–2.

27 Hume, *Treatise*, Book I, Part i, sec. 2 (pp. 7–8).

196   Morality and the Emotions

28 *Treatise*, Book II, Part i, sec. 2 (p. 277).
29 *Treatise*, Book II, Part ii, sec. 1 (p. 329). Further statements of this kind of view of emotion may be found at *Treatise*, Book II, Part i, sec. 5 (p. 286), Book II, Part i, sec. 7 (p. 296), Book II, Part ii, sec. 6 (pp. 367–8), Book II, Part ii, sec. 9 (pp. 381–2), Book II, Part iii, sec. 3 (p. 415), and Book III, Part i, sec. 2 (p. 471).
30 This interpretation of Hume's view of emotion is supported by most commentators who have considered this part of his work. See Alston, 'Emotion and Feeling', p. 480; Ardal, op. cit., esp. pp. 7–40, 61–79, 93–133; J. Bricke, 'Emotion and Thought in Hume's *Treatise*', *Canadian Journal of Philosophy*, 1974, suppl. vol. 1, Part 1; Calhoun and Solomon (eds), *What is an Emotion?* pp. 9, 94–5; D. Davidson, 'Hume's Cognitive Theory of Pride', *Journal of Philosophy*, 1976, vol. 73, no. 19; P.L. Gardiner, 'Hume's Theory of the Passions', in D.F. Pears (ed.), *David Hume: A Symposium*, London, Macmillan, 1963; Hanfling, op. cit., pp. 42–5; N. Kemp Smith, *The Philosophy of David Hume*, London, Macmillan, 1964, pp. 164–8, 179–91; Kenny, *Action, Emotion and Will*, pp. 20–8; Lyons, *Emotion*, pp. 8–12; Neu, op. cit., pp. 1–68, 77–8; Rorty, 'From Passions to Emotions and Sentiments', pp. 167–71.
     Now, perhaps evidence can be found to show that, against my presentation of Descartes's and Hume's views of emotions along the lines of prevailing interpretations, these philosophers sometimes take emotions as conceptually more complex than psychic feelings. Thus, it has been suggested recently that Hume's view of the nature of emotion is more sophisticated than that usually attributed to him. (See here A. Baier, 'Hume's Analysis of Pride', *Journal of Philosophy*, 1978, vol. 75, no. 1, esp. pp. 27–9. See also S.R. Sutherland, 'Hume on Morality and the Emotions', *Philosophical Quarterly*, 1976, vol. 26, no. 102.) However, it is beyond the scope of this chapter to examine such exegetical issues.
31 Of course, instead of claiming that emotions are exclusively either bodily or psychic feelings, one may hold that emotions are bodily and/or psychic feelings. That is, the view here would be that emotions are feelings which are sometimes bodily, sometimes psychic, and on some occasions a combination of both. In some of his writings, Freud appears to hold this view of emotions. (See, for example, 'The Unconscious', pp. 190–3, and 'Anxiety', pp. 195–6, both in Calhoun and Solomon (eds), *What is an Emotion?*) This might also be Jung's view. (See 'Psychological Types', in *The Basic Writings of C.G. Jung* (ed. V.S. de Laszlo), New York, Random House, 1959, pp. 240–1.) On Freud's conception of emotion, see Calhoun and Solomon, *What is an Emotion?*, pp. 184–6; Lyons, *Emotion*, pp. 25–31; Neu, op. cit., pp. 139–43, 155; and Solomon, *The Passions*, pp. 139–46, 159, 225. On psychic and bodily feelings in emotions, see Dewey, op. cit.; Duncker, op. cit., pp. 401–7, 426; and Scheler, op. cit., pp. 335–9.
32 Some experimental psychologists have identified emotions with determinate configurations of unusual bodily changes. See those cited by Alston, 'Emotion and Feeling', p. 482; Kenny, *Action, Emotion and Will*, pp. 33–4; Lyons, *Emotion*, p. 15n7; and Solomon, *The Passions*, pp. 135–7, 147–8.
33 Hume, *Treatise*, Book II, Part i, sec. 5 (p. 286). Cf. also Hume's description of pride (e.g. at II, i, 5, p. 287) as 'a *peculiar* impression or emotion' (my emphasis). See also Descartes, *The Passions of the Soul*, Part I, art. 26, where, after arguing that we may be mistaken in our perceptions of external objects and of changes in our bodies, Descartes says: 'we cannot be so deceived regarding the passsions, inasmuch as they are so close to, and so entirely within our soul, that it is impossible for it to feel them without their being actually such as it feels them to be'. On Descartes's view in this connection, see Kenny, *Action, Emotion and Will*, pp. 4–5, 12–13; and Rorty, 'From Passions to Emotions and Sentiments', pp. 164–5.
34 W.B. Cannon, 'Bodily Changes in Pain, Hunger, Fear and Rage', in Calhoun and Solomon (eds) *What is an Emotion?*; Schachter and Singer, 'Cognitive, Social, and Physiological Determinants of Emotional State'. See also Alston, 'Emotion and Feeling', pp. 484–5; Alston, 'Feelings', pp. 8–9; Hanfling, op. cit., pp. 45–8; E.R.

Hilgard, R.C. Atkinson, and R.L. Atkinson, *Introduction to Psychology*, New York, Harcourt Brace Jovanovich, 1975, pp. 348–52; Kenny, *Action, Emotion and Will*, pp. 38–9, 48, 70, 98–9; W. Lyons, 'Emotions and Feelings', *Ratio*, 1977, vol. 19, no. 1; Lyons, 'Physiological Changes and the Emotions', op. cit., pp. 610–12, 615–17; Lyons, *Emotion*, pp. 15–16, 19–20, 45–6, 80–1, 119–23, 126–43; A. MacIntyre, 'Emotion, Behaviour and Belief', in *Against the Self-images of the Age*, London, Duckworth, 1971, pp. 234–5; Neu, op. cit., pp. 2, 19n2; Rey, op. cit., pp. 179–80, 187–9; Rorty, 'Explaining Emotions', p. 117; Jean-Paul Sartre, *Sketch for a Theory of the Emotions* (trans. P. Mairet), London, Methuen, 1962, p. 32; Solomon, *The Passions*, pp. 147, 154, 157–8.
35 Cannon, op. cit., pp. 146–7, 149–51.
36 See Alston, 'Emotion and Feeling', pp. 482–3; Alston, 'Feelings', pp. 8–11; Bedford, op. cit., p. 111; Lyons, 'Emotions and Feelings'; Lyons, *Emotion*, pp. 130–43; MacIntyre, op. cit., pp. 234–5; Melden, op. cit., pp. 204–5; Neu, op. cit., p. 19; A.O. Rorty, 'Agent Regret', in Rorty (ed.), *Explaining Emotions*, p. 498; Ryle, op. cit., pp. 84–5; Solomon, *The Passions*, pp. 159–61.
37 See those cited in note 34 of this chapter.
38 See C.D. Broad, 'Emotion and Sentiment', in D.R. Cheney (ed.), *Broad's Critical Essays in Moral Philosophy*, London, Allen & Unwin, 1971, pp. 299–300; Melden, op. cit., p. 219.
39 Both James and Lange seem to allow that felt bodily changes which are 'unmotived' by characteristic perceptual stimuli may still constitute the particular emotions which they would be if caused by their usual perceptions. See James, 'What is an Emotion?', pp. 23–5; James, 'The Emotions', pp. 109–13; Lange, op. cit., p. 72. See also H.M. Feinstein, 'William James on the Emotions', *Journal of the History of Ideas*, 1970, vol. 31, no. 1, pp. 140–1.
40 Many philosophers have made the point that emotions are distinct from certain other phenomena, such as sensations, by arguing that emotions require *objects* (in some sense), and they have argued further that we can distinguish between particular emotions by referring to their intentional objects. (See Aquinas, *Summa Theologiae*, 1a2ae, Q. 23, arts 1–4; F. Brentano, *Psychology from an Empirical Standpoint* (trans. D.B. Terrell), London, Routledge & Kegan Paul, 1971, esp. Bk II, Ch. 1, Sec. 5; Hanfling, op. cit., pp. 45–51; Kenny, *Action, Emotion and Will*, pp. 10–28, 60–75; Kenny, *The Metaphysics of Mind*, pp. 56–7; Pitcher, op. cit., pp. 326–7; Wilson, op. cit.)
    Both of these claims have been challenged recently, for it has been pointed out that there are ambiguities in the notion of emotional 'objects', and that, at least on some construals of this notion, objects are not always required by emotions in any case. (See K.S. Donnellan, 'Causes, Objects, and Producers of the Emotions', *Journal of Philosophy*, 1970, vol. 67, no. 21; J.C. Gosling, 'Emotion and Object', *Philosophical Review*, 1965, vol. 74, no. 4; Green, 'Emotions and Belief'; R. Lamb, 'Objectless Emotions', *Philosophy and Phenomenological Research*, 1987, vol. 48, no. 1; and Neu, op. cit., pp. 37–8, 43.)
    I cannot enter into these disputes here, and so I have preferred to put what I believe many have been suggesting in their talk of emotional 'objects' in terms of 'cognition' instead. For emotions do seem to be distinct from sensations in requiring certain cognitions, and as I have argued, we can often distinguish between particular emotions in terms of their cognitions.
41 Lyons, *Emotion*, pp. 57–8. Lyons does allow that wants or desires may sometimes be involved in certain particular emotional states.
42 ibid., p. 64
43 Schachter and Singer, 'Cognitive, Social, and Physiological Determinants of Emotional State', p. 177.
44 Hampshire, op. cit., p. 239. Other exponents of this view of emotions may include MacIntyre, op. cit., pp. 233–5; Perkins, op. cit.; I. Thalberg, 'Emotion and Thought', *American Philosophical Quarterly*, 1964, vol. 1, no. 1; I. Thalberg,

'Constituents and Causes of Emotion and Action', *American Philosophical Quarterly*, 1973, vol. 23, no. 90; and perhaps also Neu, op. cit., e.g. pp. 139–40.
45 Broad, op. cit., p. 283. See also R.E. Aquila, 'Causes and Constituents of Occurrent Emotion', *Philosophical Quarterly*, 1975, vol. 25, no. 101. Greenspan, *Emotions and Reasons*, pp. 3–36, describes emotions as affective states of comfort or discomfort directed towards a corresponding evaluative proposition, which they function to 'keep in mind'. On the notion of 'affective cognitions', see S. Cohen, 'Distinctions Among Blame Concepts', *Philosophy and Phenomenological Research*, 1977, vol. 38, no. 2, p. 153; I. Dilman, 'Reason, Passion and the Will', *Philosophy*, 1984, vol. 59, no. 228, p. 203; and Lawrie, op. cit., p. 117.
46 Broad, op. cit., p. 286.
47 Sartre, op. cit., pp. 75–9, 86. See also Calhoun and Solomon (eds), *What is an Emotion?* pp. 16–17; Calhoun, 'Cognitive Emotions?', pp. 329–30; and Roberts, 'What an Emotion is: A Sketch'.
48 Solomon, 'Emotions and Choice', p. 257. See also Solomon, *The Passions*; Solomon, 'The Logic of Emotion', *Nous*, 1977, vol. 11, no. 1; Solomon, 'Sartre on Emotions', in P.A. Schlipp (ed.) *The Philosophy of Jean-Paul Sartre*, La Salle, The Open Court, 1977, esp. pp. 220–7; and Solomon, ' "I Can't Get It Out of My Mind": (Augustine's Problem)', *Philosophy and Phenomenological Research*, 1984, vol. 44, no. 3. Cf. Pitcher, op. cit., p. 338; and Davidson, op. cit., eg. p. 753: 'The theory I have constructed identifies the state someone is in if he is proud that p with his having the attitude of approving of himself because of p, and this in turn (following Hume) I have not distinguished from judging or holding that one is praiseworthy because of p.'
49 Solomon, *The Passions*, p. 187.
50 See Neu, op. cit., pp. 165–8; J. Neu, 'Jealous Thoughts', in Rorty (ed.), *Explaining Emotions*, pp. 431–2, 450–1; Robinson, op. cit., esp. pp. 731, 741; and Tov-Ruach, op. cit., p. 469. Neu also claims to find suggestions of this view in Spinoza, but I consider this doubtful, given the central role which Spinoza gives to affects and desires in his account of emotion.
51 Sartre, op. cit., esp. pp. 45, 57–8, 63–74.
52 ibid., pp. 68–9.
53 For example, Calhoun, 'Cognitive Emotions?', esp. pp. 340, 342; R. de Sousa, 'The Rationality of Emotions', in Rorty (ed.), *Explaining Emotions*, esp. pp. 137–8, 141; Roberts, 'Solomon on the Control of Emotions', esp. p. 402; and Roberts, 'What an Emotion is: A Sketch'. Solomon also says in places that in equating emotions with judgements, he has in mind 'interpretive' or 'constitutive' judgements (in a Sartrean sense). Cf., for example, Solomon, *The Passions*, pp. 195–203; Solomon, 'The Logic of Emotion', p. 46; Solomon, 'Sartre on Emotions', pp. 220–7; and Solomon, ' "I Can't Get It Out of My Mind" ', pp. 406–8.
54 See S.R. Leighton, 'Feelings and Emotion', *Review of Metaphysics*, 1984, vol. 38, no. 2, esp. pp. 308–15; S.R. Leighton, 'A New View of Emotion', *American Philosophical Quarterly*, 1985, vol. 22, no. 2, pp. 135–40; and Marks, op. cit., pp. 231–2.
55 This is Lyons's reply to the objection presented above (see *Emotion*, pp. 80–5, 94). For although he does not analyse emotion exclusively in terms of cognition, Lyons does want to argue that emotions can always be differentiated by reference to their cognitions.
56 See Alston, 'Emotion and Feeling', p. 485; Beardsley, op. cit., pp. 164–7, 172–3; F. Bergmann, 'Review of *The Passions*', *Journal of Philosophy*, 1978, vol. 75, no. 4, pp. 203–5; Green, 'Emotions and Belief', p. 37; Greenspan, 'Emotions, Reasons, and "Self-Involvement" ', esp. pp. 162–3; Leighton, 'A New View of Emotion', esp. pp. 135–40; Marks, op. cit., pp. 231–2; Marshall, op. cit., pp. 245–7; Moravcsik, op. cit., p. 215; Perkins, op. cit.; D. Sachs, 'Review of *The Passions*', *Philosophical Review*, 1978, vol. 87, no. 3, pp. 474–5; Stocker, 'Psychic Feelings', esp. pp. 18–23; and Stocker, 'Emotional Thoughts', esp. secs 4, 6, and 7.

57 See Solomon's reply to his critics in the Appendix (added later) to 'Emotions and Choice', in Rorty (ed.), *Explaining Emotions*, p. 275: 'an emotion is never a single judgment but a system of judgments, and although one might well make one or several judgments of the system without having the emotion, my claim is that one cannot make *all* of them and not have the emotion'. See also Solomon, 'The Logic of Emotion', pp. 46–9; and Solomon, ' "I Can't Get It Out of My Mind" ', pp. 406–8.

58 Unless, of course, the cognitions themselves are already described as involving affective elements. For example, Lyons proposes that the cognition which is characteristic of envying say, a famous pianist, is the judgment that he is a fine pianist and that this displeases me (*Emotion*, p. 83). According to Lyons, reference to this enables us to distinguish envy from other emotions, such as admiration, exclusively in terms of an affectless evaluative judgement. But on the contrary, I would say that being displeased by something involves an essential affective element.

59 On the importance of desire in emotion, see Ardal, op. cit., pp. 70–3, 126–8; Ewing, op. cit., esp. pp. 62, 69–71; Gordon, 'Fear'; Green, 'Emotions and Belief', p. 27; Greenspan, 'Emotions, Reasons, and "Self-Involvement" ', pp. 165–6; Kenny, *Action, Emotion and Will*, esp. p. 100; Lawrie, op. cit., pp. 113–17; Lyons, 'Physiological Changes and the Emotions', pp. 603–4; Lyons, *Emotion*, pp. 63–6, 93–7, 167–9; Marks, op. cit., esp. pp. 231–2; Neu, *Emotion, Thought and Therapy*, pp. 54–5, 99–100; Robinson, op. cit., esp. pp. 734–6. See also those mentioned in note 1 of this chapter.

60 See Blum, *Friendship, Altruism and Morality*, esp. pp. 12–20; and Blum, 'Compassion', esp. p. 511.

61 Marks, op. cit., p. 227. Others who can be read as holding this kind of view include Bedford, op. cit.; Greenspan, 'A Case of Mixed Feelings: Ambivalence and the Logic of Emotion', esp. pp. 233ff; Greenspan, 'Emotions as Evaluations', e.g. p. 165n13; Neu, *Emotion, Thought and Therapy*, pp. 59, 166–7; Pitcher, op. cit., pp. 332–5; Robinson, op. cit., e.g. pp. 736–9; and R. Warner, 'Enjoyment', *Philosophical Review*, 1980, vol. 89, no. 4. Solomon, in response to the many criticisms which have been made of his view that emotions are judgements, seems to concede in his later works that along with judgements, emotions also involve *desires* (although not affects). So Solomon's later view resembles that being considered here. See, for example, 'The Logic of Emotion', pp. 48–9; and the Appendix added later to 'Emotions and Choice', in Rorty (ed.), *Explaining Emotions*, esp. p. 274: 'emotions *essentially* involve desires, expectations, purposes, and attitudes. Emotions are motivated by desires, sometimes distinguished by desires, and in virtually every case some desire is essential to an emotion . . . But it certainly does not follow that by so "opening up" my analysis beyond the "emotions are judgments" slogan I am thereby bound to include also dispositions to behave and feelings and all sorts of things. It is the heart of my argument that "feelings" and physiology and, with qualifications, dispositions to behave, do not play an essential role in the constitution of emotions and cannot be used in even the most rudimentary account of the definitive properties of either emotions in general or particular emotions'.

62 Marks, op. cit., p. 230.

63 Cf. Shaffer, op. cit., pp. 161, 163, 168–70; Stocker, 'Psychic Feelings', p. 14. See also those mentioned in note 1 of this chapter.

64 Cf. Lyons, *Emotion*, pp. 81–5; Stocker, 'Emotional Thoughts', esp. pp. 6–12.

65 Cf. Alston, 'Emotion and Feeling', pp. 483–5; Leighton, 'Feelings and Emotion', p. 3l2; Lyons, 'Physiological Changes and the Emotions', p. 610; Lyons, 'Emotions and Feelings', pp. 4–5; Lyons, *Emotion*, pp. 120, 135; and Neu, *Emotion, Thought and Therapy*, p. 43.

66 Cf. Farrell, op. cit., p. 543.

67 See Hume, *Treatise*, Book II, Part ii, sec. 6 (pp. 366–8), Book II, Part ii, sec. 9 (pp.

381–2), Book III, Part iii, sec. 1 (p. 591); Hume, *An Enquiry Concerning the Principles of Morals*, App. II (p. 298); Spinoza, *Ethics*, Part III, prop. xl; Part III, Definition Emotion xxxii–xlviii. Alston ('Emotion and Feeling', pp. 480–1) and Lyons (*Emotion*, pp. 35–7) attribute accounts of emotion based exclusively on desire to Aquinas and Hobbes, but I believe that this is a mistaken interpretation, as both these philosophers seem to allow that emotions involve cognitions and affects, along with desires. See, for example, *Summa Theologiae*, 1a2ae, Q. 23, arts 1–4; *Leviathan*, Part I, Chapter 6.

68 On affective desire and the contrast with affectless desire, see Duncker, op. cit., pp. 414–25; Greenspan, *Emotions and Reasons*, pp. 157–9; Lawrie, op. cit.; Marshall, op. cit., pp. 247–8; Stocker, 'Psychic Feelings', pp. 14–16; Stocker, 'Affectivity and Self-Concern', pp. 216–17; and Vadas, op. cit.

69 Indeed, in some moral psychologies, such as Aristotle's, the separations between cognition, desire, and affect which I have discussed here in developing an adequate account of emotion may not be considered as real possibilities. See Stocker, 'Affectivity and Self-Concern: The Assumed Psychology in Aristotle's Ethics'.

70 I am grateful to Roger Trigg for pointing out this problem.

71 See Hume, *Treatise*, Book II, Part i, sec. 1; Book II, Part ii, sec. 9; Book II, Part iii, sec. 10; Book III, Part i, sec. 2; Book III, Part iii, sec. 1; and Blum, *Friendship, Altruism and Morality*, Chapter 2, esp. pp. 26–7. It may also be the case that through certain emotions, such as empathy, we can take a more *impartial* view of the world. For example, on a moral theory such as R.M. Hare's 'Universal Prescriptivism', where we must in deciding an action's rightness 'take on' the preferences of those affected by the action as if they were our own, and then resolve any conflicts as one would if they were intrapersonal (see *Moral Thinking*, Oxford, Clarendon Press, 1981), empathy would be an important means of taking on others' preferences, and so of overcoming our partiality.

2 THE MORAL SIGNIFICANCE OF EMOTIONS

1 This notion of an aretaic ethics is usefully outlined by W.K. Frankena, 'The Ethics of Love Conceived as an Ethics of Virtue', *Journal of Religious Ethics*, 1973, vol. 1, no. 1; and M. Stocker, 'Good Intentions in Greek and Modern Moral Virtue', *Australasian Journal of Philosophy*, 1979, vol. 57, no. 3.

2 See Aristotle, *Nicomachean Ethics*, esp. Book II, Chapter 4, 1105a28ff.

3 Indeed, Aristotle seems to hold that emotions are the *archetypal* province of moral virtue, for Aristotle's account of the virtuous life is perhaps most importantly an account of what emotional sensibilities a good person will have. For this interpretation, see W. Fortenbaugh, 'Aristotle: Emotion and Moral Virtue', *Arethusa*, 1969, vol. 2, no. 2, esp. pp. 163–4; C.M. Korsgaard, 'Aristotle on Function and Virtue', *History of Philosophy Quarterly*, 1986, vol. 3, no. 3, p. 261; and A. Preus, 'Aristotle on Healthy and Sick Souls', *Monist*, 1986, vol. 69, no. 3, pp. 419, 423.

4 Ronald de Sousa (*The Rationality of Emotion*, Cambridge, Mass., MIT Press, 1987, pp. 314–15) holds that there may be unconditionally good and bad emotion-types. As examples of the latter, he lists 'Envy, motiveless malice, certain forms of resentment, and despair' (p. 315).

5 See E. Bedford, 'Emotions', in V.C. Chappell (ed.), *The Philosophy of Mind*, Englewood Cliffs, Prentice-Hall, 1962, e.g. p. 120; R.M. Chisholm, 'Brentano's Theory of Correct and Incorrect Emotion', *Revue Internationale de Philosophie*, 1966, vol. 20, no. 75; A.C. Ewing, 'The Justification of Emotions', *Proceedings of the Aristotelian Society*, 1957, suppl. vol. 31; W. Lyons, *Emotion*, Cambridge, Cambridge University Press, 1980, pp. 72–3; J.M.E. Moravcsik, 'Understanding and the Emotions', *Dialectica*, 1982, vol. 36, nos 2–3, e.g. pp. 209–10; G. Taylor, 'Justifying the Emotions', *Mind*, 1975, vol. 84, esp. p. 393; G. Taylor, 'Love',

Proceedings of the Aristotelian Society, 1975–6, vol. 76, esp. pp. 147–51, 157; G. Taylor, *Pride, Shame, and Guilt: Emotions of Self-assessment*, Oxford, Clarendon Press, 1985, Chapter 1; and M. Warnock, 'The Justification of Emotions', *Proceedings of the Aristotelian Society*, 1957, suppl. vol. 31. See also Plato's characterisation of false pleasures in the *Philebus*, 36c–41a.

6 See R. Kraut, 'Feelings in Context', *Journal of Philosophy*, 1986, vol. 83, no. 11, p. 647; Lyons, op. cit., p. 78; J. Neu, *Emotion, Thought and Therapy*, London, Routledge & Kegan Paul, 1977, p. 60; D.L. Perry, 'Pleasure and Justification', *Personalist*, 1970, vol. 51, no. 2, pp. 178ff; S.L. Ross, 'Evaluating the Emotions', *Journal of Philosophy*, 1984, vol. 81, no. 6; and R. de Sousa, 'Self-deceptive Emotions', in A.O. Rorty (ed.), *Explaining Emotions*, Berkeley, University of California Press, 1980, esp. pp. 284–5.

7 Cf. Ross, op. cit.

8 Of course, this is not to deny that it is generally better, morally speaking, if on the whole our emotions are rational rather than irrational.

9 For discussion of such issues, see (in addition to those mentioned in notes 4 and 5 of this chapter) R. Audi, 'The Rational Assessment of Emotions', *Southwestern Journal of Philosophy*, 1977, vol. 8; C.D. Broad, 'Emotion and Sentiment', in D.R. Cheney (ed.), *Broad's Critical Essays in Moral Philosophy*, New York, Humanities Press, 1971; Alan Gibbard, *Wise Choices, Apt Feelings*, Oxford, Clarendon Press, 1990, pp. 6–9, 36–54, 274–84; P.S. Greenspan, 'A Case of Mixed Feelings: Ambivalence and the Logic of Emotion', in Rorty (ed.), *Explaining Emotions*, pp. 234ff, esp. pp. 234n14, 236n15; P.S. Greenspan, *Emotions and Reasons*, New York, Routledge, 1988, esp. pp. 14–20, 30, 79–175; C. Behan McCullagh, 'The Rationality of Emotions and of Emotional Behaviour', *Australasian Journal of Philosophy*, 1990, vol. 68, no. 1; C. Provis, 'Reason and Emotion', *Canadian Journal of Philosophy*, 1981, vol. 11, no. 3; A.O. Rorty, 'Explaining Emotions', in Rorty (ed.) *Explaining Emotions*; A.O. Rorty, 'Varieties of Rationality, Varieties of Emotion', *Social Science Information*, 1985, vol. 24, no. 2; A.O. Rorty, 'The Historicity of Psychological Attitudes: Love is Not Love Which Alters Not When It Alteration Finds', in P.A. French, T.E. Uehling, and H.K. Wettstein (eds), *Midwest Studies in Philosophy*, 1986, vol. 10, esp. pp. 408–11; E.T. Sankowski, 'The Sense of Responsibility and the Justifiability of Emotions', *Southern Journal of Philosophy*, 1975, vol. 13, no. 2; J.A. Shaffer, 'An Assessment of Emotion', *American Philosophical Quarterly*, 1983, vol. 20, no. 2, pp. 164–5; R.C. Solomon, *The Passions*, New York, Doubleday Anchor, 1976, pp. 241–52; R. de Sousa, 'The Rationality of Emotions', in Rorty (ed.), *Explaining Emotions*; R. de Sousa, *The Rationality of Emotion*.

10 See St Thomas Aquinas's discussion of this view in *Summa Theologiae*, 1a2ae, Question 24, art. 2; see also 1a2ae, Question 59, art. 2, and Question 34, art. 1.

11 St Augustine, *City of God* (trans. D.S. Wiesen), London, Heinemann, 1968, IX, 4. For a sympathetic interpretation of this Stoic view, see M. Nussbaum, 'The Stoics on the Extirpation of the Passions', *Apeiron*, 1987, vol. 20, no. 2.

12 Cf. W.W. Fortenbaugh, *Aristotle on Emotion*, London, Duckworth, 1975, pp. 33, 83–7; and R. Hursthouse, 'Plato on Commensurability and Desire: Plato on the Emotions', *Proceedings of the Aristotelian Society*, 1984, suppl. vol. 58.

13 Taylor, 'Justifying the Emotions', p. 401. Cf. also Bedford, op. cit., esp. p. 121; Fortenbaugh, *Aristotle on Emotion*, p. 18; Hursthouse, op. cit., pp. 90ff; Taylor, 'Love'; Taylor, *Pride, Shame, and Guilt*, Chapter 1.

14 Ewing, op. cit., p. 67. See also D.M. Farrell, 'Jealousy', *Philosophical Review*, 1980, vol. 89, no. 4, pp. 547–8; and W.D. Ross's claim (*The Right and the Good*, Oxford, Oxford University Press, 1930, p. 156): 'cannot we say that the moral goodness both of actions and of feelings arises from their proceeding from a certain kind of desire?' However, here we must remember that Ross is speaking of a specific desire, i.e. the desire to do one's duty, and the emotions (e.g. respect) which proceed from or involve this.

15 For this kind of approach, see Kraut, op. cit., e.g. p. 647; R. Lawrie, 'Passion', *Philosophy and Phenomenological Research*, 1980, vol. 41, no. 1; and M. Scheler, *Formalism in Ethics and Non-formal Ethics of Values* (trans. M.S. Frings and R.L. Funk), Evanston, Northwestern University Press, 1973, pp. 250–3, 264, 328–49.

16 Cf. Korsgaard, op. cit., esp. p. 262; and Neu, op. cit., p. 60.

17 Broad, op. cit., p. 293.

18 Ewing, op. cit., p. 71.

19 Shaffer, op. cit., p. 165. See also Fortenbaugh, 'Aristotle: Emotion and Moral Virtue', p. 166n7; Taylor, 'Love', e.g. p. 162; and J.D. Wallace, *Virtues and Vices*, Ithaca, Cornell University Press, 1978, pp. 132–3, 154–6.

20 Cf. L.A. Blum, *Friendship, Altruism and Morality*, London, Routledge & Kegan Paul, 1980, pp. 140–68.

21 See Ewing, op. cit., p. 72; Shaffer, op. cit., pp. 161–2.

22 Note that I am not here attempting to characterise an *emotionless* person. Afflictions such as worthlessness and alienation may in fact involve certain deeply felt emotions, including despair, fear, and self-pity. This shows that these maladies are importantly *emotional* deficiencies.

23 Aristotle, *Nicomachean Ethics*, Book IV, Chapter 5, 1126a8; and Book IV, Chapter 3, 1125a20f.

24 On such features of an emotionally deficient person, see Fortenbaugh, 'Aristotle: Emotion and Moral Virtue', pp. 168–9; R.F. Holland, 'Morality and Moral Reasoning', *Philosophy*, 1972, vol. 47, no. 181, p. 266; W. Neblett, 'Indignation: A Case Study in the Role of Feelings in Morals', *Metaphilosophy*, 1979, vol. 10, no. 2, pp. 139–40; M.S. Pritchard, 'Responsibility, Understanding, and Psychopathology', *Monist*, 1974, vol. 58, no. 4, esp. p. 644; Taylor, 'Justifying the Emotions', pp. 397–401; and R. Wollheim, 'On Persons and Their Lives', in Rorty (ed.), *Explaining Emotions*, esp. pp. 308–11.

25 See here M. Baron, 'The Alleged Moral Repugnance of Acting from Duty', *Journal of Philosophy*, 1984, vol. 81, no. 4, pp. 205–6; J. Kelly, 'Virtue and Pleasure', *Mind*, 1973, vol. 82, no. 327, p. 403; M. Stocker, 'Psychic Feelings: Their Importance and Irreducibility', *Australasian Journal of Philosophy*, 1983, vol. 61, no. 1, pp. 5–7; M. Stocker, *Plural and Conflicting Values*, Oxford, Clarendon Press, 1990, pp. 30–2, 114–17.

26 In explicating the moral significance of emotions in terms of their connections with certain goods, I should not be taken as claiming that we have emotions *in order* to achieve such goods, and so I am not defending a version of the view held by Sartre and others that emotions are had for a purpose. I cannot discuss this view here, but suffice it to be said that, as I argue in Chapter 5, the moral significance of emotions need not depend on our responsibility for them (although, as we see in Chapter 5, being responsible for an emotion may properly influence the kind of moral assessments that are appropriately made of a person in regard to their emotions). Therefore, were some form of the Sartrean thesis true, it would not affect the account which follows.

27 On this view, see M. Jefferson, 'What is Wrong with Sentimentality?', *Mind*, 1983, vol. 92, no. 368; M.W. Michaels, 'Morality Without Distinction', *Philosophical Forum*, 1986, vol. 17, no. 3; and Provis, op. cit.

28 Blum, op. cit., pp. 132–7, 166; Wallace, op. cit., pp. 143–4. Cf. also N.K. Badhwar, 'Friendship, Justice and Supererogation', *American Philosophical Quarterly*, 1985, vol. 22, no. 2, p. 129.

29 See L.A. Blum, 'Compassion', in A.O. Rorty (ed.), *Explaining Emotions*, esp. p. 516; L.M. Hinman, 'On the Purity of Our Moral Motives: A Critique of Kant's Account of the Emotions and Acting for the Sake of Duty', *Monist*, 1983, vol. 66, no. 2, pp. 263–4; Moravcsik, op. cit., esp. pp. 218–19, 223–4; Pritchard, op. cit.; and J. Walker, 'Imagination and the Passions', *Philosophy and Phenomenological Research*, 1969, vol. 29, no. 4, pp. 581–2, 586. As Nancy Sherman (*The Fabric of Character*, Oxford, Clarendon Press, 1989, p. 38) puts it: 'Through the emotions we

come to recognize what is ethically salient, what for a human being counts as suffering or cruelty, what is unfair.'

30 Cf. I. Dilman, 'Reason, Passion and the Will', *Philosophy*, 1984, vol. 59, no. 228, esp. pp. 188, 203; Iris Murdoch, *The Sovereignty of Good*, London, Routledge & Kegan Paul, 1970, esp. pp. 17–23, 34–42; and M. C. Nussbaum, *The Fragility of Goodness*, Cambridge, Cambridge University Press, 1986, pp. 15–16, 45–6, 68–70, 378–94.

31 C.S. Lewis, *An Experiment in Criticism*, Cambridge, Cambridge University Press, 1961, p. 137. I owe this reference to Davis McCaughey. See also, in the context of Bentham's famous remark that 'Pleasure for pleasure, pushpin is as good as poetry' (Jeremy Bentham, *Works*, Edinburgh, Tait, 1843, vol. 2, pp. 253–4), J.J.C. Smart's claim that 'the reading of poetry may develop imagination and sensitivity, and so as a result of his interest in poetry a man may be able to do more for the happiness of others than if he had played pushpin and let his brain deteriorate' ('An Outline of a System of Utilitarian Ethics', in J.J.C. Smart and Bernard Williams, *Utilitarianism: For and Against*, Cambridge, Cambridge University Press, 1973, p. 16).

32 See M.B. Arnold, 'Human Emotion and Action', in T. Mischel (ed.), *Human Action: Conceptual and Empirical Issues*, New York, Academic Press, 1969, pp. 189–91, 195; Lyons, op. cit., pp. 189–92; M. Stocker, 'Desiring the Bad: An Essay in Moral Psychology', *Journal of Philosophy*, 1979, vol. 76, no. 12, esp. pp. 744–6; M. Stocker, 'Affectivity and Self-Concern: The Assumed Psychology in Aristotle's Ethics', *Pacific Philosophical Quarterly*, 1983, vol. 64, no. 3, esp. pp. 213–14; Stocker, 'Psychic Feelings', p. 6 (esp. n4); and Wallace, op. cit., p. 81.

While some may not regard *courage* as an emotion, my understanding of courage is that it consists in having an appropriate mixture of fear and confidence, and so I consider that courage is an emotion, which we can *show* in action.

33 See Aristotle, *Nicomachean Ethics*, Book I, Chapter 13, Book III, Chapters 6–12, Book VII, Chapters 1–10, and Book IX, Chapter 4. See also Aquinas, *Summa Theologiae* (trans. E. D'Arcy), 1a2ae, Question 24, art. 3: 'One sees then that, just as it is better that a man should not merely have the right intention, but also perform the good action: it is better that he be bent on the good, not merely with his will, but also with his sensory orexis [which, according to Aquinas, is the seat of emotion].' On Aristotle's distinction between the good person and the merely continent person, see N.J.H. Dent, 'Virtues and Actions', *Philosophical Quarterly*, 1975, vol. 25, no. 101, esp. pp. 325–7, 330–1; A. Duff, 'Aristotelian Courage', *Ratio*, 1987, vol. 29, no. 1; and Korsgaard, op. cit., esp. pp. 264–5.

34 See Chapter 3 for the application of this point to Kantian arguments against emotions as moral motives.

35 On this notion of integrity, see Taylor, *Pride, Shame, and Guilt*, Chapter 5.

36 Aristotle, *Nicomachean Ethics*, Book IX, Chapter 4, 1166b19. See also Book I, Chapter 13, 1102b28, Book III, Chapter 12, 1119b13–18; M.F. Burnyeat, 'Aristotle on Learning to be Good', in A.O. Rorty (ed.), *Essays on Aristotle's Ethics*, Berkeley, University of California Press, 1980, esp. pp. 80, 88; Korsgaard, op. cit., pp. 264ff; P. Railton, 'Alienation, Consequentialism, and the Demands of Morality', *Philosophy and Public Affairs*, 1984, vol. 13, no. 2, pp. 137–8; B. Williams, 'A Critique of Utilitarianism', in Smart and Williams, *Utilitarianism: For and Against*, esp. pp. 103–4, 108–18; B. Williams, 'Persons, Character and Morality', in A.O. Rorty (ed.), *The Identities of Persons*, Berkeley, University of California Press, 1976.

37 Martin Benjamin, *Splitting the Difference: Compromise and Integrity in Ethics and Politics*, Lawrence, Kansas University Press, 1990, p. 52.

38 See M. Stocker, 'The Schizophrenia of Modern Ethical Theories', *Journal of Philosophy*, 1976, vol. 73, no. 4, pp. 453–66. See also M. Stocker, 'Values and Purposes: The Limits of Teleology and the Ends of Friendship', *Journal of Philosophy*, 1981, vol. 78, no. 12; and M. Stocker, 'Friendship and Morality: Some Difficult Relations', unpublished paper.

204   *Morality and the Emotions*

39 Cf. Korsgaard, op. cit., pp. 265–6, 272; Railton, op. cit., pp. 146–8.
40 See Wallace, op. cit., p. 81: 'The function of courage . . . is to preserve practical reasoning and enable it to issue in action in the face of danger.' See also Arnold, op. cit., pp. 192–3; Duff, op. cit.; A.C. Ewing, *Ethics*, London, English Universities Press, 1953, p. 150; Hursthouse, op. cit.; and Lyons, op. cit., pp. 189–92.
41 See D.B. Annis, 'The Meaning, Value, and Duties of Friendship', *American Philosophical Quarterly*, 1987, vol. 24, no. 4; Badhwar, op. cit.; Baron, op. cit., pp. 204–6; Railton, op. cit., p. 146; M. Slote, 'Morality Not a System of Imperatives', *American Philosophical Quarterly*, 1982, vol. 19, no. 4, p. 336; and C.H. Sommers, 'Filial Morality', *Journal of Philosophy*, 1986, vol. 83, no. 8, esp. pp. 447–51.
42 Aristotle, *Nicomachean Ethics*, Book IX, Chapter 5, 1166b30–1167a12; Book IV, Chapter 6, 1126b20ff. See also P. Gilbert, 'Friendship and the Will', *Philosophy*, 1986, vol. 61, no. 235, e.g. pp. 64–5; Lyons, op. cit., p. 142; and W. Lyons, 'Emotions and Feelings', *Ratio*, 1977, vol. 19, no. 1, pp. 11–12.
43 For example, Aristotle, *Nicomachean Ethics*, Book IX, Chapter 9, 1169b10; Aquinas, *Summa Theologiae*, 1a2ae, Question 24, art. 4; Question 26, arts 1, 2, and 4; Question 28, art. 5. See also Annis, op. cit.; L.A. Blum, 'Iris Murdoch and the Domain of the Moral', *Philosophical Studies*, 1986, vol. 50, no. 3; R. Brown, *Analyzing Love*, Cambridge, Cambridge University Press, 1987, e.g. pp. 124–7; Murdoch, op. cit., esp. pp. 17–23, 34–42; Nussbaum, *The Fragility of Goodness*, pp. 6–9, 200–23, 343–5, 354–72; N. Sherman, 'Aristotle on Friendship and the Shared Life', *Philosophy and Phenomenological Research*, 1987, vol. 47, no. 4; Sherman, *The Fabric of Character*, Chapter 4; and L. Thomas, 'Love and Morality: The Possibility of Altruism', in J.H. Fetzer (ed.), *Sociobiology and Epistemology*, Dordrecht, Reidel, 1985. Cf. also S. Luper-Foy, 'Competing for the Good Life', *American Philosophical Quarterly*, 1986, vol. 23, no. 2, esp. pp. 174–5, who emphasises the moral importance of love and friendship as essentially *non-competitive* relationships.
44 Railton, op. cit., p. 139. A similar point is also made by J. Cottingham, 'Ethics and Impartiality', *Philosophical Studies*, 1983, vol. 43, pp. 89–90; J. Cottingham, 'Partiality, Favouritism and Morality', *Philosophical Quarterly*, 1986, vol. 36, no. 144, pp. 368–70; and E. Sankowski, 'Love and Moral Obligation', *Journal of Value Inquiry*, 1978, vol. 12, no. 2, p. 105.
45 See B. Williams, 'Moral Luck', in *Moral Luck*, Cambridge, Cambridge University Press, 1981. For further discussion of the Gauguin case and other related cases, see M. Baron, 'On Admirable Immorality', *Ethics*, 1986, vol. 96, no. 3; T. Nagel, 'Moral Luck', in *Mortal Questions*, Cambridge, Cambridge University Press, 1979; M. Slote, *Goods and Virtues*, Oxford, Clarendon Press, 1983, pp. 79ff.
46 See Cottingham, 'Partiality, Favouritism and Morality', pp. 369–70, for further examples. But Cottingham also points out that the number of people living good lives without love and friendship has certain limits. That is, a situation where most people live without love and friendship is probably not even feasible, much less *good*.
47 The Gauguin example may be somewhat misleading, in so far as it might be thought that the assessment of his life as good involves aesthetic or primarily aesthetic value, rather than moral value. To explore the complexities raised here would take me far beyond my present concerns, but let it be said that since the Gauguin example is usually taken to involve moral value, and also to avoid unnecessary complications, I shall proceed as if this is the case.
48 See Aristotle, *Nicomachean Ethics*, Book IX, Chapter 9, 1169b28–1170b19; J.M. Cooper, 'Aristotle on Friendship', in Rorty (ed.), *Essays on Aristotle's Ethics*, pp. 317–34; M.L. Homiak, 'The Pleasure of Virtue in Aristotle's Moral Theory', *Pacific Philosophical Quarterly*, 1985, vol. 66, nos 1 and 2, pp. 103–5; A.O. Rorty, 'The Place of Contemplation in Aristotle's *Nicomachean Ethics*', in Rorty (ed.), *Essays on Aristotle's Ethics*, pp. 389–91; F. Schoeman, 'Aristotle on the Good of

Friendship', *Australasian Journal of Philosophy*, 1985, vol. 63, no. 3; Sherman, 'Aristotle on Friendship and the Shared Life', esp. pp. 607–13; Sherman, *The Fabric of Character*, pp. 138–44.

49 Of course, *other* loves and friendships (and so the emotions which are constitutive of them) may also interfere with a certain relationship of love and friendship (and this suggests that there are limits to the number of people one can have as genuine friends). But these other loves and friendships are not thereby necessarily shown to be morally bad to any extent, since each of these may be good for the reasons given above in relation to love and friendship generally. Perhaps when one love or friendship interferes *excessively* with another, the former relationship (and the emotions constitutive of it) may in this context be therefore regarded as morally bad to some extent. But, as I argue in the following chapter, it is important to recognise here that, contrary to many Kantian views, just because something might be morally bad in some situation does *not* entail that it cannot in general be morally good.

50 For further development of this point, see P.S. Greenspan, 'Identificatory Love', *Philosophical Studies*, 1986, vol. 50, no. 3, esp. pp. 325–6; and Hursthouse, op. cit., esp. pp. 90–2.

51 Solomon, op. cit., pp. 56, 93, 97, 132, 189–90, 219–20, 236, 371–8. See also Martin Heidegger, *Being and Time*, New York, Harper & Row, 1962; Jean-Paul Sartre, *Sketch for a Theory of the Emotions*, London, Methuen, 1962; and Jean-Paul Sartre, *Being and Nothingness*, London, Methuen, 1969.

52 See here de Sousa, *The Rationality of Emotion*, pp. 323–4; and R. Wollheim, *The Thread of Life*, Cambridge, Mass., Harvard University Press, 1984. See also the recent interpretations of Hume's view, in *A Treatise of Human Nature*, of the passions (and in particular, *pride*) as constituting the self by providing a unifying thread which links the disparate 'bundle of perceptions' (*Treatise*, Book I, Part iv, section 6, p. 252) which is self. In his claim (at *Treatise*, Book II, Part i, sections 2 and 5, pp. 278 and 287) that pride 'produces' the idea of self, Hume seems to misrepresent a *conceptual* relation as a *causal* relation. Some recent commentators rescue Hume from this apparent falsehood by suggesting that Hume was here describing how pride helps constitute the self by unifying the bundle of perceptions. For this view, see J. McIntyre, 'Personal Identity and the Passions', *Journal of the History of Philosophy*, 1989, vol. 27, no. 4; A. Rorty, ' "Pride Produces the Idea of Self": Hume on Moral Agency', *Australasian Journal of Philosophy*, 1990, vol. 68, no. 3, pp. 255–69; A. Baier, 'Passionate Persons', Pauline Chazan, 'Pride, Virtue and Self-hood: A Reconstruction of Hume', and J. Taylor, 'Sympathy, Self, and Others', all presented at the 17th Hume Conference, Australian National University, Canberra, June 1990.

53 D. Sachs, 'How to Distinguish Self-respect from Self-esteem', *Philosophy and Public Affairs*, 1981, vol. 10, no. 4, pp. 352–4; D. Sachs, 'Self-respect and Respect for Others: Are They Independent?' in O.H. Green (ed.), *Respect for Persons* (Tulane Studies in Philosophy, vol. 31), New Orleans, Tulane University Press, 1982, pp. 113, 116–18, 122–5. See also, J. Benson, 'Who is the Autonomous Man?' *Philosophy*, 1983, vol. 58, no. 1, e.g. p. 9.

54 On this, see M. Stocker, 'Intellectual Desire, Emotion and Action', in Rorty (ed.), *Explaining Emotions*.

55 Cf. Dilman, op. cit.

56 Stocker, 'Affectivity and Self-Concern', esp. pp. 219–20, 224–8. See also Greenspan, 'Identificatory Love', and Greenspan, *Emotions and Reasons*, Chapter 3.

57 See Dilman, op. cit., p. 191.

58 Wallace, op. cit., pp. 15, 146n, 154–6. See also F.R. Berger, 'Gratitude', *Ethics*, 1975, vol. 85, no. 4; Blum, 'Compassion', pp. 515–16; and Blum, *Friendship, Altruism and Morality*, pp. 144–51, esp. p. 150.

59 Wallace, op. cit., p. 155. It should be acknowledged, however, that there are

certain people whose sense of self-worth is not dependent on any concern which others may have for them. For example, consider here Boethius's uplifting dialogue, *The Consolation of Philosophy* (trans. V.E. Watts, Harmondsworth, Penguin, 1969), written while he was languishing in prison awaiting execution. But such people seem to be the exception. I am indebted to Brian Mooney for this reference.

60 See Kant's second formulation of the categorical imperative, *Foundations of the Metaphysics of Morals*, in *Gesammelte Werke*, Berlin, Akademie Verlag, 1911, p. 429: 'Act so that you treat humanity, whether in your own person or in that of another, always as an end and never as a means only' (trans. L.W. Beck). Cf. also John Rawls, *A Theory of Justice*, Oxford, Oxford University Press, 1972, pp. 440–6.

61 Cf. Solomon, op. cit., pp. 274, 318–23, 350–5; Lyons, *Emotion*, pp. 97–8.

62 B. Williams, 'Morality and the Emotions', in *Problems of the Self*, Cambridge, Cambridge University Press, 1973, pp. 222–3. See also C. Nabe, 'In Praise of Guilt', *Journal of Value Inquiry*, 1987, vol. 21, no. 3; and Taylor, *Pride, Shame, and Guilt*, Chapter 4.

63 See also Greenspan ('Identificatory Love', pp. 325–6) and Stocker ('Affectivity and Self-Concern', pp. 225–8) on the *distancing* involved in self-pity.

64 See Aristotle, *Nicomachean Ethics*, Book IX, Chapter 8, and Book IV, Chapter 3, 1125a20f.

65 I discuss this point in relation to Kantian views in Chapter 3. Lawrence Blum also makes this point – see his *Friendship, Altruism and Morality*, pp. 153–7.

66 R.M. Adams, 'Motive Utilitarianism', *Journal of Philosophy*, 1976, vol. 73, no. 14, p. 470.

67 See ibid., pp. 470–2. Cf. Railton, op. cit., pp. 152–60; and Slote, 'Morality Not a System of Imperatives', p. 337.

68 See Lyons, *Emotion*, pp. 97–8, 187–8.

69 On this point, see S.L. Ross, op. cit., pp. 312–14.

70 Blum, *Friendship, Altruism and Morality*: page numbers in parentheses refer to this book.

71 Aristotle, *Nicomachean Ethics*, Book IX, Chapter 8, 1168a28ff, and Book IV, Chapter 3, 1125a20f. Cf. Cottingham, 'Ethics and Impartiality', pp. 85, 90; Cottingham, 'Partiality, Favouritism and Morality', pp. 364–8; and de Sousa, *The Rationality of Emotion*, pp. 308–9.

72 See Sachs, 'How to Distinguish Self-respect from Self-esteem'; Sachs, 'Self-respect and Respect for Others: Are They Independent?'; and Stocker, 'Affectivity and Self-Concern', pp. 217–20.

73 See W.D. Falk, 'Morality, Self, and Others' in H.-N. Castaneda and G. Nakhnikian (eds), *Morality and the Language of Conduct*, Detroit, Wayne State University Press, 1965.

74 Cf. B. Herman, 'Rules, Motives, and Helping Actions', *Philosophical Studies*, 1984, vol. 45, no. 3, p. 376; Luper-Foy, op. cit., p. 175; and Slote, 'Morality Not a System of Imperatives', p. 336.

75 It should perhaps be noted here that whether something is intrinsically or unconditionally good, where these notions are understood as outlined above, does not yet speak to the issue, discussed earlier, of its place (if any) in good lives (i.e. whether it is necessary for certain good lives, all good lives, or neither of these). For even if something is good in all situations, it may not be necessary for all good lives. And something may be non-motivationally good without being good in all situations, but it may nevertheless be a necessary feature of all good lives. I cannot discuss these complex issues any further here, for to do so would take me far beyond my present concerns.

76 Wallace, op. cit., pp. 152–3. Cf. also Cottingham, 'Partiality, Favouritism and Morality', p. 363; and Luper-Foy, op. cit., pp. 169, 173–5.

77 I am indebted to Kim Lycos for help with this section.

78 Note that evaluations of emotional rightness and wrongness centre on what we *take*

to be the object of our emotion, which in some cases may not be the *real* or *actual* object of our emotion. In Ronald de Sousa's terms, I am claiming that these evaluations are directed at the 'focus' of our emotion, which may not be identical to (what de Sousa, following Wittgenstein, calls) the 'target' of our emotion. (See de Sousa, *The Rationality of Emotion*, pp. 114–39; Ludwig Wittgenstein, *Philosophical Investigations*, Oxford, Basil Blackwell, 1978, I, 476. Cf. also Helen Nissenbaum's notion of 'aspects' of emotional episodes, which is closely related if not equivalent to de Sousa's notion of emotional 'focus': Helen Fay Nissenbaum, *Emotion and Focus*, Stanford, Center for the Study of Language and Information, 1985, p. 72.) The rightness or wrongness of an emotional response is determined by whether its focus is one which in fact we ought or ought not have here (i.e. by whether a *phronimos* would take this as an object of this emotion-type).

79 In Chapter 1, at note 40, I referred to intentionality or object-directedness as a feature of emotions considered as *cognitive* phenomena (which distinguishes them from non-cognitive phenomena, such as sensations). Now, my account here of the rightness and wrongness of particular emotional responses in terms of their *objects* might be regarded as a kind of reduction of the moral significance of emotions to their constituent *cognitions*, and thus as inconsistent with my general approach in this chapter, which aims to show the value of emotions in terms of all three of their constituents: i.e. cognitions, desires, and affects. But the inconsistency here is only apparent. I am using the objects of emotions to individuate particular manifestations of general emotion-types, and I am arguing that evaluations of those objects can be transferred to evaluations of the emotions which are directed at them. But this is not to suggest that *cognitions* (which are directed at emotional objects) are the *bearers* of value in the emotions which they partly constitute. Cognitions provide a means of linking the value or disvalue of particular instances of emotion with the value or disvalue of the objects at which they are directed, but it is still the complex of cognition-desire-affect which is evaluated in particular emotions. Thus, *caring* for the promotion of evil is worse than just *believing* that evil ought to be promoted, or *desiring* the promotion of evil.

80 See Aristotle, *Nicomachean Ethics*, Book VI, Chapters 3–6, 1139b14–1141a9. In my reading of *phronesis* and its role in virtue, I have been helped enormously here and in what follows by Nancy Sherman, *The Fabric of Character*, esp. pp. 28–55. See also R. Sorabji, 'Aristotle on the Role of Intellect in Virtue', in Rorty (ed.), *Essays on Aristotle's Ethics*, esp. pp. 205–14; and E. Telfer, 'The Unity of the Moral Virtues in Aristotle's *Nicomachean Ethics*', *Proceedings of the Aristotelian Society*, 1989/90, vol. 90.

81 See Aristotle, *Nicomachean Ethics*, Book VI, Chapter 11, 1143b14, Book VI, Chapter 12, 1144a32–5; Sherman, *The Fabric of Character*, pp. 38, 44–50, 165–74; and N. Sherman, 'The Place of Emotions in Morality', unpublished paper, 1988, pp. 41–2, 50–3. *Phronesis* here plays an analogous role to what Barbara Herman calls 'Rules of Moral Salience', in her 'normative reconstruction' of Kantian moral perception, in 'The Practice of Moral Judgment', *Journal of Philosophy*, 1985, vol. 82, no. 8.

82 Sherman, *The Fabric of Character*, p. 45. See also Ronald de Sousa's argument that emotions determine *axiological salience* among the wide and disparate range of possible objects of perception in any given situation, and as such, emotions are indispensable to the proper operation of reason (*The Rationality of Emotion*, esp. pp. 190–203). Interestingly, the importance of certain emotions (particularly *empathy*) in *moral* reasoning is now recognised in some contemporary forms of Utilitarianism. For example, in explaining the derivation of Utilitarianism from meta-ethical Universal Prescriptivism, R.M. Hare claims that it is only when we have *empathy* with those affected by our (proposed) actions that we can understand their preferences sufficiently for rational moral argument to proceed. See Hare, *Moral Thinking*, Oxford, Clarendon Press, 1981, e.g. p. 92: In making a rational moral judgement about how cautiously I ought to drive, I must know, with regard

to any potential accident victims, ' "What it is like to be those people in that situation" . . . In so far as they will *suffer* if they are in the collision (it will *hurt* to have one's neck broken), I shall not know what it will be like for them . . . unless I know what it is like to suffer like that. It will not do to know that someone's neck will be broken in the sense that the X-ray will show a fracture. I have to know what it will be *like* for the patient . . . It is the latter kind of knowledge which . . . [is] required for the full information which rationality in making moral judgements demands . . . If the experience of suffering were absent, both the object and the means of knowledge would be absent'. This claim is prefigured in Hare's earlier account of moral reasoning, in *Freedom and Reason*, Oxford, Oxford University Press, 1963, e.g. pp. 92–3: 'if B [the moral agent] were a completely apathetic person, who literally did not mind what happened to himself or to anybody else, the argument [about what ought to be done] would not touch him. The three necessary ingredients [for moral argument] which we have noticed, then, are (1) facts; (2) logic; (3) inclinations'.

83 While the perceptual and responsive elements of particular manifestations of emotion operate together when guided by *phronesis*, it might be noted that these two elements may diverge and so be evaluated differently when not directed by *phronesis*, or when *phronesis* has been inadequately inculcated. For example, imagine a generally sympathetic person, recently divorced by her husband, who hears that her ex-husband has suffered some misfortune. Because of her enduring sympathy, she may well be able to recognise more about the nature and extent of his suffering here than most others; however, due to their recent separation, she may respond to his situation with *Schadenfreude* instead of compassion. In this type of case, the sympathy which enables heightened perception might be evaluated as right, while the emotional response of *Schadenfreude* may be considered wrong. This shows that an important function of *phronesis* in good character is to harmonise the perceptual and the responsive elements of the emotions we have. On this variability of moral character, see Rosalind Hursthouse, *Beginning Lives*, Oxford, Basil Blackwell, 1987, pp. 266–8.

84 This should not be taken as suggesting that, in any given situation, there will always be *one* kind of emotional response which we ought to have. Michael Stocker (in *Plural and Conflicting Values*, pp. 9–36, 51–84, 112–23) discusses cases of 'dirty hands', such as torturing a person in order to obtain information which will save many innocent lives, and argues that in such cases we are justified in performing an act which is none the less ineliminably morally wrong. Stocker argues that we ought to feel shame at the morally unavoidable wrong we have brought about here (even though it might also be right to feel proud here at having saved innocent lives). So the *phronimos* may well have two conflicting emotional responses to a situation. See Aristotle's discussion of 'mixed' actions in *Nicomachean Ethics*, Book III, Chapter 1, 1109b30–1111b4.

85 It should be noted that those who believe in the Platonic and Aristotelian notion of the 'unity of the virtues' would hold that emotions such as love and care, which help constitute certain virtues and which therefore have significant first-level moral goodness, cannot be directed at objects which are (either subjectively, or in fact) evil. On this view, it is conceptually impossible to 'care' for what is or is taken as bad, *qua* bad, in the same sense that we care for the good. In my discussion here, it is clear that I reject this view, and I do so largely because I find it at odds with what we do seem able to care about in life. However, I will not argue explicitly against the unity of the virtues thesis here; suffice to say that those who believe that the emotions which help constitute certain virtues cannot be directed at morally bad objects, would not move from the first to the second level of moral significance in their evaluations of emotional responses. Thus, in so far as one cares for a murderous dictator at all, the view would be that we must be caring here for some morally good object, and so our emotional response here is both good and right, *qua* caring for the good. In contrast to this interpretation, I want to allow for the

possibility that the moral goodness and badness of emotions may come apart at the first and second level of moral significance.

86 See the parallel distinction in Kantian ethics between right action, which is action *in accordance with* duty, and morally worthy action, which is action performed *out of* duty. For Kantians, only the latter reflects well on the agent.

3 KANTIAN ARGUMENTS AGAINST EMOTIONS AS MORAL MOTIVES

1 See I. Kant, *Foundations of the Metaphysics of Morals*, in *Gesammelte Werke*, Berlin, Akademie Verlag, 1911, pp. 397–9, 405–7, 411, 428.

2 ibid., pp. 400–1, esp. p. 401n. Whether or not Kant can *consistently* allow that acting out of an emotion such as respect for duty has moral worth is a question I do not consider here. On this issue, see L.M. Hinman, 'On the Purity of Our Moral Motives: A Critique of Kant's Account of the Emotions and Acting for the Sake of Duty', *Monist*, 1983, vol. 66, no. 2, pp. 254–7; S. Palmquist, 'Is Duty Kant's "Motive" for Moral Action?', *Ratio*, 1986, vol. 28, no. 2; and R.P. Wolff, *The Autonomy of Reason*, New York, Harper & Row, 1973, pp. 83–4.

3 See W. Neblett, 'Feelings of Obligation', *Mind*, 1976, vol. 85, no. 339. A.C. Ewing (*Ethics*, London, English Universities Press, 1953, pp. 147–8) and W.D. Ross (*The Right and the Good*, Oxford, Clarendon Press, 1930, pp. 157–60, 164) make a similar claim about motivation by the sense of duty, and *desire*, to the effect that although action motivated by duty does indeed have special moral value, this need not entail that action motivated by desire is altogether without moral value, since one can be motivated by a desire to do one's duty. Indeed, Ewing and Ross believe that this is the best motive to action we can have.

4 Perhaps the view that a motive which involves devotion to duty from an emotion other than respect may be morally good would be disputed by Kant, on the grounds that such an attachment to duty would be fluctuating and unreliable. But, particularly if some of my later arguments are correct, there is no good reason to suppose that a person who, for example, loved acting conscientiously would be any less reliable in this regard than a person who acted conscientiously out of respect for the moral law, or a person who acted conscientiously without being emotionally committed to doing so.

5 It should be noted that there may be circumstances in which lacking a supererogatory good can be viewed as a moral failing. For example, consider a person who never 'puts himself out' for anyone, or a soldier lacking a medal in an Anzac Day march (cf. G.W. Trianosky, 'Supererogation, Wrongdoing, and Vice: On the Autonomy of the Ethics of Virtue', *Journal of Philosophy*, 1986, vol. 83, no. 1, esp. p. 30). This indicates that, as I suggested in Chapter 2, a good life consists in more than just not acting wrongly, but since it would only strengthen my claim that Kant fails to accord moral value to motivation by emotion, this complication can be ignored here. I take up this point briefly in Section 4.

6 See B. Herman, 'On the Value of Acting from the Motive of Duty', *Philosophical Review*, 1981, vol. 90, no. 3; Neblett, op. cit.; and T. Sorell, 'Kant's Good Will and Our Good Nature', *Kant-Studien*, 1987, band 78, heft 1. Herman's reasons for making such a claim are discussed later in this chapter.

7 R.G. Henson, 'What Kant Might Have Said: Moral Worth and the Overdetermination of Dutiful Action', *Philosophical Review*, 1979, vol. 88, no. 1, p. 50. Cf. also E.L. Beardsley's notion of 'moral credit' in 'Moral Worth and Moral Credit', *Philosophical Review*, 1957, vol. 66, esp. p. 326.

8 It is unclear whether Henson's Kant would regard the performance of acts which lack moral worth in battle (e.g. fighting but losing the battle) as morally defective.

9 I might say that I find Henson's interpretation of Kant as claiming that we are on the whole better without moral worth rather implausible, and quite at odds with some of Kant's comments in the *Foundations*. But I will not pursue this issue.

10 Schiller's verse runs:
   I readily serve my friends, but unfortunately
       I like doing it,
   and so it vexes me to think that I lack virtue.
   There is no other remedy; you must endeavour to
       despise them,
   and then perform with aversion what Duty bids
       you do.
   Quoted in W. Witte, *Schiller*, Oxford, Blackwell, 1949, p. 85.
11 Henson, op. cit., pp. 45ff.
12 ibid., p. 44n7.
13 This view that acting from duty and thus gaining moral worth requires the absence
   of cooperating inclinations is also attributed to Kant by Sorell (op. cit.). But on
   Sorell's interpretation, Kantian morality comes out as more demanding than it does
   on Henson's account, for unlike Henson, Sorell takes Kant as holding that lacking
   moral worth (e.g. through having cooperating inclinations *present* when acting from
   duty) may as such be morally defective.
      Also, since acting from a sense of duty seems prima facie compatible with the
   presence of cooperating inclinations, Henson and Sorell's interpretation might
   have been more intuitively plausible (although in my opinion, still objectionable as
   an account of the truth of the matter) if they had taken Kant as claiming that one
   may act from duty in the presence of cooperating inclinations, but only when one
   acts from duty without such inclinations present does one's act have moral worth.
   Perhaps Henson and Sorell should have recognised this possibility, and given
   reasons why their interpretation is to be preferred to this one.
14 See, for example, Henson's claim (op. cit., p. 45) that 'Kant would not deny moral
   worth to a dutiful act which was done in *opposition* to strong inclinations'. Indeed, on
   Henson's interpretation this would seem to be the typical picture of morally worthy
   action, given that, according to Henson, Kant's notion of moral worth (in the
   Foundations) is like a citation for winning the struggle against opposing forces. I might
   point out that this account of the morally worthy person as one who typically must
   overcome contrary inclinations in doing what is right, is directly contrary to Aristotle's
   account of the good person as one who does what is right with the full support of their
   desires and emotions. In Aristotle's view, the morally worthy person as portrayed by
   Henson's Kant would be a merely *continent* and so morally inferior person.
      Now in Chapter 2 I argued for this Aristotelian view of harmony between
   evaluation, motivation, and affectivity as a characteristic feature of a good person,
   and I also argued that having this psychic harmony is important for acting in
   accordance with our values. Nevertheless, I did allow that we may sometimes carry
   out our values in the face of psychic disharmony, and further, that we may show
   moral goodness to some degree in performing such action. However, I suggested
   that a person who acts on their values with psychic harmony is morally better than
   one who does so with disharmony. I shall not take up this issue again here, for in
   any case, as we shall see shortly, we need not interpret Kant (in the *Foundations*) as
   holding that morally worthy action typically involves acting against contrary inclinations or acting without any potentially supporting inclinations present (as
   Henson would have it). I discuss Henson's interpretation of Kantian moral worth
   further in Section 6 of this chapter.
15 It may be worth noting here that Henson's understanding of gaining moral worth
   for an act done from duty as akin to being awarded a citation for gallantry in the
   battle against evil fits Schiller's position better than the present one. For acting
   from duty in the face of contrary inclinations may be more like winning a battle
   against 'evil' (in Kant's eyes) than acting from duty without inclinations (or
   inclinations relevant to the act) present at all.
16 Herman, op. cit., pp. 371, 375–7, 382; cf. also R.B. Louden, 'Kant's Virtue Ethics',
   Philosophy, 1986, vol. 61, no. 238, pp. 487–8.

17 Herman, op. cit., pp. 363–6. In Section 2 I argue that contrary to this claim, which I believe Herman wrongly attributes to Kant, we can and sometimes do perform wrong acts (in Kantian terms) from a sense of duty.

18 Herman, op. cit., pp. 361–71, 376.

19 Cf. ibid., pp. 375n17, 377.

20 ibid., pp. 373–5; B. Herman, 'Integrity and Impartiality', *Monist*, 1983, vol. 66, no. 2, p. 236. Some recent defenders of Kantian or quasi-Kantian accounts of moral motivation have developed a similar notion of the duty motive as a condition governing our acting on other motives (such as desires and emotions). Indeed, these writers have argued that morally good action which reflects moral worth on the agent is characteristically motivated by duty in this sense. For these accounts, see M. Baron, 'The Alleged Moral Repugnance of Acting from Duty', *Journal of Philosophy*, 1984, vol. 81, no. 4; M. Baron, 'Kantian Ethics and Supererogation', *Journal of Philosophy*, 1987, vol. 84, no. 5, esp. pp. 252–3; P. Benson, 'Moral Worth', *Philosophical Studies*, 1987, vol. 51, no. 3, pp. 377–9; Louden, op. cit., esp. pp. 478–9, 484–9; A.M.S. Piper, 'Moral Theory and Moral Alienation', *Journal of Philosophy*, 1987, vol. 84, no. 2; and W.E. Schaller, 'Kant on Virtue and Moral Worth', *Southern Journal of Philosophy*, 1987, vol. 25, no. 4, esp. pp. 569–70. Earlier suggestions of this understanding of the duty motive can be found in Ewing, op. cit., pp. 147–8, and Ross, op. cit., pp. 172–3.

21 Kant, *Foundations*, pp. 393–4, 399–400, 428. See Ewing, op. cit., pp. 51–4; Herman, 'On the Value of Acting from the Motive of Duty', p. 377n19; Herman, 'Integrity and Impartiality', p. 237n16; C.M. Korsgaard, 'Aristotle and Kant on the Source of Value', *Ethics*, 1986, vol. 96, no. 3, p. 499; Louden, op. cit.; M. Midgley, 'The Objection to Systematic Humbug', *Philosophy*, 1978, vol. 53, pp. 161–2; and H.J. Paton, 'Kant on Friendship', *Proceedings of the British Academy*, 1956, vol. 42, pp. 49–51. See also Michael Slote's discussion of 'dependent goods' in Chapter 3 of *Goods and Virtues*, Oxford, Clarendon Press, 1983, esp. p. 64.

22 See K. Baier, 'Moral Value and Moral Worth', *Monist*, 1970, vol. 54, no. 1, p. 29; L.A. Blum, *Friendship, Altruism and Morality*, London, Routledge & Kegan Paul, 1980, pp. 158–9; L.A. Blum, 'Iris Murdoch and the Domain of the Moral', *Philosophical Studies*, 1986, vol. 50, no. 3, pp. 360–3; B.E.A. Liddell, *Kant on the Foundation of Morality*, Bloomington, Indiana University Press, 1970, pp. 39–43; K. Simmons, 'Kant on Moral Worth', *History of Philosophy Quarterly*, 1989, vol. 6, no. 1, esp. pp. 94–7; Sorell, op. cit., p. 101; and Wolff, op. cit., pp. 57–8.

23 See Kant, *Foundations*, pp. 390, 398, 411–12, 454.

24 Cf. Herman, 'On the Value of Acting from the Motive of Duty', pp. 363–6; Herman, 'Integrity and Impartiality', p. 234.

25 See Blum, *Friendship, Altruism and Morality*, pp. 30–3.

26 On this point, see J. Campbell, 'Kantian Conceptions of Moral Goodness', *Canadian Journal of Philosophy*, 1983, vol. 13, no. 4, pp. 536–9.

27 See B. Williams, 'Morality and the Emotions', in *Problems of the Self*, Cambridge, Cambridge University Press, 1973, esp. p. 226.

28 Kant, *Foundations* (trans. L.W. Beck), p. 427.

29 See Kant, *Foundations*, pp. 399, 413n3, and 451.

30 In Kant, *The Doctrine of Virtue*, in *Gesammelte Werke*, Berlin, Akademie Verlag, 1914, pp. 456–7 (trans. M.J. Gregor). See pp. 407–9, where Kant describes various emotions in terms of bodily sensations. Thus, enthusiasm is an 'agitation' which gives us 'the illusory strength of one sick with a fever'. And see p. 401: 'love is a matter of *feeling*, not of *will*'; and p. 377: 'feeling, no matter by what it is aroused, always belongs to the order of *nature*'; and we read again on p. 409: 'agitation [*Affekten*] always belongs to sensibility, no matter by what kind of object it is aroused'.

On the inadequacies of Kant's account of emotions, see D. Cartwright, 'Kant's View of the Moral Significance of Kindhearted Emotions and the Moral Insignificance of Kant's View', *Journal of Value Inquiry*, 1987, vol. 21, no. 4;

Hinman, op. cit., esp. pp. 252–4, 257–61; and M. Scheler, *Formalism in Ethics and Non-formal Ethics of Values* (trans. M.S. Frings and R.L. Funk), Evanston, Northwestern University Press, 1973, e.g. pp. 239–41.

31 See Kant, *Anthropology from a Pragmatic Point of View*, in *Gesammelte Werke*, Berlin, Akademie Verlag, 1917, Book III.

32 Kant, *Anthropology from a Pragmatic Point of View* (trans. V.L. Dowdell), p. 251. See also p. 266: the passions are 'cancerous sores for pure practical reason, and most of them are incurable because the sick person does not want to be cured and avoids the dominion of the principle by which alone a cure could be effected'.

33 This point is admitted by Ross (op. cit., p. 5), in arguing that action from a good motive is never morally obligatory.

34 Campbell (op. cit., pp. 536–9) pursues this issue in more depth than I have space to do here, and makes a similar point.

35 Blum, *Friendship, Altruism and Morality*, p. 32.

36 See W.K. Frankena, 'Obligation and Motivation in Recent Moral Philosophy', in K.E. Goodpaster (ed.), *Perspectives on Morality: Essays by William K. Frankena*, Notre Dame, University of Notre Dame Press, 1976, for a thorough discussion of this view, which he calls 'internalism', and its opposite, which he calls 'externalism'.

37 Cf. Blum, *Friendship, Altruism and Morality*, p. 31.

38 Herman, 'On the Value of Acting from the Motive of Duty', pp. 364–6; Herman, 'Integrity and Impartiality', pp. 234–5. See Kant, *Foundations*, p. 398. On the construal of this notion of a moral interest, see Benson, op. cit., esp. pp. 376ff.

39 Herman, 'On the Value of Acting from the Motive of Duty', p. 363. See also p. 382; and Benson, op. cit., p. 377.

40 For this criticism, see Blum, *Friendship, Altruism and Morality*, e.g. pp. 15, 99–101; and B. Williams, 'Persons, Character and Morality', in A.O. Rorty (ed.), *The Identities of Persons*, Berkeley, University of California Press, 1976, pp. 214–15.

41 See B. Herman, 'Rules, Motives, and Helping Actions', *Philosophical Studies*, 1984, vol. 45, no. 3. Piper (op. cit., pp. 111–17) also uses this argument based on the motive/object distinction to rebut Blum and Williams's above criticism of acting from duty. See also Baron ('The Alleged Moral Repugnance of Acting from Duty'), who agrees with Herman that helping another from duty is compatible with having a direct concern for their welfare. See also here J. Baker, 'Do One's Motives Have to be Pure?' in R.E. Grandy and R. Warner (eds), *Philosophical Grounds of Rationality: Intentions, Categories, Ends*, Oxford, Clarendon Press, 1986, esp. pp. 470–3; and Simmons, op. cit., e.g. pp. 91–2.

42 Cf. Blum, *Friendship, Altruism and Morality*, Chapters III, IV, and V; Blum, 'Iris Murdoch and the Domain of the Moral', esp. p. 346n14. See also J. Cottingham, 'Ethics and Impartiality', *Philosophical Studies*, 1983, vol. 43; and J. Cottingham, 'Partiality, Favouritism and Morality', *Philosophical Quarterly*, 1986, vol. 36, no. 144, esp. p. 369.

43 Herman, 'On the Value of Acting from the Motive of Duty', pp. 364–5; Herman, 'Rules, Motives, and Helping Actions', pp. 376–7. A similar argument for duty and against emotion as moral motivation is put forward by Baier (op. cit., p. 29) and Ewing (op. cit., pp. 53–4).

44 Kant, *Foundations* (trans. L.W. Beck), p. 394. See also pp. 407, 399–400; and Campbell, op. cit., p. 546; Korsgaard, op. cit., p. 503; and Louden, op. cit., p. 477.

45 Cf. Campbell, op. cit., pp. 545–6.

46 See Herman, 'Integrity and Impartiality', p. 235.

47 W.D. Ross (op. cit., e.g. p. 7) appears to hold such a view, as would Kant (see my note 44). See also Michael Slote's discussion of 'admirable immorality', in *Goods and Virtues*, Chapter 4.

48 Plato and Aristotle both take this approach. For two contemporary defences of this kind of view, see P. Geach, *The Virtues*, Cambridge, Cambridge University Press, 1977; and J. Smith, 'Can Virtue be in the Service of Bad Acts?', *New Scholasticism*,

1984, vol. 58, no. 3. On this issue, cf. P. Foot, 'Virtues and Vices', in *Virtues and Vices*, Berkeley, University of California Press, 1979; and G.E. Pence, 'Recent Work on Virtues', *American Philosophical Quarterly*, 1984, vol. 21, no. 4, esp. p. 288.
49 See Hinman, op. cit., pp. 263–4. Cf. also E. Brown, 'Sympathy and Moral Objectivity', *American Philosophical Quarterly*, 1986, vol. 23, no. 2, e.g. p. 179.
50 Kant, *Foundations*, p. 428.
51 See Barbara Herman's 'normative reconstruction' of Kant's view of the role of moral judgement in an agent who has properly internalised the motive of duty: 'It is useful to think of the moral knowledge needed by Kantian agents (prior to making moral judgments) as knowledge of a kind of moral rule. Let us call these "rules of moral salience". Acquired as elements in a moral education, they structure an agent's perception of his situation so that what he perceives is a world with moral features. They enable him to pick out those elements of his circumstances or of his proposed actions which require moral attention' ('The Practice of Moral Judgment', *Journal of Philosophy*, 1985, vol. 82, no. 8, p. 418).
52 Cf. Blum, *Friendship, Altruism and Morality*, pp. 132–7, 166.
53 ibid., Chapters II, III, and V. See also Robert Brown's contrast between personal love and what he (somewhat confusingly) calls 'disinterested care', in *Analyzing Love*, Cambridge, Cambridge University Press, 1987, pp. 26–9.
54 Of course, this is not to deny that it is indeed unprofessional to become so 'emotionally involved' with a particular patient or client that they become overly dependent on one, or that one is then led to neglect *other* patients or clients who also have a legitimate claim on one's emotional and other resources. However, instead of showing the inappropriateness of sympathy and compassion here, this just shows the importance of taking responsibility for having these emotional capacities, and, as Aristotle said, taking care that we have them on the right occasions, to the right degree, and towards the right objects.
55 Cf. Nancy Sherman, *The Fabric of Character*, Oxford, Clarendon Press, 1989, pp. 46–7. Note that emotions unguided by *phronesis* may still be directed at the right objects, and may still motivate right action. I am claiming that *phronesis* is necessary for *reliable* emotional direction and motivation.
56 B. Herman, 'The Practice of Moral Judgment', p. 424. See also B. Herman, 'Mutual Aid and Respect for Persons', *Ethics*, 1984, vol. 94, no. 4, pp. 601–2. Similar views or interpretations are expressed by Baron, 'The Alleged Moral Repugnance of Acting from Duty'; Cartwright, op. cit.; B. Gert, *The Moral Rules*, New York, Harper & Row, 1970, pp. 143–9; Louden, op. cit.; Piper, op. cit.; Sherman, op. cit., pp. 45–6; and N. Sherman, 'The Place of Emotions in Kantian Morality', in O. Flanagan and A.O. Rorty (eds), *Essays in Moral Psychology*, Cambridge, Mass., MIT Press, 1990.
The parallel here with Sidgwick and Hare's 'indirect utilitarianism' should be noted. That is, Sidgwick realised that being directly motivated by a desire to maximise utility would not, in some situations, *in fact* maximise utility. So one ought, if one is to be a good utilitarian, to act directly from various *other* motives, including some partial emotional motives (such as love for particular persons), as long as one's *overall* motivation is regulated by an underlying commitment to maximising utility. See H. Sidgwick, *The Methods of Ethics*, Chicago, University of Chicago Press, 1962, Book IV, Chapter III; and R.M. Hare, *Moral Thinking*, Oxford, Clarendon Press, 1981. For a critical discussion of indirect utilitarianism, see Bernard Williams, *Ethics and the Limits of Philosophy*, London, Fontana, 1985, Chapter 6.
57 See especially *The Doctrine of Virtue*, e.g. Akademie, pp. 399, 456–7, 484. See also *Anthropology from a Pragmatic Point of View*, Akademie, p. 282; and *Religion Within the Limits of Reason Alone*, New York, Harper & Row, 1960, p. 19n.
58 See R.M. Adams, 'Involuntary Sins', *Philosophical Review*, 1985, vol. 94, no. 1, esp. pp. 4–6, 11, 27–8; L.A. Blum, 'Compassion', in A.O. Rorty (ed.), *Explaining*

Emotions, Berkeley, University of California Press, 1980, pp. 514–16; Blum, *Friendship, Altruism and Morality*, pp. 140–68; A.C. Ewing, 'The Justification of Emotions', *Proceedings of the Aristotelian Society*, 1957, suppl. vol. 31, esp. pp. 67–8; P.S. Greenspan, 'Identificatory Love', *Philosophical Studies*, 1986, vol. 50, no. 3, pp. 321, 328, 335–6, 340–1; R. Hursthouse, 'Plato on Commensurability and Desire: Plato on the Emotions', *Proceedings of the Aristotelian Society*, 1984, suppl. vol. 58, esp. pp. 90–2; Midgley, op. cit.; and E. Sankowski, 'Love and Moral Obligation', *Journal of Value Inquiry*, 1978, vol. 12, no. 2, pp. 103–4, 108.

59 Cf. Greenspan, op. cit., p. 335.

60 *Lectures on Ethics* (trans. L. Infield), New York, Harper & Row, 1963, p. 200.

61 Cf. David Hume, *A Treatise of Human Nature*, Book III, Part iii, sec. 1.

62 See E. D'Arcy, *Human Acts*, Oxford, Clarendon Press, 1963, pp. 160–1; N.J.H. Dent, 'Virtues and Actions', *Philosophical Quarterly*, 1975, vol. 25, no. 101, esp. pp. 318–21, 326–7; J. Kekes, 'Moral Sensitivity', *Philosophy*, 1984, vol. 59, no. 227, esp. pp. 7, 11, 18; J. Kekes, '"Ought Implies Can" and Two Kinds of Morality', *Philosophical Quarterly*, 1984, vol. 34, no. 137; Ross, op. cit., pp. 132–3, 155–7; and J.D. Wallace, *Virtues and Vices*, Ithaca, Cornell University Press, 1978, pp. 76–7.

63 O.H. Green, 'Obligations Regarding Passions', *Personalist*, 1979, vol. 60, no. 2, p. 136.

64 L.A. Kosman, 'Being Properly Affected: Virtues and Feelings in Aristotle's Ethics', in A.O. Rorty (ed.), *Essays on Aristotle's Ethics*, Berkeley, University of California Press, 1980, p. 108. See Aristotle, *Nicomachean Ethics*, Book II, Chapter 6, 1106b15–23.

65 See Adams, op. cit., pp. 27–8. The distinction between motives which are accidentally good/bad and motives which are intrinsically good/bad is not intended to be exhaustive.

66 See, for example, *The Doctrine of Virtue*, pp. 399–400, 456–7.

67 Cf. Green, op. cit.; W. Lyons, *Emotion*, Cambridge, Cambridge University Press, 1980, pp. 202–6; Sankowski, op. cit., eg. pp. 105–6; and C.H. Sommers, 'Filial Morality', *Journal of Philosophy*, 1986, vol. 83, no. 8, esp. pp. 446–7, 450.

68 Aristotle, *Nicomachean Ethics*, Book III, Chapter 1, 1111a30–1, and Book IV, Chapter 5, 1125b30–3.

69 Here 'ought' means 'it is defective, if not...'. On this usage, see S.D. Hudson, 'Taking Virtues Seriously', *Australasian Journal of Philosophy*, 1981, vol. 59, no. 2, p. 192; and J. Kelly, 'Virtue and Pleasure', *Mind*, 1973, vol. 82, no. 327, p. 407.

70 Wallace, op. cit., pp. 135–41. See also note 5 in this chapter.

71 This view is taken by Baron, 'The Alleged Moral Repugnance of Acting from Duty', pp. 205, 210; Paton, op. cit., esp. pp. 49–51; Schaller, op. cit.; and Sommers, 'Filial Morality'. See also Louden, op. cit., esp. pp. 486–8.

72 A. MacIntyre, *After Virtue: A Study in Moral Theory*, Notre Dame, University of Notre Dame Press, 1981, pp. 142–3.

73 See Kant, *Foundations*, pp. 446, 453–5, 457–8; *Critique of Practical Reason*, in *Gesammelte Werke*, Berlin, Akademie Verlag, 1913, pp. 80–1.

74 See Hinman, op. cit., pp. 252–4; and Wolff, op. cit., p. 66.

75 See Kant, *Foundations*, p. 412; Wolff, op. cit., pp. 115–17, 216.

76 See Wolff, op. cit., pp. 122, 135–6, 172–3, 211.

77 See Kant, *Foundations*, pp. 457–8: '[Man] does not even hold himself responsible for these inclinations and impulses or attribute them to his proper self, ie. his will, *though he does ascribe to his will the indulgence which he may grant to them when he permits them an influence on his maxims to the detriment of the rational laws of his will*' (trans. L.W. Beck, my italics). See also *The Metaphysic of Morals*, in *Gesammelte Werke*, Berlin, Akademie Verlag, 1914, Introduction, p. 226. See Liddell, op. cit., pp. 105–7, 146–9.

78 For a contemporary argument for the view that being motivated by reason is sufficient for acting freely, see G. Watson, 'Free Agency', *Journal of Philosophy*, 1975, vol. 72, no. 8.

79 See Kant, *Anthropology from a Pragmatic Point of View*, Akademie, p. 267; and Hinman, op. cit., p. 258. For a detailed defence of this interpretation of Kant, see H.E. Allison, 'Morality and Freedom: Kant's Reciprocity Thesis', *Philosophical Review*, 1986, vol. 95, no. 3, esp. pp. 418–25. Cf. also the Stoic view of emotions mentioned in my Chapter 2, Section 1.

80 See Campbell, op. cit., pp. 543–4.

81 See M. Stocker, 'Intellectual Desire, Emotion, and Action', in A.O. Rorty (ed.), *Explaining Emotions*, Berkeley, University of California Press, 1980.

82 See Herman, 'On the Value of Acting from the Motive of Duty', pp. 376–82; and Herman, 'Integrity and Impartiality', p. 237, esp. n. 14.

83 Henson, op. cit., p. 52.

84 See ibid., p. 50.

4 RESPONSIBILITY FOR EMOTIONS

1 H.L.A. Hart, 'Responsibility', in J. Feinberg and H. Gross (eds), *Responsibility: Selected Readings*, Encino, Dickenson, 1975, p. 26. Of course, as we see later, ascriptions of causality may involve considerable complexity.

2 See ibid., pp. 30–2; and R. Audi, 'Moral Responsibility, Freedom, and Compulsion', *American Philosophical Quarterly*, 1974, vol. 11, no. 1, p. 2.

3 See Hart, op. cit., p. 33; Audi, op. cit., p. 2; and T.H. Irwin, 'Reason and Responsibility in Aristotle', in A.O. Rorty (ed.), *Essays on Aristotle's Ethics*, Berkeley, University of California Press, 1980, pp. 118, 125, 134.

4 J. Feinberg, 'Action and Responsibility' (in *Doing and Deserving: Essays in the Theory of Responsibility*, Princeton, Princeton University Press, 1970), pp. 128–39, seems to appreciate these distinctions.

5 For example, Descartes, *The Passions of the Soul*, esp. Part I, articles 17–29, 45–7; A.C. Ewing, *Ethics*, London, English Universities Press, 1953, p. 150; L.A. Kosman, 'Being Properly Affected: Virtues and Feelings in Aristotle's Ethics', in A.O. Rorty (ed.), *Essays on Aristotle's Ethics*, pp. 112–13; W. Lyons, *Emotion*, Cambridge, Cambridge University Press, 1980, pp. 180–1; G.E. Moore, 'The Nature of Moral Philosophy', in *Philosophical Studies*, London, Routledge & Kegan Paul, 1922, pp. 316ff; and R. Trigg, *Pain and Emotion*, Oxford, Clarendon Press, 1970, p. 49. Cf. also Kant, *The Doctrine of Virtue* (trans. M. Gregor), New York, Harper & Row, 1964, secs 34–5; W.D. Ross, *Foundations of Ethics*, Oxford, Clarendon Press, 1939, pp. 115–16; and H. Sidgwick, *The Methods of Ethics*, Chicago, University of Chicago Press, 1962, p. 239. For an excellent discussion of the claims of Kant and Sidgwick in this regard, see L.A. Blum, *Friendship, Altruism and Morality*, London, Routledge & Kegan Paul, 1980, Chapter 8. See also those writers cited in the following note.

6 For example, see R. Taylor, *Good and Evil*, New York, Macmillan, 1970, p. 241; and see also R.S. Peters, 'Emotions and the Category of Passivity', *Proceedings of the Aristotelian Society*, 1961–2, vol. 62, pp. 119f; both cited in I. Thalberg, 'Mental Activity and Passivity', *Mind*, 1978, vol. 87, p. 381.

7 See M. Stocker, 'Responsibility Especially for Beliefs', *Mind*, 1982, vol. 91, pp. 408–9. Cf. also M. Midgley, 'The Objection to Systematic Humbug', *Philosophy*, 1978, vol. 53, pp. 152–4, 167; R.C. Solomon, 'Emotions and Choice', in A.O. Rorty (ed.), *Explaining Emotions*, Berkeley, University of California Press, 1980, pp. 261–2; and R.C. Solomon, ' "I Can't Get It Out of My Mind": (Augustine's Problem)', *Philosophy and Phenomenological Research*, 1984, vol. 44, no. 3, esp. pp. 409–10.

8 See Stocker's consideration of this view with regard to belief, op. cit., p. 409.

9 Cf. R.M. Adams, 'Involuntary Sins', *Philosophical Review*, 1985, vol. 94, no. 1, pp. 7–10.

10 Stocker, op. cit., pp. 409–10.

11 ibid., p. 411. See also R.M. Gordon, 'The Passivity of Emotions', *Philosophical*

216   *Morality and the Emotions*

Review, 1986, vol. 95, no. 3; and R.M. Gordon, *The Structure of Emotions*, Cambridge, Cambridge University Press, 1987, pp. 110–20.

12 See R. Taylor, *Action and Purpose*, Englewood Cliffs, Prentice-Hall, 1966, p. 59, cited in Thalberg, op. cit., p. 387.

13 See Stocker, op. cit., p. 415.

14 There is an interesting analogy here between the views of those who hold an 'at will' requirement of responsibility, and those who in debates about abortion insist that there must be some morally significant 'marker event' at which a foetus gains independent moral status. For the impoverishment of both approaches is shown when we reflect that many of what various moral theories consider to be the most important features of a person and a life (such as self-awareness, an ability to reason and understand, and a capacity for happiness and suffering) are acquired only *gradually*, and yet this is no obstacle to their having moral significance or (at least to the extent that we participate in their development) to our having responsibility for them. For a convincing argument in support of this 'developmental' view of our morally significant capacities, see Stephen Buckle, 'Biological Processes and Natural Events', *Journal of Medical Ethics*, 1988, vol. 14, no. 3, pp. 144–7.

15 On this, see H. Frankfurt, 'The Importance of What We Care About', *Synthese*, 1982, vol. 53, p. 264.

16 For just some of its adherents, see Audi, op. cit., pp. 5, 13; F.B. Buckley, 'Analysis of "X Could Have Acted Otherwise"', *Philosophical Studies*, 1956, vol. 7, no. 5; R.M. Chisholm, 'Responsibility and Avoidability', in J. Feinberg (ed.), *Reason and Responsibility*, Belmont, Dickenson, 1965, pp. 255–6; E. D'Arcy, *Human Acts*, Oxford, Clarendon Press, 1963, p. 103; P.J. Fitzgerald, 'Voluntary and Involuntary Acts', in A.R. White (ed.), *The Philosophy of Action*, Oxford, Oxford University Press, 1968, p. 143; J. Glover, *Responsibility*, London, Routledge & Kegan Paul, 1970, pp. 10–11; H.L.A. Hart, 'Negligence, *Mens Rea*, and Criminal Responsibility', in *Punishment and Responsibility*, Oxford, Oxford University Press, 1968; H.L.A. Hart, 'Responsibility', p. 32; J. Plamenatz, 'Responsibility, Blame and Punishment', in P. Laslett and W.G. Runciman (eds), *Philosophy, Politics and Society* (Third Series), Oxford, Blackwell, 1967, p. 173; E. Sankowski, 'Responsibility of Persons for Their Emotions', *Canadian Journal of Philosophy*, 1977, vol. 7, no. 4, pp. 835–8; C.L. Stevenson, 'Ethical Judgments and Avoidability', in Feinberg, *Reason and Responsibility*, pp. 354–6; and White, op. cit., p. 6.

17 On this issue, see R. Lawrie, 'Passion', *Philosophy and Phenomenological Research*, 1980, vol. 41, no. 1; and G.D. Marshall, 'On Being Affected', *Mind*, 1968, vol. 77, no. 306, pp. 249–59.

18 A. Kenny, *Action, Emotion and Will*, London, Routledge & Kegan Paul, 1963, p. 98.

19 J.-P. Sartre, *Sketch for a Theory of the Emotions* (trans. P. Mairet), London, Methuen, 1962, pp. 75–6; R.C. Solomon, *The Passions*, Garden City, Doubleday Anchor, 1976, pp. 151–64, 192–3; R.C. Solomon, 'The Logic of Emotion', *Nous*, 1977, vol. 11, no. 1, p. 47; and Solomon, '"I Can't Get It Out of My Mind": (Augustine's Problem)', esp. p. 411. See also Descartes, *The Passions of the Soul*, Part I, article 46; and M. Scheler, *Formalism in Ethics and Non-formal Ethics of Values* (trans. M.S. Frings and R.L Funk), Evanston, Northwestern University Press, 1973, pp. 336–7, 350. On Sartre's view here, see A.G. Pleydell-Pearce, 'Freedom, Emotion and Choice in the Philosophy of Jean-Paul Sartre', *Journal of the British Society for Phenomenology*, 1970, vol. 1, no. 1, esp. pp. 40–1.

20 See H.G. Classen, 'Will, Belief and Knowledge', *Dialogue*, 1979, vol. 18, no. 1; J.L. Evans, 'Error and the Will', *Philosophy*, 1963, vol. 38, no. 144; B. Grant, 'Descartes, Belief and the Will', *Philosophy*, 1976, vol. 51, no. 4; Lyons, op. cit., pp. 181–2; J.M.E. Moravcsik, 'Understanding and the Emotions', *Dialectica*, 1982, vol. 36, nos 2–3, p. 214; L. Pojman, 'Belief and Will', *Religious Studies*, 1978, vol.

14, no. 1; L. Pojman, 'Believing and Willing', *Canadian Journal of Philosophy*, 1985, vol. 15, no. 1; H.H. Price, 'Belief and Will', in S. Hampshire (ed.), *Philosophy of Mind*, New York, Harper & Row, 1966, esp. pp. 106–12; and B. Williams, 'Deciding to Believe', in *Problems of the Self*, Cambridge, Cambridge University Press, 1973. For some arguments in support of the contrary view that we can and, indeed, often do adopt and reject our beliefs at will, see R. Holyer, 'Belief and Will Revisited', *Dialogue*, 1983, vol. 22, no. 2; M.B. Naylor, 'Voluntary Belief', *Philosophy and Phenomenological Research*, 1985, vol. 45, no. 3; and Sidgwick, op. cit., pp. 72–4. Whether or not we can have or give up beliefs at will, it nevertheless seems that there is much we can do to influence and control our beliefs, and that our doing so often amounts to our being responsible for them. On this, see M. Jefferson, 'What is Wrong with Sentimentality?', *Mind*, 1983, vol. 1, no. 368, p. 526; J. Montmarquet, 'The Voluntariness of Belief', *Analysis*, 1986, vol. 46, no. 1; I. Murdoch, *The Sovereignty of Good*, London, Routledge & Kegan Paul, 1970, esp. p. 40; and Stocker, op. cit.

21 Notoriously however, emotions can involve beliefs which are ill-founded, and to this extent beliefs may not be constrained by the way the world is. But this is not yet to say that these unconstrained emotional beliefs can be had or given up simply at will.

22 On this 'inertia' of the emotions, see A. Baier, 'Actions, Passions, and Reasons', in *Postures of the Mind: Essays on Mind and Morals*, London, Methuen, 1985. See also A.O. Rorty, 'Explaining Emotions'; R. de Sousa, 'The Rationality of Emotions', esp. pp. 140–1; and P.S. Greenspan, 'A Case of Mixed Feelings: Ambivalence and the Logic of Emotion', esp. pp. 236, 241–2; all in A.O. Rorty (ed.), *Explaining Emotions*.

23 Cf. Adams, op. cit., pp. 7–10. There is a certain peculiarity in asking whether desire is directly controllable by the will, since the will has often been identified with the faculty of desire (e.g. see Descartes, *The Passions of the Soul*, Part I, articles 17–18). Thus to will that something were the case is often interpreted as equivalent to wanting that it would be the case. But even if willing and desiring are taken as equivalent, it can still be meaningfully asked whether we can have or stop having our desires at will, for on the above view this would be like asking whether wanting to have or give up a certain desire is sufficient for having or giving up that desire, which is a familiar enough question.

24 See Adams, op. cit., pp. 10–11.

25 T. Nagel, 'Moral Luck', in *Mortal Questions*, Cambridge, Cambridge University Press, 1979. See also B. Williams, 'Moral Luck', in *Moral Luck*, Cambridge, Cambridge University Press, 1981; and J. Feinberg, 'Sua Culpa', in *Doing and Deserving*. For some defences of the contrary view, see J. Andre, 'Nagel, Williams, and Moral Luck', *Analysis*, 1983, vol. 43, no. 4; and H. Jensen, 'Morality and Luck', *Philosophy*, 1984, vol. 59, no. 229.

26 J. Feinberg, 'Problematic Responsibility in Law and Morals', in *Doing and Deserving*, p. 26. See also pp. 27–9.

27 Audi, op. cit., p. 3. Cf. M.A. Slote, 'Understanding Free Will', *Journal of Philosophy*, 1980, vol. 77, no. 3, pp. 147–8.

28 See Stocker, op. cit., p. 404. See also R. Taylor, 'Thought and Purpose', in M. Brand (ed.), *The Nature of Human Action*, Glenview, Scott-Foresman, 1970, p. 282.

29 See Stocker, op. cit., pp. 404–7.

30 See Adams, op. cit., pp. 14–16; C. Calhoun and R.C. Solomon (eds), *What is an Emotion?* New York, Oxford University Press, 1984, pp. 36–40 (Introduction); Descartes, *The Passions of the Soul*, Part I, article 50, Part III, articles 161 and 211; de Sousa, op. cit., e.g. p.141; R. de Sousa, *The Rationality of Emotion*, Cambridge, Mass., MIT Press, 1987, pp. 10–12; O.H. Green, 'Obligations Regarding Passions', *Personalist*, 1979, vol. 60, no. 2, p. 37; L.M. Hinman, 'On the Purity of Our Moral Motives: A Critique of Kant's Account of the Emotions and Acting for the Sake of

Duty', *Monist*, 1983, vol. 66, no. 2, pp. 262–6; P.J. Koch, 'Expressing Emotion', *Pacific Philosophical Quarterly*, 1983, vol. 64, no. 2, e.g. p. 181; Lyons, op. cit., pp. 195ff; Marshall, op. cit., esp. pp. 250–1; Midgley, op. cit., pp. 164–9; Murdoch, op. cit., e.g. pp. 17–23; W. Neblett, 'Indignation: A Case Study in the Role of Feelings in Morals', *Metaphilosophy*, 1979, vol. 10, no. 2, pp. 148–9; R.C. Roberts, 'Solomon on the Control of the Emotions', *Philosophy and Phenomenological Research*, 1984, vol. 44, no. 3; R.C. Roberts, 'Will Power and the Virtues', *Philosophical Review*, 1984, vol. 93, no. 2, pp. 245–6; Sankowski, op. cit., *passim*; R. Scruton, 'Emotion, Practical Knowledge and Common Culture', in Rorty (ed.), *Explaining Emotions*; and N. Sherman, 'The Place of Emotions in Morality', unpublished paper, pp. 22–33.

31 Murdoch, op. cit., pp. 17–18.

32 On the importance of fiction in developing and controlling our emotions, see K.L. Walton, 'Fearing Fictions', *Journal of Philosophy*, 1978, vol. 75, no. 1, esp. pp. 24–7.

33 Kosman, op. cit., pp. 112–13. Cf. M.F. Burnyeat, 'Aristotle on Learning to be Good', in Rorty (ed.), *Essays on Aristotle's Ethics*, pp. 76, 82. See also W. James, 'What is an Emotion?' in K. Dunlap (ed.), *The Emotions*, New York, Hafner, 1967, p. 22: 'There is no more valuable precept in moral education than this, as all who have experience know: If we wish to conquer undesirable emotional tendencies in ourselves, we must assiduously and in the first instance cold-bloodedly go through the *outward motions* of those contrary dispositions we prefer to cultivate . . . Soothe the brow, brighten the eye . . . pass the genial compliment, and your heart must be frigid indeed if it does not gradually thaw!' (cited in Solomon, *The Passions*, p. 168). Although here, of course, it must be remembered that James's account of emotions differs from mine, since (as we saw in Chapter 1) James held that emotions are just the feelings or awareness of bodily changes.

34 See Gordon, *The Structure of Emotions*, p. 154, for this suggestion.

35 See E. Sankowski, 'Love and Moral Obligation', *Journal of Value Inquiry*, 1978, vol. 12, no. 2, p. 106.

36 Cf. H. Frankfurt, 'Identification and Externality', in A.O. Rorty (ed.), *The Identities of Persons*, Berkeley, University of California Press, 1976; and T. Penelhum, 'Human Nature and External Desires', *Monist*, 1979, vol. 62, no. 3.

37 See Blum, op. cit., pp. 192–207.

38 Nancy Sherman, *The Fabric of Character*, Oxford, Clarendon Press, 1989, p. 171.

39 See also here, R.C. Roberts, 'What an Emotion is: A Sketch', *Philosophical Review*, 1988, vol. 97, no. 2, pp. 192–5.

40 Sherman, *The Fabric of Character*, p. 172.

41 Irwin, op. cit., p. 135. See Aristotle, *Nicomachean Ethics*, Book III, Chapter 1, 1111a27–b3.

42 See E. D'Arcy, *Human Acts*, Oxford, Clarendon Press, 1963, p. 41.

43 See Audi, op. cit., pp. 2–3; M. Stocker, '"Ought" and "Can"', *Australasian Journal of Philosophy*, 1971, vol. 49, no. 3, esp. pp. 314–16; and M.J. Zimmerman, 'Negligence and Moral Responsibility', *Nous*, 1986, vol. 20, no. 2.

44 In terms of the two kinds of foresight distinguished earlier, that we had (or culpably lacked) either (or both) act or schematic foresight of the consequences of our action seems sufficient for extending our responsibility to those consequences, as I discuss later. Since the present point seems to hold for either kind of foresight, I shall ignore such complications here, and speak only in terms of 'foresight'.

45 Sankowski, 'Responsibility of Persons for Their Emotions', p. 836. See also H.G. Frankfurt, 'Coercion and Moral Responsibility', in T. Honderich (ed.), *Essays on Freedom of Action*, London, Routledge & Kegan Paul, 1973, p. 78; Jefferson, op. cit., p. 526; and Midgley, op. cit., pp. 164–9.

46 David Hume, *A Treatise of Human Nature*, Book II, Part i, sec. 4.

47 Kosman, op. cit., p. 113.

48 Sankowski, 'Responsibility of Persons for Their Emotions', p. 840.

49 See Aristotle, *Nicomachean Ethics*, Book III, Chapter 1, 1111b1–4.
50 Frankfurt, 'The Importance of What We Care About', esp. p. 264.
51 A. Baier, 'Caring About Caring: A Reply to Frankfurt', *Synthese*, 1982, vol. 53, p. 275.
52 See Sankowski, 'Responsibility of Persons for Their Emotions', pp. 833–4; and M.B. Arnold, 'Human Emotion and Action', in T. Mischel (ed.), *Human Action: Conceptual and Empirical Issues*, New York, Academic Press, 1969, esp. pp. 177, 189–90. See also my discussion of emotion, psychic harmony, and strength of will in Chapter 2.
53 See Green, op. cit., p. 136.
54 See D. Davidson, 'Freedom to Act', and D.C. Dennett, 'Mechanism and Responsibility', both in T. Honderich (ed.), *Essays on Freedom of Action*, for two contemporary representatives, but the view has a long and distinguished history. Indeed, Irwin (op. cit., pp. 123ff) finds traces of it in Aristotle's ethics.
55 See M. Brand, 'Ability, Possibility, and Power', in Brand (ed.), *The Nature of Human Action*, pp. 130–1; G.E. Moore, *Ethics*, London, Oxford University Press, 1978, pp. 11–13, 84–95; and P.H. Nowell-Smith, *Ethics*, Harmondsworth, Penguin, 1954, pp. 273ff. Indeed, many of those writers cited in note 16 of this chapter as holding avoidability as a *necessary* condition of responsibility also take it, along with these writers here, to be a *sufficient* condition of responsibility.
56 See R.M. Chisholm, 'Freedom and Action', in K. Lehrer (ed.), *Freedom and Determinism*, New York, Random House, 1966, pp. 14–16; and Davidson, op. cit., pp. 141–4.
57 See J. Feinberg, 'Causing Voluntary Actions', in *Doing and Deserving*, pp. 185–6; H. Frankfurt, 'Alternate Possibilities and Moral Responsibility', *Journal of Philosophy*, 1969, vol. 66, no. 23, esp. pp. 832–6; and K. Lehrer, 'Comments', in W.H. Capitan and D.D. Merrill (eds), *Metaphysics and Explanation*, Pittsburgh, University of Pittsburgh Press, 1966, pp. 53–4. The example is taken from Lehrer, who in turn takes it from Locke, *An Essay Concerning Human Understanding*, Book 11, Chapter xxi, sec. 10.
58 Aristotle, *Nicomachean Ethics*, Book III, Chapter 5, 1114a4–31. It may be objected by libertarians and some Kantians here that no matter how fixed our character, we can always then and there make an effective choice to act against it. Whether or not such a claim is true, which (as may already be apparent from my arguments in this chapter) I doubt, I shall not consider it here, as it broadens the notions of voluntariness and responsibility so much that it would only aid my argument that we can be responsible for our emotions.
59 D'Arcy, op. cit., p. 125. See also Stocker, 'Responsibility Especially for Beliefs', p. 404.
60 D'Arcy, op. cit., pp. 32–4, 48–50.
61 Audi, op. cit., pp. 3–4.
62 W.H.F. Barnes, 'Intention, Motive and Responsibility', *Proceedings of the Aristotelian Society*, 1945, suppl. vol. 19, pp. 236–7.
63 See R.E. Keeton, 'The Basic Rule of Legal Cause in Negligence Cases', in Feinberg and Gross, op. cit., pp. 48–9.
64 See H.L.A. Hart and A.M. Honore, 'Causation and Responsibility', in Feinberg and Gross, op. cit., p. 38.
65 See Feinberg, 'Causing Voluntary Actions', pp. 166–7; and 'Sua Culpa', pp. 195ff.
66 See L. Kenner, 'On Blaming', *Mind*, 1967, vol. 76, no. 302, pp. 240–1, 248. See also R.B. Brandt, 'Blameworthiness and Obligation', in A.I. Melden (ed.), *Essays in Moral Philosophy*, Seattle, University of Washington Press, 1958, p. 36.
67 See J. Brown, 'Moral Theory and the Ought-Can Principle', *Mind*, 1977, vol. 86, no. 342, pp. 217–22; and J. Feinberg, 'On Being "Morally Speaking a Murderer"', in *Doing and Deserving*, p. 48.
68 See Glover, op. cit., esp. p. 3; and Hart, 'Negligence, *Mens Rea*, and Criminal Responsibility', pp. 152–7.

220   Morality and the Emotions

69 See John Rawls, 'Outline of a Decision Procedure for Ethics', *Philosophical Review*, 1951, vol. 60, no. 2, esp. pp. 178–80. While Rawls uses his sketch of a competent moral judge as a device for the resolution of conflicts between competing interests, the notion can be usefully extended to the context of determining moral responsibility for consequences of actions and omissions. This theoretical device is an old one, and in Rawls's idea one can find echoes of Rousseau's notion of the 'General Will'. For Rousseau conceived of the General Will in terms of a judgement of justice which would be arrived at if people in a community are adequately informed, are motivated by good will, and have a concern for common human interests. See Jean-Jacques Rousseau, *The Social Contract* (trans. G. Hopkins), Book II, Chapters III and IV, in Ernest Barker (ed.), *Social Contract: Essays by Locke, Hume, Rousseau*, London, Oxford University Press, 1971, pp. 193–8.

70 Cf. *Palsgraf* v. *Long Island R.R. Co.* (1928), cited in Feinberg, 'Problematic Responsibility in Law and Morals', p. 28n; *Larrimore* v. *American Nat. Ins. Co.*, 184 Okl. 614 (1939), cited in Keeton, op. cit., p. 46; Feinberg, 'Sua Culpa', pp. 195ff; J.G. Fleming, *The Law of Torts*, Sydney, Law Book Co., 1987, Chapter 7, esp. pp. 96–104; and W.A. Seavey, 'Negligence – Subjective or Objective?' in H. Morris (ed.), *Freedom and Responsibility*, Stanford, Stanford University Press, 1961.

71 Sankowski, 'Responsibility of Persons for Their Emotions', pp. 835–6; Adams, op. cit., pp. 17–21.

72 Feinberg, 'Causing Voluntary Actions', pp. 169–71. See also his 'Action and Responsibility', esp. pp. 139–51; 'Sua Culpa', pp. 200ff; Rorty, 'Explaining Emotions'; and G. Marshall, 'Overdetermination and the Emotions', in Rorty (ed.), *Explaining Emotions*.

73 See Robert I. Levy, 'Emotion, Knowing, and Culture', in R.A. Shweder and R.A. LeVine (eds), *Culture Theory: Essays on Mind, Self, and Emotion*, Cambridge, Cambridge University Press, 1984. I am indebted to Zoe Sweett for this reference. See also Marshall, 'Overdetermination and the Emotions'; and Rorty, 'Explaining Emotions', esp. pp. 118ff.

74 See, for example, Anthony Kenny's defence of compatibilism against physiological and psychological determinism, in *The Metaphysics of Mind*, Oxford, Clarendon Press, 1989, Chapter 10.

5   MORAL ASSESSMENTS OF PERSONS FOR THEIR EMOTIONS

1 I adopt 'credit' rather than praise as the positive correlate of blame because, as I suggest in Section 1, credit and creditworthiness seem parallel to blame and blameworthiness in that both types of assessments seem to require that the person at whom they are directed is responsible for what he is being assessed for, whereas praise and praiseworthiness seem to have no such requirement.

2 Hereafter, unless otherwise indicated, I intend 'blame' and 'credit' to refer to moral (rather than non-moral) blame and credit. On the issue of how to determine whether an assessment is a *moral* assessment, see Section 4 of this chapter.

3 For this account, see E.L. Beardsley, 'Moral Worth and Moral Credit', *Philosophical Review*, 1957, vol. 66, no. 3; E.L. Beardsley, 'Moral Disapproval and Moral Indignation', *Philosophy and Phenomenological Research*, 1970, vol. 31, no. 2; L.A. Blum, *Friendship, Altruism and Morality*, London, Routledge & Kegan Paul, 1980, pp. 187–90; S. Cohen, 'Distinctions among Blame Concepts', *Philosophy and Phenomenological Research*, 1977, vol. 38, no. 2; J. Feinberg, 'Action and Responsibility' and 'Sua Culpa', both in *Doing and Deserving: Essays in the Theory of Responsibility*, Princeton, Princeton University Press, 1970; L.C. Holborow, 'Blame, Praise and Credit', *Proceedings of the Aristotelian Society*,

1971–2, vol. 72; L. Kenner, 'On Blaming', *Mind*, 1967, vol. 76, no. 302; R.D. Milo, *Immorality*, Princeton, Princeton University Press, 1984, pp. 3–4, 21, and Chapter 8, esp. pp. 219–25; M. Philips, 'Rationality, Responsibility and Blame', *Canadian Journal of Philosophy*, 1987, vol. 17, no. 1, esp. pp. 143–4; E. Sankowski, 'Responsibility of Persons for Their Emotions', *Canadian Journal of Philosophy*, 1977, vol. 7, no. 4, esp. pp. 829, 832, 838; E. Sankowski, 'Love and Moral Obligation', *Journal of Value Inquiry*, 1978, vol. 12, no. 2, pp. 102, 108–10; J.E.R. Squires, 'Blame', *Philosophical Quarterly*, 1968, vol. 18, no. 70; and A.R. White, 'Responsibility, Liability, Excuses and Blame', *Studi Internazionale di Filosofia*, 1973, vol. 5.

Some writers accept the *necessity* of these conditions but would argue that this is not yet an account of the *sufficient* conditions for blameworthiness and creditworthiness unless we add a third condition stipulating that X is the justified subject of some blaming or crediting responses because of Z. This view is held by R.B. Brandt, 'Blameworthiness and Obligation', in A.I. Melden (ed.), *Essays in Moral Philosophy*, Seattle, University of Washington Press, 1958, esp. pp. 6–7, 14–17, 24–6; N.O. Dahl, '"Ought" and Blameworthiness', *Journal of Philosophy*, 1967, vol. 64, no. 13, esp. pp. 420, 427; J. Glover, *Responsibility*, London, Routledge & Kegan Paul, 1970, pp. 19–20, 49–50, 54–61, 70–3; and W. Lyons, *Emotion*, Cambridge, Cambridge University Press, 1980, pp. 193ff.

4 For discussion of the variety of blaming and crediting responses, see E.L. Beardsley, 'A Plea for Deserts', *American Philosophical Quarterly*, 1969, vol. 6, no. 1, esp. pp. 33–5, 42; E.L. Beardsley, 'Blaming', *Philosophia*, 1978, vol. 8, no. 4; E.L. Beardsley, 'Moral Disapproval and Moral Indignation'; E.L. Beardsley, 'Moral Worth and Moral Credit'; Brandt, op. cit., esp. pp. 5–14, 24–30; Cohen, op. cit.; J. Feinberg, 'Problematic Responsibility in Law and Morals', pp. 30–1, 'On Being "Morally Speaking a Murderer"', pp. 53–4, 'The Expressive Function of Punishment', pp. 98–118, 'Action and Responsibility', pp. 124–9, all in *Doing and Deserving*; Glover, op. cit., pp. 56–7; G.P. Henderson, 'Censure Under Control', *Ratio*, 1973, vol. 15, no. 1; Holborow, op. cit.; Kenner, op. cit.; Lyons, op. cit., pp. 193–5; Milo, op. cit., pp. 220–1; Philips, op. cit., pp. 143–5; and Squires, op. cit.

My use of the term blaming and crediting 'responses' may be thought a little misleading in so far as these responses are often *expressions* of blame and credit. However, I have avoided using the terms 'blaming expressions' and 'crediting expressions' here, because we may have a blaming or crediting attitude or emotion towards someone without expressing it to them, or indeed to anyone. In any case, by the notions of 'blaming responses' and 'crediting responses' I do not have in mind responses to blaming and crediting, but responses (to wrong or right emotions, actions, etc.) which themselves are *embodiments* of blame or credit.

5 See Beardsley, 'Blaming', pp. 579–80; P. Foot, 'Free Will as Involving Determinism', *Philosophical Review*, 1957, vol. 66, no. 4, pp. 447–9; Henderson, op. cit., pp. 49–54; Holborow, op. cit., pp. 92–100; T.H. Irwin, 'Reason and Responsibility in Aristotle', in A.O. Rorty (ed.), *Essays on Aristotle's Ethics*, Berkeley, University of California Press, 1980, pp. 134–5; Milo, op. cit., pp. 221–2; and J.D. Wallace, *Virtues and Vices*, Ithaca, Cornell University Press, 1978, pp. 55–8.

6 See Aristotle, *Nicomachean Ethics*, Book VI, Chapter 12, 1144a18, Book VI, Chapter 13, 1144b26–8.

7 See Hume, *A Treatise of Human Nature*, Book II, Part iii, sec. 2: 'Actions are by their very nature temporary and perishing; and where they proceed not from some cause in the characters and disposition of the person, who perform'd them, they infix not themselves upon him, and can neither redound to his honour, if good, nor infamy, if evil. The action itself may be blameable . . . But the person is not responsible for it; and as it proceeded from nothing in him, that is durable or constant, and leaves nothing of that nature behind it, 'Tis impossible he can, upon its account, become the object of punishment or vengeance' (cf. II, i, 6; II, ii, 3; and

222   Morality and the Emotions

Hume, *An Enquiry Concerning Human Understanding*, Section VIII, Part ii). See also Brandt, op. cit., pp. 12–19, 31–2; Glover, op. cit., p. 64; P.H. Nowell-Smith, *Ethics*, Harmondsworth, Penguin, 1964, pp. 270, 294–307.

8 On this point, see Cohen, op. cit., pp. 151–2, 157–8.

9 See Milo, op. cit., pp. 222–5.

10 For example, Susan Wolf ('Asymmetrical Freedom', *Journal of Philosophy*, 1980, vol. 77, no. 3, esp. p. 156) claims that creditworthiness does not require responsibility in the sense of being able to do otherwise.

11 Brandt, op. cit., p. 8n5. See also J. Andre, 'Nagel, Williams, and Moral Luck', *Analysis*, 1983, vol. 43, no. 4, p. 205; Glover, op. cit., p. 64; and J.J.C. Smart, 'Free Will, Praise and Blame', in G. Dworkin (ed.), *Determinism, Free Will, and Moral Responsibility*, Englewood Cliffs, Prentice-Hall, 1970, pp. 210–11.

12 There is also a second discontinuity between praise and blame which does not exist between credit and blame. That is, to praise a person for something seems to involve some kind of praising *act*, such as rewarding, congratulating, commending, or thanking, whereas neither crediting nor blaming a person for something need involve performing an action at all. Crediting or blaming someone may sometimes involve only having certain attitudes and emotions about them, without expressing them in action. Thus, where blame can take the form of having disapproval or unexpressed indignation towards the blameworthy person, similarly, to credit someone for their compassion may involve just thinking well of or admiring them on account of their compassion, without expressing this to them or others. However, were such thoughts or emotions to remain unexpressed, we could not really be said to have *praised* this person for their compassion, although we could still have *credited* them for it.

Of course, I am not denying that, as with blameworthiness and creditworthiness, someone can be praiseworthy without the question of whether praising responses towards them would be justified having been settled. Rather, the point here is that praise is already a certain kind of response to a person for their good qualities – namely, a response which involves (a certain kind of) action, whereas credit and blame may take the form of attitudes and emotions, quite apart from whether they are also expressed in action. So, the negative correlate of praise is not blame, but rather is located among those forms of 'speaking ill of' someone which do not require responsibility – such as dispraise, disparagement, and deprecation.

13 For this view, see for example Brandt, op. cit., pp. 29–30; H.H. Price, 'Belief and Will', in S. Hampshire (ed.), *Philosophy of Mind*, New York, Harper & Row, 1966, pp. 101, 112–13; and R. Taylor, *Good and Evil*, New York, Macmillan, 1970, pp. 241, 252.

14 Among the various proponents of this view are Dahl, op. cit., p. 420; B. Gert, *The Moral Rules*, New York, Harper & Row, 1970, pp. 143–9; and Lyons, op. cit., pp. 195, 202–3.

15 Price, op. cit., p. 113. See also pp. 101, 112.

16 John Stuart Mill, *On Liberty*, Cleveland, Meridian, 1962, Chapter IV, pp. 205–25. See also G. Dworkin and D. Blumenfeld, 'Punishment for Intentions', *Mind*, 1966, vol. 75, no. 299; H. Morris, 'Punishment for Thoughts', in *On Guilt and Innocence*, Berkeley, University of California Press, 1976, esp. pp. 12–13, 26; and Sankowski, 'Responsibility of Persons for Their Emotions', pp. 830–1, 838–40.

17 See those cited in note 4 of this chapter.

18 See R.M. Adams, 'Involuntary Sins', *Philosophical Review*, 1985, vol. 94, no. 1, pp. 21–4.

19 This view is held by Brandt, op. cit., pp. 6–7, 14, 16–17, 24–6; Dahl, op. cit., pp. 420f; Lyons, op. cit., pp. 194f; and Price, op. cit., pp. 101, 112–13; who were cited in notes 13 and 14 as explicitly denying that we can be blameworthy and creditworthy for our emotions. The view that blameworthiness and creditworthiness is sufficient for justified blaming and crediting responses is also held by Glover, op. cit., pp. 19, 49, 56ff; G.E. Moore, *Ethics*, London, Oxford University Press, 1978,

pp. 79–82; and Nowell-Smith, op. cit., pp. 271ff; although these writers are unclear on whether they allow us to be blameworthy and creditworthy for our emotions.

20 Indeed, it seems less important for crediting responses to be justified than for blaming responses to be justified. That is, given that one is creditworthy or blameworthy for something in the first place, to be the subject of unjustified crediting responses seems less bad (in so far as it is bad at all) than being the subject of unjustified blaming responses. One explanation for this asymmetry might be that, as Susan Wolf (op. cit., pp. 155–6) points out, reproaching or punishing a person is likely to cause them some pain, whereas praising or rewarding them will probably only add to their pleasures, and causing someone pain is something we think needs to be justified, while giving a person pleasure does not. So, to reproach or punish someone unjustifiably is to do them an injustice, whereas to praise someone unjustifiably is apt to be just a harmless mistake. (Of course, this is not to deny that it *can* be bad to have certain crediting responses, such as rewarding, towards a creditworthy person when they are unjustified in a particular case, especially if this is at the expense of other creditworthy people who are justified in being the subjects of those responses.) See also Glover, op. cit., pp. 68n2, 198; and Holborow, op. cit., p. 90.

21 Mill, *On Liberty*, p. 209.

22 ibid., p. 207. See also Sankowski, 'Responsibility of Persons for Their Emotions', pp. 838–9.

23 See Brandt, op. cit., pp. 7–8, 16–17, 26–7; Cohen, op. cit.; Feinberg, 'Action and Responsibility', op. cit., pp. 127–9; H. Jensen, 'Morality and Luck', *Philosophy*, 1984, vol. 59, no. 229, p. 325; and Milo, op. cit., p. 220.

24 See Brandt, op. cit., pp. 6–7; L. Hertzberg, 'Blame and Causality', *Mind*, 1975, vol. 84, no. 336, p. 510; and Squires, op. cit., pp. 58–60.

25 See Adams, op. cit., pp. 21–4; Beardsley, 'A Plea for Deserts', pp. 40–2; Brandt, op. cit., pp. 17n17, 25–7; and Squires, op. cit., pp. 54ff.

26 This view seems to be advocated by Brandt, op. cit., pp. 6–7, 14, 16–17, 24–6; Glover, op. cit., pp. 19, 49, 56ff; and Lyons, op. cit., pp. 194ff; among others.

27 See Beardsley, 'Moral Disapproval and Moral Indignation', op. cit., esp. pp. 161, 166, 174–6; Beardsley, 'A Plea for Deserts', pp. 41–2; and Irwin, op. cit., p. 134.

28 Cf. Augustine's dictum: 'Hate the sin, not the sinner.' On pardoning and forgiving as excluding blaming responses while preserving blameworthiness, see Cohen, op. cit., p. 164; E. D'Arcy, *Human Acts*, Oxford, Clarendon Press, 1963, p. 80; A.C. Ewing, *Ethics*, London, English Universities Press, 1953, pp. 170–1; Holborow, op. cit., p. 88; J. King, 'Elenchus, Self-Blame and the Socratic Paradox', *Review of Metaphysics*, 1987, vol. 41, no. 1, esp. pp. 119–20; A. Kolnai, 'Forgiveness', *Proceedings of the Aristotelian Society*, 1973–4, vol. 74, esp. p. 101; and J. North, 'Wrongdoing and Forgiveness', *Philosophy*, 1987, vol. 62, no. 242, esp. p. 507.

The fact that forgiveness may sometimes consist in just an internal change of heart, without any change in external actions (e.g. in cases where the wrongdoer is abroad or now deceased), also shows that blaming responses may sometimes be only attitudes and emotions. For *these* are what one gives up in forgiveness here.

29 Adams, op. cit., p. 23; see also p. 24. And Sankowski, 'Love and Moral Obligation', pp. 109–10.

30 This shows that it may be misleading of Strawson ('Freedom and Resentment', in *Freedom and Resentment and Other Essays*, London, Methuen, 1974) to argue that if no one was responsible for anything, then the emotional responses embodying moral assessments which we could legitimately have towards others on account of what they do and have would be deeply impoverished. For although the absence of responsibility may exclude the justifiedness of our having *some* such emotional responses, such as indignation and gratitude, nevertheless as we can see here, we could still justifiably have a wide range of emotions involving moral assessments towards others on account of what they do and have.

31 Of course, the former person may be *enviable* and the latter *pitiable* in regard to

such things, but there are important differences between envy and thinking well of or esteem, as there are between pity and thinking poorly of or disesteem. Thus, in contrast to thinking well of and esteem, envying a person for something (such as their popularity or their abundance of spare time) does not necessarily imply that we thereby think any better of *them*; and unlike thinking poorly of and disesteem, pitying someone for their bad features (such as racist beliefs or uncontrollable anger) need not imply that we thereby think any less of *them*. Indeed, we might wonder whether envy and pity are agent (or person) evaluations at all, for envy seems to be just an affective desire for something possessed by another which one acutely feels one is lacking, and pity seems to be more like just regarding a certain state of affairs with sorrow. On envy here, see J. Neu, 'Jealous Thoughts', in A.O. Rorty (ed.), *Explaining Emotions*, Berkeley, University of California Press, 1980. For further discussion of pity in the context of this issue, see M. Stocker, 'Affectivity and Self-Concern: The Assumed Psychology in Aristotle's Ethics', *Pacific Philosophical Quarterly*, 1983, vol. 64, no. 3, secs 5 and 7.

32 It should be noted that while these assessments do not require responsibility, they may of course still be applied to people for features which they *are* responsible for. Indeed, crediting and blaming (which we have already seen, do seem to require responsibility) are themselves ways of thinking well or poorly of people, respectively, but importantly here, the reverse is not the case. That is, we can think well of a person for their good qualities, such as their wit or their athleticism, without thereby *crediting* them for those qualities. And likewise, we can think poorly of a person for defects such as laziness or ugliness, without thereby *blaming* them for those features. For in making such assessments we need not presuppose (as do credit and blame) that the person involved is responsible for their good or bad feature. Thus, the range of crediting and blaming responses which we can have towards people form a subset of the full variety of esteeming and disesteeming responses which we can have towards people.

33 This might be regarded as a somewhat unorthodox way of proceeding, in so far as it is thought that we have a better grasp of the notions of esteem and disesteem than we do of pride and shame. Nevertheless, I believe that this approach will prove useful in helping us understand what we can be estimable and disestimable for.

34 See Hume, *A Treatise of Human Nature*, Book II, Part i; P.S. Ardal, *Passion and Value in Hume's Treatise*, Edinburgh, Edinburgh University Press, 1966, Chapter 2; A. Isenberg, 'Natural Pride and Natural Shame', and G. Taylor, 'Pride', both in Rorty (ed.), *Explaining Emotions*; and G. Taylor, *Pride, Shame, and Guilt: Emotions of Self-Assessment*, Oxford, Clarendon Press, 1985, esp. pp. 20–35, 41–2, 71–3, 90–2. While Hume speaks of pride and *humility*, as Ardal (op. cit., p. 34) points out, much of what Hume says about humility actually seems closer to our present notion of *shame*, and so I shall speak of shame rather than humility as the contrary of pride.

Given my presentation in Chapter 1 of Hume's theory of emotions as just simple unanalysable impressions, he cannot (or cannot consistently) see these features of pride and shame as *conceptually* involved in these emotions, but rather must take these features as typical causal antecedents of pride and shame. However, as has often been pointed out, Hume's discussion is more illuminating of pride and shame when interpreted as making conceptual points about these emotions, and this is how I shall read him here.

Strictly speaking, the requirement that pride and shame be directed at objects which are *in fact* related to the self in some way, is a requirement only of *rational* pride and shame. That is, it is of course possible for a person to have pride or shame about something which they believe is related to them in the appropriate way, even though *in fact* it is not, but this would be an example of *irrational* pride or shame. I shall ignore this complication in the text, since even in such cases of irrational pride and shame the appropriate relation is still *believed* necessary for having these emotions, and it is this relation itself which I am interested in here.

So when I speak of pride and shame, I am referring to pride and shame about things which are actually related to us in the manner required for these emotions to be rational.

35 Hume, *Treatise*, Book II, Part i, sec. 6.

36 ibid.

37 On these possibilities, see Hume, *Treatise*, Book II, Part i, sec. 6; Ardal, op. cit., Chapter 2; A. Baier, 'Hume's Analysis of Pride', *Journal of Philosophy*, 1978, vol. 75, no. 1; D. Davidson, 'Hume's Cognitive Theory of Pride', *Journal of Philosophy*, 1976, vol. 73, no. 19; Isenberg, op. cit.; Stocker, 'Affectivity and Self-Concern', esp. pp. 218–20; Taylor, 'Pride'; and Taylor, *Pride, Shame and Guilt*.

38 Adams, op. cit., p. 11. See also Aristotle, *Nicomachean Ethics*, Book III, Chapter 1, 1111b1–3; M.C. Aufhauser, 'Guilt and Guilt Feeling', *Ethics*, 1975, vol. 85, no. 4, esp. pp. 293–4; Blum, op. cit., pp. 169–90; and E. Schlossberger, 'Why We Are Responsible for Our Emotions', *Mind*, 1986, vol. 95, no. 377.

39 To be sure, we may feel great regret and maybe even shame simply at being involved in (e.g. just being a causal agent in) the production of something bad or wrong, such as accidentally running over someone, where what is done did not (or not in an appropriate way) proceed from our beliefs, desires, intentions, or emotions. But importantly, we could justifiably have shame here only at *having done what is bad or wrong*; we would not be justified in having shame about *ourselves* for this (although of course, such a reaction would be perfectly natural), and so *we* would not be disestimable for this.

40 See St Thomas Aquinas, *Summa Theologiae*, 1a2ae, 24, 1. See also H. Sidgwick, *The Methods of Ethics*, Chicago, Chicago University Press, 1962, pp. 72ff.

41 Aquinas, *Summa Theologiae*, 1a2ae, 24, 1.

42 Cf. Susan Wolf's critique of the apparent overridingness of certain moralities in determining the sorts of character-ideals which we should aspire to ('Moral Saints', *Journal of Philosophy*, 1982, vol. 79, no. 8). For Wolf's negative assessments of people who would seem to embody those ideals could be thought equally important from a life-guiding point of view as any *moral* assessments of such people. (Indeed, Wolf's argument may be taken not as making *extramoral* points here, but rather as making *moral* assessments of various deficient moralities, and therefore as suggestions about what any adequate conception of morality must as such involve.)

43 For discussions of some of these issues, see M. Baron, 'On Admirable Immorality', *Ethics*, 1986, vol. 96, no. 3; O. Flanagan, 'Admirable Immorality and Admirable Imperfection', *Journal of Philosophy*, 1986, vol. 83, no. 1; M. Slote, *Goods and Virtues*, Oxford, Clarendon Press, 1983, Chapter 4; and M. Stocker, *Plural and Conflicting Values*, Oxford, Clarendon Press, 1990, esp. Chapter 1.

44 Kant himself seems to deny the possibility of a person being pathologically incapable of acting from duty. Nevertheless, the existence of pathological liars is all too familiar for many of us.

45 Cf. J. Brown, 'Moral Theory and the Ought-Can Principle', *Mind*, 1977, vol. 86, esp. pp. 216–17; and Ewing, op. cit., pp. 146–7.

46 See Adams, op. cit., p. 23. It should be remembered that here I am discussing moral assessments of *persons* for their morally significant features, but I am not discussing morally significant natural events, such as earthquakes.

47 Blum, op. cit., pp. 172–83. See also J. Kekes, 'Moral Sensitivity', *Philosophy*, 1984, vol. 59, no. 227; and J. Kekes, '"Ought Implies Can" and Two Kinds of Morality', *Philosophical Quarterly*, 1984, vol. 34, no. 137, esp. pp. 463–7.

48 Adams, op. cit., p. 12. See also Andre, op. cit., p. 205; and N.J.H. Dent, 'Virtues and Actions', *Philosophical Quarterly*, 1975, vol. 25, no. 101, esp. pp. 331–2.

49 On the distinction between these two types of evaluations, see T. Nagel, 'Moral Luck', in *Mortal Questions*, Cambridge, Cambridge University Press, 1979, p. 36.

50 See L.A. Blum, 'Iris Murdoch and the Domain of the Moral', *Philosophical Studies*, 1986, vol. 50, no. 3, esp. pp. 360ff; and S.L. Ross, 'Evaluating the

Emotions', *Journal of Philosophy*, 1984, vol. 81, no. 6, pp. 315–16. See also my Chapter 2, Section 7.

51 Hume, *Treatise*, Book III, Part iii, sec. 4. See Aristotle, *Nicomachean Ethics*, Books I, II, III (Chapters 1–5), VII (Chapter 13), and IX (Chapter 9). See also Martha C. Nussbaum, *The Fragility of Goodness*, Cambridge, Cambridge University Press, 1986, esp. Chapters 11 and 12, for an excellent discussion of how so much that is morally valuable in our lives and which we can be estimable and disestimable for is importantly beyond our control.

52 R.C. Roberts, 'Will Power and the Virtues', *Philosophical Review*, 1984, vol. 93, no. 2, p. 227. See also Nagel, op. cit., pp. 32–3. Here we might think of G.E. Moore, who was often thought of as good on account of the natural qualities of kindness, politeness, and generosity which he displayed.

53 See Blum, *Friendship, Altruism and Morality*, pp. 188–90.

Bibliography

Adams, R.M., 'Motive utilitarianism', *Journal of Philosophy*, 1976, vol. 73, no. 14.
—— 'Saints', *Journal of Philosophy*, 1984, vol. 81, no. 7.
—— 'Involuntary Sins', *Philosophical Review*, 1985, vol. 94, no. 1.
Allison, H.E., 'Morality and Freedom: Kant's Reciprocity Thesis', *Philosophical Review*, 1986, vol. 95, no. 3.
Alston, W.P., 'Emotion and Feeling', in P. Edwards (ed.), *The Encyclopedia of Philosophy* (Vol. 2), New York, Collier Macmillan, 1967.
—— 'Feelings', *Philosophical Review*, 1969, vol. 78, no. 1.
Andre, J., 'Nagel, Williams, and Moral Luck', *Analysis*, 1983, vol. 43, no. 4.
Annis, D.B., 'The Meaning, Value, and Duties of Friendship', *American Philosophical Quarterly*, 1987, vol. 24, no. 4.
Aquila, R.E., 'Causes and Constituents of Occurrent Emotion', *Philosophical Quarterly*, 1975, vol. 25, no. 101.
Aquinas, St Thomas, *Summa Theologiae, Vol. 19, The Emotions* (trans. E. D'Arcy), London, Eyre & Spottiswoode, 1967.
—— *Summa Theologiae, Vol. 20, Pleasure* (trans. E. D'Arcy), London, Eyre & Spottiswoode, 1975.
Ardal, P.S., *Passion and Value in Hume's Treatise*, Edinburgh, Edinburgh University Press, 1966.
Aristotle, *The Nicomachean Ethics* (trans. W.D. Ross), Oxford, Oxford University Press, 1915.
—— *De Anima* (trans. J.A. Smith), Oxford, Clarendon Press, 1931.
—— *The Eudemian Ethics* (trans. A. Rackham), London, Heinemann, 1935.
—— *The Rhetoric* (trans. W.R. Roberts), Oxford, Clarendon Press, 1946.
Armstrong, R.L., 'Friendship', *Journal of Value Inquiry*, 1985, vol. 19, no. 3.
Arnold, M.B., 'Human Emotion and Action', in T. Mischel (ed.), *Human Action: Conceptual and Empirical Issues*, New York, Academic Press, 1969.
Audi, R., 'Moral Responsibility, Freedom, and Compulsion', *American Philosophical Quarterly*, 1974, vol. 11, no. 1.
—— 'The Rational Assessment of Emotions', *Southwestern Journal of Philosophy*, 1977, vol. 8.
Aufhauser, M.C., 'Guilt and Guilt Feeling: Power and the Limits of Power', *Ethics*, 1975, vol. 85.

Augustine, St, *City of God* (trans. D.S. Wiesen), London, Heinemann, 1968.
Aune, B., 'Feelings, Moods, and Introspection', *Mind*, 1963, vol. 72, no. 286.
Badhwar, N.K., 'Friendship, Justice and Supererogation', *American Philosophical Quarterly*, 1985, vol. 22, no. 2.
—— 'Friends as Ends in Themselves', *Philosophy and Phenomenological Research*, September 1987, vol. 48, no. 1.
Baier, A., 'Hume's Analysis of Pride', *Journal of Philosophy*, 1978, vol. 75, no. 1.
—— 'Master Passions', in A.O. Rorty (ed.), *Explaining Emotions*, Berkeley, University of California Press, 1980.
—— 'Caring about Caring: A Reply to Frankfurt', *Synthese*, 1982, vol. 53, no. 2.
—— *Postures of the Mind*, London, Methuen, 1985.
—— 'Trust and Anti-trust', *Ethics*, 1986, vol. 96, no. 2.
—— 'Passionate Persons', 17th Hume Conference, Australian National University, Canberra, June 1990.
—— 'Hume on Pride and Virtue', unpublished paper.
Baier, K., 'Moral Value and Moral Worth', *Monist*, 1970, vol. 54, no. 1.
Bailey, C., 'Morality, Reason and Feeling', *Journal of Moral Education*, 1980, vol. 9, no. 2.
Baker, J., 'Do One's Motives Have to be Pure?', in R.E. Grandy and R. Warner (eds), *Philosophical Grounds of Rationality: Intentions, Categories, Ends*, Oxford, Clarendon Press, 1986.
Barnes, W.H.F., 'Intention, Motive and Responsibility', *Proceedings of the Aristotelian Society*, 1945, suppl. vol. 19.
Baron, M., 'The Alleged Moral Repugnance of Acting from Duty', *Journal of Philosophy*, 1984, vol. 81, no. 4.
—— 'Varieties of Ethics of Virtue', *American Philosophical Quarterly*, 1985, vol. 22, no. 1.
—— 'On Admirable Immorality', *Ethics*, 1986, vol. 96, no. 3.
—— 'Kantian Ethics and Supererogation', *Journal of Philosophy*, 1987, vol. 84, no. 5.
Beardsley, E.L., 'Moral Worth and Moral Credit', *Philosophical Review*, 1957, vol. 66, no. 3.
—— 'A Plea for Deserts', *American Philosophical Quarterly*, 1969, vol. 6, no. 1.
—— 'Moral Disapproval and Moral Indignation', *Philosophy and Phenomenological Research*, 1970, vol. 31.
—— 'Blaming', *Philosophia*, 1978, vol. 8, no. 4.
Bedford, E., 'Emotions', in V.C. Chappell (ed.), *The Philosophy of Mind*, Englewood Cliffs, Prentice-Hall, 1962.
Benjamin, M., *Splitting the Difference: Compromise and Integrity in Ethics and Politics*, Lawrence, Kansas University Press, 1990.
Bennett, J., *A Study of Spinoza's Ethics*, Indianapolis, Hackett, 1984.
Benson, J., 'Emotion and Expression', *Philosophical Review*, 1967, vol. 76, no. 3.
—— 'Who is the Autonomous Man?', *Philosophy*, 1983, vol. 58, no. 1.
Benson, P., 'Moral Worth', *Philosophical Studies*, 1987, vol. 51, no. 3.
Bentham, J., *Works*, Edinburgh, Tait, 1843.

Ben-Zeev, A., 'The Nature of Emotions', *Philosophical Studies*, 1987, vol. 52, no. 3.

Berger, F.R., 'Gratitude', *Ethics*, 1975, vol. 85, no. 4.

Bergmann, F., 'Review of R. Solomon, *The Passions*', *Journal of Philosophy*, 1978, vol. 75, no. 4.

Blum, L.A., 'Compassion', in A.O. Rorty (ed.), *Explaining Emotions*, Berkeley, University of California Press, 1980.

—— *Friendship, Altruism and Morality*, London, Routledge & Kegan Paul, 1980.

—— 'Kant's and Hegel's Moral Rationalism: A Feminist Perspective', *Canadian Journal of Philosophy*, 1982, vol. 12, no. 2.

—— 'Iris Murdoch and the Domain of the Moral', *Philosophical Studies*, 1986, vol. 50, no. 3.

Boethius, *The Consolation of Philosophy* (trans. V.E. Watts), Harmondsworth, Penguin, 1969.

Brand, M., 'Ability, Possibility, and Power', in M. Brand (ed.), *The Nature of Human Action*, Glenview, Scott-Foresman, 1970.

—— (ed.), *The Nature of Human Action*, Glenview, Scott-Foresman, 1970.

Brandt, R.B., 'Blameworthiness and Obligation', in A.I. Melden (ed.), *Essays in Moral Philosophy*, Seattle, University of Washington Press, 1958.

—— *Value and Obligation*, New York, Harcourt, Brace & World, 1961.

Brentano, F., *Psychology from an Empirical Standpoint* (trans. D.B. Terrell), London, Routledge & Kegan Paul, 1971.

Bricke, J., 'Emotion and Thought in Hume's *Treatise*', *Canadian Journal of Philosophy*, 1974, suppl. vol. 1, part 1.

Britton, K., 'Feelings and Their Expressions', *Philosophy*, 1957, vol. 32, no. 121.

Broad, C.D., 'Emotion and Sentiment', in *Broad's Critical Essays in Moral Philosophy* (ed. D.R. Cheney), London, Allen & Unwin, 1971.

Brown, E., 'Sympathy and Moral Objectivity', *American Philosophical Quarterly*, 1986, vol. 23, no. 2.

Brown, J., 'Moral Theory and the Ought–Can Principle', *Mind*, 1977, vol. 86, no. 342.

Brown, R., *Analyzing Love*, Cambridge, Cambridge University Press, 1987.

Buchanan, A., 'Categorical Imperatives and Moral Principles', *Philosophical Studies*, 1977, vol. 31, no. 2.

Buckle, S., 'Biological Processes and Natural Events', *Journal of Medical Ethics*, 1988, vol. 14, no. 3.

Buckley, F.B., 'Analysis of "X Could Have Acted Otherwise"', *Philosophical Studies*, 1956, vol. 7, no. 5.

Burnyeat, M.F., 'Aristotle on Learning to be Good', in A.O. Rorty (ed.), *Essays on Aristotle's Ethics*, Berkeley, University of California Press, 1980.

Calhoun, C.C.H., 'The Humean Moral Sentiment: A Unique Feeling', *Southwestern Journal of Philosophy*, 1980, vol. 11.

—— 'Cognitive Emotions?' in C. Calhoun and R.C. Solomon (eds), *What is an Emotion?* New York, Oxford University Press, 1984.

Calhoun, C., and Solomon, R.C. (eds), *What is an Emotion?* New York, Oxford University Press, 1984.

230   *Morality and the Emotions*

Campbell, J., 'Kantian Conceptions of Moral Goodness', *Canadian Journal of Philosophy*, 1983, vol. 13, no. 4.
Cannon, W.B., 'Bodily Changes in Pain, Hunger, Fear and Rage', in C. Calhoun and R.C. Solomon (eds), *What is an Emotion?* New York, Oxford University Press, 1984.
Capaldi, N., 'Hume's Theory of the Passions', in D.W. Livingstone and J.T. King (eds), *Hume: A Re-evaluation*, New York, Fordham University Press, 1976.
Capitan, W.H., and Merrill, D.D. (eds), *Metaphysics and Explanation*, Pittsburgh, University of Pittsburgh Press, 1966.
Cartwright, D., 'Kant's View of the Moral Significance of Kindhearted Emotions and the Moral Insignificance of Kant's View', *Journal of Value Inquiry*, 1987, vol. 21, no. 4.
Cassin, C., 'Emotions and Evaluations', *Personalist*, 1968, vol. 49.
Castaneda, H.-N., and Nakhnikian, G. (eds), *Morality and the Language of Conduct*, Detroit, Wayne State University Press, 1965.
Chappell, V.C. (ed.), *The Philosophy of Mind*, Englewood Cliffs, Prentice-Hall, 1962.
Chazan, P., 'Pride, Virtue and Self-hood: A Reconstruction of Hume', 17th Hume Conference, Australian National University, Canberra, June 1990.
Chisholm, R.M., 'Responsibility and Avoidability', in J. Feinberg (ed.), *Reason and Responsibility*, Belmont, Dickenson, 1965.
—— 'Brentano's Theory of Correct and Incorrect Emotion', *Revue Internationale de Philosophie*, 1966, vol. 20, no. 4.
—— 'Freedom and Action', in K. Lehrer (ed.), *Freedom and Determinism*, New York, Random House, 1966.
Clarke, S.G., 'Emotions: Rationality Without Cognitivism', *Dialogue*, 1986, vol. 25, no. 4.
Classen, H.G., 'Will, Belief and Knowledge', *Dialogue*, 1979, vol. 18, no. 1.
Cohen, S., 'Distinctions Among Blame Concepts', *Philosophy and Phenomenological Research*, 1977, vol. 38, no. 2.
Cooper, J.M., 'Aristotle on Friendship', in A.O. Rorty (ed.), *Essays on Aristotle's Ethics*, Berkeley, University of California Press, 1980.
Cottingham, J., 'Ethics and Impartiality', *Philosophical Studies* 1983, vol. 43, no. 1.
—— 'Partiality, Favouritism and Morality', *Philosophical Quarterly*, 1986, vol. 36, no. 144.
Coyne, M.U., 'Moral Luck?', *Journal of Value Inquiry*, 1985, vol. 19, no. 4.
Dahl, N.O., '"Ought" and Blameworthiness', *Journal of Philosophy*, 1967, vol. 64, no. 13.
D'Arcy, E., *Human Acts: An Essay in their Moral Evaluation*, Oxford, Clarendon Press, 1963.
Davidson, D., 'Freedom to Act', in T. Honderich (ed.), *Essays on Freedom of Action*, London, Routledge & Kegan Paul, 1973.
—— 'Hume's Cognitive Theory of Pride', *Journal of Philosophy*, 1976, vol. 73, no. 19.
Davis, W.A., 'The Varieties of Fear', *Philosophical Studies*, 1987, vol. 51, no. 3.
Dent, N.J.H., 'Virtues and Actions', *Philosophical Quarterly*, 1975, vol. 25, no. 101.

—— *The Moral Psychology of the Virtues*, Cambridge, Cambridge University Press, 1987.

Descartes, R., *The Passions of the Soul* (trans. E.S. Haldane and G.R.T. Ross), Cambridge, Cambridge University Press, 1931.

De Sousa, R.B., 'Review of R. Solomon, *The Passions*', *Canadian Journal of Philosophy*, 1979, vol. 9, no. 2.

—— 'Self-deceptive Emotions', in A.O. Rorty (ed.), *Explaining Emotions*, Berkeley, University of California Press, 1980.

—— 'The Rationality of Emotions', in A.O. Rorty (ed.), *Explaining Emotions*, Berkeley, University of California Press, 1980.

—— *The Rationality of Emotion*, Cambridge, Mass., MIT Press, 1987.

Deutscher, M., 'Conceptual Connection and Causal Relation', *Australasian Journal of Philosophy*, 1976, vol. 54, no. 1.

Dewey, J., 'The Theory of Emotions', in C. Calhoun and R.C. Solomon (eds), *What is an Emotion?* New York, Oxford University Press, 1984.

Dilman, I., 'Reason, Passion and the Will', *Philosophy*, 1984, vol. 59, no. 228.

Diorio, J.A., 'Do Altruistic Emotions Have Intrinsic Value?' *Journal of Value Inquiry*, 1984, vol. 28, no. 1.

Donnellan, K., 'Causes, Objects, and Producers of the Emotions', *Journal of Philosophy*, 1970, vol. 67, no. 21.

Duff, A., 'Aristotelian Courage', *Ratio*, 1987, vol. 29, no. 1.

Duncker, K., 'On Pleasure, Emotion, and Striving', *Philosophy and Phenomenological Research*, 1940, vol. 1, no. 4.

Dunlap, K. (ed.), *The Emotions*, New York, Hafner, 1967.

Dworkin, G. (ed.), *Determinism, Free Will, and Moral Responsibility*, Englewood Cliffs, Prentice-Hall, 1970.

Dworkin, G., and Blumenfeld, D., 'Punishment for Intentions', *Mind*, 1966, vol. 75, no. 299.

Ewing, A.C., *Ethics*, London, English Universities Press, 1953.

—— 'The Justification of Emotions', *Proceedings of the Aristotelian Society*, 1957, suppl. vol. 31.

Falk, W.D., 'Intention, Motive and Responsibility', *Proceedings of the Aristotelian Society*, 1945, suppl. vol. 19.

—— 'Morality, Self, and Others', in H.-N. Castaneda and G. Nakhnikian (eds), *Morality and the Language of Conduct*, Detroit, Wayne State University Press, 1965.

Farrell, D.M., 'Jealousy', *Philosophical Review*, 1980, vol. 89, no. 4.

Feinberg, J. (ed.), *Reason and Responsibility*, Belmont, Dickenson, 1965.

—— *Doing and Deserving: Essays in the Theory of Responsibility*, Princeton, Princeton University Press, 1970.

Feinberg, J., and Gross, H. (eds), *Responsibility: Selected Readings*, Encino, Dickenson, 1975.

Feinstein, H.M., 'William James on the Emotions', *Journal of the History of Ideas*, 1970, vol. 31, no. 1.

Fischer, J.M., 'Responsibility and Failure', *Proceedings of the Aristotelian Society*, 1985/6, vol. 86.

Fisher, M., 'Reason, Emotion and Love', *Inquiry*, 1977, vol. 20.

Fitzgerald, P.J., 'Voluntary and Involuntary Acts', in A.R. White (ed.), *The Philosophy of Action*, Oxford, Oxford University Press, 1968.

Flanagan, O., 'Admirable Immorality and Admirable Imperfection', *Journal of Philosophy*, 1986, vol. 83, no. 1.

Fleming, J.G., *The Law of Torts*, Sydney, Law Book Co., 1987.

Foot, P., 'Free Will as Involving Determinism', *Philosophical Review*, 1957, vol. 66, no. 4.

—— 'Virtues and Vices', in *Virtues and Vices*, Oxford, Blackwell, 1978.

Fortenbaugh, W.W., 'Aristotle: Emotion and Moral Virtue', *Arethusa*, 1969, vol. 2, no. 2.

—— 'Aristotle's Rhetoric on Emotions', *Archiv fur Geschichte der Philosophie*, 1970, band 52, heft 1.

—— *Aristotle on Emotion*, London, Duckworth, 1975.

Frankena, W.K., *Ethics*, Englewood Cliffs, Prentice-Hall, 1963.

—— 'The Ethics of Love Conceived as an Ethics of Virtue', *Journal of Religious Ethics*, 1973, vol. 1, no. 1.

—— 'Obligation and Motivation in Recent Moral Philosophy', in K.E. Goodpaster (ed.), *Perspectives on Morality: Essays by William K. Frankena*, Notre Dame, University of Notre Dame Press, 1976.

Frankfurt, H., 'Alternate Possibilities and Moral Responsibility', *Journal of Philosophy*, 1969, vol. 66, no. 23.

—— 'Coercion and Moral Responsibility', in T. Honderich (ed.), *Essays on Freedom of Action*, London, Routledge & Kegan Paul, 1973.

—— 'Identification and Externality', in A.O. Rorty (ed.), *The Identities of Persons*, Berkeley, University of California Press, 1976.

—— 'The Importance of What We Care About', *Synthese*, 1982, vol. 53, no. 2.

Freud, S., 'Anxiety', in C. Calhoun and R.C. Solomon (eds), *What is an Emotion?* New York, Oxford University Press, 1984.

—— 'The Unconscious', in C. Calhoun and R.C. Solomon (eds), *What is an Emotion?* New York, Oxford University Press, 1984.

Gaita, R., '"Better One Than Ten"', *Philosophical Investigations*, 1982, vol. 5.

Gardiner, P.L., 'Hume's Theory of the Passions', in D.F. Pears (ed.), *David Hume: A Symposium*, London, Macmillan, 1963.

Geach, P., *The Virtues*, Cambridge, Cambridge University Press, 1977.

Gert, B., *The Moral Rules*, New York, Harper & Row, 1970.

—— 'Review of R. Solomon, *The Passions*', *Metaphilosophy*, 1979, vol. 10, no. 2.

Gibbard, A., *Wise Choices, Apt Feelings*, Oxford, Clarendon Press, 1990.

Gilbert, P., 'Friendship and the Will', *Philosophy*, 1986, vol. 61, no. 235.

Glover, J., *Responsibility*, London, Routledge & Kegan Paul, 1970.

Goldman, A.I., *A Theory of Human Action*, Englewood Cliffs, Prentice-Hall, 1970.

Gordon, R.M., 'Emotions and Knowledge', *Journal of Philosophy*, 1969, vol. 66, no. 13.

—— 'Judgmental Emotions', *Analysis*, 1973, vol. 34, no. 2.

—— 'The Aboutness of Emotions', *American Philosophical Quarterly*, 1974, vol. 11, no. 1.

—— 'Fear', *Philosophical Review*, 1980, vol. 89, no. 4.

—— 'The Passivity of Emotions', *Philosophical Review*, 1986, vol. 95, no. 3.

—— *The Structure of Emotions*, New York, Cambridge University Press, 1987.

Gosling, J.C., 'Emotion and Object', *Philosophical Review*, 1965, vol. 74, no. 4.
—— *Pleasure and Desire*, Oxford, Clarendon Press, 1969.
Grant, B., 'Descartes, Belief and the Will', *Philosophy*, 1976, vol. 51.
Green, O.H., 'The Expression of Emotion', *Mind*, 1970, vol. 79.
—— 'Emotions and Belief', in *American Philosophical Quarterly, Monograph no. 6: Studies in the Philosophy of Mind*, Oxford, Blackwell, 1972.
—— 'Obligations Regarding Passions', *Personalist*, 1979, vol. 60, no. 2.
—— 'Wittgenstein and the Possibility of a Philosophical Theory of Emotion', *Metaphilosophy*, 1987, vol. 10, nos 3 and 4.
Greenspan, P.S., 'A Case of Mixed Feelings: Ambivalence and the Logic of Emotion', in A.O. Rorty (ed.), *Explaining Emotions*, Berkeley, University of California Press, 1980.
—— 'Emotions, Reasons, and "Self-involvement" ', *Philosophical Studies*, 1980, vol. 38, no. 2.
—— 'Emotions as Evaluations', *Pacific Philosophical Quarterly*, 1981, vol. 62, no. 2.
—— 'Identificatory Love', *Philosophical Studies*, 1986, vol. 50, no. 3.
—— *Emotions and Reasons*, New York, Routledge, 1988.
Guignon, C., 'Moods in Heidegger's *Being and Time*', in C. Calhoun and R.C. Solomon (eds), *What is an Emotion?* New York, Oxford University Press, 1984.
Gustafson, D.F. (ed.), *Essays in Philosophical Psychology*, Garden City, Anchor Books, 1964.
Hamlyn, D.W., 'The Phenomena of Love and Hate', *Philosophy*, 1978, vol. 53.
Hampshire, S. (ed.), *Philosophy of Mind*, New York, Harper & Row, 1966.
—— 'Sincerity and Single-mindedness', in *Freedom of Mind and Other Essays*, Princeton, Princeton University Press, 1971.
Hanfling, O., *The Grammar of Feelings*, Milton Keynes, Open University Press, 1976.
Hare, R.M., *Freedom and Reason*, Oxford, Oxford University Press, 1963.
—— *Moral Thinking*, Oxford, Clarendon Press, 1981.
Harrison, B., 'Moral Judgment, Action and Emotion', *Philosophy*, 1984, vol. 59, no. 229.
Hart, H.L.A., 'Negligence, *Mens Rea*, and Criminal Responsibility', in *Punishment and Responsibility*, Oxford, Oxford University Press, 1968.
—— 'Responsibility', in J. Feinberg and H. Gross (eds), *Responsibility: Selected Readings*, Encino, Dickenson, 1975.
Hart, H.L.A., and Honore, A.M., 'Causation and Responsibility', in J. Feinberg and H. Gross (eds), *Responsibility: Selected Readings*, Encino, Dickenson, 1975.
Heidegger, M., *Being and Time*, New York, Harper & Row, 1962.
Henderson, G.P., 'Censure Under Control', *Ratio*, 1973, vol. 15, no. 1.
Henson, R.G., 'What Kant Might Have Said: Moral Worth and the Overdetermination of Dutiful Action', *Philosophical Review*, 1979, vol. 88, no. 1.
Herman, B., 'On the Value of Acting from the Motive of Duty', *Philosophical Review*, 1981, vol. 90, no. 3.

—— 'Integrity and Impartiality', *Monist*, 1983, vol. 66, no. 2.
—— 'Mutual Aid and Respect for Persons', *Ethics*, 1984, vol. 94, no. 4.
—— 'Rules, Motives, and Helping Actions', *Philosophical Studies*, 1984, vol. 45, no. 3.
—— 'The Practice of Moral Judgement', *Journal of Philosophy*, 1985, vol. 82, no. 8.
Hertzberg, L., 'Blame and Causality', *Mind*, 1975, vol. 84.
Hilgard, E.R., Atkinson, R.C., and Atkinson, R.L., *Introduction to Psychology*, New York, Harcourt Brace Jovanovich, 1975.
Hinman, L.M., 'On the Purity of Our Moral Motives: A Critique of Kant's Account of the Emotions and Acting for the Sake of Duty', *Monist*, 1983, vol. 66, no. 2.
Hobbes, T., *Leviathan* (ed. C.B. Macpherson), Harmondsworth, Penguin, 1968.
Holborow, L.C., 'Blame, Praise and Credit', *Proceedings of the Aristotelian Society*, 1971–2, vol. 72.
Holland, R.F., 'Morality and Moral Reasoning', *Philosophy*, 1972, vol. 47, no. 181.
Holyer, R., 'Belief and Will Revisited', *Dialogue*, 1983, vol. 22, no. 2.
Homiak, M.L., 'The Pleasure of Virtue in Aristotle's Moral Theory', *Pacific Philosophical Quarterly*, 1985, vol. 66, nos 1 and 2.
Honderich, T. (ed.), *Essays on Freedom of Action*, London, Routledge & Kegan Paul, 1973.
Hudson, S.D., 'Taking Virtues Seriously', *Australasian Journal of Philosophy*, 1981, vol. 59, no. 2.
Hume, D., *An Enquiry Concerning the Principles of Morals* (ed. L.A. Selby-Bigge), Oxford, Oxford University Press, 1975.
—— *A Treatise of Human Nature* (ed. L.A. Selby-Bigge), Oxford, Oxford University Press, 1978.
Hursthouse, R., 'Plato on Commensurability and Desire: Plato on the Emotions', *Proceedings of the Aristotelian Society*, 1984, suppl. vol. 58.
—— *Beginning Lives*, Oxford, Basil Blackwell, 1987.
Hyslop, A., 'Emotions and Fictional Characters', *Australasian Journal of Philosophy*, 1986, vol. 64, no. 3.
Irwin, T.H., 'Reason and Responsibility in Aristotle', in A.O. Rorty (ed.), *Essays on Aristotle's Ethics*, Berkeley, University of California Press, 1980.
Isenberg, A., 'Natural Pride and Natural Shame', in A.O. Rorty (ed.), *Explaining Emotions*, Berkeley, University of California Press, 1980.
James, W., 'The Emotions', in K. Dunlap (ed.), *The Emotions*, New York, Hafner, 1967.
—— 'What is an Emotion?' in K. Dunlap (ed.), *The Emotions*, New York, Hafner, 1967.
—— *The Principles of Psychology* (Vol. 1), Cambridge, Mass., Harvard University Press, 1981.
Jefferson, M., 'What is Wrong with Sentimentality?', *Mind*, 1983, vol. 92, no. 368.
Jensen, H., 'Morality and Luck', *Philosophy*, 1984, vol. 59, no. 229.
Jung, C.G., 'Psychological Types', in *The Basic Writings of C.G. Jung* (ed. V.S. DeLaszlo), New York, Random House, 1959.

Kagan, S., 'Causation, Liability and Internalism', *Philosophy and Public Affairs*, 1986, vol. 15, no. 1.

Kant, I., *Critique of Practical Reason* (trans. L.W. Beck), Indianapolis, Bobbs-Merrill, 1956 (originally in *Gesammelte Werke*, Berlin, Akademie Verlag, 1913).

—— *Foundations of the Metaphysics of Morals* (trans. L.W. Beck), Indianapolis, Bobbs-Merrill, 1959 (originally in *Gesammelte Werke*, Berlin, Akademie Verlag, 1911).

—— *Religion Within the Limits of Reason Alone* (trans. T.M. Greene and H.M. Hudson), New York, Harper & Row, 1960.

—— *Lectures on Ethics* (trans. L. Infield), New York, Harper & Row, 1963.

—— *The Doctrine of Virtue* (trans. M. Gregor), New York, Harper & Row, 1964 (originally in *Gesammelte Werke*, Berlin, Akademie Verlag, 1914).

—— *Anthropology from a Pragmatic Point of View* (trans. V.L. Dowdell), Carbondale, Southern Illinois University Press, 1978 (originally in *Gesammelte Werke*, Berlin, Akademie Verlag, 1917).

Kavka, G.S., 'Some Paradoxes of Deterrence', *Journal of Philosophy*, 1978, vol. 75, no. 6.

Keeton, R.E., 'The Basic Rule of Legal Cause in Negligence Cases', in J. Feinberg and H. Gross (eds), *Responsibility: Selected Readings*, Encino, Dickenson, 1975.

Kekes, J., 'Moral Sensitivity', *Philosophy*, 1984, vol. 59, no. 227.

—— '"Ought Implies Can" and Two Kinds of Morality', *Philosophical Quarterly*, 1984, vol. 31, no. 137.

Kelly, J., 'Reason and Emotion', *Southern Journal of Philosophy*, 1972, vol. 10, no. 3.

—— 'Virtue and Pleasure', *Mind*, 1973, vol. 82, no. 327.

Kemp Smith, N., *The Philosophy of David Hume*, London, Macmillan, 1964.

Kenner, L., 'On Blaming', *Mind*, 1967, vol. 76, no. 302.

Kenny, A., *Action, Emotion and Will*, London, Routledge & Kegan Paul, 1963.

—— *The Metaphysics of Mind*, Oxford, Clarendon Press, 1989.

Kerner, G.C., 'Passions and the Cognitive Foundation of Ethics', *Philosophy and Phenomenological Research*, 1970, vol. 31, no. 2.

King, J., 'Elenchus, Self-blame and the Socratic Paradox', *Review of Metaphysics*, 1987, vol. 41, no. 1.

Koch, P.J., 'Expressing Emotion', *Pacific Philosophical Quarterly*, 1983, vol. 64, no. 2.

—— 'Bodily Feeling in Emotion', *Dialogue*, 1987, vol. 26, no. 1.

—— 'Emotional Ambivalence', *Philosophy and Phenomenological Research*, 1987, vol. 48, no. 2.

Kolnai, A., 'Forgiveness', *Proceedings of the Aristotelian Society*, 1973–4, vol. 74.

Korsgaard, C.M., 'Aristotle and Kant on the Source of Value', *Ethics*, 1986, vol. 96, no. 3.

—— 'Aristotle on Function and Virtue', *History of Philosophy Quarterly*, 1986, vol. 3, no. 3.

Kosman, L.A., 'Being Properly Affected: Virtues and Feelings in Aristotle's Ethics', in A.O. Rorty (ed.), *Essays on Aristotle's Ethics*, Berkeley,

University of California Press, 1980.

Kraut, R., 'Feelings in Context', *Journal of Philosophy*, 1986, vol. 83, no. 11.

—— 'Love *De Re*', in P.A. French, T.E. Uehling, and H.K. Wettstein (eds), *Midwest Studies in Philosophy*, 1986, vol. 10.

Lamb, R., 'Objectless Emotions', *Philosophy and Phenomenological Research*, 1987, vol. 48, no. 1.

Lange, C.G., 'The Emotions: A Psychophysiological Study', in K. Dunlap (ed.), *The Emotions*, New York, Hafner, 1967.

Lawrie, R., 'Passion', *Philosophy and Phenomenological Research*, 1980, vol. 41, no. 1.

Lehrer, K., 'Comments', in W.H. Capitan and D.D. Merrill (eds), *Metaphysics and Explanation*, Pittsburgh, University of Pittsburgh Press, 1966.

—— (ed.), *Freedom and Determinism*, New York, Random House, 1966.

Leighton, S.R., 'Feelings and Emotion', *Review of Metaphysics*, 1984, vol. 38, no. 2.

—— 'A New View of Emotion', *American Philosophical Quarterly*, 1985, vol. 22, no. 2.

—— 'Unfelt Feelings in Pain and Emotion', *Southern Journal of Philosophy*, 1986, vol. 24, no. 1.

Lemmon, E.J., 'Moral Dilemmas', *Philosophical Review*, 1962, vol. 71, no. 2.

Levi, A., *French Moralists: The Theory of the Passions, 1585 to 1649*, Oxford, Clarendon Press, 1964.

Levy, R.I., 'Emotion, Knowing, and Culture', in R.A. Shweder and R.A. LeVine (eds), *Culture Theory: Essays on Mind, Self, and Emotion*, Cambridge, Cambridge University Press, 1984.

Lewis, C.S., *An Experiment in Criticism*, Cambridge, Cambridge University Press, 1961.

Liddell, B.E.A., *Kant on the Foundation of Morality*, Bloomington, Indiana University Press, 1970.

Lloyd, G., *The 'Man' of Reason: Male and Female in Western Philosophy*, London, Methuen, 1984.

Locke, J., *An Essay Concerning Human Understanding* (ed. A.S. Pringle-Pattison), Oxford, Clarendon Press, 1924.

Losin, P., 'Aristotle's Doctrine of the Mean', *History of Philosophy Quarterly*, 1987, vol. 4, no. 3.

Louden, R.B., 'Kant's Virtue Ethics', *Philosophy*, 1986, vol. 61, no. 238.

Luper-Foy, S., 'Competing for the Good Life', *American Philosophical Quarterly*, 1986, vol. 23, no. 2.

Lyons, W., 'Physiological Changes and the Emotions', *Canadian Journal of Philosophy*, 1974, vol. 3, no. 4.

—— 'Emotions and Feelings', *Ratio*, 1977, vol. 19, no. 1.

—— *Emotion*, Cambridge, Cambridge University Press, 1980.

McCullagh, C.B., 'The Rationality of Emotions and of Emotional Behaviour', *Australasian Journal of Philosophy*, 1990, vol. 68, no. 1.

McDowell, J., 'Are Moral Requirements Hypothetical Imperatives?', *Proceedings of the Aristotelian Society*, 1978, suppl. vol. 52.

—— 'Virtue and Reason', *Monist*, 1979, vol. 62, no. 3.

—— 'Non-cognitivism and Rule-following', in S.H. Holtzman and C.M.

Leich (eds), *Wittgenstein: To Follow a Rule*, London, Routledge & Kegan Paul, 1981.

MacIntyre, A., 'Emotion, Behavior and Belief', in *Against the Self-images of the Age*, London, Duckworth, 1971.

—— *After Virtue: A Study in Moral Theory*, Notre Dame, University of Notre Dame Press, 1981.

—— 'Comments on Frankfurt', *Synthese*, 1982, vol. 53, no. 2.

McIntyre, J., 'Personal Identity and the Passions', *Journal of the History of Philosophy*, 1989, vol. 27, no. 4.

Marcus, R.B., 'Moral Dilemmas and Consistency', *Journal of Philosophy*, 1980, vol. 77, no. 3.

Marks, J., 'A Theory of Emotion', *Philosophical Studies*, 1982, vol. 42, no. 2.

Marshall, G.D., 'On Being Affected', *Mind*, 1968, vol. 77, no. 306.

—— 'Overdetermination and the Emotions', in A.O. Rorty (ed.), *Explaining Emotions*, Berkeley, University of California Press, 1980.

Mayeroff, M., *On Caring*, New York, Harper & Row, 1971.

Melden, A.I. (ed.), *Essays in Moral Philosophy*, Seattle, University of Washington Press, 1958.

—— 'The Conceptual Dimensions of Emotions', in T. Mischel (ed.), *Human Action*, New York, Academic Press, 1969.

Michaels, M., 'Morality Without Distinction', *Philosophical Forum*, 1986, vol. 17, no. 3.

Midgley, M., 'The Objection to Systematic Humbug', *Philosophy*, 1978, vol. 53, no. 2.

—— *Heart and Mind*, London, Methuen, 1983.

—— *Wickedness: A Philosophical Essay*, London, Routledge & Kegan Paul, 1984.

Mill, J.S., *On Liberty*, Cleveland, Meridian, 1962.

Millgram, E., 'Aristotle on Making Other Selves', *Canadian Journal of Philosophy*, 1987, vol. 17, no. 2.

Milo, R.D., *Immorality*, Princeton, Princeton University Press, 1984.

Mischel, T. (ed.), *Human Action: Conceptual and Empirical Issues*, New York, Academic Press, 1969.

Montmarquet, J., 'The Voluntariness of Belief', *Analysis*, 1986, vol. 46, no. 1.

Moore, G.E., 'The Nature of Moral Philosophy', in *Philosophical Studies*, London, Routledge & Kegan Paul, 1922.

—— *Ethics*, London, Oxford University Press, 1978.

Moravcsik, J.M.E., 'Understanding and the Emotions', *Dialectica*, 1982, vol. 36, nos 2 and 3.

Morris, H., 'Punishment for Thoughts', in *On Guilt and Innocence*, Berkeley, University of California Press, 1976.

Murdoch, I., *The Sovereignty of Good*, London, Routledge & Kegan Paul, 1970.

Nabe, C., 'In Praise of Guilt', *Journal of Value Inquiry*, 1987, vol. 21, no. 3.

Nagel, T., *The Possibility of Altruism*, Oxford, Clarendon Press, 1970.

—— 'Moral Luck', in *Mortal Questions*, Cambridge, Cambridge University Press, 1979.

Naylor, M.B., 'Voluntary Belief', *Philosophy and Phenomenological*

Research, 1985, vol. 45, no. 3.

Neblett, W., 'Feelings of Obligation', *Mind*, 1976, vol. 85.

—— 'Indignation: A Case Study in the Role of Feelings in Morals', *Metaphilosophy*, 1979, vol. 10, no. 2.

—— *The Role of Feelings in Morals*, Washington, University Press of America, 1981.

Neu, J., *Emotion, Thought and Therapy*, London, Routledge & Kegan Paul, 1977.

—— 'Jealous Thoughts', in A.O. Rorty (ed.), *Explaining Emotions*, Berkeley, University of California Press, 1980.

Nissenbaum, H.F., *Emotion and Focus*, Stanford, Center for the Study of Language and Information, 1985.

North, J., 'Wrongdoing and Forgiveness', *Philosophy*, 1987, vol. 62, no. 242.

Nowell-Smith, P.H., *Ethics*, Harmondsworth, Penguin, 1954.

Nussbaum, M.C., *The Fragility of Goodness: Luck and Ethics in Greek Tragedy and Philosophy*, Cambridge, Cambridge University Press, 1986.

—— 'The Stoics on the Extirpation of the Passions', *Apeiron*, 1987, vol. 20, no. 2.

Oaklander, L.N., and Gull, R., 'Review of R. Solomon, *The Passions*', *Nous*, 1978, vol. 12, no. 1.

Oakley, J., 'A Critique of Kantian Arguments Against Emotions as Moral Motives', *History of Philosophy Quarterly*, 1990, vol. 7, no. 4.

Palmer, D., 'Unfelt Pains', *American Philosophical Quarterly*, 1975, vol. 12, no. 4.

Palmquist, S., 'Is Duty Kant's "Motive" for Moral Action?', *Ratio*, 1986, vol. 28, no. 2.

Parfit, D., 'Later Selves and Moral Principles', in A. Montefiore (ed.), *Philosophy and Personal Relations*, London, Routledge & Kegan Paul, 1973.

Parker, R., 'Blame, Punishment, and the Role of Result', *American Philosophical Quarterly*, 1984, vol. 21, no. 3.

Pascal, B., *Pensées* (trans. M. Turnell), London, Harvill Press, 1962.

Paton, H.J., 'Kant on Friendship', *Proceedings of the British Academy*, 1956, vol. 42.

Pears, D.F., 'Causes and Objects of Some Feelings and Psychological Reactions', *Ratio*, 1962, vol. 4, no. 2.

—— (ed.), *David Hume: A Symposium*, London, Macmillan, 1963.

Pence, G.E., 'Recent Work on Virtues', *American Philosophical Quarterly*, 1984, vol. 21, no. 4.

Penelhum, T., 'Human Nature and External Desires', *Monist*, 1979, vol. 62, no. 3.

Perkins, M., 'Emotion and Feeling', *Philosophical Review*, 1966, vol. 75, no. 2.

Perry, D.L., 'Pleasure and Justification', *Personalist*, 1970, vol. 51, no. 2.

Peters, R.S., 'Emotions and the Category of Passivity', *Proceedings of the Aristotelian Society*, 1961–2, vol. 62.

Phillips, M., 'Rationality, Responsibility and Blame', *Canadian Journal of Philosophy*, 1987, vol. 17, no. 1.

Piper, A.M.S., 'Moral Theory and Moral Alienation', *Journal of Philosophy*, 1987, vol. 84, no. 2.

Pitcher, G., 'Emotion', *Mind*, 1965, vol. 74, no. 295.
Plamenatz, J., 'Responsibility, Blame and Punishment', in P. Laslett and W.G. Runciman (eds), *Philosophy, Politics and Society* (Third Series), Oxford, Blackwell, 1967.
Plato, *The Symposium* (trans. W. Hamilton), Harmondsworth, Penguin, 1951.
—— *Phaedrus* (trans. W. Hamilton), Harmondsworth, Penguin, 1973.
—— *Philebus* (trans. J.C.B. Gosling), Oxford, Clarendon Press, 1975.
—— *The Republic* (trans. A. Bloom), New York, Basic Books, 1978.
Pleydell-Pearce, A.G., 'Freedom, Emotion and Choice in the Philosophy of Jean-Paul Sartre', *Journal of the British Society for Phenomenology*, 1970, vol. 1, no. 1.
Pojman, L., 'Belief and Will', *Religious Studies*, 1978, vol. 14, no. 1.
—— 'Believing and Willing', *Canadian Journal of Philosophy*, 1985, vol. 15, no. 1.
Preus, A., 'Aristotle on Healthy and Sick Souls', *Monist*, 1986, vol. 69, no. 3.
Price, H.H., 'Belief and Will', in S. Hampshire (ed.), *Philosophy of Mind*, New York, Harper & Row, 1966.
Pritchard, M.S., 'Responsibility, Understanding, and Psychopathology', *Monist*, 1974, vol. 58, no. 4.
Provis, C., 'Reason and Emotion', *Canadian Journal of Philosophy*, 1981, vol. 11, no. 3.
Railton, P., 'Alienation, Consequentialism, and the Demands of Morality', *Philosophy and Public Affairs*, 1984, vol. 13, no. 2.
Rawls, J., 'Outline of a Decision Procedure for Ethics', *Philosophical Review*, 1951, vol. 60, no. 2.
—— *A Theory of Justice*, Oxford, Oxford University Press, 1972.
Rey, G., 'Functionalism and the Emotions', in A.O. Rorty (ed.), *Explaining Emotions*, Berkeley, University of California Press, 1980.
Richards, N., 'Luck and Desert', *Mind*, 1986, vol. 95, no. 378.
Roberts, R.C., 'Solomon on the Control of the Emotions', *Philosophy and Phenomenological Research*, 1984, vol. 44, no. 3.
—— 'Will Power and the Virtues', *Philosophical Review*, 1984, vol. 93, no. 2.
—— 'What an Emotion is: A Sketch', *Philosophical Review*, 1988, vol. 97, no. 2.
Robinson, J., 'Emotion, Judgement, and Desire', *Journal of Philosophy*, 1983, vol. 80, no. 11.
Rorty, A.O. (ed.), *The Identities of Persons*, Berkeley, University of California Press, 1976.
—— 'Agent Regret', in A.O. Rorty (ed.), *Explaining Emotions*, Berkeley, University of California Press, 1980.
—— (ed.), *Essays on Aristotle's Ethics*, Berkeley, University of California Press, 1980.
—— (ed.), *Explaining Emotions*, Berkeley, University of California Press, 1980.
—— 'Explaining Emotions', in A.O. Rorty (ed.), *Explaining Emotions*, Berkeley, University of California Press, 1980.
—— 'The Place of Contemplation in Aristotle's *Nicomachean Ethics*', in A.O. Rorty (ed.), *Essays on Aristotle's Ethics*, Berkeley, University of California Press, 1980.

—— 'From Passions to Emotions and Sentiments', *Philosophy*, 1982, vol. 57, no. 220.

—— 'Varieties of Rationality, Varieties of Emotion', *Social Science Information*, 1985, vol. 24.

—— 'The Historicity of Psychological Attitudes: Love is Not Love Which Alters Not When it Alteration Finds', in P.A. French, T.E. Uehling, and H.K. Wettstein (eds), *Midwest Studies in Philosophy*, 1986, vol. 10.

—— ' "Pride Produces the Idea of Self": Hume on Moral Agency', *Australasian Journal of Philosophy*, 1990, vol. 68, no. 3.

Ross, S.L., 'Evaluating the Emotions', *Journal of Philosophy*, 1984, vol. 81, no. 6.

Ross, W.D., *The Right and the Good*, Oxford, Clarendon Press, 1930.

—— *Foundations of Ethics*, Oxford, Clarendon Press, 1939.

Rousseau, J.-J., *The Social Contract* (trans. G. Hopkins), in E. Barker (ed.), *Social Contract: Essays by Locke, Hume, Rousseau*, London, Oxford University Press, 1971.

Ryle, G., *The Concept of Mind*, Harmondsworth, Penguin, 1963.

Sachs, D., 'Review of R. Solomon, *The Passions*', *Philosophical Review*, 1978, vol. 87, no. 3.

—— 'How to Distinguish Self-respect from Self-esteem', *Philosophy and Public Affairs*, 1981, vol. 10, no. 4.

—— 'Self-respect and Respect for Others: Are They Independent?' in O.H. Green (ed.), *Respect for Persons* (Tulane Studies in Philosophy, vol. 31), New Orleans, Tulane University Press, 1982.

Sankowski, E.T., 'The Sense of Responsibility and the Justifiability of Emotions', *Southern Journal of Philosophy*, 1975, vol. 13, no. 2.

—— 'Responsibility of Persons for their Emotions', *Canadian Journal of Philosophy*, 1977, vol. 7, no. 4.

—— 'Love and Moral Obligation', *Journal of Value Inquiry*, 1978, vol. 12, no. 2.

Sartre, J.-P., *Sketch for a Theory of the Emotions* (trans. P. Mairet), London, Methuen, 1962.

—— *Being and Nothingness* (trans. H.E. Barnes), London, Methuen, 1969.

Schachter, S., and Singer, J.E., 'Cognitive, Social, and Physiological Determinants of Emotional State', in C. Calhoun and R.C. Solomon (eds), *What is an Emotion?* New York, Oxford University Press, 1984.

Schaller, W.E., 'Kant on Virtue and Moral Worth', *Southern Journal of Philosophy*, 1987, vol. 25, no. 4.

Scheler, M., *Formalism in Ethics and Non-formal Ethics of Values* (trans. M.S. Frings and R.L. Funk), Evanston, Northwestern University Press, 1973.

Scheman, N., 'On Sympathy', *Monist*, 1979, vol. 62, no. 3.

Schilpp, P.A. (ed.), *The Philosophy of Jean-Paul Sartre*, La Salle, Open Court, 1977.

Schlossberger, E., 'Why We Are Responsible for Our Emotions', *Mind*, 1986, vol. 95, no. 377.

Schneider, M., 'Review of R. Solomon, *The Passions*', *Review of Metaphysics*, 1977, vol. 31, no. 1.

Schoeman, F., 'Aristotle on the Good of Friendship', *Australasian Journal of Philosophy*, 1985, vol. 63, no. 3.

Scruton, R., 'Emotion, Practical Knowledge and Common Culture', in A.O. Rorty (ed.), *Explaining Emotions*, Berkeley, University of California Press, 1980.

Seavey, W.A., 'Negligence – Subjective or Objective?' in H. Morris (ed.), *Freedom and Responsibility*, Stanford, Stanford University Press, 1961.

Shaffer, J.A., 'An Assessment of Emotion', *American Philosophical Quarterly*, 1983, vol. 20, no. 2.

Sharp, F.C., 'Voluntarism and Objectivity in Ethics', *Philosophical Review*, 1941, vol. 50.

Sherman, N., 'Aristotle on Friendship and the Shared Life', *Philosophy and Phenomenological Research*, 1987, vol. 47, no. 4.

—— *The Fabric of Character*, Oxford, Clarendon Press, 1989.

—— 'The Place of Emotions in Kantian Morality', in O. Flanagan and A.O. Rorty (eds), *Essays in Moral Psychology*, Cambridge, MIT Press, 1990.

—— 'The Place of Emotions in Morality', unpublished paper.

Shibles, W., *Emotion: The Method of Philosophical Therapy*, Whitewater, Language Press, 1974.

Shope, R.K., 'Physical and Psychic Energy', *Philosophy of Science*, 1971, vol. 38, no. 1.

Sidgwick, H., *The Methods of Ethics*, Chicago, University of Chicago Press, 1962.

Simmons, K., 'Kant on Moral Worth', *History of Philosophy Quarterly*, 1989, vol. 6, no. 1.

Slote, M.A., 'Understanding Free Will', *Journal of Philosophy*, 1980, vol. 77, no. 3.

—— 'Morality Not a System of Imperatives', *American Philosophical Quarterly*, 1982, vol. 19, no. 4.

—— *Goods and Virtues*, Oxford, Clarendon Press, 1983.

—— 'Morality and Self–Other Asymmetry', *Journal of Philosophy*, 1984, vol. 81, no. 4.

Smart, J.J.C., 'Free Will, Praise and Blame', in G. Dworkin (ed.), *Determinism, Free Will, and Moral Responsibility*, Englewood Cliffs, Prentice-Hall, 1970.

Smart, J.J.C., and Williams, B., *Utilitarianism: For and Against*, Cambridge, Cambridge University Press, 1973.

Smith, J., 'Can Virtue be in the Service of Bad Acts?', *New Scholasticism*, 1984, vol. 58, no. 3.

Solomon, R.C., *The Passions*, Garden City, Doubleday, Anchor, 1976.

—— 'The Logic of Emotion', *Nous*, 1977, vol. 11, no. 1.

—— 'The Rationality of the Emotions', *Southwestern Journal of Philosophy*, 1977, vol. 8.

—— 'Sartre on Emotions', in P.A. Schilpp (ed.), *The Philosophy of Jean-Paul Sartre*, La Salle, Open Court, 1977.

—— 'Emotions and Choice', in A.O. Rorty (ed.), *Explaining Emotions*, Berkeley, University of California Press, 1980.

—— '"I Can't Get It Out of My Mind": (Augustine's Problem)', *Philosophy and Phenomenological Research*, 1984, vol. 44, no. 3.

—— 'Emotions, Feelings and Contexts', *Journal of Philosophy*, 1986, vol. 83, no. 11.

Sommers, C.H., 'Filial Morality', *Journal of Philosophy*, 1986, vol. 83, no. 8.

Sorell, T., 'Kant's Good Will and Our Good Nature: Second Thoughts About Henson and Herman', *Kant-Studien*, 1987, band 78, heft 1.

Spinoza, *Ethics* (trans. R.H.M. Elwes), New York, Dover Publications, 1955.

Squires, J.E.R., 'Blame', *Philosophical Quarterly*, 1968, vol. 18, no. 70.

Staude, M., 'Irving Thalberg's Component Analysis of Emotion and Action', *Philosophical Quarterly*, 1974, vol. 24, no. 95.

Sterling, M.C., 'The Cognitive Theory of the Emotions', *Southwestern Journal of Philosophy*, 1979, vol. 10.

Stevenson, C.L., 'Ethical Judgments and Avoidability', in J. Feinberg (ed.), *Reason and Responsibility*, Belmont, Dickenson, 1965.

Stocker, M., 'Intentions and Act Evaluations', *Journal of Philosophy*, 1970, vol. 67, no. 17.

—— ' "Ought" and "Can" ', *Australasian Journal of Philosophy*, 1971, vol. 49, no. 3.

—— 'Act and Agent Evaluations', *Review of Metaphysics*, 1973, vol. 27, no. 1.

—— 'Agent and Other: Against Ethical Universalism', *Australasian Journal of Philosophy*, 1976, vol. 54, no. 3.

—— 'The Schizophrenia of Modern Ethical Theories', *Journal of Philosophy*, 1976, vol. 73, no. 4.

—— 'Desiring the Bad: An Essay in Moral Psychology', *Journal of Philosophy*, 1979, vol. 76, no. 12.

—— 'Good Intentions in Greek and Modern Moral Virtue', *Australasian Journal of Philosophy*, 1979, vol. 57, no. 3.

—— 'Intellectual Desire, Emotion, and Action', in A.O. Rorty (ed.), *Explaining Emotions*, Berkeley, University of California Press, 1980.

—— 'Values and Purposes: The Limits of Teleology and the Ends of Friendship', *Journal of Philosophy*, 1981, vol. 78, no. 12.

—— 'Responsibility Especially for Beliefs', *Mind*, 1982, vol. 91, no. 363.

—— 'Affectivity and Self-concern: The Assumed Psychology in Aristotle's Ethics', *Pacific Philosophical Quarterly*, 1983, vol. 64, no. 3.

—— 'Psychic Feelings: Their Importance and Irreducibility', *Australasian Journal of Philosophy*, 1983, vol. 61, no. 1.

—— 'Dirty Hands and Conflicts of Values and of Desires in Aristotle's Ethics', *Pacific Philosophical Quarterly*, 1986, vol. 67, no. 1.

—— 'Emotional Thoughts', *American Philosophical Quarterly*, 1987, vol. 24, no. 1.

—— *Plural and Conflicting Values*, Oxford, Clarendon Press, 1990.

—— 'Friendship and Morality: Some Difficult Relations', unpublished paper.

Strasser, M., 'Guilt, Regret and Prima Facie Duties', *Southern Journal of Philosophy*, 1987, vol. 25, no. 1.

Strawson, P.F., 'Freedom and Resentment', in *Freedom and Resentment and Other Essays*, London, Methuen, 1974.

—— 'Imagination and Perception', in *Freedom and Resentment and Other Essays*, London, Methuen, 1974.

Sutherland, S., 'Hume on Morality and the Emotions', *Philosophical Quarterly*, 1976, vol. 26, no. 102.

Swabey, W.C., 'Benevolence and Virtue', *Philosophical Review*, 1943, vol. 52, no. 5.

Taylor, G., 'Justifying the Emotions', *Mind*, 1975, vol. 84, no. 335.

—— 'Love', *Proceedings of the Aristotelian Society*, 1975–6, vol. 76.
—— 'Pride', in A.O. Rorty (ed.), *Explaining Emotions*, Berkeley, University of California Press, 1980.
—— *Pride, Shame, and Guilt: Emotions of Self-assessment*, Oxford, Clarendon Press, 1985.
Taylor, G., and Wolfram, S., 'Virtues and Passions', *Analysis*, 1970–1, vol. 31, no. 3.
Taylor, J., 'Sympathy, Self, and Others', 17th Hume Conference, Australian National University, Canberra, June 1990.
Taylor, R., *Good and Evil*, New York, Macmillan, 1970.
—— 'Thought and Purpose', in M. Brand (ed.), *The Nature of Human Action*, Glenview, Scott-Foresman, 1970.
Telfer, E., 'The Unity of the Moral Virtues in Aristotle's *Nicomachean Ethics*', *Proceedings of the Aristotelian Society*, 1989/90, vol. 90.
Thalberg, I., 'Emotion and Thought', *American Philosophical Quarterly*, 1964, vol. 1, no. 1.
—— 'Constituents and Causes of Emotion and Action', *Philosophical Quarterly*, 1973, vol. 23, no. 90.
—— 'Could Affects be Effects?', *Australasian Journal of Philosophy*, 1978, vol. 56, no. 2.
—— 'Mental Activity and Passivity', *Mind*, 1978, vol. 87, no. 347.
Thomas, L., 'Love and Morality: The Possibility of Altruism', in J.H. Fetzer (ed.), *Sociobiology and Epistemology*, Dordrecht, Reidel, 1985.
—— 'Friendship', *Synthese*, 1987, vol. 72, no. 2.
Thomson, J.J., 'A Note on Internalism', *Philosophy and Public Affairs*, 1986, vol. 15, no. 1.
Tietz, J., 'Emotional Objects and Criteria', *Canadian Journal of Philosophy*, 1973, vol. 3, no. 2.
—— 'Knowledge Requiring Emotions', *Southwestern Journal of Philosophy*, 1975, vol. 6, no. 3.
Tiles, J.E., 'The Combat of Passion and Reason', *Philosophy*, 1977, vol. 52, no. 3.
Tov-Ruach, L., 'Jealousy, Attention, and Loss', in A.O. Rorty (ed.), *Explaining Emotions*, Berkeley, University of California Press, 1980.
Trebilcot, J., 'Dr Kenny's Perceptions', *Mind*, 1970, vol. 79.
Trianosky, G.W., 'Supererogation, Wrongdoing and Vice: On the Autonomy of the Ethics of Virtue', *Journal of Philosophy*, 1986, vol. 83, no. 1.
Trigg, R., *Pain and Emotion*, Oxford, Clarendon Press, 1970.
Vadas, M., 'Affective and Non-affective desire', *Philosophy and Phenomenological Research*, 1984, vol. 45, no. 2.
Von Wright, G.H., *The Varieties of Goodness*, London, Routledge & Kegan Paul, 1963.
Walker, J., 'Imagination and the Passions', *Philosophy and Phenomenological Research*, 1969, vol. 29, no. 4.
Wallace, J.D., *Virtues and Vices*, Ithaca, Cornell University Press, 1978.
Walsh, W.H., 'Pride, Shame and Responsibility', *Philosophical Quarterly*, 1970, vol. 20, no. 78.
Walter, E., 'The Logic of Emotions', *Southern Journal of Philosophy*, 1972, vol. 10.

Walton, K.L, 'Fearing Fictions', *Journal of Philosophy*, 1978, vol. 75, no. 1.
Warner, R., 'Enjoyment', *Philosophical Review*, 1980, vol. 89, no. 4.
Warnock, M., 'The Justification of Emotions', *Proceedings of the Aristotelian Society*, 1957, suppl. vol. 31.
Watson, G., 'Free Agency', *Journal of Philosophy*, 1975, vol. 72, no. 8.
White, A.R., 'The Concept of Care', *Philosophical Quarterly*, 1960, vol. 10, no. 40.
—— (ed.), *The Philosophy of Action*, Oxford, Oxford University Press, 1968.
—— 'Responsibility, Liability, Excuses and Blame', *Studi Internazionali di Filosofia*, 1973, vol. 5.
Williams, B., 'Deciding to Believe', in *Problems of the Self*, Cambridge, Cambridge University Press, 1973.
—— 'Ethical Consistency', in *Problems of the Self*, Cambridge, Cambridge University Press, 1973.
—— 'Morality and the Emotions', in *Problems of the Self*, Cambridge, Cambridge University Press, 1973.
—— 'Persons, Character and Morality', in A.O. Rorty (ed.), *The Identities of Persons*, Berkeley, University of California Press, 1976.
—— 'Moral Luck', in *Moral Luck*, Cambridge, Cambridge University Press, 1981.
—— *Ethics and the Limits of Philosophy*, London, Fontana, 1985.
Wilson, J.R.S., *Emotion and Object*, Cambridge, Cambridge University Press, 1972.
Winch, P., 'Trying', in *Ethics and Action*, London, Routledge & Kegan Paul, 1972.
Witte, W., *Schiller*, Oxford, Blackwell, 1949.
Wittgenstein, L., *Philosophical Investigations*, Oxford, Basil Blackwell, 1978.
Wolf, S., 'Asymmetrical Freedom', *Journal of Philosophy*, 1980, vol. 77, no. 3.
—— 'The Importance of Free Will', *Mind*, 1981, vol. 90, no. 359.
—— 'Moral Saints', *Journal of Philosophy*, 1982, vol. 79, no. 8.
Wolff, R.P., *The Autonomy of Reason*, New York, Harper & Row, 1973.
Wollheim, R., 'On Persons and Their Lives', in A.O. Rorty (ed.), *Explaining Emotions*, Berkeley, University of California Press, 1980.
—— *The Thread of Life*, Cambridge, Mass., Harvard University Press, 1984.
Zimmerman, M., 'Negligence and Moral Responsibility', *Nous*, 1986, vol. 20, no. 2.
—— 'Luck and Moral Responsibility', *Ethics*, 1987, vol. 97, no. 2.

Index